Don't Sweat

the Small Stuff . . .

Omnibus

Don't Sweat the Small Stuff . . . Omnibus

Simple ways to keep the little things from taking over your life

Richard Carlson, P.h.D

HODDER
MOBIUS

This omnibus edition first published in Great Britain in 2007
by Hodder & Stoughton
An Hachette Livre UK company

11

Copyright © Richard Carlson 1997 and 1998

The right of Richard Carlson to be identified as the Author
of the Work has been asserted by him in accordance with
the Copyright, Designs and Patents Act 1988.

All rights reserved. No part of this publication may be reproduced, stored
in a retrieval system, or transmitted, in any form or by any means without
the prior written permission of the publisher, nor be otherwise circulated in
any form of binding or cover other than that in which it is published and
without a similar condition being imposed on the subsequent purchaser.

A CIP catalogue record for this title is available from the British Library

ISBN 978 0 340 96381 4

Printed and bound by CPI Group (UK) Ltd, Croydon, CR0 4YY

Hodder & Stoughton policy is to use papers that are natural, renewable
and recyclable products and made from wood grown in sustainable forests.
The logging and manufacturing processes are expected to conform
to the environmental regulations of the country of origin.

Hodder & Stoughton Ltd
338 Euston Road
London NW1 3BH

www.hodder.co.uk

Don't Sweat the Small Stuff . . . and It's All Small Stuff

Simple ways to keep the little things from taking over your life

I dedicate this book to my daughters, Jazzy and Kenna, who remind me every day how important it is to remember not to "sweat the small stuff." I love you both so much. Thank you for being just the way you are.

Acknowledgments

I would like to acknowledge the following people for assisting me in the creation of this book: Patti Breitman for her enthusiasm and encouragement surrounding this book and for her dedication and wisdom in not sweating the small stuff. And Leslie Wells for her vision and for her insightful editorial skill. Thank you both very much.

Contents

Introduction

*The greatest discovery of my generation is that a human being can
alter his life by altering his attitude.*

—WILLIAM JAMES

Whenever we're dealing with bad news, a difficult person,
or a disappointment of some kind, most of us get into
certain habits, ways of reacting to life—particularly adversity—
that don't serve us very well. We overreact, blow things out of
proportion, hold on too tightly, and focus on the negative aspects of life. When we are immobilized by little things—when
we are irritated, annoyed, and easily bothered—our (over-) reactions not only make us frustrated but actually get in the way
of getting what we want. We lose sight of the bigger picture,
focus on the negative, and annoy other people who might otherwise help us. In short, we live our lives as if they were one
great big emergency! We often rush around looking busy, trying
to solve problems, but in reality, we are often compounding
them. Because everything seems like such a big deal, we end up
spending our lives dealing with one drama after another.

After a while, we begin to believe that everything really *is*

1

a big deal. We fail to recognize that the way we relate to our problems has a lot to do with how quickly and efficiently we solve them. As I hope you will soon discover, when you learn the habit of responding to life with more ease, problems that seemed "insurmountable" will begin to seem more manageable. And even the "biggies," things that are truly stressful, won't throw you off track as much as they once did.

Happily, there is another way to relate to life—a softer, more graceful path that makes life seem easier and the people in it more compatible. This "other way" of living involves replacing old habits of "reaction" with new habits of perspective. These new habits enable us to have richer, more satisfying lives.

I'd like to share a personal story that touched my heart and reinforced an important lesson—a story that demonstrates the essential message of this book. As you will see, the events of this story planted the seed for the title of the book you are about to read.

About a year ago a foreign publisher contacted me and requested that I attempt to get an endorsement from best-selling author Dr. Wayne Dyer for a foreign edition of my book *You Can Feel Good Again*. I told them that while Dr. Dyer had given me an endorsement for an earlier book, I had no idea whether or not he would consider doing so again. I told them, however, that I would try.

As is often the case in the publishing world, I sent out my request, but did not hear back. After some time had gone by, I came to the conclusion that Dr. Dyer was either too busy or unwilling to write an endorsement. I honored this decision and let the publisher know that we wouldn't be able to use his name to promote the book. I considered the case closed.

About six months later, however, I received a copy of the foreign edition and to my surprise, right on the cover was the old endorsement for the earlier book from Dr. Dyer! Despite my specific instructions to the contrary, the foreign publisher had used his earlier quote and transferred it to the new book. I was extremely upset, and worried about the implications as well as the possible consequences. I called my literary agent, who immediately contacted the publisher and demanded that the books be taken off the shelves.

In the meantime, I decided to write Dr. Dyer an apology, explaining the situation and all that was being done to rectify the problem. After a few weeks of wondering about what his response might be, I received a letter in the mail that said the following: "Richard. There are two rules for living in harmony. #1) Don't sweat the small stuff and #2) It's all small stuff. Let the quote stand. Love, Wayne."

That was it! No lectures, no threats. No hard feelings and no confrontation. Despite the obvious unethical use of his very famous name, he responded with grace and humility; no feathers ruffled. His response demonstrated the important concepts of "going with the flow," and of learning to respond to life gracefully, with ease.

For more than a decade I have worked with clients, helping them to approach life in this more accepting way. Together, we deal with all types of issues—stress, relationship problems, work-related issues, addictions, and general frustration.

In this book, I will share with you very specific strategies—things you can start doing today—that will help you respond to life more gracefully. The strategies you are going to read about are the ones that have proven themselves to be the most successful by clients and readers of mine over the years. They also represent the way I like to approach my own life: the path of least resistance. Each strategy is simple, yet powerful, and will act as a navigational guide to point you in the direction of greater perspective and more relaxed living. You'll find that many of the strategies will apply not only to isolated events but to many of life's most difficult challenges.

When you "don't sweat the small stuff," your life won't be perfect, but you *will* learn to accept what life has to offer with far less resistance. As we learn in the Zen philosophy, when you learn to "let go" of problems instead of resisting with all your might, your life will begin to flow. You will, as the serenity prayer suggests, "Change the things that can be changed, accept those that cannot, and have the wisdom to know the difference." I'm confident that if you give these strategies a try, you will learn the two rules of harmony. #1) Don't sweat the small stuff, and #2) It's all small stuff. As you incorporate these ideas into your life you will begin to create a more peaceful and loving you.

1.

Don't Sweat the Small Stuff

O ften we allow ourselves to get all worked up about things that, upon closer examination, *aren't* really that big a deal. We focus on little problems and concerns and blow them way out of proportion. A stranger, for example, might cut in front of us in traffic. Rather than let it go, and go on with our day, we convince ourselves that we are justified in our anger. We play out an imaginary confrontation in our mind. Many of us might even tell someone else about the incident later on rather than simply let it go.

Why not instead simply allow the driver to have his accident somewhere else? Try to have compassion for the person and remember how painful it is to be in such an enormous hurry. This way, we can maintain our own sense of well-being and avoid taking other people's problems personally.

There are many similar, "small stuff" examples that occur every day in our lives. Whether we had to wait in line, listen to unfair criticism, or do the lion's share of the work, it pays enormous dividends if we learn not to worry about little things. So many people spend so much of their life energy "sweating the small stuff" that they completely lose touch with the magic and beauty of life. When you commit to working toward this goal you will find that you will have far more energy to be kinder and gentler.

2.

Make Peace with Imperfection

I've yet to meet an absolute perfectionist whose life was filled with inner peace. The need for perfection and the desire for inner tranquility conflict with each other. Whenever we are attached to having something a certain way, better than it already is, we are, almost by definition, engaged in a losing battle. Rather than being content and grateful for what we have, we are focused on what's wrong with something and our need to fix it. When we are zeroed in on what's wrong, it implies that we are dissatisfied, discontent.

Whether it's related to ourselves—a disorganized closet, a scratch on the car, an imperfect accomplishment, a few pounds we would like to lose—or someone else's "imperfections"—the way someone looks, behaves, or lives their life—the very act of focusing on imperfection pulls us away from our goal of being kind and gentle. This strategy has nothing to do with ceasing to do your very best but with being overly attached and focused on what's wrong with life. It's about realizing that while there's always a better way to do something, this doesn't mean that you can't enjoy and appreciate the way things already are.

The solution here is to catch yourself when you fall into your habit of insisting that things should be other than they are. Gently remind yourself that life is okay the way it is, right now. In the absence of your judgment, everything would be fine. As you begin to eliminate your need for perfection in all areas of your life, you'll begin to discover the perfection in life itself.

3.

Let Go of the Idea that Gentle, Relaxed People Can't Be Superachievers

One of the major reasons so many of us remain hurried, frightened, and competitive, and continue to live life as if it were one giant emergency, is our fear that if we were to become more peaceful and loving, we would suddenly stop achieving our goals. We would become lazy and apathetic.

You can put this fear to rest by realizing that the opposite is actually true. Fearful, frantic thinking takes an enormous amount of energy and drains the creativity and motivation from our lives. When you are fearful or frantic, you literally immobilize yourself from your greatest potential, not to mention enjoyment. Any success that you do have is despite your fear, not because of it.

I have had the good fortune to surround myself with some very relaxed, peaceful, and loving people. Some of these people are best-selling authors, loving parents, counselors, computer experts, and chief executive officers. All of them are fulfilled in what they do and are very proficient at their given skills.

I have learned the important lesson: When you have what you want (inner peace), you are *less* distracted by your wants, needs, desires, and concerns. It's thus easier to concentrate, focus, achieve your goals, and to give back to others.

4.

Be Aware of the Snowball Effect of Your Thinking

A powerful technique for becoming more peaceful is to be aware of how quickly your negative and insecure thinking can spiral out of control. Have you ever noticed how uptight you feel when you're caught up in your thinking? And, to top it off, the more absorbed you get in the details of whatever is upsetting you, the worse you feel. One thought leads to another, and yet another, until at some point, you become incredibly agitated.

For example, you might wake up in the middle of the night and remember a phone call that needs to be made the following day. Then, rather than feeling relieved that you remembered such an important call, you start thinking about everything else you have to do tomorrow. You start rehersing a probable conversation with your boss, getting yourself even more upset. Pretty soon you think to yourself, "I can't believe how busy I am. I must make fifty phone calls a day. Whose life is this anyway?" and on and on it goes until you're feeling sorry for yourself. For many people, there's no limit to how long this type of "thought attack" can go on. In fact, I've been told by clients that many of their days and nights are spent in this type of mental rehearsal. Needless to say, it's impossible to feel peaceful with your head full of concerns and annoyances.

The solution is to notice what's happening in your head before your thoughts have a chance to build any momentum. The sooner you catch yourself in the act of building your mental snowball, the easier it is to stop. In our example here, you might notice your snowball thinking right when you start running through the list of what you have to do the next day. Then, instead of obsessing on your upcoming day, you say to yourself, "Whew, there I go again," and consciously nip it in the bud. You stop your train of thought before it has a chance to get going. You can then focus, not on how overwhelmed you are, but on how grateful you are for remembering the phone call that needed to be made. If it's the middle of the night, write it down on a piece of paper and go back to sleep. You might even consider keeping a pen and paper by the bed for such moments.

You may indeed be a very busy person, but remember that

filling your head with thoughts of how overwhelmed you are only exacerbates the problem by making you feel even more stressed than you already do. Try this simple little exercise the next time you begin to obsess on your schedule. You'll be amazed at how effective it can be.

5.

Develop Your Compassion

Nothing helps us build our perspective more than developing compassion for others. Compassion is a sympathetic feeling. It involves the willingness to put yourself in someone else's shoes, to take the focus off yourself and to imagine what it's like to be in someone else's predicament, and simultaneously, to feel love for that person. It's the recognition that other people's problems, their pain and frustrations, are every bit as real as our own—often far worse. In recognizing this fact and trying to offer some assistance, we open our own hearts and greatly enhance our sense of gratitude.

Compassion is something you can develop with practice. It involves two things: intention and action. Intention simply means you remember to open your heart to others; you expand what and who matters, from yourself to other people. Action is simply the "what you do about it." You might donate a little money or time (or both) on a regular basis to a cause near to your heart. Or perhaps you'll offer a beautiful smile and genuine

17

"hello" to the people you meet on the street. It's not so important what you do, just that you do something. As Mother Teresa reminds us, "We cannot do great things on this earth. We can only do small things with great love."

Compassion develops your sense of gratitude by taking your attention off all the little things that most of us have learned to take too seriously. When you take time, often, to reflect on the miracle of life—the miracle that you are even able to read this book—the gift of sight, of love, and all the rest, it can help to remind you that many of the things that you think of as "big stuff" are really just "small stuff" that you are *turning into* big stuff.

6.

Remind Yourself that When You Die, Your "In Basket" Won't Be Empty

So many of us live our lives as if the secret purpose is to somehow get everything done. We stay up late, get up early, avoid having fun, and keep our loved ones waiting. Sadly, I've seen many people who put off their loved ones so long that the loved ones lose interest in maintaining the relationship. I used to do this myself. Often, we convince ourselves that our obsession with our "to do" list is only temporary—that once we get through the list, we'll be calm, relaxed, and happy. But in reality, this rarely happens. As items are checked off, new ones simply replace them.

The nature of your "in basket" is that it's *meant* to have items to be completed in it—it's not meant to be empty. There will always be phone calls that need to be made, projects to complete, and work to be done. In fact, it can be argued that a full "in basket" is essential for success. It means your time is in demand!

Regardless of who you are or what you do, however, remember that *nothing* is more important than your own sense of happiness and inner peace and that of your loved ones. If you're obsessed with getting everything done, you'll never have a sense of well-being! In reality, almost everything can wait. Very little in our work lives truly falls into the "emergency" category. If you stay focused on your work, it will all get done in due time.

I find that if I remind myself (frequently) that the purpose of life *isn't* to get it all done but to enjoy each step along the way and live a life filled with love, it's far easier for me to control my obsession with completing my list of things to do. Remember, when you die, there *will* still be unfinished business to take care of. And you know what? Someone else will do it for you! Don't waste any more precious moments of your life regretting the inevitable.

7.

Don't Interrupt Others or
Finish Their Sentences

It wasn't until a few years ago that I realized how often I interrupted others and/or finished their sentences. Shortly thereafter, I also realized how destructive this habit was, not only to the respect and love I received from others but also for the tremendous amount of energy it takes to try to be in two heads at once! Think about it for a moment. When you hurry someone along, interrupt someone, or finish his or her sentence, you have to keep track not only of your own thoughts but of those of the person you are interrupting as well. This tendency (which, by the way, is extremely common in busy people), encourages both parties to speed up their speech and their thinking. This, in turn, makes both people nervous, irritable, and annoyed. It's downright exhausting. It's also the cause of many arguments, because if there's one thing almost everyone resents, it's someone who doesn't listen to what they are saying. And how can you really listen to what someone is saying when you are speaking for that person?

Once you begin noticing yourself interrupting others, you'll see that this insidious tendency is nothing more than an innocent habit that has become invisible to you. This is good news because it means that all you really have to do is to begin catching yourself when you forget. Remind yourself (before a conversation begins, if possible) to be patient and wait. Tell yourself to allow the other person to finish speaking before you take your turn. You'll notice, right away, how much the interactions with the people in your life will improve as a direct result of this simple act. The people you communicate with will feel much more relaxed around you when they feel heard and listened to. You'll also notice how much more relaxed *you'll* feel when you stop interrupting others. Your heart and pulse rates will slow down, and you'll begin to enjoy your conversations rather than rush through them. This is an easy way to become a more relaxed, loving person.

8.

Do Something Nice for Someone Else—
and Don't Tell *Anyone* About It

While many of us frequently do nice things for others, we are almost certain to mention our acts of kindness to someone else, secretly seeking their approval.

When we share our own niceness or generosity with someone else, it makes us feel like we are thoughtful people, it reminds us of how nice we are and how deserving we are of kindness.

While all acts of kindness are inherently wonderful, there is something even more magical about doing something thoughtful but mentioning it to no one, ever. You always feel good when you give to others. Rather than diluting the positive feelings by telling others about your own kindness, by keeping it to yourself you get to retain *all* the positive feelings.

It's really true that one should give for the sake of giving, not to receive something in return. This is precisely what you

are doing when you don't mention your kindness to others—
your rewards are the warm feelings that come from the act of
giving. The next time you do something really nice for someone else, keep it to yourself and revel in the abundant joy of
giving.

9.

Let Others Have the Glory

There is something magical that happens to the human spirit, a sense of calm that comes over you, when you cease needing all the attention directed toward yourself and instead allow others to have the glory.

Our need for excessive attention is that ego-centered part of us that says, "Look at me. I'm special. My story is more interesting than yours." It's that voice inside of us that may not come right out and say it, but that wants to believe that "my accomplishments are slightly more important than yours." The ego is that part of us that wants to be seen, heard, respected, considered special, often at the expense of someone else. It's the part of us that interrupts someone else's story, or impatiently waits his turn to speak so that he can bring the conversation and attention back to himself. To varying degrees, most of us engage in this habit, much to our own detriment. When you immediately dive in and bring the conversation back toward you, you can subtly minimize the joy that person has in sharing, and in doing so, create distance between yourself and others. Everyone loses.

The next time someone tells you a story or shares an accomplishment with you, notice your tendency to say something about yourself in response.

Although it's a difficult habit to break, it's not only enjoyable but actually peaceful to have the quiet confidence to be able to surrender your need for attention and instead share in the joy of someone else's glory. Rather than jumping right in and saying, "Once I did the same thing" or "Guess what I did today," bite your tongue and notice what happens. Just say, "That's wonderful," or "Please tell me more," and leave it at that. The person you are speaking to will have so much more fun and, because you are so much more "present," because you are listening so carefully, he or she won't feel in competition with you. The result will be that the person will feel more relaxed around you, making him or her more confident as well as more interesting. You too will feel more relaxed because you won't be on the edge of your seat, waiting your turn.

Obviously, there are many times when it's absolutely appropriate to exchange experience back and forth, and to share *in* the glory and attention rather than giving it all away. I'm re-

ferring here to the compulsive need to grab it from others. Ironically, when you surrender your need to hog the glory, the
attention you used to need from other people is replaced by a
quiet inner confidence that is derived from letting others
have it.

10.

Learn to Live in the Present Moment

To a large degree, the measure of our peace of mind is determined by how much we are able to live in the present moment. Irrespective of what happened yesterday or last year, and what may or may not happen tomorrow, the present moment is where you are—always!

Without question, many of us have mastered the neurotic art of spending much of our lives worrying about a variety of things—all at once. We allow past problems and future concerns to dominate our present moments, so much so that we end up anxious, frustrated, depressed, and hopeless. On the flip side, we also postpone our gratification, our stated priorities, and our happiness, often convincing ourselves that "someday" will be better than today. Unfortunately, the same mental dynamics that tell us to look toward the future will only repeat themselves so that "someday" never actually arrives. John Lennon once said, "Life is what's happening while we're busy making other plans." When we're busy making "other plans," our children are busy growing up, the people we love are moving away and dying, our bodies are getting out of shape, and our dreams are slipping away. In short, we miss out on life.

Many people live as if life were a dress rehearsal for some later date. It isn't. In fact, no one has a guarantee that he or she will be here tomorrow. Now is the only time we have, and the only time that we have any control over. When our attention is in the present moment, we push fear from our minds. Fear is the concern over events that might happen in the future—we won't have enough money, our children will get into trouble, we will get old and die, whatever.

To combat fear, the best strategy is to learn to bring your attention back to the present. Mark Twain said, "I have been through some terrible things in my life, some of which actually happened." I don't think I can say it any better. Practice keeping your attention on the here and now. Your efforts will pay great dividends.

11.

Imagine that Everyone Is Enlightened
Except You

This strategy gives you a chance to practice something that is probably completely unacceptable to you. However, if you give it a try, you might find that it's one of the most helpful exercises in self-improvement.

As the title suggests, the idea is to imagine that everyone you know and everyone you meet is perfectly enlightened. That is, everyone except you! The people you meet are all here to teach you something. Perhaps the obnoxious driver or disrespectful teenager is here to teach you about patience, the punk rocker might be here to teach you to be less judgmental.

Your job is to try to determine what the people in your life are trying to teach you. You'll find that if you do this, you'll be far less annoyed, bothered, and frustrated by the actions and imperfections of other people. You can actually get yourself in the habit of approaching life in this manner and, if you do, you'll be glad you did. Often, once you discover what someone is trying to teach you, it's easy to let go of your frustration. For example, suppose you're in the post office and the postal clerk appears to be intentionally moving slowly. Rather than feeling frustrated, ask yourself the question, "What is he trying to teach me?" Maybe you need to learn about compassion—how hard it would be to have a job that you don't like. Or perhaps you could learn a little more about being patient. Standing in line is an excellent opportunity to break your habit of feeling impatient.

You may be surprised at how fun and easy this is. All you're really doing is changing your perception from "Why are they doing this?" to "What are they trying to teach me?" Take a look around today at all the enlightened people.

12.

Let Others Be "Right" Most of the Time

One of the most important questions you can ever ask your-self is, "Do I want to be 'right'—or do I want to be happy?" Many times, the two are mutually exclusive!

Being right, defending our positions, takes an enormous amount of mental energy and often alienates us from the people in our lives. Needing to be right—or needing someone else to be wrong—encourages others to become defensive, and puts pressure on us to keep defending. Yet, many of us (me too, at times) spend a great deal of time and energy attempting to prove (or point out) that we are right—and/or others are wrong. Many people, consciously or unconsciously, believe that it's somehow their job to show others how their positions, statements, and points of view are incorrect, and that in doing so, the person they are correcting is going to somehow appreciate it, or at least learn something. Wrong!

Think about it. Have you *ever* been corrected by someone and said to the person who was trying to be right, "Thank you so much for showing me that I'm wrong and you're right. Now I see it. Boy, you're great!" Or, has anyone you know ever thanked you (or even agreed with you) when you corrected them, or made yourself "right" at their expense? Of course not. The truth is, all of us hate to be corrected. We all want our positions to be respected and understood by others. Being listened to and heard is one of the greatest desires of the human heart. And those who learn to listen are the most loved and respected. Those who are in the habit of correcting others are often resented and avoided.

It's not that it's *never* appropriate to be right—sometimes you genuinely need to be or want to be. Perhaps there are certain philosophical positions that you don't want to budge on such as when you hear a racist comment. Here, it's important to speak your mind. Usually, however, it's just your ego creeping in and ruining an otherwise peaceful encounter—a habit of wanting or needing to be right.

A wonderful, heartfelt strategy for becoming more peaceful and loving is to practice allowing others the joy of being right— give them the glory. Stop correcting. As hard as it may be to change this habit, it's worth any effort and practice it takes. When someone says, "I really feel it's important to . . ." rather than jumping in and saying, "No, it's more important to . . ." or any of the hundreds of other forms of conversational editing, simply let it go and allow their statement to stand. The people in your life will become less defensive and more loving. They will appreciate you more than you could ever have dreamed possible, even if they don't exactly know why. You'll discover the joy of participating in and witnessing other people's happiness, which is far more rewarding than a battle of egos. You don't have to sacrifice your deepest philosophical truths or most heartfelt opinions, but, starting today, let others be "right," *most* of the time!

13.

Become More Patient

The quality of patience goes a long way toward your goal of creating a more peaceful and loving self. The more patient you are, the more accepting you will be of what is, rather than insisting that life be exactly as you would like it to be. Without patience, life is extremely frustrating. You are easily annoyed, bothered, and irritated. Patience adds a dimension of ease and acceptance to your life. It's essential for inner peace.

Becoming more patient involves opening your heart to the present moment, even if you don't like it. If you are stuck in a traffic jam, late for an appointment, opening to the moment would mean catching yourself building a mental snowball before your thinking got out of hand and gently reminding yourself to relax. It might also be a good time to breathe as well as an opportunity to remind yourself that, in the bigger scheme of things, being late is "small stuff."

Patience also involves seeing the innocence in others. My wife, Kris, and I have two young children ages four and seven.

On many occasions while writing this book, our four-year-old daughter has walked into my office and interrupted my work, which can be disruptive to a writer. What I have learned to do (most of the time) is to see the innocence in her behavior rather than to focus on the potential implications of her interruption ("I won't get my work done, I'll lose my train of thought, this was my only opportunity to write today," and so forth). I remind myself *why* she is coming to see me—because she loves me, not because she is conspiring to ruin my work. When I remember to see the innocence, I immediately bring forth a feeling of patience, and my attention is brought back to the moment. Any irritation that may have been building is eliminated and I'm reminded, once again, of how fortunate I am to have such beautiful children. I have found that, if you look deeply enough, you can almost always see the innocence in other people as well as in potentially frustrating situations. When you do, you will become a more patient and peaceful person and, in some strange way, you begin to enjoy many of the moments that used to frustrate you.

14.

Create "Patience Practice Periods"

Patience is a quality of heart that can be greatly enhanced with deliberate practice. An effective way that I have found to deepen my own patience is to create actual practice periods—periods of time that I set up in my mind to practice the art of patience. Life itself becomes a classroom, and the curriculum is patience.

You can start with as little as five minutes and build up your capacity for patience, over time. Start by saying to yourself, "Okay, for the next five minutes I won't allow myself to be bothered by anything. I'll be patient." What you'll discover is truly amazing. Your intention to be patient, especially if you know it's only for a short while, immediately strengthens your capacity for patience. Patience is one of those special qualities where success feeds on itself. Once you reach little milestones—five minutes of successful patience—you'll begin to see that you do, indeed, have the capacity to be patient, even for longer periods of time. Over time, you may even become a patient person.

Since I have young children at home, I have many possibilities to practice the art of patience. For example, on a day when both girls are firing questions at me as I'm trying to make important phone calls, I'll say to myself, "Now is a great time to be patient. For the next half hour I'm going to be as patient as possible (see, I've worked hard, I'm up to thirty minutes)!" All kidding aside, it really works—and it has worked in our family. As I keep my cool and don't allow myself to be annoyed and upset, I can calmly, yet firmly, direct my children's behavior far more effectively than when I get crazy. The simple act of gearing my mind toward patience allows me to remain in the present moment far more than I would if I were upset, thinking about all the times this has happened before and feeling like a martyr. What's more, my patient feelings are often contagious—they rub off on the kids, who then decide, on their own, that it's no fun to bother Dad.

Being patient allows me to keep my perspective. I can remember, even in the midst of a difficult situation, that what's before me—my present challenge—isn't "life or death" but simply a minor obstacle that must be dealt with. Without patience, the same scenario can become a major emergency complete with yelling, frustration, hurt feelings, and high blood pressure. It's really not worth all that. Whether you're needing to deal with children, your boss, or a difficult person or situation—if you don't want to "sweat the small stuff," improving your patience level is a great way to start.

15.

Be the First One to Act Loving or Reach Out

So many of us hold on to little resentments that may have stemmed from an argument, a misunderstanding, the way we were raised, or some other painful event. Stubbornly, we wait for someone else to reach out to us—believing this is the *only* way we can forgive or rekindle a friendship or family relationship.

An acquaintance of mine, whose health isn't very good, recently told me that she hasn't spoken to her son in almost three years. "Why not?" I asked. She said that she and her son had had a disagreement about his wife and that she wouldn't speak to him again unless he called first. When I suggested that she be the one to reach out, she resisted initially and said, "I can't do that. He's the one who should apologize." She was literally willing to die before reaching out to her only son. After a little gentle encouragement, however, she did decide to be the first one to reach out. To her amazement, her son was grateful for her willingness to call and offered an apology of his own. As is usually the case when someone takes the chance and reaches out, everyone wins.

Whenever we hold on to our anger, we turn "small stuff" into really "big stuff" in our minds. We start to believe that our positions are more important than our happiness. They are not. If you want to be a more peaceful person you must understand that being right is almost never more important than allowing yourself to be happy. The way to be happy is to let go, and reach out. Let other people be right. This doesn't mean that you're wrong. Everything will be fine. You'll experience the peace of letting go, as well as the joy of letting others be right. You'll also notice that, as you reach out and let others be "right," they will become less defensive and more loving toward you. They might even reach back. But, if for some reason they don't, that's okay too. You'll have the inner satisfaction of knowing that you have done your part to create a more loving world, and certainly you'll be more peaceful yourself.

44

16.

Ask Yourself the Question,
"Will This Matter a Year from Now?"

Almost every day I play a game with myself that I call "time warp." I made it up in response to my consistent, erroneous belief that what I was all worked up about was really important.

To play "time warp," all you have to do is imagine that whatever circumstance you are dealing with isn't happening right now but a year from now. Then simply ask yourself, "Is this situation really as important as I'm making it out to be?" Once in a great while it may be—but a vast majority of the time, it simply isn't.

Whether it be an argument with your spouse, child, or boss, a mistake, a lost opportunity, a lost wallet, a work-related rejection, or a sprained ankle, chances are, a year from now you aren't going to care. It will be one more irrelevant detail in your life. While this simple game won't solve all your problems, it can give you an enormous amount of needed perspective. I find myself laughing at things that I used to take far too seriously. Now, rather than using up my energy feeling angry and over-whelmed, I can use it instead on spending time with my wife and children or engaging in creative thinking.

17.

Surrender to the Fact that Life Isn't Fair

A friend of mine, in response to a conversation we were having about the injustices of life, asked me the question, "Who said life was going to be fair, or that it was even meant to be fair?" Her question was a good one. It reminded me of something I was taught as a youngster: Life isn't fair. It's a bummer, but it's absolutely true. Ironically, recognizing this sobering fact can be a very liberating insight.

One of the mistakes many of us make is that we feel sorry for ourselves, or for others, thinking that life *should be* fair, or that someday it will be. It's not and it won't. When we make this mistake we tend to spend a lot of time wallowing and/or complaining about what's wrong with life. We commiserate with others, discussing the injustices of life. "It's not fair," we complain, not realizing that, perhaps, it was never intended to be.

One of the *nice* things about surrendering to the fact that life isn't fair is that it keeps us from feeling sorry for ourselves by encouraging us to do the very best we can with what we have. We know it's not "life's job" to make everything perfect, it's our own challenge. Surrendering to this fact also keeps us from feeling sorry for others because we are reminded that everyone is dealt a different hand, and everyone has unique strengths and challenges. This insight has helped me to deal with the problems of raising two children, the difficult decisions I've had to make about who to help and who I can't help, as well as with my own personal struggles during those times that I have felt victimized or unfairly treated. It almost always wakes me up to reality and puts me back on track.

The fact that life isn't fair doesn't mean we shouldn't do everything in our power to improve our own lives or the world as a whole. To the contrary, it suggests that we should. When we don't recognize or admit that life isn't fair, we tend to feel pity for others and for ourselves. Pity, of course, is a self-defeating emotion that does nothing for anyone, except to make everyone feel worse than they already do. When we *do* recognize that life isn't fair, however, we feel *compassion* for others and for ourselves. And compassion is a heartfelt emotion that delivers loving-kindness to everyone it touches. The next time you find yourself thinking about the injustices of the world, try reminding yourself of this very basic fact. You may be surprised that it can nudge you out of self-pity and into helpful action.

18.

Allow Yourself to Be Bored

For many of us, our lives are so filled with stimuli, not to mention responsibilities, that it's almost impossible for us to sit still and do nothing, much less relax—even for a few minutes. A friend of mine said to me, "People are no longer human beings. We should be called human doings."

I was first exposed to the idea that occasional boredom can actually be good for me while studying with a therapist in La Conner, Washington, a tiny little town with very little "to do." After finishing our first day together, I asked my instructor, "What is there to do around here at night?" He responded by saying, "What I'd like you to do is allow yourself to be bored. Do nothing. This is part of your training." At first I thought he was kidding! "Why on earth would I choose to be bored?" I asked. He went on to explain that if you allow yourself to be bored, even for an hour—or less—and don't fight it, the feelings of boredom will be replaced with feelings of peace. And after a little practice, you'll learn to relax.

Much to my surprise, he was absolutely right. At first, I could barely stand it. I was so used to doing something every second that I really struggled to relax. But after a while I got used to it, and have long since learned to enjoy it. I'm not talking about hours of idle time or laziness, but simply learning the art of relaxing, of just "being," rather than "doing," for a few minutes each day. There isn't a specific technique other than to consciously do nothing. Just sit still, perhaps look out the window and notice your thoughts and feelings. At first you may get a little anxious, but each day it will get a little easier. The payback is tremendous.

Much of our anxiety and inner struggle stems from our busy, overactive minds always needing something to entertain them, something to focus on, and always wondering "What's next?" While we're eating dinner we wonder what's for dessert. While eating dessert, we ponder what we should do afterward. After that evening, it's "What should we do this weekend?" After we've been out, we walk into the house and immediately turn on the television, pick up the phone, open a book, or start cleaning. It's almost as though we're frightened at the thought of not having something to do, even for a minute.

The beauty of doing nothing is that it teaches you to clear your mind and relax. It allows your mind the freedom to "not know," for a brief period of time. Just like your body, your mind needs an occasional break from its hectic routine. When you allow your mind to take a break, it comes back stronger, sharper, more focused and creative.

When you allow yourself to be bored, it takes an enormous amount of pressure off you to be performing and doing something every second of every day. Now, when either of my two children says to me, "Daddy, I'm bored," I respond by saying, "Great, be bored for a while. It's good for you." Once I say this, they always give up on the idea of me solving their problem. You probably never thought someone would actually suggest that you allow yourself to be bored. I guess there's a first for everything!

19.

Lower Your Tolerance to Stress

It seems that we have it backward in our society. We tend to look up to people who are under a great deal of stress, who can handle loads of stress, and those who are under a great deal of pressure. When someone says, "I've been working really hard," or "I'm really stressed out," we are taught to admire, even emulate their behavior. In my work as a stress consultant I hear the proud words "I have a very high tolerance to stress" almost every day. It probably won't come as a surprise that when these stressed-out people first arrive at my office, more often than not, what they are hoping for are strategies to *raise* their tolerance to stress even higher so they can handle even more!

Fortunately, there is an inviolable law in our emotional environment that goes something like this: Our current level of stress will be exactly that of our tolerance to stress. You'll notice that the people who say, "I can handle lots of stress" will *always* be under a great deal of it! So, if you teach people to raise their tolerance to stress, that's exactly what will happen. They will accept even more confusion and responsibility until again, their external level of stress matches that of their tolerance. Usually it takes a crisis of some kind to wake up a stressed-out person to their own craziness—a spouse leaves, a health issue emerges, a serious addiction takes over their life—something happens that jolts them into a search for a new kind of strategy.

It may seem strange, but if you were to enroll in the average stress management workshop, what you would probably learn is to *raise* your tolerance to stress. It seems that even stress consultants are stressed out!

What you want to start doing is noticing your stress early, *before* it gets out of hand. When you feel your mind moving too quickly, it's time to back off and regain your bearings. When your schedule is getting out of hand, it's a signal that it's time to slow down and reevaluate what's important rather than power through everything on the list. When you're feeling out of control and resentful of all you have to do, rather than roll up your sleeves and "get to it," a better strategy is to relax, take a few deep breaths, and go for a short walk. You'll find that when you catch yourself getting too stressed out—early, before it gets out of control—your stress will be like the proverbial snowball rolling down the hill. When it's small, it's manageable and easy to control. Once it gathers momentum, however, it's difficult, if not impossible, to stop.

There's no need to worry that you won't get it all done. When your mind is clear and peaceful and your stress level is reduced, you'll be more effective and you'll have more fun. As you lower your tolerance to stress, you will find that you'll have far less stress to handle, as well as creative ideas for handling the stress that is left over.

20.

Once a Week, Write a Heartfelt Letter

This is an exercise that has helped to change many lives, assisting people in becoming more peaceful and loving. Taking a few minutes each week to write a heartfelt letter does many things for you. Picking up a pen or typing on a keyboard slows you down long enough to remember the beautiful people in your life. The act of sitting down to write helps to fill your life with gratitude.

Once you decide to try this, you'll probably be amazed at how many people appear on your list. I had one client who said, "I probably don't have enough weeks left in my life to write everyone on my list." This may or may not be true for you, but chances are, there are a number of people in your life, or from your past, who are quite deserving of a friendly, heartfelt letter. Even if you don't have people in your life to whom you feel you can write, go ahead and write the letter to someone you don't know instead—perhaps to an author who may not even be living, whose works you admire. Or to a great inventor or thinker from the past or present. Part of the value of the letter is to gear your thinking toward gratitude. Writing the letter, even if it isn't sent, would do just that.

The purpose of your letter is very simple: to express love and gratitude. Don't worry if you're awkward at writing letters. This isn't a contest from the head but a gift from the heart. If you can't think of much to say, start with short little notes like, "Dear Jasmine. I woke up this morning thinking of how lucky I am to have people like you in my life. Thank you so much for being my friend. I am truly blessed, and I wish for you all the happiness and joy that life can bring. Love, Richard."

Not only does writing and sending a note like this focus your attention on what's right in your life, but the person receiving it will, in all likelihood, be extremely touched and grateful. Often, this simple action starts a spiral of loving actions whereby the person receiving your letter may decide to do the same thing to someone else, or perhaps will act and feel more loving toward others. Write your first letter this week. I'll bet you'll be glad you did.

21.

Imagine Yourself
at Your Own Funeral

This strategy is a little scary for some people but universally effective at reminding us of what's most important in our lives.

When we look back on our lives, how many of us are going to be pleased at how uptight we were? Almost universally, when people look back on their lives while on their deathbed, they wish that their priorities had been quite different. With few exceptions, people wish they hadn't "sweated the small stuff" so much. Instead, they wish they had spent more time with the people and activities that they truly loved and less time worrying about aspects of life that, upon deeper examination, really don't matter all that much. Imagining yourself at your own funeral allows you to look back at your life while you still have the chance to make some important changes.

While it can be a little scary or painful, it's a good idea to consider your own death and, in the process, your life. Doing so will remind you of the kind of person you want to be and the priorities that are most important to you. If you're at all like me, you'll probably get a wake-up call that can be an excellent source of change.

22.

Repeat to Yourself,

"Life Isn't an Emergency"

I n some ways, this strategy epitomizes the essential message of this book. Although most people believe otherwise, the truth is, life *isn't* an emergency.

I've had hundreds of clients over the years who have all but neglected their families as well as their own dreams because of their propensity to believe that life is an emergency. They justify their neurotic behavior by believing that if they don't work eighty hours a week, they won't get everything done. Sometimes I remind them that when they die, their "in basket" won't be empty!

A client who is a homemaker and mother of three children recently said to me, "I just can't get the house cleaned up the way I like it before everyone leaves in the morning." She was so upset over her inability to be perfect that her doctor had prescribed her anti-anxiety medicine. She was acting (and feeling) like there was a gun pointed at her head and the sniper was demanding that every dish be put away and every towel folded—or else! Again, the silent assumption was, *this is an emergency!* The truth was, no one other than she had created the pressure she was experiencing.

I've never met anyone (myself included) who hasn't turned little things into great big emergencies. We take our own goals so seriously that we forget to have fun along the way, and we forget to cut ourselves some slack. We take simple preferences and turn them into conditions for our own happiness. Or, we beat ourselves up if we can't meet our self-created deadlines. The first step in becoming a more peaceful person is to have the humility to admit that, in most cases, you're creating your own emergencies. Life will usually go on if things don't go according to plan. It's helpful to keep reminding yourself and repeating the sentence, "Life isn't an emergency."

23.

Experiment with Your Back Burner

Your back burner is an excellent tool for remembering a fact or bringing forth an insight. It's an almost effortless yet effective way of using your mind when you might otherwise start feeling stressed out. Using your back burner means allowing your mind to solve a problem while you are busy doing something else, here in the present moment.

The back burner of your mind works in the same way as the back burner of a stove. While on low heat, the cooking process mixes, blends, and simmers the ingredients into a tasty meal. The way you prepared this meal was to throw the various ingredients into the pot, mix them up, and leave them alone. Often the less you interfere, the better the result.

In much the same way, we can solve many of life's problems (serious and otherwise) if we feed the back burner of our mind with a list of problems, facts, and variables, and possible solutions. Just as when we make soup or a sauce, the thoughts and ideas we feed the back burner of our mind must be left alone to simmer properly.

Whether you are struggling to solve a problem or can't remember a person's name, your back burner is always available to help you. It puts our quieter, softer, and sometimes most intelligent source of thinking to work for us on issues that we have no immediate answer for. The back burner is *not* a prescription for denial or procrastination. In other words, while you *do* want to put your problems on your back burner, you *don't* want to turn the burner off. Instead, you want to gently hold the problem in your mind without actively analyzing it. This simple technique will help you solve many problems and will greatly reduce the stress and effort in your life.

24.

Spend a Moment Every Day Thinking of
Someone to Thank

This simple strategy, which may take only a few seconds to complete, has long been one of the most important habits I have ever engaged in. I try to remember to start my day thinking of someone to thank. To me, gratitude and inner peace go hand in hand. The more genuinely grateful I feel for the gift of my life, the more peaceful I feel. Gratitude, then, is worthy of a little practice.

If you're anything like me, you probably have many people in your life to feel grateful for: friends, family members, people from your past, teachers, gurus, people from work, someone who gave you a break, as well as countless others. You may want to thank a higher power for the gift of life itself, or for the beauty of nature.

As you think of people to be grateful for, remember that it can be anyone—someone who allowed you to merge into traffic, someone who held the door open for you, or a physician who saved your life. The point is to gear your attention toward gratitude, preferably first thing in the morning.

I learned a long time ago that it's easy to allow my mind to slip into various forms of negativity. When I do, the first thing that leaves me is my sense of gratitude. I begin to take the people in my life for granted, and the love that I often feel is replaced with resentment and frustration. What this exercise reminds me to do is to focus on the good in my life. Invariably as I think of one person to feel gratitude for, the image of another person pops into my head, then another and another. Pretty soon I'm thinking of other things to be grateful for—my health, my children, my home, my career, the readers of my books, my freedom, and on and on it goes.

It may seem like an awfully simple suggestion, but it really works! If you wake up in the morning with gratitude on your mind, it's pretty difficult, in fact almost impossible, to feel anything but peace.

25.

Smile at Strangers, Look into Their Eyes, and Say Hello

Have you ever noticed or thought about how little eye contact most of us have with strangers? Why? Are we afraid of them? What keeps us from opening our hearts to people we don't know?

I don't really know the answers to these questions, but I do know that there is virtually always a parallel between our attitude toward strangers and our overall level of happiness. In other words, it's unusual to find a person who walks around with her head down, frowning and looking away from people, who is secretly a peaceful, joyful person.

I'm not suggesting it's better to be outgoing than introverted, that you need to expend tons of extra energy trying to brighten others' days, or that you should pretend to be friendly. I am suggesting, however, that if you think of strangers as being a little more like you and treat them not only with kindness and respect but with smiles and eye contact as well, you'll probably notice some pretty nice changes in yourself. You'll begin to see that most people are just like you—most of them have families, people they love, troubles, concerns, likes, dislikes, fears, and so forth. You'll also notice how nice and grateful people can be when you're the first one to reach out. When you see how similar we all are, you begin to see the innocence in all of us. In other words, even though we often mess up, most of us are doing the best that we know how with the circumstances that surround us. Along with seeing the innocence in people comes a profound feeling of inner happiness.

26.

Set Aside Quiet Time, Every Day

As I begin to write this strategy it's exactly 4:30 in the morning, my favorite time of the day. I still have at least an hour and a half before my wife and children get out of bed and the phone begins to ring; at least an hour before anyone can ask me to do anything. It's absolutely silent outside and I'm in complete solitude. There is something rejuvenating and peaceful about being alone and having some time to reflect, work, or simply enjoy the quiet.

I've been working in the stress management field for well over a decade. In that time I've met some extraordinary people. I can't think of a single person whom I would consider to be inwardly peaceful who doesn't carve out at least a little quiet time, virtually every day. Whether it's ten minutes of meditation or yoga, spending a little time in nature, or locking the bathroom door and taking a ten-minute bath, quiet time to yourself is a vital part of life. Like spending time alone, it helps to balance the noise and confusion that infiltrate much of our day.

Personally, when I set aside quiet time for myself, it makes the rest of my day seem manageable. When I don't, I really notice the difference.

There's a little ritual that I do that I've shared with many friends. Like many people, I drive to and from my office on a daily basis. On my way home from work, as I get close to my driveway, I pull my car over and stop. There is a nice spot where I can spend a minute or two looking at the view or closing my eyes and breathing. It slows me down and helps me feel centered and grateful. I've shared this strategy with dozens of people who used to complain about having "no time for quiet." They would speed into their driveways with the radio blaring in their ears. Now, with a simple shift in their actions, they enter their homes feeling much more relaxed.

27.

Imagine the People in Your Life
as Tiny Infants and
as One-Hundred-Year-Old Adults

I learned this technique almost twenty years ago. It has proven to be extremely successful for releasing feelings of irritation toward other people.

Think of someone who truly irritates you, who makes you feel angry. Now, close your eyes and try to imagine this person as a tiny infant. See their tiny little features and their innocent little eyes. Know that babies can't help but make mistakes and each of us was, at one time, a little infant. Now, roll forward the clock one hundred years. See the same person as a very old person who is about to die. Look at their worn-out eyes and their soft smile, which suggests a bit of wisdom and the admission of mistakes made. Know that each of us will be one hundred years old, alive or dead, before too many decades go by.

You can play with this technique and alter it in many ways. It almost always provides the user with some needed perspective and compassion. If our goal is to become more peaceful and loving, we certainly don't want to harbor negativity toward others.

28.

Seek First to Understand

This is adopted from one of Stephen Covey's "Seven Habits of Highly Effective People." Using this strategy is a shortcut to becoming a more content person (and you'll probably become more effective too).

Essentially, "seek first to understand" implies that you become more interested in understanding others and less in having other people understand you. It means mastering the idea that if you want quality, fulfilling communication that is nourishing to you and others, understanding others must come first. When you understand where people are coming from, what they are trying to say, what's important to them, and so forth, *being* understood flows naturally; it falls into place with virtually no effort. When you reverse this process, however (which is what most of us do most of the time), you are putting the cart before the horse. When you try to *be* understood *before* you understand, the effort you exert will be felt by you and the person or people you are trying to reach. Communication will break down, and you may end up with a battle of two egos.

I was working with a couple who had spent the first ten years of their marriage frustrated, arguing about their finances. He couldn't understand why she wanted to save every penny they earned, and she couldn't understand why he was a spendthrift. Any rationale on either position had been lost in their joint frustration. While many problems are more complex than this couple's, their solutions were relatively simple. Neither person felt understood. They needed to learn to stop interrupting each other and to listen carefully. Rather than defending their own positions, each needed to seek first to understand. This is precisely what I got them to do. He learned that she was saving to avoid her parents' financial disasters. Essentially, she was frightened of being broke. She learned that he felt embarrassed that he wasn't able to "take care of her" as well as his father did his mother. Essentially, he wanted her to be proud of him. As each learned to understand the other, their frustration with each other was replaced by compassion. Today, they have a nice balance between spending and saving.

Seeking first to understand isn't about who's right or wrong; it is a philosophy of effective communication. When you practice this method you'll notice that the people you communicate with will feel listened to, heard, and understood. This will translate into better, more loving relationships.

29.

Become a Better Listener

I grew up believing I was a good listener. And although I have become a better listener than I was ten years ago, I have to admit I'm still only an *adequate* listener.

Effective listening is more than simply avoiding the bad habit of interrupting others while they are speaking or finishing their sentences. It's being content to listen to the *entire* thought of someone rather than waiting impatiently for your chance to respond.

In some ways, the way we fail to listen is symbolic of the way we live. We often treat communication as if it were a race. It's almost like our goal is to have no time gaps between the conclusion of the sentence of the person we are speaking with and the beginning of our own. My wife and I were recently at a café having lunch, eavesdropping on the conversations around us. It seemed that no one was really listening to one another; instead they were taking turns not listening to one another. I asked my wife if I still did the same thing. With a smile on her face she said, "Only sometimes."

Slowing down your responses and becoming a better listener aids you in becoming a more peaceful person. It takes pressure from you. If you think about it, you'll notice that it takes an enormous amount of energy and is very stressful to be sitting at the edge of your seat trying to guess what the person in front of you (or on the telephone) is going to say so that you can fire back your response. But as you wait for the people you are communicating with to finish, as you simply listen more intently to what is being said, you'll notice that the pressure you feel is off. You'll immediately feel more relaxed, and so will the people you are talking to. They will feel safe in slowing down their own responses because they won't feel in competition with you for "airtime"! Not only will becoming a better listener make you a more patient person, it will also enhance the quality of your relationships. Everyone loves to talk to someone who truly listens to what they are saying.

30.

Choose Your Battles Wisely

C hoose your battles wisely" is a popular phrase in parenting but is equally important in living a contented life. It suggests that life is filled with opportunities to choose between making a big deal out of something or simply letting it go, realizing it doesn't really matter. If you choose your battles wisely, you'll be far more effective in winning those that are truly important.

Certainly there will be times when you will want or need to argue, confront, or even fight for something you believe in. Many people, however, argue, confront, and fight over practically anything, turning their lives into a series of battles over relatively "small stuff." There is so much frustration in living this type of life that you lose track of what is truly relevant.

The tiniest disagreement or glitch in your plans can be made into a big deal if your goal (conscious or unconscious) is to have everything work out in your favor. In my book, this is nothing more than a prescription for unhappiness and frustration.

The truth is, life is rarely exactly the way we want it to be, and other people often don't act as we would like them to. Moment to moment, there are aspects of life that we like and others that we don't. There are always going to be people who disagree with you, people who do things differently, and things that don't work out. If you fight against this principle of life, you'll spend most of your life fighting battles.

A more peaceful way to live is to decide consciously which battles are worth fighting and which are better left alone. If your primary goal isn't to have everything work out perfectly but instead to live a relatively stress-free life, you'll find that most battles pull you *away from* your most tranquil feelings. Is it really important that you prove to your spouse that you are right and she is wrong, or that you confront someone simply because it appears as though he or she has made a minor mistake? Does your preference of which restaurant or movie to go to matter enough to argue over it? Does a small scratch on your car really warrant a suit in small claims court? Does the fact that your neighbor won't park his car on a different part of the street have to be discussed at your family dinner table? These and thousands of other small things are what many people spend their lives fighting about. Take a look at your own list.

If it's like mine used to be, you might want to reevaluate your priorities.

If you don't want to "sweat the small stuff," it's critical that you choose your battles wisely. If you do, there will come a day when you'll rarely feel the need to do battle at all.

31.

Become Aware of Your Moods and Don't Allow Yourself to Be Fooled by the Low Ones

Your own moods can be extremely deceptive. They can, and probably do, trick you into believing your life is far worse than it really is. When you're in a good mood, life looks great. You have perspective, common sense, and wisdom. In good moods, things don't feel so hard, problems seem less formidable and easier to solve. When you're in a good mood, relationships seem to flow and communication is easy. If you are criticized, you take it in stride.

On the contrary, when you're in a bad mood, life looks unbearably serious and difficult. You have very little perspective. You take things personally and often misinterpret those around you, as you impute malignant motives into their actions.

Here's the catch: People don't realize their moods are always on the run. They think instead that their lives have suddenly become worse in the past day, or even the last hour. So, someone who is in a good mood in the morning might love his wife, his job, and his car. He is probably optimistic about his future and feels grateful about his past. But by late afternoon, if his mood is bad, he claims he hates his job, thinks of his wife as a nuisance, thinks his car is a junker, and believes he's going nowhere in his career. If you ask him about his childhood while he's in a low mood, he'll probably tell you it was extremely difficult. He will probably blame his parents for his current plight.

Such quick and drastic contrasts may seem absurd, even funny—but we're all like that. In low moods we lose our perspective and everything seems urgent. We completely forget that when we are in a good mood, everything seems so much better. We experience the *identical* circumstances—who we are married to, where we work, the car we drive, our potential, our childhood—entirely differently, depending on our mood! When we are low, rather than blaming our mood as would be appropriate, we instead tend to feel that our whole life is wrong. It's almost as if we actually believe that our lives have fallen apart in the past hour or two.

The truth is, life is almost *never* as bad as it seems when you're in a low mood. Rather than staying stuck in a bad temper, convinced you are seeing life realistically, you can learn to question your judgment. Remind yourself, "Of course I'm feeling defensive [or angry, frustrated, stressed, depressed]; I'm in a bad mood. I always feel negative when I'm low." When you're in an ill mood, learn to pass it off as simply that: an unavoidable human condition that *will* pass with time, if you leave it alone. A low mood is not the time to analyze your life. To do so is emotional suicide. If you have a legitimate problem, it will still be there when your state of mind improves. The trick is to be grateful for our good moods and graceful in our low moods— not taking them too seriously. The next time you feel low, for whatever reason, remind yourself, "This too shall pass." It will.

32.

Life Is a Test. It Is Only a Test

One of my favorite posters says, "Life is a test. It is only a test. Had this been a real life you would have been instructed where to go and what to do." Whenever I think of this humorous bit of wisdom, it reminds me to not take my life so seriously.

When you look at life and its many challenges as a test, or series of tests, you begin to see each issue you face as an opportunity to grow, a chance to roll with the punches. Whether you're being bombarded with problems, responsibilities, even insurmountable hurdles, when looked at as a test, you always have a chance to succeed, in the sense of rising above that which is challenging you. If, on the other hand, you see each new issue you face as a serious battle that must be won in order to survive, you're probably in for a very rocky journey. The only time you're likely to be happy is when everything is working out just right. And we all know how often that happens.

As an experiment, see if you can apply this idea to something you are forced to deal with. Perhaps you have a difficult teenager or a demanding boss. See if you can redefine the issue you face from being a "problem" to being a test. Rather than struggling with your issue, see if there is something you can learn from it. Ask yourself, "Why is this issue in my life? What would it mean and what would be involved to rise above it? Could I possibly look at this issue any differently? Can I see it as a test of some kind?"

If you give this strategy a try you may be surprised at your changed responses. For example, I used to struggle a great deal over the issue of my perception of not having enough time. I would rush around trying to get everything done. I blamed my schedule, my family, my circumstances, and anything else I could think of for my plight. Then it dawned on me. If I wanted to be happy, my goal didn't necessarily have to be to organize my life perfectly so that I had more time, but rather to see whether I could get to the point where I felt it was okay that I couldn't get everything done that I felt I must. In other words, my real challenge was to see my struggle as a test. Seeing this issue as a test ultimately helped me to cope with one of my biggest personal frustrations. I still struggle now and then about my perceived lack of time, but less than I used to. It has become far more acceptable to me to accept things as they are.

33.

Praise and Blame Are All the Same

One of the most unavoidable life lessons is having to deal with the disapproval of others. Praise and blame are all the same is a fancy way of reminding yourself of the old cliché that you'll never be able to please all the people all the time. Even in a landslide election victory in which a candidate secures 55 percent of the vote, he or she is left with 45 percent of the population that wishes someone else were the winner. Pretty humbling, isn't it?

Our approval rating from family, friends, and the people we work with isn't likely to be much higher. The truth is, everyone has their own set of ideas with which to evaluate life, and our ideas don't always match those of other people. For some reason, however, most of us struggle against this inevitable fact. We get angry, hurt, or otherwise frustrated when people reject our ideas, tell us no, or give us some other form of disapproval.

The sooner we accept the inevitable dilemma of not being able to win the approval of everyone we meet, the easier our lives will become. When you expect to be dished out your share of disapproval instead of struggling against this fact, you'll develop a helpful perspective to assist your life journey. Rather than feeling rejected by disapproval, you can remind yourself, "Here it is again. That's okay." You can learn to be pleasantly surprised, even grateful when you receive the approval you're hoping for.

I find that there are many days when I experience both praise and blame. Someone will hire me to speak and someone else won't want to; one phone call delivers good news, another announces a new issue to deal with. One of my children is happy with my behavior, the other struggles against it. Someone says what a nice guy I am, someone else thinks I'm selfish because I don't return his phone call. This back and forth, good and bad, approval and disapproval is a part of everyone's life. I'm the first to admit that I always prefer approval over disapproval. It feels better and it's certainly easier to deal with. The more content I've become, however, the less I depend on it for my sense of well-being.

34.

Practice Random Acts of Kindness

There is a bumper sticker that has been out for some time now. You see it on cars all across the nation (in fact, I have one on my own car). It says, "Practice Random Acts of Kindness and Senseless Acts of Beauty." I have no idea who thought of this idea, but I've never seen a more important message on a car in front of me. Practicing random kindness is an effective way to get in touch with the joy of giving without expecting anything in return. It's best practiced without letting anyone know what you are doing.

There are five toll bridges in the San Francisco Bay Area. A while back, some people began paying the tolls of the cars immediately behind them. The drivers would drive to the toll window, and pull out their dollar bill, only to be informed, "Your toll has been paid by the car ahead of you." This is an example of a spontaneous, random gift, something given without expectation of or demand for anything in return. You can imagine the impact that tiny gift had on the driver of the car! Perhaps it encouraged him to be a nicer person that day. Often a single act of kindness sets a series of kind acts in motion.

There is no prescription for how to practice random kindness. It comes from the heart. Your gift might be to pick up litter in your neighborhood, make an anonymous contribution to a charity, send some cash in an unmarked envelope to make someone experiencing financial stress breathe a little easier, save an animal by bringing it to an animal rescue agency, or get a volunteer position feeding hungry people at a church or shelter. You may want to do all these things, and more. The point is, giving is fun and it doesn't have to be expensive.

Perhaps the greatest reason to practice random kindness is that it brings great contentment into your life. Each act of kindness rewards you with positive feelings and reminds you of the important aspects of life—service, kindness, and love. If we all do our own part, pretty soon we will live in a nicer world.

35.

Look Beyond Behavior

Have you ever heard yourself, or someone else, say: "Don't mind John, he didn't know what he was doing"? If so, you have been exposed to the wisdom of "looking beyond behavior." If you have children, you know very well the importance of this simple act of forgiveness. If we all based our love on our children's behavior, it would often be difficult to love them at all. If love were based purely on behavior, then perhaps none of us would ever have been loved as a teenager!

Wouldn't it be nice if we could try to extend this same loving-kindness toward everyone we meet? Wouldn't we live in a more loving world if, when someone acted in a way that we didn't approve of, we could see their actions in a similar light as our teenagers' offbeat behavior?

This doesn't mean that we walk around with our heads in the sand, pretend that everything is always wonderful, allow others to "walk all over us," or that we excuse or approve of negative behavior. Instead, it simply means having the perspective to give others the benefit of the doubt. Know that when the postal clerk is moving slowly, he is probably having a bad day, or perhaps all of his days are bad. When your spouse or close friend snaps at you, try to understand that, beneath this isolated act, your loved one really wants to love you, and to feel loved by you. Looking beyond behavior is easier than you might think. Try it today, and you'll see and feel some nice results.

36.

See the Innocence

For many people, one of the most frustrating aspects of life is not being able to understand other people's behavior. We see them as "guilty" instead of "innocent." It's tempting to focus on people's seemingly irrational behavior—their comments, actions, mean-spirited acts, selfish behavior—and get extremely frustrated. If we focus on behavior too much, it can seem like other people are making us miserable.

But as I once heard Wayne Dyer sarcastically suggest in a lecture, "Round up all the people who are making you miserable and bring them to me. I will treat them [as a counselor], and you'll get better!" Obviously, this is absurd. It's true that other people do weird things (who doesn't?), but *we* are the ones getting upset, so we are the ones who need to change. I'm not talking about accepting, ignoring, or advocating violence or any other deviant behavior. I'm merely talking about learning to be less *bothered* by the actions of people.

Seeing the innocence is a powerful tool for transformation

that means when someone is acting in a way that we don't like, the best strategy for dealing with that person is to distance our-selves from the behavior; to "look beyond it," so that we can see the innocence in where the behavior is coming from. Very often, this slight shift in our thinking immediately puts us into a state of compassion.

Occasionally, I work with people who are pressuring me to hurry up. Often, their technique for getting me to hurry along is obnoxious, even insulting. If I focus on the words they use, the tone of their voices, and the urgency of their messages, I can get annoyed, even angry in my responses. I see them as "guilty." However, if I remember the urgency *I* feel when I'm in a hurry to do something, it allows me to see the innocence in their behavior. Underneath even the most annoying behavior is a frustrated person who is crying out for compassion.

The next time (and hopefully from now on), when someone acts in a strange way, look for the innocence in his behavior. If you're compassionate, it won't be hard to see. When you see the innocence, the same things that have always frustrated you no longer do. And, when you're not frustrated by the actions of others, it's a lot easier to stay focused on the beauty of life.

37.

Choose Being Kind over Being Right

As I first introduced in strategy number 12, you are given many opportunities to choose between being kind and being right. You have chances to point out to someone their mistakes, things they could or should have done differently, ways they can improve. You have chances to "correct" people, privately as well as in front of others. What all these opportunities amount to are chances to make someone else feel bad, and yourself feel bad in the process.

Without getting too psychoanalytical about it, the reason we are tempted to put others down, correct them, or show them how we're right and they're wrong is that our ego mistakenly believes that if we point out how someone else is wrong, we must be right, and therefore we will feel better.

In actuality, however, if you pay attention to the way you feel after you put someone down, you'll notice that you feel worse than before the put-down. Your heart, the compassionate part of you, knows that it's impossible to feel better at the expense of someone else.

Luckily, the opposite is true—when your goal is to build people up, to make them feel better, to share in their joy, you too reap the rewards of their positive feelings. The next time you have the chance to correct someone, even if their facts are a little off, resist the temptation. Instead, ask yourself, "What do I really want out of this interaction?" Chances are, what you want is a peaceful interaction where all parties leave feeling good. Each time you resist "being right," and instead choose kindness, you'll notice a peaceful feeling within.

Recently my wife and I were discussing a business idea that had turned out really well. I was talking about "my" idea, clearly taking credit for our success! Kris, in her usual loving manner, allowed me to have the glory. Later that day, I remembered that the idea was actually her idea, not mine. Whoops! When I called her to apologize, it was obvious to me that she cared more for my joy than she did her own need to take credit. She said that she enjoys seeing me happy and that it doesn't matter whose idea it was. (Do you see why she's so easy to love?)

Don't confuse this strategy with being a wimp, or not standing up for what you believe in. I'm not suggesting that it's not okay for you to be right—only that if you *insist* on being right, there is often a price to pay—your inner peace. In order to be a person filled with equanimity, you must choose kindness over being right, most of the time. The best place to start is with the next person you speak to.

38.

Tell Three People (Today) How Much You Love Them

A uthor Stephen Levine asks the question, "If you had an hour to live and could make only one phone call—who would you call, what would you say, and why are you waiting?" What a powerful message!

Who knows what we are waiting for? Perhaps we want to believe we will live forever, or that "someday" we will get around to telling the people we love how much we love them. Whatever the reasons, most of us simply wait too long.

As fate would have it, I'm writing this strategy on my grandmother's birthday. Later today, my father and I are driving out to visit her grave site. She died about two years ago. Before she passed away, it became obvious how important it was to her to let her family know how much she loved us all. It was a good reminder that there is no good reason to wait. Now is the time to let people know how much you care.

Ideally, you can tell someone in person or over the phone. I wonder how many people have been on the receiving end of a phone call where the caller says, "I just called to tell you how much I love you!" You may be surprised that almost nothing in the world means so much to a person. How would you like to receive the same message?

If you're too shy to make such a phone call, write a heartfelt letter instead. Either way, you may find that as you get used to it, letting people know how much you love them will become a regular part of your life. It probably won't shock you to know that, if it does, you'll probably begin receiving more love as a result.

39.

Practice Humility

Humility and inner peace go hand in hand. The less compelled you are to try to prove yourself to others, the easier it is to feel peaceful inside.

Proving yourself is a dangerous trap. It takes an enormous amount of energy to be continually pointing out your accomplishments, bragging, or trying to convince others of your worth as a human being. Bragging actually dilutes the positive feelings you receive from an accomplishment or something you are proud of. To make matters worse, the more you try to prove yourself, the more others will avoid you, talk behind your back about your insecure need to brag, and perhaps even resent you.

Ironically, however, the less you care about seeking approval, the more approval you seem to get. People are drawn to those with a quiet, inner confidence, people who don't need to *make* themselves look good, be "right" all the time, or steal the glory. Most people love a person who doesn't need to brag, a person who shares from his or her heart and not from his or her ego.

The way to develop genuine humility is to practice. It's nice because you will get immediate inner feedback in the way of calm, easy feelings. The next time you have an opportunity to brag, resist the temptation. I discussed this strategy with a client, and he shared the following story: He was with a group of friends a few days after he had been promoted at work. His friends didn't know it yet, but my client was chosen to be promoted instead of another friend of theirs. He was a little competitive with this person, and had the very strong temptation to sneak in the fact that he had been chosen and their other friend *wasn't*. He felt himself about ready to say something, when a little voice inside him said, "Stop. Don't do it!" He went ahead and shared with his friends, but didn't cross the line and turn the sharing into gloating. He never mentioned how their other friend didn't get promoted. He told me that he couldn't remember ever feeling so calm and proud of himself. He was able to enjoy his success without bragging. Later, when his friends did find out what had happened, they let him know that they were extremely impressed with his good judgment and humility. He received more positive feedback and attention from practicing humility—not less.

40.

When in Doubt about Whose Turn It Is
to Take Out the Trash,
Go Ahead and Take It Out

I f we're not careful, it's easy to become resentful about all the responsibilities of daily living. Once, in a very low mood, I figured out that on an average day, I do over 1,000 different things. Of course, when I'm in a better mood, that number is significantly lower.

As I think about it, it's astounding to me how easy it is for me to remember all the chores that I do, as well as all the other responsibilities that I take care of. But, at the same time, it's easy for me to forget all the things that my wife does on a daily basis. How convenient!

It's really difficult to become a contented person if you're keeping score of all you do. Keeping track only discourages you by cluttering your mind with who's doing what, who's doing more, and so forth. If you want to know the truth about it, this is the epitome of "small stuff." It will bring you far more joy to your life to know that you have done your part and someone else in your family has one less thing to do, than it will to worry and fret over whose turn it is to take out the trash.

The strongest argument against this strategy is the concern that you'll be taken advantage of. This mistake is similar to believing it's important that you're right. Most of the time it's *not* important that you're right, and neither is it important if you take the trash out a few more times than your spouse or housemate. Making things like garbage less relevant in your life will undoubtedly free up more time and energy for truly important things.

41.

Avoid Weatherproofing

The idea of weatherproofing as it pertains to peaceful living is a metaphor to explain one of our most neurotic, ungrateful tendencies. It comes from a friend of mind, Dr. George Pransky.

Just as we can weatherproof a home for the winter by looking for cracks, leaks, and imperfections, we can also weatherproof our relationships, even our lives, by doing the very same thing. Essentially, weatherproofing means that you are on the careful lookout for what needs to be fixed or repaired. It's finding the cracks and flaws of life, and either trying to fix them, or at least point them out to others. Not only does this tendency alienate you from other people, it makes you feel bad, too. It encourages you to think about what's *wrong* with everything and everyone—what you don't like. So, rather than appreciating our relationships and our lives, weatherproofing encourages us to end up thinking that life isn't all it's cracked up to be. Nothing is ever good enough the way it is.

In our relationships, weatherproofing typically plays itself out like this: You meet someone and all is well. You are attracted to his or her appearance, personality, intellect, sense of humor, or some combination of these traits. Initially, you not only approve of your differences with this person, you actually appreciate them. You might even be attracted to the person, in part because of how different you are. You have different opinions, preferences, tastes, and priorities.

After a while, however, you begin to notice little quirks about your new partner (or friend, teacher, whoever), that you feel could be improved upon. You bring it to their attention. You might say, "You know, you sure have a tendency to be late." Or, "I've noticed you don't read very much." The point is, you've begun what inevitably turns into a way of life—looking for and thinking about what you *don't like* about someone, or something that isn't quite right.

Obviously, an occasional comment, constructive criticism, or helpful guidance isn't cause for alarm. I have to say, however, that in the course of working with hundreds of couples over the years, I've met very few people who didn't feel that they were weatherproofed at times by their partner. Occasional harmless comments have an insidious tendency to become a way of looking at life.

When you are weatherproofing another human being, it says

106

nothing about them—but it does define you as someone who needs to be critical.

Whether you have a tendency to weatherproof your relationships, certain aspects of your life, or both, what you need to do is write off weatherproofing as a bad idea. As the habit creeps into your thinking, catch yourself and seal your lips. The less often you weatherproof your partner or your friends, the more you'll notice how super your life really is.

42.

Spend a Moment, Every Day,
Thinking of Someone to Love

Earlier in this book I introduced the idea of spending a moment, each day, thinking of someone to thank. Another excellent source of gratitude and inner peace is to spend a moment, every day, thinking of someone to love. Remember the old saying, "An apple a day keeps the doctor away?" The love equivalent might read, "Thinking of someone to love each day keeps your resentment away!"

I started consciously choosing to think of people to love when I realized how often I could get caught up in thinking about the opposite—people who irritate me. My mind would focus on negative or strange behavior, and within seconds I was filled with negativity. Once I made the conscious decision, however, to spend a moment each morning thinking of someone to love, my attention was redirected toward the positive, not only toward that one person, but in general throughout the day. I don't mean to suggest that I never get irritated anymore, but without question it happens much less frequently than it used to. I credit this exercise with much of my improvement.

Every morning when I wake up, I close my eyes and take a few deep breaths. Then I ask myself the question, "Who shall I send love to today?" Instantly, a picture of someone will pop into my mind—a family member, a friend, someone I work with, a neighbor, someone from my past, even a stranger I may have seen on the street. To me, it doesn't really matter who it is because the idea is to gear my mind toward love. Once the person to whom I'm directing the love is clear, I simply wish them a day filled with love. I might say to myself something like, "I hope you have a wonderful day filled with loving kindness." When I'm finished, which is within seconds, I usually feel that my heart is ready to begin my day. In some mystical way that I can't explain, those few seconds stick with me for many hours. If you give this little exercise a try, I think you'll find that your day is a little more peaceful.

43.

Become an Anthropologist

Anthropology is a science dealing with man and his origins. In this strategy, however, I'll conveniently redefine anthropology as "being interested, without judgment, in the way other people choose to live and behave." This strategy is geared toward developing your compassion, as well as a way of becoming more patient. Beyond that, however, being interested in the way other people act is a way of replacing judgments with loving-kindness. When you are genuinely curious about the way someone reacts or the way they feel about something, it's unlikely that you will also be annoyed. In this way, becoming an anthropologist is a way of becoming less frustrated by the actions of others.

When someone acts in a way that seems strange to you, rather than reacting in your usual way, such as, "I can't believe they would do that," instead say something to yourself like "I see, that must be the way she sees things in her world. Very interesting." In order for this strategy to help you, you have to be genuine. There's a fine line between being "interested" and being arrogant, as if secretly you believe that your way is better.

Recently I was at a local shopping mall with my six-year-old daughter. A group of punk rockers walked by with orange spiked hair and tattoos covering much of their bodies. My daughter immediately asked me, "Daddy, why are they dressed up like that? Are they in costumes?" Years ago I would have felt very judgmental and frustrated about these young people— as if their way was wrong and my more conservative way was right. I would have blurted out some judgmental explanation to my daughter and passed along to her my judgmental views. Pretending to be an anthropologist, however, has changed my perspective a great deal; it's made me softer. I said to my daughter, "I'm not really sure, but it's interesting how different we all are, isn't it?" She said, "Yeah, but I like my own hair." Rather than focusing on the behavior and continuing to give it energy, we both dropped it and continued to enjoy our time together.

When you are interested in other perspectives, it doesn't imply, even slightly, that you're advocating it. I certainly wouldn't choose a punk rock lifestyle or suggest it to anyone else. At the same time, however, it's really not my place to judge it either. One of the cardinal rules of joyful living is that judging others takes a great deal of energy and, without exception, pulls you away from where you want to be.

112

44.

Understand Separate Realities

While we're on the subject of being interested in the way other people do things, let's take a moment to discuss separate realities.

If you have traveled to foreign countries or seen depictions of them in movies, you are aware of vast differences among cultures. The principle of separate realities says that the differences among individuals is every bit as vast. Just as we wouldn't expect people of different cultures to see or do things as we would (in fact, we'd be disappointed if they did), this principle tells us that the individual differences in our ways of seeing the world prohibit this as well. It's not a matter of merely tolerating differences but of truly understanding and honoring the fact that it literally can't be any other way.

I have seen an understanding of this principle change lives. It can virtually eliminate quarrels. When we expect to see things differently, when we take it as a given that others will do things differently and react differently to the same stimuli, the compassion we have for ourselves and for others rises dramatically. The moment we expect otherwise, the potential for conflict exists.

I encourage you to consider deeply and respect the fact that we are all very different. When you do, the love you feel for others as well as the appreciation you have for your own uniqueness will increase.

45.

Develop Your Own Helping Rituals

If you want your life to stand for peace and kindness, it's helpful to do kind, peaceful things. One of my favorite ways to do this is by developing my own helping rituals. These little acts of kindness are opportunities to be of service and reminders of how good it feels to be kind and helpful.

We live in a rural area of the San Francisco Bay Area. Most of what we see is beauty and nature. One of the exceptions to the beauty is the litter that some people throw out of their windows as they are driving on the rural roads. One of the few drawbacks to living out in the boondocks is that public services, such as litter collection, are less available than they are closer to the city.

A helping ritual that I practice regularly with my two children is picking up litter in our surrounding area. We've become so accustomed to doing this that my daughters will often say to me in animated voices, "There's some litter, Daddy, stop the car!" And if we have time, we will often pull over and pick it up. It may seem strange, but we actually enjoy it. We pick up litter in parks, on sidewalks, practically anywhere. Once I even saw a complete stranger picking up litter close to where we live. He smiled at me and said, "I saw you doing it, and it seemed like a good idea."

Picking up litter is only one of an endless supply of possible helping rituals. You might like holding a door open for people, visiting lonely elderly people in nursing homes, or shoveling snow off someone else's driveway. Think of something that seems effortless yet helpful. It's fun, personally rewarding, and sets a good example. Everyone wins.

46.

Every Day, Tell at Least One Person Something You Like, Admire, or Appreciate about Them

How often do you remember (or take the time), to tell people how much you like, admire, or appreciate them? For many people, it's not often enough. In fact, when I ask people how often they *receive* heartfelt compliments from others, I hear answers like "I can't remember the last time I received a compliment," "Hardly ever," and, sadly, "I never receive them."

There are several reasons why we don't vocally let others know about our positive feelings toward them. I've heard excuses like, "They don't need to hear me say that—they already know," and "I do admire her, but I'm too embarrassed to say anything." But when you ask the would-be recipient if he or she enjoys being given genuine compliments and positive feedback, the answer nine times out of ten is, "I love it." Whether your reason for *not* giving compliments on a regular basis is not knowing what to say, embarrassment, feeling that other people already know their strengths and don't need to be told, or simply not being in the habit of doing it, it's time for a change.

Telling someone something that you like, admire, or appreciate about them is a "random act of kindness." It takes almost no effort (once you get used to it), yet it pays enormous dividends. Many people spend their entire lifetimes wishing that other people would acknowledge them. They feel this especially about their parents, spouses, children, and friends. But even compliments from strangers feel good if they are genuine. Letting someone know how you feel about them also feels good to the person offering the compliment. It's a gesture of loving-kindness. It means that your thoughts are geared toward what's right with someone. And when your thoughts are geared in a positive direction, your feelings are peaceful.

The other day I was in the grocery store and witnessed an incredible display of patience. The checkout clerk had just been chewed out by an angry customer, clearly without good cause. Rather than being reactive, the clerk defused the anger by remaining calm. When it was my turn to pay for my groceries I said to her, "I'm so impressed at the way you handled that customer." She looked me right in the eye and said, "Thank you, sir. Do you know you are the first person ever to give me a compliment in this store?" It took less than two seconds to let her know, yet it was a highlight of her day, and of mine.

118

47.

Argue for Your Limitations,
and They're Yours

M any people spend a great deal of energy arguing for their own limitations; "I can't do that," "I can't help it, I've always been that way," "I'll never have a loving relationship," and thousands of other negative and self-defeating statements.

Our minds are powerful instruments. When we decide that something is true or beyond our reach, it's very difficult to pierce through this self-created hurdle. When we argue for our position, it's nearly impossible. Suppose, for example, you tell yourself, "I can't write." You'll look for examples to prove your position. You'll remember your poor essays in high school, or recall how awkward you felt the last time you sat down to write a letter. You'll fill your head with limitations that will frighten you from trying. In order to become a writer or anything else, the first step is to silence your greatest critic—you.

I had a client who told me, "I'll never have a good relationship. I always screw them up." Sure enough, she was right. Whenever she met someone, she would, without even knowing it, look for reasons for her new partner to leave her. If she were late for a date, she would tell him, "I'm always late." If they had a disagreement, she would say, "I'm always getting into arguments." Sooner or later, she would convince him that she wasn't worthy of his love. Then she would say to herself, "See, it happens every time. I'll never have a good relationship."

She had to learn to stop expecting things to go wrong. She needed to "catch herself" in the act of arguing for her own limitations. When she started to say, "I always do that," she needed instead to say, "That's ridiculous. I don't *always* do anything." She had to see that arguing for her limitations was just a negative habit that could easily be replaced with a more positive habit. Today, she's doing much better. When she reverts to her old habit, she usually laughs at herself.

I have learned that when I argue for my own limitations, very seldom do I disappoint myself. I suspect the same is true for you.

48.

Remember that Everything Has
God's Fingerprints on It

Rabbi Harold Kushner reminds us that everything that God has created is potentially holy. Our task as humans is to find that holiness in what appear to be unholy situations. He suggests that when we can learn to do this, we will have learned to nurture our souls. It's easy to see God's beauty in a beautiful sunrise, a snow-capped mountain, the smile of a healthy child, or in ocean waves crashing on a sandy beach. But can we learn to find the holiness in seemingly ugly circumstances—difficult life lessons, a family tragedy, or a struggle for life?

When our life is filled with the desire to see the holiness in everyday things, something magical begins to happen. A feeling of peace emerges. We begin to see nurturing aspects of daily living that were previously hidden to us. When we remember that everything has God's fingerprints on it, that alone makes it special. If we remember this spiritual fact while we are dealing with a difficult person or struggling to pay our bills, it broadens our perspective. It helps us to remember that God also created the person you are dealing with or that, despite your struggle to pay your bills, you are truly blessed to have all that you do.

Somewhere, in the back of your mind, try to remember that everything has God's fingerprints on it. The fact that we can't see the beauty in something doesn't suggest that it's not there. Rather, it suggests that we are not looking carefully enough or with a broad enough perspective to see it.

49.

Resist the Urge to Criticize

When we judge or criticize another person, it says nothing about that person; it merely says something about our own need to be critical.

If you attend a gathering and listen to all the criticism that is typically levied against others, and then go home and consider how much good all that criticism actually does to make our world a better place, you'll probably come up with the same answer that I do: Zero! It does no good. But that's not all. Being critical not only solves nothing; it contributes to the anger and distrust in our world. After all, none of us likes to be criticized. Our reaction to criticism is usually to become defensive and/or withdrawn. A person who feels attacked is likely to do one of two things: he will either retreat in fear or shame, or he will attack or lash out in anger. How many times have you criticized someone and had them respond by saying, "Thank you so much for pointing out my flaws. I really appreciate it"?

Criticism, like swearing, is actually nothing more than a bad

123

habit. It's something we get used to doing; we're familiar with how it feels. It keeps us busy and gives us something to talk about.

If, however, you take a moment to observe how you actually feel immediately after you criticize someone, you'll notice that you will feel a little deflated and ashamed, almost like *you're* the one who has been attacked. The reason this is true is that when we criticize, it's a statement to the world and to ourselves, "I have a need to be critical." This isn't something we are usually proud to admit.

The solution is to catch yourself in the act of being critical. Notice how often you do it and how bad it makes you feel. What I like to do is turn it into a game. I still catch myself being critical, but as my need to criticize arises, I try to remember to say to myself, "There I go again." Hopefully, more often than not, I can turn my criticism into tolerance and respect.

50.

Write Down Your Five Most Stubborn
Positions and See if You Can Soften Them

The first time I tried this strategy, I was so stubborn that I insisted that I *wasn't* stubborn! Over time, as I have worked toward becoming a gentler person, I have found it far easier to see where I'm being stubborn.

Here are a few examples from my clients: "People who aren't stressed are lazy." "My way is the only way." "Men aren't good listeners." "Women spend too much money." "Children are too much work." "People in business don't care about anything except money." You can see that the list itself is potentially endless. The point here isn't the specifics of what you are stubborn about but rather the fact that you hold on so tightly to any given idea you might have.

It doesn't make you weak to soften your positions. In fact, it makes you stronger. I have a male client who was adamant, to the point of being obnoxious about it, that his wife spent too much money. As he relaxed a little, and noticed his own rigidity, he discovered something that he's now a little embarrassed about, but laughs at. He found out that, in reality, he spent *more* discretionary money on himself than his wife spent on herself! His objectivity had become muddled by his own rigid belief.

As he has become wiser and gentler, his marriage has improved immensely. Rather than resenting his wife for something she wasn't even doing, he now appreciates her restraint. She, in turn, feels his new acceptance and appreciation and loves him more than before.

51.

Just for Fun, Agree with Criticism Directed Toward You (Then Watch It Go Away)

So often we are immobilized by the slightest criticism. We treat it like an emergency, and defend ourselves as if we were in a battle. In truth, however, criticism is nothing more than an observation by another person about us, our actions, or the way we think about something, that doesn't match the vision we have of ourselves. Big deal!

When we react to criticism with a knee-jerk, defensive response, it hurts. We feel attacked, and we have a need to defend or to offer a countercriticism. We fill our minds with angry or hurtful thoughts directed at ourselves or at the person who is being critical. All this reaction takes an enormous amount of mental energy.

An incredibly useful exercise is to agree with criticism directed toward you. I'm not talking about turning into a doormat or ruining your self-esteem by believing all negativity that comes in your direction. I'm only suggesting that there are many times when simply agreeing with criticism defuses the situation, satisfies a person's need to express a point of view, offers you a chance to learn something about yourself by seeing a grain of truth in another position, and, perhaps most important, provides you an opportunity to remain calm.

One of the first times I consciously agreed with criticism directed toward me was many years ago when my wife said to me, "Sometimes you talk too much." I remember feeling momentarily hurt before deciding to agree. I responded by saying, "You're right, I do talk too much sometimes." I discovered something that changed my life. In agreeing with her, I was able to see that she had a good point. I often do talk too much! What's more, my nondefensive reaction helped her to relax. A few minutes later she said, "You know, you're sure easy to talk to." I doubt she would have said that had I become angry at her observation. I've since learned that reacting to criticism never makes the criticism go away. In fact, negative reactions to criticism often convince the person doing the criticizing that they are accurate in their assessment of you.

Give this strategy a try. I think you'll discover that agreeing with an occasional criticism has more value than it costs.

52.

Search for the Grain of Truth
in Other Opinions

I f you enjoy learning as well as making other people happy, you'll love this idea.

Almost everyone feels that their own opinions are good ones, otherwise they wouldn't be sharing them with you. One of the destructive things that many of us do, however, is compare someone else's opinion to our own. And, when it doesn't fall in line with our belief, we either dismiss it or find fault with it. We feel smug, the other person feels diminished, and we learn nothing.

Almost every opinion has some merit, especially if we are looking for merit, rather than looking for errors. The next time someone offers you an opinion, rather than judge or criticize it, see if you can find a grain of truth in what the person is saying.

If you think about it, when you judge someone else or their opinion, it really doesn't say *anything* about the other person, but it says quite a bit about your need to be judgmental.

I still catch myself criticizing other points of view, but far

129

less than I used to. All that changed was my intention to find the grain of truth in other positions. If you practice this simple strategy, some wonderful things will begin to happen: You'll begin to understand those you interact with, others will be drawn to your accepting and loving energy, your learning curve will be enhanced, and, perhaps most important, you'll feel much better about yourself.

53.

See the Glass as Already Broken
(and Everything Else Too)

This is a Buddhist teaching that I learned over twenty years ago. It has provided me, again and again, with greatly needed perspective to guide me toward my goal of a more accepting self.

The essence of this teaching is that all of life is in a constant state of change. Everything has a beginning and everything has an end. Every tree begins with a seed and will eventually transform back into earth. Every rock is formed and every rock will vanish. In our modern world, this means that every car, every machine, every piece of clothing is created and all will wear out and crumble; it's only a matter of when. Our bodies are born and they will die. A glass is created and will eventually break.

There is peace to be found in this teaching. When you expect something to break, you're not surprised or disappointed when it does. Instead of becoming immobilized when something is destroyed, you feel grateful for the time you have had.

The easiest place to start is with the simple things, a glass of water, for example. Pull out your favorite drinking glass. Take a moment to look at and appreciate its beauty and all it does for you. Now, imagine that same glass as already broken, shattered all over the floor. Try to maintain the perspective that, in time, everything disintegrates and returns to its initial form.

Obviously, no one wants their favorite drinking glass, or anything else, to be broken. This philosophy is not a prescription for becoming passive or apathetic, but for making peace with the way things are. When your drinking glass does break, this philosophy allows you to maintain your perspective. Rather than thinking, "Oh my God," you'll find yourself thinking, "Ah, there it goes." Play with this awareness and you'll find yourself not only keeping your cool but appreciating life as never before.

54.

Understand the Statement,
"Wherever You Go, There You Are"

This is the title of a super book by Jon Kabat-Zinn. As the title suggests, wherever you go, you take yourself with you! The significance of this statement is that it can teach you to stop constantly wishing you were somewhere else. We tend to believe that if we were somewhere else—on vacation, with another partner, in a different career, a different home, a different circumstance—somehow we would be happier and more content. We wouldn't!

The truth is, if you have destructive mental habits—if you get annoyed and bothered easily, if you feel angry and frustrated a great deal of the time, or if you're constantly wishing things were different, these identical tendencies will follow you, wherever you go. And the reverse is also true. If you are a generally happy person who rarely gets annoyed and bothered, then you can move from place to place, from person to person, with very little negative impact.

Someone once asked me, "What are the people like in California?" I asked him, "What are the people like in your home state?" He replied, "Selfish and greedy." I told him that he would probably find the people in California to be selfish and greedy.

Something wonderful begins to happen with the simple realization that life, like an automobile, is driven from the inside out, not the other way around. As you focus more on becoming more peaceful with where you are, rather than focusing on where you would *rather* be, you begin to find peace right now, in the present. Then, as you move around, try new things, and meet new people, you carry that sense of inner peace with you. It's absolutely true that "Wherever you go, there you are."

55.

Breathe Before You Speak

This simple strategy has had remarkable results for virtually everyone I know who has tried it. The almost immediate results include increased patience, added perspective, and, as a side benefit, more gratitude and respect from others.

The strategy itself is remarkably simple. It involves nothing more than pausing—breathing—after the person to whom you are speaking is finished. At first, the time gap between your voices may seem like an eternity—but in reality, it amounts to only a fraction of a second of actual time. You will get used to the power and beauty of breathing, and you will come to appreciate it as well. It will bring you closer to, and earn you more respect from, virtually everyone you come in contact with. You'll find that being listened to is one of the rarest and most treasured gifts you can offer. All it takes is intention and practice.

If you observe the conversations around you, you'll notice

that, often, what many of us do is simply wait for *our* chance to speak. We're not *really* listening to the other person, but simply waiting for an opening to express our own view. We often complete other people's sentences, or say things like, "Yeah, yeah," or "I know," very rapidly, urging them to hurry up so that we can have our turn. It seems that talking to one another is sometimes more like sparring back and forth like fighters or Ping-Pong balls than it is enjoying or learning from the conversation.

This harried form of communication encourages us to criticize points of view, overreact, misinterpret meaning, impute false motives, and form opinions, all before our fellow communicator is even finished speaking. No wonder we are so often annoyed, bothered, and irritated with one another. Sometimes, with our poor listening skills, it's a miracle that we have any friends at all!

I spent most of my life waiting for my turn to speak. If you're at all like me, you'll be pleasantly amazed at the softer reactions and looks of surprise as you let others completely finish their thought before you begin yours. Often, you will be allowing someone to feel listened to for the very first time. You will sense a feeling of relief coming from the person to whom you are speaking—and a much calmer, less rushed feeling between the two of you. No need to worry that you won't get your turn to speak—you will. In fact, it will be more rewarding to speak because the person you are speaking to will pick up on your respect and patience and will begin to do the same.

56.

Be Grateful when You're Feeling Good and
Graceful when You're Feeling Bad

The happiest person on earth isn't always happy. In fact, the happiest people *all* have their fair share of low moods, problems, disappointments, and heartache. Often the difference between a person who is happy and someone who is unhappy isn't how often they get low, or even how low they drop, but instead, it's what they do with their low moods. How do they relate to their changing feelings?

Most people have it backward. When they are feeling down, they roll up their sleeves and get to work. They take their low moods very seriously and try to figure out and analyze what's wrong. They try to force themselves out of their low state, which tends to compound the problem rather than solve it.

When you observe peaceful, relaxed people, you find that when they are feeling good, they are very grateful. They understand that both positive and negative feelings come and go, and that there will come a time when they won't be feeling so good. To happy people, this is okay, it's the way of things. They accept the inevitability of passing feelings. So, when they are feeling depressed, angry, or stressed out, they relate to these feelings with the same openness and wisdom. Rather than fight their feelings and panic simply because they are feeling bad, they accept their feelings, knowing that this too shall pass. Rather than stumbling and fighting against their negative feelings, they are graceful in their acceptance of them. This allows them to come gently and gracefully out of negative feeling states into more positive states of mind. One of the happiest people I know is someone who also gets quite low from time to time. The difference, it seems, is that he has become comfortable with his low moods. It's almost as though he doesn't really care because he knows that, in due time, he will be happy again. To him, it's no big deal.

The next time you're feeling bad, rather than fight it, try to relax. See if, instead of panicking, you can be graceful and calm. Know that if you don't fight your negative feelings, if you are graceful, they will pass away just as surely as the sun sets in the evening.

57.

Become a Less Aggressive Driver

Where do you get the most uptight? If you're like most people, driving in traffic is probably high on your list. To look at most major freeways these days, you'd think you were on a racetrack instead of a roadway.

There are three excellent reasons for becoming a less aggressive driver. First, when you are aggressive, you put yourself and everyone around you in extreme danger. Second, driving aggressively is extremely stressful. Your blood pressure goes up, your grip on the wheel tightens, your eyes are strained, and your thoughts are spinning out of control. Finally, you end up saving no time in getting to where you want to go.

Recently I was driving south from Oakland to San Jose. Traffic was heavy, but moving. I noticed an extremely aggressive and angry driver weaving in and out of the lanes, speeding up and slowing down. Clearly, he was in a hurry. For the most part I remained in the same lane for the entire forty-mile journey. I was listening to a new audiotape I had just purchased and day-dreaming along the way. I enjoyed the trip a great deal because

141

driving gives me a chance to be alone. As I was exiting off the freeway, the aggressive driver came up behind me and raced on by. Without realizing it, I had actually arrived in San Jose ahead of him. All of his weaving, rapid acceleration, and putting families at risk had earned him nothing except perhaps some high blood pressure and a great deal of wear and tear on his vehicle. On average, he and I had driven at the same speed.

The same principle applies when you see drivers speeding past you so that they can beat you to the next stoplight. It simply doesn't pay to speed. This is especially true if you get a ticket and have to spend eight hours in traffic school. It will take you years of dangerous speeding to make up this time alone.

When you make the conscious decision to become a less aggressive driver, you begin using your time in the car to relax. Try to see your driving not only as a way of getting you somewhere, but as a chance to breathe and to reflect. Rather than tensing your muscles, see if you can relax them instead. I even have a few audiotapes that are specifically geared toward muscular relaxation. Sometimes I pop one in and listen. By the time I reach my destination I feel more relaxed than I did before getting into the car. During the course of your lifetime, you're probably going to spend a great deal of time driving. You can spend those moments being frustrated, or you can use them wisely. If you do the latter, you'll be a more relaxed person.

58.

Relax

What does it mean to relax? Despite hearing this term thousands of times during the course of our lives, very few people have deeply considered what it's really about.

When you ask people (which I have done many times) what it means to relax, most will answer in a way that suggests that relaxing is something you plan to do later—you do it on vacation, in a hammock, when you retire, or when you get everything done. This implies, of course, that most other times (the other 95 percent of your life) should be spent nervous, agitated, rushed, and frenzied. Very few actually come out and say so, but this is the obvious implication. Could this explain why so many of us operate as if life were one great big emergency? Most of us postpone relaxation until our "in basket" is empty. Of course it never is.

It's useful to think of relaxation as a quality of heart that you can access on a regular basis rather than something reserved for some later time. You can relax now. It's helpful to remember that relaxed people can still be superachievers and, in fact, that relaxation and creativity go hand in hand. When I'm feeling uptight, for example, I don't even try to write. But when I feel relaxed, my writing flows quickly and easily.

Being more relaxed involves training yourself to respond differently to the dramas of life—turning your melodrama into a mellow-drama. It comes, in part, from reminding yourself over and over again (with loving kindness and patience) that you have a choice in how you respond to life. You can learn to relate to your thinking as well as your circumstances in new ways. With practice, making these choices will translate into a more relaxed self.

59.

Adopt a Child Through the Mail

While I don't want to turn this book into an advertisement for service agencies, I do have to say that my experience of adopting children through the mail has been extremely positive. No, you don't actually *adopt* a child, but you do get to help one out while, at the same time, getting to know them. The experience has brought tremendous joy and satisfaction to my entire family. My six-year-old daughter has an adoptee, and has enjoyed and learned from the experience a great deal. My daughter and her pal regularly write to each other, and draw pictures that we hang up. They enjoy hearing about each other's lives.

Each month you contribute a very small amount of money to the agency in charge of helping the children. The money is used to help the children and their parents with the necessities of life, which makes sending the children to school and caring for their needs a little easier.

I think that the reason we enjoy this type of giving so much is that it's interactive. So often, when you give to a charity, you have no way of knowing who you are helping. In this instance, you not only get to know who, but you have the privilege of getting to know them as well. Also, the regularity of the ongoing relationship reminds you how fortunate you are to be in a position to help. For me and for many people that I know, this type of giving brings forth feelings of gratitude. There are many fine agencies to choose from, but my personal favorite is Children, Inc., out of Richmond, Virginia, (800) 538-5381.

60.

Turn Your Melodrama into a Mellow-Drama

In a certain respect, this strategy is just another way of saying, "Don't sweat the small stuff." Many people live as if life were a melodrama—"an extravagantly theatrical play in which action and plot predominate." Sound familiar? In dramatic fashion, we blow things out of proportion, and make a big deal out of little things. We forget that life isn't as bad as we're making it out to be. We also forget that when we're blowing things out of proportion, *we* are the ones doing the blowing.

I've found that simply reminding myself that life doesn't have to be a soap opera is a powerful method of calming down. When I get too worked up or start taking myself too seriously (which happens more than I like to admit), I say to myself something like, "Here I go again. My soap opera is starting." Almost always, this takes the edge off my seriousness and helps me laugh at myself. Often, this simple reminder enables me to change the channel to a more peaceful station. My melodrama is transformed into a "mellow-drama."

If you've ever watched a soap opera, you've seen how the characters will take little things so seriously as to ruin their lives over them—someone says something to offend them, looks at them wrong, or flirts with their spouse. Their response is usually, "Oh my gosh. How could this happen to me?" Then they exacerbate the problem by talking to others about "how awful it is." They turn life into an emergency—a melodrama.

The next time you feel stressed out, experiment with this strategy—remind yourself that life isn't an emergency and turn your melodrama into a mellow-drama.

61.

Read Articles and Books with Entirely
Different Points of View from Your Own
and Try to Learn Something

Have you ever noticed that practically everything you read justifies and reinforces your own opinions and views on life? The same is true with our radio and television listening and viewing choices as well. In fact, on America's most popular radio talk show, callers often identify themselves as "ditto heads," meaning "I already agree with everything you say. Tell me more." Liberals, conservatives—we're all the same. We form opinions and then spend our entire lifetimes validating what we believe to be true. This rigidity is sad, because there is so much we can learn from points of view that are different from our own. It's also sad because the stubbornness it takes to keep our heart and mind closed to everything other than our own point of view creates a great deal of inner stress. A closed mind is always fighting to keep everything else at arm's length.

We forget that we're all equally convinced that our way of

looking at the world is the only correct way. We forget that two people who disagree with one another can often use the *identical* examples to prove their own point of view—and both sides can be articulate and convincing.

Knowing this, we can either buckle down and get even more stubborn—or we can lighten up and try to learn something new! For just a few minutes a day—whatever your slant on life—try making a gentle effort to read articles and/or books with different points of view. You don't need to change your core beliefs or your deepest held positions. All you're doing is expanding your mind and opening your heart to new ideas. This new openness will reduce the stress it takes to keep other points of view away. In addition to being very interesting, this practice helps you see the innocence in others as well as helping you become more patient. You'll become a more relaxed, philosophic person, because you'll begin to sense the logic in other points of view. My wife and I subscribe to both the most conservative as well as the most liberal newsletters in America. I'd say that both have broadened our perspective on life.

62.

Do One Thing at a Time

The other day I was driving on the freeway and noticed a man who, while driving in the fast lane, was shaving, drinking a cup of coffee, and reading the newspaper! "Perfect," I thought to myself, as just that morning I was trying to think of an appropriate example to point out the craziness of our frenzied society.

How often do we try to do more than one thing at once? We have cordless phones that are supposed to make our lives easier, but in some respects, they make our lives more confusing. My wife and I were at a friend's home for dinner a while ago and noticed her talking on the phone while simultaneously answering the door, checking on dinner, and changing her daughter's diaper (after she washed her hands, of course)! Many of us have the same tendency when we're speaking to someone and our mind is somewhere else, or when we're doing three or four chores all at the same time.

When you do too many things at once, it's impossible to

be present-moment oriented. Thus, you not only lose out on much of the potential enjoyment of what you are doing, but you also become far less focused and effective.

An interesting exercise is to block out periods of time where you commit to doing only one thing at a time. Whether you're washing dishes, talking on the phone, driving a car, playing with your child, talking to your spouse, or reading a magazine, try to focus only on that one thing. Be present in what you are doing. Concentrate. You'll notice two things beginning to happen. First, you'll actually enjoy what you are doing, even something mundane like washing dishes or cleaning out a closet. When you're focused, rather than distracted, it enables you to become absorbed and interested in your activity, whatever it might be. Second, you'll be amazed at how quickly and efficiently you'll get things done. Since I've become more present-moment oriented, my skills have increased in virtually all areas of my life— writing, reading, cleaning house, and speaking on the phone. You can do the same thing. It all starts with your decision to do one thing at a time.

63.

Count to Ten

When I was growing up my father used to count out loud to ten when he was angry with my sisters and me. It was a strategy he, and many other parents, used to cool down before deciding what to do next.

I've improved this strategy by incorporating the use of the breath. All you have to do is this: When you feel yourself getting angry, take a long, deep inhalation, and as you do, say the number one to yourself. Then, relax your entire body as you breathe out. Repeat the same process with the number two, all the way through *at least* ten (if you're really angry, continue to twenty-five). What you are doing here is clearing your mind with a mini version of a meditation exercise. The combination of counting and breathing is so relaxing that it's almost impossible to remain angry once you are finished. The increased oxygen in your lungs and the time gap between the moment you became angry and the time you finish the exercise enables you to increase your perspective. It helps make "big stuff" look like "little

153

stuff." The exercise is equally effective in working with stress or frustration. Whenever you feel a little off, give it a try.

The truth is, this exercise is a wonderful way to spend a minute or two whether or not you're angry. I've incorporated this strategy into my daily life simply because it's relaxing and I enjoy it. Often, it helps me to keep from getting angry in the first place.

64.

Practice Being in the "Eye of the Storm"

The eye of the storm is that one specific spot in the center of a twister, hurricane, or tornado that is calm, almost isolated from the frenzy of activity. Everything around the center is violent and turbulent, but the center remains peaceful. How nice it would be if we too could be calm and serene in the midst of chaos—in the eye of the storm.

Surprisingly enough, it's much easier that you might imagine to be in the eye of a "human storm." What it takes is intention and practice. Suppose, for example, that you are going to a family gathering that is going to be chaotic. You can tell yourself that you are going to use the experience as an opportunity to remain calm. You can commit to being the one person in the room who is going to be an example of peace. You can practice breathing. You can practice listening. You can let others be right and enjoy the glory. The point is, you can do it if you set your mind to it.

By starting out with harmless scenarios like family gatherings, cocktail parties, and birthday parties for children, you can build a track record and enjoy some success. You'll notice that by being in the eye of the storm, you will be more present-moment oriented. You'll enjoy yourself more than ever before. Once you have mastered harmless circumstances like these, you can practice on more difficult areas of life—dealing with conflict, hardship, or grief. If you start slowly, have some success, and keep practicing, pretty soon you'll know how to live in the eye of the storm.

65.

Be Flexible with Changes in Your Plans

Once I get something in my mind (a plan), it can be tricky to let go of it and go with the flow. I was taught, and to some degree it's certainly true, that success, or successfully completing a project, requires perseverance. At the same time, however, inflexibility creates an enormous amount of inner stress and is often irritating and insensitive to other people.

I like to do the majority of my writing in the wee hours of the morning. I might have the goal, in this book for example, to complete one or two strategies before anyone else in the house wakes up. But what happens if my four-year-old wakes up early and walks upstairs to see me? My plans have certainly been altered, but how do I react? Or, I might have the goal to go out for a run before going to the office. What happens if I get an emergency call from the office and have to skip my run?

There are countless potential examples for all of us—times when our plans suddenly change, something we thought was going to take place doesn't, someone doesn't do what they said they would do, you make less money than you thought you would, someone changes your plans without your consent, you have less time than previously planned, something unexpected comes up—and on and on it goes. The question to ask yourself is, What's *really* important?

We often use the excuse that it's natural to be frustrated when our plans change. That depends, however, on what your priorities are. Is it more important to stick to some rigid writing schedule or to be available to my four-year-old? Is missing a thirty-minute run worth getting upset over? The more general question is, "What's more important, getting what I want and keeping my plans, or learning to go with the flow?" Clearly, to become a more peaceful person, you must prioritize being flexible over rigidity most of the time (obviously there will be exceptions). I've also found it helpful to *expect* that a certain percentage of plans will change. If I make allowances in my mind for this inevitability, then when it happens I can say, "Here is one of those inevitabilities."

You'll find that if you create the goal to become more flexible, some wonderful things will begin to happen: You'll feel more relaxed, yet you won't sacrifice any productivity. You may even become *more* productive because you won't need to expend so much energy being upset and worried. I've learned to trust that I will keep my deadlines, achieve most of my goals, and honor my responsibilities despite the fact that I may have to alter my plans slightly (or even completely). Finally, the people around you will be more relaxed too. They won't feel like they have to walk around on eggshells if, by some chance, your plans have to change.

.

66.

Think of What You Have Instead of What You Want

In over a dozen years as a stress consultant, one of the most pervasive and destructive mental tendencies I've seen is that of focusing on what we *want* instead of what we *have*. It doesn't seem to make any difference how much we have; we just keep expanding our list of desires, which guarantees we will remain dissatisfied. The mind-set that says "I'll be happy when this desire is fulfilled" is the same mind-set that will repeat itself once that desire is met.

A friend of ours closed escrow on his new home on a Sunday. The very next time we saw him he was talking about his next house that was going to be even bigger! He isn't alone. Most of us do the very same thing. We want this or that. If we don't get what we want we keep thinking about all that we don't have—and we remain dissatisfied. If we do get what we want, we simply re-create the same thinking in our new circumstances. So, despite getting what we want, we still remain unhappy. Happiness can't be found when we are yearning for new desires.

Luckily, there is a way to be happy. It involves changing the emphasis of our thinking from what we want to what we have. Rather than wishing your spouse were different, try thinking about her wonderful qualities. Instead of complaining about your salary, be grateful that you have a job. Rather than wishing you were able to take a vacation to Hawaii, think of how much fun you have had close to home. The list of possibilities is endless! Each time you notice yourself falling into the "I wish life were different" trap, back off and start over. Take a breath and remember all that you have to be grateful for. When you focus not on what you want, but on what you have, you end up getting more of what you want anyway. If you focus on the good qualities of your spouse, she'll be more loving. If you are grateful for your job rather than complaining about it, you'll do a better job, be more productive, and probably end up getting a raise anyway. If you focus on ways to enjoy yourself around home rather than waiting to enjoy yourself in Hawaii, you'll end up having more fun. If you ever do get to Hawaii, you'll be in the habit of enjoying yourself. And, if by some chance you don't, you'll have a great life anyway.

Make a note to yourself to start thinking more about what you have than what you want. If you do, your life will start appearing much better than before. For perhaps the first time in your life, you'll know what it means to feel satisfied.

67.

Practice Ignoring Your Negative Thoughts

It has been estimated that the average human being has around 50,000 thoughts per day. That's a lot of thoughts. Some of these thoughts are going to be positive and productive. Unfortunately, however, many of them are also going to be negative—angry, fearful, pessimistic, worrisome. Indeed, the important question in terms of becoming more peaceful isn't whether or not you're going to have negative thoughts—you are—it's what you choose to do with the ones that you have.

In a practical sense, you really have only two options when it comes to dealing with negative thoughts. You can analyze your thoughts—ponder, think through, study, think some more—or you can learn to ignore them—dismiss, pay less attention to, not take so seriously. This later option, learning to take your negative thoughts less seriously, is infinitely more effective in terms of learning to be more peaceful.

When you have a thought—any thought—that's all it is, a thought! It can't hurt you without your consent. For example, if you have a thought from your past, "I'm upset because my parents didn't do a very good job," you can get into it, as many do, which will create inner turmoil for you. You can give the thought significance in your mind, and you'll convince yourself that you should indeed be unhappy. Or, you can recognize that your mind is about to create a mental snowball, and you can choose to dismiss the thought. This doesn't mean your childhood wasn't difficult—it may very well have been—but in *this* present moment, you have a choice of which thoughts to pay attention to.

The same mental dynamic applies to thoughts of this morning, even five minutes ago. An argument that happened while you were walking out the door on your way to work is no longer an actual argument, it's a thought in your mind. This dynamic also applies to future-oriented thoughts of this evening, next week, or ten years down the road. You'll find, in all cases, that if you ignore or dismiss a negative thought that fills your mind, a more peaceful feeling is only a moment away. And, in a more peaceful state of mind, your wisdom and common sense will tell you what to do. This strategy takes practice but is well worth the effort.

68.

Be Willing to Learn
from Friends and Family

One of the saddest observations I've made centers around how reluctant many of us are to learn from the people closest to us—our parents, spouses, children, and friends. Rather than being open to learning, we close ourselves off out of embarrassment, fear, stubbornness, or pride. It's almost as if we say to ourselves, "I have already learned all that I can [or want to learn] from this person; there is nothing else I can [or need to] learn."

It's sad, because often the people closest to us know us the best. They are sometimes able to see ways in which we are acting in a self-defeating manner and can offer very simple solutions. If we are too proud or stubborn to learn, we lose out on some wonderful, simple ways to improve our lives.

I have tried to remain open to the suggestions of my friends and family. In fact, I have gone so far as to ask certain members of my family and a few of my friends, "What are some of my blind spots?" Not only does this make the person you are asking feel wanted and special, but you end up getting some terrific advice. It's such a simple shortcut for growth, yet almost no one uses it. All it takes is a little courage and humility, and the ability to let go of your ego. This is especially true if you are in the habit of ignoring suggestions, taking them as criticism, or tuning out certain members of your family. Imagine how shocked they will be when you ask them, sincerely, for their advice.

Pick something that you feel the person whom you are asking is qualified to answer. For example, I often ask my father for advice on business. Even if he happens to give me a bit of a lecture, it's well worth it. The advice he gives usually prevents me from having to learn something the hard way.

69.

Be Happy Where You Are

Sadly, many of us continually postpone our happiness—indefinitely. It's not that we consciously set out to do so, but that we keep convincing ourselves, "Someday I'll be happy." We tell ourselves we'll be happy when our bills are paid, when we get out of school, get our first job, a promotion. We convince ourselves that life will be better after we get married, have a baby, then another. Then we are frustrated that the kids aren't old enough—we'll be more content when they are. After that, we're frustrated that we have teenagers to deal with. We will certainly be happy when they are out of that stage. We tell ourselves that our life will be complete when our spouse gets his or her act together, when we get a nicer car, are able to go on a nice vacation, when we retire. And on and on and on!

Meanwhile, life keeps moving forward. The truth is, there's no better time to be happy than right now. If not now, when? Your life will always be filled with challenges. It's best to admit this to yourself and decide to be happy anyway. One of my favorite quotes comes from Alfred D' Souza. He said, "For a long time it had seemed to me that life was about to begin—real life. But there was always some obstacle in the way, something to be got through first, some unfinished business, time still to be served, a debt to be paid. Then life would begin. At last it dawned on me that these obstacles were my life." This perspective has helped me to see that there is no way *to* happiness. Happiness *is* the way.

70.

Remember that You Become
What You Practice Most

Repeated practice is one of the most basic principles of most spiritual and meditative paths. In other words, whatever you practice most is what you will become. If you are in the habit of being uptight whenever life isn't quite right, repeatedly reacting to criticism by defending yourself, insisting on being right, allowing your thinking to snowball in response to adversity, or acting like life is an emergency, then, unfortunately, your life will be a reflection of this type of practice. You will be frustrated because, in a sense, you have practiced being frustrated.

Likewise, however, you can choose to bring forth in yourself qualities of compassion, patience, kindness, humility, and peace—again, through what you practice. I guess it's safe to say that practice makes perfect. It makes sense, then, to be careful what you practice.

This isn't to suggest that you make your entire life into a great big project where the goal is to be constantly improving

171

yourself. Only that it's immensely helpful to become conscious of your own habits, both internal and external. Where is your attention? How do you spend your time? Are you cultivating habits that are helpful to your stated goals? Is what you say you want your life to stand for consistent with what your life really stands for? Simply asking yourself these and other important questions, and answering them honestly, helps to determine which. strategies will be most useful to you. Have you always said to yourself, "I'd like to spend more time by myself" or "I've always wanted to learn to meditate," yet somehow you've never found the time? Sadly, many people spend far more time washing their car or watching reruns of television shows they don't even enjoy than they do making time for aspects of life that nurture their hearts. If you remember that what you practice you will become, you may begin choosing different types of practice.

71.

Quiet the Mind

P ascal said, "All of humanity's problems stem from man's inability to sit quietly in a room alone." I'm not sure I would go quite this far, but I am certain that a quiet mind is the foundation of inner peace. And inner peace translates into outer peace.

Although there are many techniques for quieting the mind, such as reflection, deep breathing, contemplation, and visualization, the most universally accepted and regularly used technique is meditation. In as little as five to ten minutes a day, you can train your mind to be still and quiet. This stillness can be incorporated into your daily life, making you less reactive and irritable, and giving you greater perspective to see things as small stuff rather than as emergencies. Meditation teaches you to be calm by giving you the experience of absolute relaxation. It teaches you to be at peace.

There are many different forms and variations of meditation. Essentially, however, meditation involves emptying your mind. Usually, meditation is done alone in a quiet environment. You close your eyes and focus your attention on your breath— in and out, in and out. As thoughts enter your mind, you gently let them go and bring your attention back to your breath. Do this over and over again. Over time, you'll train yourself to keep your attention on your breath as you gently dismiss any stray thoughts.

You'll quickly discover that meditation isn't easy. You will notice that your mind will fill with thoughts the moment you attempt to keep it still. It's rare for a beginner to be able to focus attention for more than a few seconds. The trick to becoming an effective meditator is to be gentle on yourself and to be consistent. Don't be discouraged. A few minutes each day will reap tremendous benefits, over time. You can probably find a meditation class in your community. Or, if you prefer, you can learn from a book or, better yet, an audiotape. (It's hard to read with your eyes closed.) My favorite resource is Larry Le Shan's *How to Meditate*, available in both book and audio format. I don't know many people I would consider to be at peace with themselves who haven't spent at least a little time experimenting with meditation.

72.

Take Up Yoga

L ike meditation, yoga is an extremely popular and effective method for becoming a more relaxed, easygoing person. For centuries, yoga has been used to clear and free the mind, giving people feelings of ease and equanimity. It's easy to do and takes only a few minutes a day. What's more, people of virtually any age and fitness level can participate. I once took a class at the health club that included both a ten-year-old boy and an eighty-seven-year-old man. Yoga is noncompetitive in nature. You work and progress at your own speed and comfort level.

Although yoga is physical in nature, its benefits are both physical and emotional. On the physical side, yoga strengthens the muscles and the spine, creating flexibility and ease of motion. On the emotional side, yoga is a tremendous stress reducer. It balances the body-mind-spirit connection, giving you a feeling of ease and peace.

Yoga is practiced by engaging in a series of stretches, both gentle and challenging. The stretches are designed to open the body and lengthen the spine. The stretches focus on very specific, usually tight and constricted places—the neck, back, hips, legs, and spine. While you are stretching, you are also concentrating, focusing your attention on what you are doing.

The effects of yoga are truly amazing. After only a few minutes, you feel more alive and open, peaceful and relaxed. Your mind is clear. The rest of your day is easier and more focused. I used to believe that I was too busy to practice yoga. I felt I didn't have time. I'm now certain that the opposite is true—I don't have time not to practice yoga. It's too important not to do. It keeps me feeling young and energized. It's also a wonderful and peaceful way to spend time with family and/or friends. Rather than watching television together, my two daughters and I often flip on a yoga video and spend a few minutes stretching together.

Like meditation, it's easy to find a local class at a community center, the YMCA, or health club. If you prefer to learn from a book, my favorite is *Richard Hittleman's Yoga Twenty-eight-Day Exercise Plan*. There are also many fine videos you can learn from as well as a magazine dedicated solely to yoga called *Yoga Journal*.

73.

Make Service an Integral Part
of Your Life

To become a kinder, more loving individual requires action. Yet, ironically, there is nothing specific you have to do, no prescription to follow. Rather, most genuine acts of kindness and generosity seem natural; they stem from a type of thinking where service and giving have been integrated into the person's thought process.

Several teachers and philosophers that I have learned from have suggested that I begin my day by asking myself the question, "How can I be of service?" I have found this to be useful in reminding me of the multitude of ways that I can be helpful to others. When I take the time to ask this question, I find answers popping up all day long.

If one of your goals is to be of help to others, you will find the most appropriate ways. Your chances to be of service are endless. Sometimes the best way that I can be of service is to offer my home to a friend (or even a stranger) in need. Other times, it's to give my seat to an elderly person on the train, help a youngster across the monkey bars, speak to a group, write a book, help out in my daughter's school, write a check to a charity, or pick up litter on the road. The key, I believe, is to remember that being of service isn't a one-time effort. It's not doing something nice for someone and then wondering why others aren't being nice too, or doing things for us. Instead, a life of service *is* a lifelong process, a way of thinking about life. Does the trash need to be taken out? If so, go ahead and take it out even if it's not your turn. Is someone you know being difficult? Maybe they need a hug or someone to listen to them. Are you aware of a charity that is in trouble? Could you possibly give a little extra this month?

I have learned that the best way to be of service is often very simple—it's those little, quiet, often unnoticed acts of kindness that I can choose on a daily basis—being supportive of a new endeavor by my spouse, or simply taking the time and energy to listen. I know that I have a long way to go toward my goal of becoming a more selfless person. However, I also know that as I have attempted to integrate service into my life, I have felt better and better about the way I choose to live. There is an ancient saying, "Giving is its own reward." It's really true. When you give, you also receive. In fact, what you receive is directly proportional to what you give. As you give more freely of yourself in your own unique ways, you will experience more feelings of peace than you ever thought possible. Everyone wins, especially you.

74.

Do a Favor and Don't Ask For, or Expect, One in Return

This is a strategy that can help you practice integrating service into your life. It will show you how easy it is and how good it feels to do something nice for someone without expecting anything in return.

So often, either consciously or unconsciously, we want something from others, especially when we have done something for them—"I cleaned the bathroom, she should clean the kitchen." Or, "I took care of her child last week, she should offer this week." It's almost as though we keep score of our own good deeds rather than remembering that giving *is* its own reward.

When you do something nice for someone, just to do it, you'll notice (if you're quiet enough inside yourself) a beautiful feeling of ease and peace. Just as vigorous exercise releases endorphins in your brain that make you feel good physically, your acts of loving-kindness release the emotional equivalent. Your reward is the feeling you receive in knowing that you participated in an act of kindness. You don't need something in return or even a "thank you." In fact, you don't even need to let the person know what you have done.

What interferes with this peaceful feeling is our expectation of reciprocity. Our own thoughts interfere with our peaceful feelings as they clutter our minds, as we get caught up in what we think we want or need. The solution is to notice your "I want something in return" thoughts and gently dismiss them. In the absence of these thoughts, your positive feelings will return.

See if you can think of something really thoughtful to do for someone, and don't expect anything in return—whether it's surprising your spouse with a clean garage or organized desk, mowing your neighbor's lawn, or coming home early from work to give your spouse a break from the kids. When you complete your favor, see if you can tap into the warm feeling of knowing you have done something really nice without expecting anything from the person you have just helped. If you practice, I think you'll discover that the feelings themselves are reward enough.

75.

Think of Your Problems
as Potential Teachers

Most people would agree that one of the greatest sources of stress in our lives is our problems. To a certain degree this is true. A more accurate assessment, however, is that the amount of stress we feel has more to do with how we relate to our problems than it does with the problems themselves. In other words, how much of a problem do we make our problems? Do we see them as emergencies, or as potential teachers?

Problems come in many shapes, sizes, and degrees of seriousness, but all have one thing in common: They present us with something that we wish were different. The more we struggle with our problems and the more we want them to go away, the worse they seem and the more stress they cause us.

Ironically, and luckily, the opposite is also true. When we accept our problems as an inevitable part of life, when we look at them as potential teachers, it's as if a weight has been lifted off our shoulders.

Think of a problem that you have struggled with for quite

some time. How have you dealt with this problem up until now? If you're like most, you've probably struggled with it, mentally rehearsed it, analyzed it again and again, but have come up short. Where has all this struggle led you? Probably to even more confusion and stress.

Now think of the same problem in a new way. Rather than push away the problem and resist it, try to embrace it. Mentally, hold the problem near to your heart. Ask yourself what valuable lesson(s) this problem might be able to teach you. Could it be teaching you to be more careful or patient? Does it have anything to do with greed, envy, carelessness, or forgiveness? Or something equally powerful? Whatever problems you are dealing with, chances are they could be thought of in a softer way that includes a genuine desire to learn from them. When you hold your problems in this light, they soften like a clenched fist that is opening. Give this strategy a try, and I think you'll agree that most problems aren't the emergencies we think they are. And usually, once we learn what we need to learn, they begin to go away.

76.

Get Comfortable Not Knowing

There once was a village that had among its people a very wise old man. The villagers trusted this man to provide them answers to their questions and concerns.

One day, a farmer from the village went to the wise man and said in a frantic tone, "Wise man, help me. A horrible thing has happened. My ox has died and I have no animal to help me plow my field! Isn't this the worst thing that could have possibly happened?" The wise old man replied, "Maybe so, maybe not." The man hurried back to the village and reported to his neighbors that the wise man had gone mad. Surely this *was* the worst thing that could have happened. Why couldn't he see this?

The very next day, however, a strong, young horse was seen near the man's farm. Because the man had no ox to rely on, he had the idea to catch the horse to replace his ox—and he did. How joyful the farmer was. Plowing the field had never been easier. He went back to the wise man to apologize. "You were right, wise man. Losing my ox wasn't the worst thing that could have happened. It was a blessing in disguise! I never would have captured my new horse had that not happened. You must agree that this is the *best* thing that could have happened." The wise man replied once again, "Maybe so, maybe not." Not again, thought the farmer. Surely the wise man had gone mad now.

But, once again, the farmer did not know what was to happen. A few days later the farmer's son was riding the horse and was thrown off. He broke his leg and would not be able to help with the crop. Oh no, thought the man. Now we will starve to death. Once again, the farmer went to the wise man. This time he said, "How did you know that capturing my horse was not a good thing? You were right again. My son is injured and won't be able to help with the crop. This time I'm sure that this is the *worst* thing that could have possibly happened. You must agree this time." But, just as he had done before, the wise man calmly looked at the farmer and in a compassionate tone replied once again, "Maybe so, maybe not." Enraged that the wise man could be so ignorant, the farmer stormed back to the village.

The next day troops arrived to take every able-bodied man to the war that had just broken out. The farmer's son was the only young man in the village who didn't have to go. He would live, while the others would surely die.

The moral of this story provides a powerful lesson. The truth is, we *don't* know what's going to happen—we just think we do. Often we make a big deal out of something. We blow up scenarios in our minds about all the terrible things that are going to happen. Most of the time we are wrong. If we keep our cool and stay open to possibilities, we can be reasonably certain that, eventually, all will be well. Remember: maybe so, maybe not.

77.

Acknowledge the Totality of Your Being

Zorba the Greek was said to have described himself as "the whole catastrophe." The truth is, we're all the whole catastrophe, only we wish that we weren't. We deny the parts of ourselves that we deem unacceptable rather than accepting the fact that we're all less than perfect.

One of the reasons it's important to accept all aspects of yourself is that it allows you to be easier on yourself, more compassionate. When you act or feel insecure, rather than pretending to be "together," you can open to the truth and say to yourself, "I'm feeling frightened and that's okay." If you're feeling a little jealous, greedy, or angry, rather than deny or bury your feelings, you can open to them, which helps you move through them quickly and grow beyond them. When you no longer think of your negative feelings as a big deal, or as something to fear, you will no longer be as frightened by them. When you open to the totality of your being you no longer have to pretend that your life is perfect, or even hope that it will be. Instead you can accept yourself as you are, right now.

When you acknowledge the less than perfect parts of yourself, something magical begins to happen. Along with the negative, you'll also begin to notice the positive, the wonderful aspects of yourself that you may not have given yourself credit for, or perhaps even been aware of. You'll notice that while you may, at times, act with self-interest in mind, at other times you're incredibly selfless. Sometimes you may act insecure or frightened, but most often you are courageous. While you can certainly get uptight, you can also be quite relaxed.

Opening to the totality of your being is like saying to yourself, "I may not be perfect, but I'm okay just the way I am." When negative characteristics arise you can begin to recognize them as part of a bigger picture. Rather than judging and evaluating yourself simply because you're human, see if you can treat yourself with loving-kindness and great acceptance. You may indeed be "the whole catastrophe," but you can relax about it. So are the rest of us.

78.

Cut Yourself Some Slack

Each of the strategies in this book is geared toward helping you become more relaxed, peaceful, and loving. One of the most important pieces of this puzzle, however, is to remember that your goal is to stay relaxed, to not get too worked up or concerned about how you are doing. Practice the strategies, keep them in mind, yet don't worry about being perfect. Cut yourself some slack! There will be many times when you lose it, when you revert to being uptight, frustrated, stressed, and reactive—get used to it. When you do, it's okay. Life is a process—just one thing after another. When you lose it, just start again.

One of the most common mistakes I see when people are attempting to become more inwardly peaceful is that they become frustrated by little setbacks. An alternative is to see your mistakes as learning opportunities, ways to navigate your growth and perspective. Say to yourself, "Woops, I lost it again. Oh well, next time I'll handle it differently." Over time, you'll notice drastic changes in your responses to life, but it won't happen all at once.

I once heard of a proposed book title that sums up the message of this strategy: *I'm Not Okay, You're Not Okay, and That's Okay.* Give yourself a break. No one is going to bat 100 percent, or even close to it. All that's important is that, generally speaking, you are doing your best and that you are moving in the right direction. When you can learn to keep your perspective and to stay loving toward yourself, even when you prove you are human, you'll be well on your way to a happier life.

79.

Stop Blaming Others

When something doesn't meet our expectations, many of us operate with the assumption, "When in doubt, it must be someone else's fault." You can see this assumption in action almost everywhere you look—something is missing, so someone else must have moved it; the car isn't working right, so the mechanic must have repaired it incorrectly; your expenses exceed your income, so your spouse must be spending too much money; the house is a mess, so you must be the only person doing your part; a project is late, so your colleagues at work must not have done their share—and on and on it goes.

This type of blaming thinking has become extremely common in our culture. On a personal level, it has led us to believe that we are never completely responsible for our own actions, problems, or happiness. On a societal level, it has led to frivolous lawsuits and ridiculous excuses that get criminals off the hook. When we are in the habit of blaming others, we will blame others for our anger, frustration, depression, stress, and unhappiness.

In terms of personal happiness, you *cannot* be peaceful while at the same time blaming others. Surely there are times when other people and/or circumstances contribute to our problems, but it is we who must rise to the occasion and take responsibility for our own happiness. Circumstances don't make a person, they reveal him or her.

As an experiment, notice what happens when you stop blaming others for anything and everything in your life. This doesn't mean you don't hold people accountable for their actions, but that you hold *yourself* accountable for your own happiness and for your reactions to other people and the circumstances around you. When the house is a mess, rather than assuming you're the only person doing your part, clean it up! When you're over budget, figure out where *you* can spend less money. Most important, when you're unhappy, remind yourself that only you can make yourself happy.

Blaming others takes an enormous amount of mental energy. It's a "drag-me-down" mind-set that creates stress and disease. Blaming makes you feel powerless over your own life because your happiness is contingent on the actions and behavior of others, which you can't control. When you stop blaming others, you will regain your sense of personal power. You will see yourself as a choice maker. You will know that when you are upset, you are playing a key role in the creation of your own feelings. This means that you can also play a key role in creating new, more positive feelings. Life is a great deal more fun and much easier to manage when you stop blaming others. Give it a try and see what happens.

80.

Become an Early Riser

I have seen this simple, practical strategy help many people discover a more peaceful, even a more meaningful life.

So many people wake up, rush to get ready, grab a cup of coffee, and charge out the door to work. After working all day, they return home, tired. The same is usually true for men and women who stay home with their children: They get up just in time to start doing things for the kids. There is virtually no time for anything else. Whether you work, raise a family, or both, for the most part you are too tired to enjoy any time left for you. As a solution to the tiredness, the assumption is often made, "I'd better get as much sleep as I can." So, your free time is spent sleeping. For many people this creates a deep longing in the heart. Surely there must be more to life than work, children, and sleep!

Another way of looking at your fatigue is to consider that a lack of fulfillment and a sense of being overwhelmed both contribute to your tiredness. And, contrary to popular logic, a little *less* sleep and a little more time for you might be just what you need to combat your sense of fatigue.

An hour or two that is reserved just for you—*before* your day begins—is an incredible way to improve your life. I usually get up between 3 and 4 in the morning. After a quiet cup of coffee, I usually spend some time doing yoga and a few minutes of meditation. After that, I will usually go upstairs and write for a while, but I also have time to read a chapter or two in whatever book I'm enjoying. Sometimes I'll just sit for a few minutes and do nothing. Virtually every day, I stop whatever I'm doing to enjoy the sunrise as it comes up over the mountain. The phone never rings, no one is asking me to do anything for them, and there is nothing I absolutely have to do. It's by far the most quiet time of the day.

By the time my wife and children wake up, I feel as though I've had a full day of enjoyment. No matter how busy I am that day or whatever demands there are on my time, I know I've had "my time." I never feel ripped off (as so many people unfortunately do), as if my life isn't my own. I believe this makes me more available for my wife and children, as well as my clients at work and other people who depend on me.

Many people have told me that this one shift in their routine was the single most important change they have ever made in their lives. For the first time ever, they are able to participate in those quiet activities they never found the time to do. All of a sudden, the books are getting read, the meditation gets done, the sunrise is appreciated. The fulfillment you experience more than makes up for any sleep you miss out on. If you must, turn off the television at night and get to sleep an hour or two earlier.

81.

When Trying to Be Helpful,
Focus on Little Things

Mother Teresa once said, "We cannot do great things on this earth. We can only do little things with great love." Sometimes our grandiose plans to do great things at some later time interfere with our chances to do little things right now. A friend once told me, "I want my life to be about service, but I can't do anything yet. Someday, when I'm really successful, I'll do lots of things for others." Meanwhile, there are hungry people in the streets, elderly people who could use some company, mothers who need help with their children, people who can't read, neighbors whose homes need paint, streets with litter, people who need to be listened to, and thousands and thousands of other little things that need to be done.

Mother Teresa was right. We can't change the world, but to make the world a brighter place we don't need to. All we really have to do is focus on those little acts of kindness, things we can do right now. My favorite ways to be of service are to develop my own helping rituals and to practice random acts of kindness—almost always little things that give me enormous satisfaction and peace of mind. Often the most appreciated acts of kindness aren't the million-dollar grants from giant corporations but the one hour of volunteer work in a home for the elderly or the five-dollar gift from someone who can't afford anything at all.

If we focus on how little difference our acts of kindness really make in the scheme of things, surely we will end up frustrated—and will probably use our hopelessness as an excuse to do nothing. If, however, we take great care in doing something—anything—we will feel the joy of giving and will help to make our world just a little bit brighter.

82.

Remember, One Hundred Years from Now, All New People

My good friend Patti recently shared this bit of wisdom with me that she learned from one of her favorite authors. It has added a great deal of perspective to my life.

In the scheme of things, one hundred years isn't all that long a time. However, one thing's for sure: A hundred years from now we will all be gone from this planet. And when kept in mind, this idea can fill us with needed perspective during times of perceived crisis or stress.

If you have a flat tire or lock yourself out of your house, what's it going to mean one hundred years from now? How about if someone acted unkindly toward you or if you had to stay up most of the night working? What if your house didn't get cleaned or your computer breaks down? Suppose you can't afford to go on a much needed vacation, buy a new car, or move to a larger apartment? All of these things and most others are brought into a deeper perspective when looked at with a hundred-year view.

Just this morning I found myself at a mental fork in the road, about to get uptight about a mini crisis at work. There was a double booking and two people showed up at the same time for the same appointment. What saved me from getting overly stressed and too uptight was remembering that one hundred years from now, no one will remember this moment, no one will care. I calmly took responsibility for the error and one of the people was happy to reschedule. As usual, this was "small stuff" that could easily have been turned into "big stuff."

83.

Lighten Up

These days, it seems that almost all of us are too serious. My older daughter often says to me, "Daddy, you've got that serious look again." Even those of us who are committed to nonseriousness are probably too serious. People are frustrated and uptight about virtually everything—being five minutes late, having someone else show up five minutes late, being stuck in traffic, witnessing someone look at us wrong or say the wrong thing, paying bills, waiting in line, overcooking a meal, making an honest mistake—you name it, we all lose perspective over it.

The root of being uptight is our unwillingness to accept life as being different, in any way, from our expectations. Very simply, we want things to be a certain way but they're *not* a certain way. Life is simply as it is. Perhaps Benjamin Franklin said it best: "Our limited perspective, our hopes and fears become our measure of life, and when circumstances don't fit our ideas, they become our difficulties." We spend our lives wanting things, people, and events to be just as we want them to be—and when they're not, we fight and we suffer.

The first step in recovering from overseriousness is to admit that you have a problem. You have to want to change, to become more easygoing. You have to see that your own uptightness is largely of your own creation—it's composed of the way you have set up your life and the way you react to it.

The next step is to understand the link between your expectations and your frustration level. Whenever you expect something to be a certain way and it isn't, you're upset and you suffer. On the other hand, when you let go of your expectations, when you accept life as it is, you're free. To hold on is to be serious and uptight. To let go is to lighten up.

A good exercise is to try to approach a single day without expectations. Don't expect people to be friendly. When they're not, you won't be surprised or bothered. If they are, you'll be delighted. Don't expect your day to be problem free. Instead, as problems come up, say to yourself, "Ah, another hurdle to overcome." As you approach your day in this manner you'll notice how graceful life can be. Rather than fighting against life, you'll be dancing with it. Pretty soon, with practice, you'll lighten up your entire life. And when you lighten up, life is a lot more fun.

84.

Nurture a Plant

At first glance this may seem like a strange or superficial suggestion. What good could it possibly do to nurture a plant?

One of the goals of spiritual life and one of the requirements of inner peace is to learn to love unconditionally. The problem is, it's really hard to love a person, any person, unconditionally. The person we are trying to love inevitably says or does the wrong thing, or fails to meet our expectations in some way. So, we get upset and put conditions on our love: "I'll love you, but you have to change. You must act the way I want you to act."

Some people are better at loving their pets than the people in their lives. But to love a pet unconditionally is hard too. What happens when your dog wakes you up with unnecessary barking in the middle of the night or ruins your favorite carpet with an accident? Do you love him just as much? My children have a bunny. It was really hard to love that bunny when he chewed a hole in my beautifully crafted wooden gate!

A plant, however, is easy to love just the way it is. Therefore, nurturing a plant offers us an excellent opportunity to practice unconditional love.

Why does virtually every spiritual tradition advocate unconditional love? Because love has such transformational power. Unconditional love brings forth peaceful feelings in both the giver and the receiver.

Select a plant, indoor or outdoor, that you will see every day. Practice taking care of and loving that plant as if it were your baby (it's easier to care for your plant than your baby—no sleepless nights, no diapers, no crying). Talk to your plant, tell it how much you love it. Love your plant whether it blooms or not, whether it lives or dies. Just love it. Notice how you feel as you offer this plant your unconditional love. When you offer this type of love you're never agitated, irritated, or hurried. You're simply in a loving space. Practice this type of love each time you see your plant, at least once a day.

After a short while, you'll be able to extend your loving-kindness beyond your plant as well. As you notice how good it feels to love, see if you can offer a similar love to the people in your life. Practice not needing them to change or be different to receive your love. Love them just the way they are. Your plant can be a wonderful teacher—showing you the power of love.

85.

Transform Your Relationship
to Your Problems

Obstacles and problems are a part of life. True happiness comes not when we get rid of all of our problems, but when we change our relationship to them, when we see our problems as a potential source of awakening, opportunities to practice patience, and to learn. Perhaps the most basic principle of spiritual life is that our problems are the best places to practice keeping our hearts open.

Certainly some problems need to be solved. Many others, however, are problems we create for ourselves by struggling to make our life different than it actually is. Inner peace is accomplished by understanding and accepting the inevitable contradictions of life—the pain and pleasure, success and failure, joy and sorrow, births and deaths. Problems can teach us to be gracious, humble, and patient.

In the Buddhist tradition, difficulties are considered to be so important to a life of growth and peace that a Tibetan prayer actually asks for them. It says, "Grant that I may be given appropriate difficulties and sufferings on this journey so that my heart may be truly awakened and my practice of liberation and universal compassion may be truly fulfilled." It is felt that when life is too easy, there are fewer opportunities for genuine growth.

I wouldn't go so far as to recommend that you seek out problems. I would, however, suggest that if you spend less time running away from problems and trying to rid yourself of them—and more time accepting problems as an inevitable, natural, even important part of life—you will soon discover that life can be more of a dance and less of a battle. This philosophy of acceptance is the root of going with the flow.

86.

The Next Time You Find Yourself in an Argument, Rather than Defend Your Position, See if You Can See the Other Point of View First

It's interesting to consider that when you disagree with someone, the person you are disagreeing with is every bit as certain of his or her position as you are of yours. Yet we always take sides—ours! This is our ego's way of refusing to learn anything new. It's also a habit that creates a lot of unnecessary stress.

The first time I consciously tried the strategy of seeing the other point of view first, I found out something truly wonderful: It didn't hurt, and it brought me closer to the person with whom I was disagreeing.

Suppose a friend says to you, "Liberals [or conservatives] are the major cause of our social problems." Rather than automatically defending your own position (whatever it is), see if you can learn something new. Say to your friend, "Tell me why you think that's true." Don't say this with a hidden agenda or in preparation to defend or prove your position, but simply to learn a different point of view. Don't try to correct or make your friend see how he is wrong. Let your friend have the satisfaction of being right. Practice being a good listener.

Contrary to popular belief, this attitude does not make you weak. It doesn't mean you aren't passionate about your beliefs, or that you're admitting that you're wrong. You're simply trying to see another point of view—you're seeking first to understand. It takes enormous energy to constantly prove a rigid position. On the other hand, it takes no energy to allow someone else to be right. In fact, it's outright energizing.

When you understand other positions and points of view, several wonderful things begin to happen. First, you often learn something new. You expand your horizons. Second, when the person you are talking to feels listened to, he or she will appreciate and respect you far more than when you habitually jump in with your own position. Jumping in only makes him or her more determined and defensive. Almost always, if *you* are softer, the other person will be softer too. It might not happen right away, but in time, it will. By seeking first to understand, you are putting your love and respect for the person to whom you are speaking above your need to be right. You are practicing a form of unconditional love. A side benefit is that the person you are speaking to may even listen to your point of view. While there is no guarantee that he will listen to you, one thing is guaranteed: If you don't listen, he or she won't. By being the first person to reach out and listen, you stop the spiral of stubbornness.

87.

Redefine a "Meaningful Accomplishment"

Sometimes it's easy to get carried away with our so-called accomplishments. We spend our lifetimes collecting achievements, earning praise and recognition, and seeking approval—so much so that we lose sight of what is truly meaningful.

If you ask the average person (as I have done many times), "What is a meaningful accomplishment?" the typical responses will be things like, "Achieving a long-term goal," "earning lots of money," "winning a game," "getting a promotion," "being the best," "earning praise," and so forth. The emphasis is almost always on the *external* aspects of life—things that happen outside of ourselves. Certainly, there is nothing wrong with these types of accomplishments—they are way of keeping score and improving our circumstances. They are not, however, the most important types of accomplishments if your primary goal is one of happiness and inner peace. Seeing your photograph in the local newspaper may be a nice thing to achieve but isn't as meaningful as learning to stay centered in the face of adversity. Yet many people would point to their photo in the paper as being a great accomplishment, but wouldn't necessarily think of "staying centered" as an accomplishment at all. Where are our priorities?

If being peaceful and loving are among your primary goals, then why not redefine your most meaningful accomplishments as being those that support and measure qualities such as kindness and happiness?

I think of my most meaningful accomplishments as stemming from inside myself: Was I kind to myself and others? Did I overreact to a challenge, or was I calm and collected? Am I happy? Did I hold on to anger or was I able to let go and move on? Was I too stubborn? Did I forgive? These questions, and others like them, remind us that the true measure of our success comes not from what we do, but from who we are and how much love we have in our hearts.

Rather than being consumed exclusively with external accomplishments, try putting more emphasis on what's really important. When you redefine what it means to achieve a meaningful accomplishment, it helps you to stay on your path.

88.

Listen to Your Feelings
(They Are Trying to Tell You Something)

You have at your disposal a foolproof guidance system to navigate you through life. This system, which consists solely of your own feelings, lets you know whether you are off track and headed toward unhappiness and conflict—or on track, headed toward peace of mind. Your feelings act as a barometer, letting you know what your internal weather is like.

When you're not caught up in your thinking, taking things too seriously, your feelings will be generally positive. They will be affirming that you are using your thinking to your advantage. No mental adjustment needs to be made.

When your experience of life is other than pleasant—when you're feeling angry, resentful, depressed, stressed out, frustrated, and so forth, your warning system of feelings kicks in like a red flag to remind you that you are off track, that it's time to ease up on your thinking, you've lost perspective. Mental adjustment does need to be made. You can think of your negative feelings in the same way you think of the warning lights on the dashboard of your car. When flashing, they let you know that it's time to ease up.

Contrary to popular belief, negative feelings don't need to be studied and analyzed. When you analyze your negative feelings, you'll usually end up with more of them to contend with.

The next time you're feeling bad, rather than getting stuck in "analysis paralysis," wondering why you feel the way you do, see if instead you can use your feelings to guide you back in the direction toward serenity. Don't pretend that the negative feelings don't exist, but try to recognize that the reason you're feeling sad, angry, stressed, or whatever is that you are taking life too seriously—you are "sweating the small stuff." Instead of rolling up your sleeves and fighting life, back off, take a few deep breaths, and relax. Remember, life isn't an emergency unless you make it so.

89.

If Someone Throws You the Ball,
You Don't Have to Catch It

My best friend, Benjamin Shield, taught me this valuable lesson. Often our inner struggles come from our tendency to jump on board someone else's problem; someone throws you a concern and you assume you must catch it, and respond. For example, suppose you're really busy when a friend calls in a frantic tone and says, "My mother is driving me crazy. What should I do?" Rather than saying, "I'm really sorry but I don't know what to suggest," you automatically catch the ball and try to solve the problem. Then later, you feel stressed or resentful that you are behind schedule and that everyone seems to be making demands on you. It's easy to lose sight of your willing participation in the dramas of your own life.

Remembering that you don't have to catch the ball is a very effective way to reduce the stress in your life. When your friend calls, you *can* drop the ball, meaning you don't have to participate simply because he or she is attempting to lure you in. If you don't take the bait, the person will probably call someone else to see if they will become involved.

This doesn't mean you never catch the ball, only that it's your choice to do so. Neither does this mean that you don't care about your friend, or that you're crass or unhelpful. Developing a more tranquil outlook on life requires that we know our own limits and that we take responsibility for our part in the process. Most of us get balls thrown at us many times each day—at work, from our children, friends, neighbors, salespeople, even strangers. If I caught all the balls thrown in my direction, I would certainly go crazy—and I suspect that you would too! The key is to know when we're catching another ball so that we won't feel victimized, resentful, or overwhelmed.

Even something terribly simple like answering your phone when you're really too busy to talk is a form of catching the ball. By answering the phone, you are willingly taking part in an interaction that you may not have the time, energy, or mind-set for at the present time. By simply not answering the phone, you are taking responsibility for your own peace of mind. The same idea applies to being insulted or criticized. When someone throws an idea or comment in your direction, you can catch it and feel hurt, or you can drop it and go on with your day.

The idea of "not catching the ball" simply because it's thrown to you is a powerful tool to explore. I hope you'll experiment with this one. You may find that you catch the ball a lot more than you think you do.

90.

One More Passing Show

This is a strategy that I have recently adopted into my own life. It's a subtle reminder that everything—the good and bad, pleasure and pain, approval and disapproval, achievements and mistakes, fame and shame—all come and go. Everything has a beginning and an ending and that's the way it's supposed to be.

Every experience you have ever had is over. Every thought you've ever had, started and finished. Every emotion and mood you've experienced has been replaced by another. You've been happy, sad, jealous, depressed, angry, in love, shamed, proud, and every other conceivable human feeling. Where did they all go? The answer is, no one really knows. All we know is that, eventually, everything disappears into nothingness. Welcoming this truth into your life is the beginning of a liberating adventure.

Our disappointment comes about in essentially two ways. When we're experiencing pleasure we want it to last forever. It never does. Or, when we're experiencing pain, we want it to go away—now. It usually doesn't. Unhappiness is the result of struggling against the natural flow of experience.

It's enormously helpful to experiment with the awareness that life is just one thing after another. One present moment followed by another present moment. When something is happening that we enjoy, know that while it's wonderful to experience the happiness it brings, it will eventually be replaced by something else, a different type of moment. If that's okay with you, you'll feel peace even when the moment changes. And if you're experiencing some type of pain or displeasure, know that this too shall pass. Keeping this awareness close to your heart is a wonderful way to maintain your perspective, even in the face of adversity. It's not always easy, but it is usually helpful.

91.

Fill Your Life with Love

I don't know anyone who doesn't want a life filled with love. In order for this to happen, the effort must start within us. Rather than waiting for other people to provide the love we desire, *we* must be a vision and a source of love. We must tap into our own loving-kindness in order to set an example for others to follow suit.

It has been said that "the shortest distance between two points is an intention." This is certainly true with regard to a life filled with love. The starting point or foundation of a life filled with love is the desire and commitment to be a source of love. Our attitude, choices, acts of kindness, and willingness to be the first to reach out will take us toward this goal.

The next time you find yourself frustrated at the lack of love in your own life or at the lack of love in the world, try an experiment. Forget about the world and other people for a few minutes. Instead, look into your own heart. Can you become a source of greater love? Can you think loving thoughts for yourself and others? Can you extend these loving thoughts outward toward the rest of the world—even to people whom you feel don't deserve it?

By opening your heart to the possibility of greater love, and by making yourself a source of love (rather than getting love) as a top priority, you will be taking an important step in getting the love you desire. You'll also discover something truly remarkable. The more love you give, the more you will receive. As you put more emphasis on being a loving person, which is something you can control—and less emphasis on receiving love, which is something you can't control—you'll find that you have plenty of love in your life. Soon you'll discover one of the greatest secrets in the world: Love is its own reward.

92.

Realize the Power of Your Own Thoughts

If you were to become aware of only one mental dynamic, the most important one to know about would be the relationship between your thinking and the way you feel.

It's important to realize that you are constantly thinking. Don't be fooled into believing that you are already aware of this fact! Think, for a moment, about your breathing. Until this moment, when you are reading this sentence, you had certainly lost sight of the fact that you were doing it. The truth is, unless you are out of breath, you simply forget that it's occurring.

Thinking works in the same way. Because you're always doing it, it's easy to forget that it's happening, and it becomes invisible to you. Unlike breathing, however, forgetting that you are thinking can cause some serious problems in your life, such as unhappiness, anger, inner conflicts, and stress. The reason this is true is that your thinking will always come back to you as a feeling; there is a point-to-point relationship.

Try getting angry without first having angry thoughts! Okay,

227

now try feeling stressed out without first having stressful thoughts—or sad without sad thoughts—or jealous without thoughts of jealousy. You can't do it—it's impossible. The truth is, in order to experience a feeling, you must first have a thought that produces that feeling.

Unhappiness doesn't and can't exist on its own. Unhappiness is the feeling that accompanies negative thinking about your life. In the absence of that thinking, the unhappiness, or stress, or jealousy, can't exist. There is nothing to hold your negative feelings in place other than your own thinking. The next time you're feeling upset, notice your thinking—it will be negative. Remind yourself that it's your thinking that is negative, not your life. This simple awareness will be the first step in putting you back on the path toward happiness. It takes practice, but you can get to the point where you treat your negative thoughts in much the same way you would treat flies at a picnic: You shoo them away and get on with your day.

93.

Give Up on the Idea that "More Is Better"

We live in the most affluent culture the world has ever seen. Estimates are that although we have only 6 percent of the world's population in America, we use almost half of the natural resources. It seems to me that if more were actually better, we would live in the happiest, most satisfied culture of all time. But we don't. Not even close. In fact, we live in one of the most dissatisfied cultures on record.

It's not that having a lot of things is bad, wrong, or harmful in and of itself, only that the desire to have more and more and more is insatiable. As long as you think more is better, you'll never be satisfied.

As soon as we get something, or achieve something, most of us simply go on to the next thing—immediately. This squelches our appreciation for life and for our many blessings. I know a man, for example, who bought a beautiful home in a nice area. He was happy until the day after he moved in. Then the thrill was gone. Immediately, he wished he'd bought a bigger, nicer home. His "more is better" thinking wouldn't allow him to enjoy his new home, even for a day. Sadly, he is not unique. To varying degrees, we're all like that. It's gotten to the point that when the Dalai Lama won the Nobel Prize for Peace in 1989, one of the first questions he received from a reporter was "What's next?" It seems that whatever we do—buy a home or a car, eat a meal, find a partner, purchase some clothes, even win a prestigious honor—it's never enough.

The trick in overcoming this insidious tendency is to convince yourself that more isn't better and that the problem doesn't lie in what you don't have, but in the longing for more. Learning to be satisfied doesn't mean you can't, don't, or shouldn't ever want more than you have, only that your happiness isn't contingent on it. You can learn to be happy with what you have by becoming more present-moment oriented, by not focusing so much on what you want. As thoughts of what would make your life better enter your mind, gently remind yourself that, even if you got what you think you want, you wouldn't be one bit more satisfied, because the same mind-set that wants more now would want more then.

Develop a new appreciation for the blessings you already enjoy. See your life freshly, as if for the first time. As you develop this new awareness, you'll find that as new possessions or accomplishments enter your life, your level of appreciation will be heightened.

An excellent measure of happiness is the differential between what you have and what you want. You can spend your lifetime wanting more, always chasing happiness—or you can simply decide to consciously want less. This latter strategy is infinitely easier and more fulfilling.

94.

Keep Asking Yourself,
"What's Really Important?"

It's easy to get lost and overwhelmed in the chaos, responsibilities, and goals of life. Once overwhelmed, it's tempting to forget about and postpone that which is most near and dear to your heart. I've found that it's helpful to keep asking myself, "What's really important?"

As part of my early morning routine, I take a few seconds to ask myself this question. Reminding myself of what's really important helps me keep my priorities straight. It reminds me that, despite my multitude of responsibilities, I have a choice of what is most important in my life and where I put my greatest amount of energy—being available for my wife and children, writing, practicing my inner work, and so forth.

Despite the appearance of being overly simplistic, I have found this strategy to be immensely helpful in keeping me on track. When I take a few moments to remind myself of what's really important, I find that I'm more present-moment oriented, in less of a hurry, and that being right loses its appeal. Conversely, when I forget to remind myself of what's really important, I find that I can quickly lose sight of my priorities and, once again, get lost in my own busyness. I'll rush out the door, work late, lose my patience, skip my exercise, and do other things that are in conflict with the goals of my life.

If you regularly take a minute to check in with yourself, to ask yourself, "What's really important?" you may find that some of the choices you are making are in conflict with your own stated goals. This strategy can help you align your actions with your goals and encourage you to make more conscious, loving decisions.

95.

Trust Your Intuitive Heart

How often have you said to yourself, after the fact, "I knew I should have done that"? How often do you intuitively know something but allow yourself to think yourself out of it?

Trusting your intuitive heart means listening to and trusting that quiet inner voice that knows what it is you need to do, what actions need to be taken, or changes need to be made in your life. Many of us *don't* listen to our intuitive heart for fear that we couldn't possibly know something without thinking it through, or for fear that legitimate answers could possibly be so obvious. We say things to ourselves like, "That couldn't possibly be right" or "I couldn't possibly do that." And, as soon as we allow our thinking mind to enter into the picture, we think ourselves out of it. We then argue for our limitations, and they become ours.

If you can overcome your fear that your intuitive heart will give you incorrect answers, if you can learn to trust it, your life will become the magical adventure it was meant to be. Trusting your intuitive heart is like removing the barriers to enjoyment and wisdom. It's the way to open your eyes and your heart to your greatest source of wisdom and grace.

If you're unfamiliar with trusting your intuition, start by setting aside a little quiet time to clear your mind and listen. Ignore and dismiss any habitual, self-defeating thoughts that enter your mind and pay attention only to the calm thoughts that begin to surface. If you find that unusual yet loving thoughts are appearing in your mind, take note of them and take action. If, for example, you get the message to write or call someone you love, go ahead and do it. If your intuitive heart says you need to slow down or take more time for yourself, try to make it happen. If you're reminded of a habit that needs attention, pay attention. You'll find that when your intuition gives you messages and you respond with action, you'll often be rewarded with positive, loving experiences. Start trusting your intuitive heart today and you'll see a world of difference in your life.

96.

Be Open to "What Is"

One of the most basic spiritual principles in many philosophies is the idea of opening your heart to "what is" instead of insisting that life be a certain way. This idea is so important because much of our internal struggle stems from our desire to control life, to insist that it be different than it actually is. But life isn't always (or even rarely is) the way we would like it to be—it is simply the way it is. The greater our surrender to the truth of the moment, the greater will be our peace of mind.

When we have preconceived ideas about the way life should be, they interfere with our opportunity to enjoy or learn from the present moment. This prevents us from honoring what we are going through, which may be an opportunity for great awakening.

Rather than reacting to a child's complaining or your spouse's disapproval, try opening your heart and accepting the moment for what it is. Make it okay that they aren't acting exactly the way you would like them to. Or, if a project you have been working on is rejected, instead of feeling defeated, see if you can say to yourself, "Ah, rejection. Next time I'll get it approved." Take a deep breath and soften your response.

You open your heart in these ways, not to pretend that you enjoy complaints, disapproval, or failure, but to transcend them—to make it all right with you that life isn't performing the way you planned. If you can learn to open your heart in the midst of the difficulties of daily life, you will soon find that many of the things that have always bothered you will cease to be concerns. Your perspective will deepen. When you fight that which you struggle with, life can be quite a battle, almost like a Ping-Pong game where you are the ball. But when you surrender to the moment, accept what is going on, make it okay, more peaceful feelings will begin to emerge. Try this technique on some of the little challenges you face. Gradually you'll be able to extend the same awareness to bigger things. This is a truly powerful way to live.

97.

Mind Your Own Business

It's tough enough trying to create a life of serenity when dealing with your own mental tendencies, issues, real-life problems, habits, and the contradictions and complexities of life. But when you feel compelled to deal with other people's issues, your goal of becoming more peaceful becomes all but impossible.

How often do you find yourself saying things like, "I wouldn't do that if I were her," or "I can't believe he did that," or "What is she thinking about?" How often are you frustrated, bothered, annoyed, or concerned about things that you not only *cannot* control or be of actual help with, but are also none of your business?

This is not a prescription to avoid being of help to people. Rather, it's about knowing when to help and when to leave something alone. I used to be the type of person who would jump in and try to solve a problem without being asked. Not only did my efforts prove fruitless, they were also almost always unappreciated, and sometimes even resented. Since recovering from my need to be overly involved, my life has become much simpler. And, now that I'm not butting in where I'm not wanted, I'm far more available to be of help when I am asked or truly needed.

Minding your own business goes far beyond simply avoiding the temptation to try to solve other people's problems. It also includes eavesdropping, gossiping, talking behind other people's backs, and analyzing or trying to figure out other people. One of the major reasons most of us focus on the shortcomings or problems of others is to avoid looking at ourselves.

When you catch yourself involved where you really don't belong, congratulate yourself for having the humility and wisdom to back off. In no time at all, you'll free up tons of extra energy to focus your attention where it's truly relevant or needed.

98.

Look for the Extraordinary in the Ordinary

I heard a story about two workers who were approached by a
reporter. The reporter asked the first worker, "What are you
doing?" His response was to complain that he was virtually a
slave, an underpaid bricklayer who spent his days wasting his
time, placing bricks on top of one another.

The reporter asked the second worker the same question.
His response, however, was quite different. "I'm the luckiest
person in the world," he said. "I get to be a part of important
and beautiful pieces of architecture. I help turn simple pieces of
brick into exquisite masterpieces."

They were both right.

The truth is, we see in life what we want to see. If you
search for ugliness you'll find plenty of it. If you want to find
fault with other people, your career, or the world in general,
you'll certainly be able to do so. But the opposite is also true.
If you look for the extraordinary in the ordinary, you can train
yourself to see it. This bricklayer sees cathedrals within pieces

of brick. The question is, can you? Can you see the extraordinary synchronicity that exists in our world; the perfection of the universe in action; the extraordinary beauty of nature; the incredible miracle of human life? To me, it's all a matter of intention. There is so much to be grateful for, so much to be in awe about. Life is precious and extraordinary. Put your attention on this fact and little, ordinary things will take on a whole new meaning.

99.

Schedule Time for Your Inner Work

In the field of financial planning there is a universally accepted principle that it's critical to pay yourself first, before you pay your other bills—to think of yourself as a creditor. The rationale for this financial wisdom is that if you wait to put money into savings until after everybody else is paid, there will be nothing left for you! The result is that you'll keep postponing your savings plan until it's too late to do anything about it. But, lo and behold, if you pay yourself first, somehow there will be just enough to pay everyone else too.

The identical principle is critical to implement into your program of spiritual practice. If you wait until all your chores, responsibilities, and everything else is done before you get started, it will never happen. Guaranteed.

I have found that scheduling a little time each day as if it were an actual appointment is the only way to ensure that you will take some time for yourself. You might become an early riser, for example, and schedule one hour that is reserved for reading, praying, reflecting, meditating, yoga, exercise, or however you want to use the time. How you choose to use the time is up to you. The important thing is that you do schedule the time and that you stick to it.

I had a client who actually hired a baby-sitter on a regular basis to ensure that she had the chance to do the things she felt she needed to do. Today, more than a year later, her efforts have paid enormous dividends. She's happier than she ever thought possible. She told me that there was a time that she never would have imagined hiring a baby-sitter to ensure this type of quality time for herself. Now that she has done it, she can't imagine not doing it! If you set your mind to it, you can find the time you need.

100.

Live This Day as if It Were Your Last.
It Might Be!

When are you going to die? In fifty years, twenty, ten, five, today? Last time I checked, no one had told me. I often wonder, when listening to the news, did the person who died in the auto accident on his way home from work remember to tell his family how much he loved them? Did he live well? Did he love well? Perhaps the only thing that is certain is that he still had things in his "in basket" that weren't yet done.

The truth is, none of us has any idea how long we have to live. Sadly, however, we act as if we're going to live forever. We postpone the things that, deep down, we know we want to do—telling the people we love how much we care, spending time alone, visiting a good friend, taking that beautiful hike, running a marathon, writing a heartfelt letter, going fishing with your daughter, learning to meditate, becoming a better listener, and on and on. We come up with elaborate and sophisticated rationales to justify our actions, and end up spending most of our time and energy doing things that aren't all that important. We argue for our limitations, and they become our limitations.

I felt it appropriate to end this book by suggesting that you live each day as if it were your last on this earth. I suggest this not as a prescription to be reckless or to abandon your responsibilities, but to remind you of how precious life really is. A friend of mine once said, "Life is too important to take too seriously." Ten years later, I know he was right. I hope that this book has been, and will continue to be, helpful to you. Please don't forget the most basic strategy of all, *Don't sweat the small stuff!* I will end this book by sincerely saying that I wish you well.

Treasure Yourself

Suggested Reading

The following are a few of my favourite related books that can bring additional light on the strategies listed in this book.

Bailey, Joseph. *The Serenity Principle*. San Francisco: Harper & Row, 1990*

Boorstein, Sylvia. *It's Easier Than You Think*. San Francisco: HarperCollins, 1996*

Carlson, Richard. *You Can Be Happy No Matter What*. San Rafael, Calif.: New World Library, 1992

———. *You Can Feel Good Again*. London: Thorsons, 1993

———. *Short Cut Through Therapy*. New York: Plume, 1995*

———. *Handbook for the Soul*. London: Piatkus, 1996

———. *Handbook for the Heart*. New York: Little, Brown, 1996*

Chopra, Deepak. *The Seven Spiritual Laws of Success*. London: Bantam, 1996

———. *Ageless Body, Timeless Mind*. London: Rider, 1993

Dyer, Wayne. *Real Magic*. New York: HarperCollins, 1992*

———. *The Sky's the Limit*. New York: Pocket Books, 1980*

———. *Your Sacred Self*. New York: Harper Paperback, 1995

———. *Your Erroneous Zones*. London: Warner, 1992

Hay, Louise. *Life. Carson*, Calif: Hay House, 1995

Hittleman, Richard. *Richard Hittleman's Twenty-eight-Day Yoga Exercise Plan*. New York: Workman, 1994

Kabat-Zinn, Jon. *Wherever You Go, There You Are*. New York: Hyperion, 1994*

Kornvield, Jack. *A Path with Heart*. London: Rider, 1995

Le Shan, Larry. *How to Mediate*. (Audio Tape) Los Angeles: Audio Renaissance, 1987*

Levine, Stephen, and Ondrea Levine. *Embracing the Beloved*. Avon: Gateway, 1995

Salzberg, Sharon. *Loving Kindness*. Boston: Shambhala, 1995*

Schwartz, Tony. *What Really Matters?* New York: Bantam, 1995*

Siegel, Bernie. *Love, Medicine and Miracles*. London: Arrow, 1989

Williamson, Marianne. *A Return to Love*. London: Thorsons, 1996

*Titles marked with * are not available in the UK.*

DON'T SWEAT THE SMALL STUFF AT WORK

SMALL STUFF AT WORK

Simple Ways to Minimize Stress
and Conflict While Bringing out the
Best in Yourself and Others

This book is dedicated to you, my readers.
I hope it makes your life at work a little easier
and less stressful!

ACKNOWLEDGMENTS

I'd like to thank Bob Miller for his continued belief in my message and Leslie Wells who, once again, shared her insightful editorial skills with me. I'd also like to acknowledge the staff at Hyperion for their ongoing efforts. As always, I'd like to thank Patti Breitman and Linda Michaels for their enthusiasm, friendship and support. Finally, I'd like to thank my good friend Rhonda Hull for her assistance in keeping me focused and on-track while writing this book, and my incredible family who didn't "sweat the small stuff" while I was dedicated to this important project. Thank you all very much.

CONTENTS

INTRODUCTION

M any of us spend an enormous amount of time and energy engaged in work—eight, ten, even twelve hours a day isn't at all uncommon. And whether we work for a giant corporation, a smaller company, or on Wall Street—or, whether we are self-employed, work for the government, or in retail—or for that matter any other industry or business, there's no doubt about it: Work can be, and usually is, stressful.

Each industry and career has its own unique set of problems and sources of stress, and each job carries its specific burdens and occasional nightmares. From time to time, most of us must deal with some combination of a variety of unpleasant issues—unrealistic deadlines and expectations, bureaucracies, difficult and demanding bosses, ridiculous meetings and memos, quotas, back-stabbing and criticism, harassment, uncertainty, and rejection. In addition, there are government regulations and high taxes, lack of appreciation, fierce competition, insensitive or selfish coworkers, demanding schedules, poor working conditions, long commutes, and downsizing. It seems that virtually no one is exempt from the hassles of having a job and doing business.

Indeed, the questions aren't whether or not stress exists in the workplace or whether or not you will be exposed to it—it most certainly does and you most certainly will. Rather, the more relevant question is, "How are you going to deal with it?" You can surrender to the fact that work is inherently stressful and there's nothing you can do about it, or you can begin to walk a slightly different path and learn to respond in new, more peaceful ways to the demands of work. It's clear to me that if you are going to find a way to work with less stress, you're going to have to find the answer within yourself. There simply isn't any job available, or any way to set up your life, that doesn't contain its own unique set of challenges.

If you've read any of my earlier books, you know that I'm an optimist. I believe that practically anyone can make at least incremental improvements in the quality of their lives by making small daily changes in attitude and behavior. Without minimizing any of the difficult issues that are out there, I know in my heart that we are not victims of the status quo. We *can* change. But change won't come about as a result of our work dishing out fewer demands or having an easier life. Rather, change must come from within us. The good news is, when it does, our work lives—in fact, our entire lives—will seem easier and less stressful.

This book came about as a result of thousands of letters and phone calls I received after writing *Don't Sweat the Small Stuff . . . And It's All Small Stuff.* Many people were pleased to discover that, after reading the book, their lives were becoming less stressful and more enjoyable. Time and time again, I received requests from readers to write a similar type of book, only this time focused on specific applications and issues in the workplace. Because, to a large extent, I have overcome my own tendency to sweat the small stuff at work and because I know many others who have done the same, I decided to embark on another *Don't Sweat the Small Stuff* journey geared toward work.

It's fascinating to examine the way people deal with the most serious work-related issues, such as being fired or overtaken by a larger competitor, internal theft or violence, or being forced to relocate to a new city. When you stop to think about it, it's quite impressive, if not amazing. For the most part, people are courageous, innovative, and resilient when forced to deal with these truly challenging problems. But, as in other areas of life, when dealing with the smaller daily "stuff," it's quite a different story. In fact, if you take a step back, you may realize that, despite the occasional significant problems in the workplace, much of what bugs us on a day-to-day basis is actually the "small stuff." Hopefully, for most of us, the truly serious and tragic issues are few and far between. Indeed, it's all those little hassles that tend to drive us crazy.

Imagine, for a moment, how much energy is expended being stressed-out, frustrated, and angry over relatively minor things. How about being offended and bothered, or feeling criticized? And think about the implications of worry, fear, and commiseration. What impact do these emotions have on our productivity and on our enjoyment of our work? It's exhausting just thinking about it! Now imagine what might happen if you could use that same energy—or even some of it—on being more productive, creative, and solution-oriented.

While there may be little we can do about the really "big stuff," you must admit that there are many instances when we blow little problems out of proportion and turn things into giant emergencies. Often, we become frustrated or overwhelmed by the accumulation of all the little things we have to deal with. So much so, that we begin to lump together the day-to-day hassles and begin to treat everything as if it were "big stuff."

Because there is so much "small stuff" to deal with at work, there is a correlation between the way you handle small stuff and the overall quality of your experience. There's no question that, if you can learn to treat the smaller hassles with more perspective, wisdom, patience and with a better sense of humor, you'll begin to bring out the best in your-self as well as in others. You'll spend far less time being bothered, annoyed, and frustrated, and more time being creative and productive. Solutions will seem as plentiful in a calmer state of mind as the problems appear in a more bothered state.

One of the nice by-products of learning not to sweat the small stuff so much is that, eventually, you begin to see more and more of what you have to deal with on a daily basis as "small stuff." Whereas before you may have treated practically everything as if it were a really big deal, you may get better at differentiating between the truly significant and that which is far more benign.

As you learn to stop sweating the small stuff at work, you'll still have many of the same problems to deal with. However, you'll experience them quite differently. Rather than reacting to each issue with knee-jerk negativity, you'll learn to respond with far more grace and ease. Your stress level will lower, and you'll begin to have a lot more fun. I know that work can be difficult, but I also know we can learn to respond to that difficulty in a more positive way. I wish you the very best of luck in your work life, and hope that this book makes it a little bit easier.

Let's go to it!

1.

DARE TO BE HAPPY

Many people don't allow themselves the luxury of being enthusiastic, light-hearted, inspired, relaxed, or happy—especially at work. To me, this is a very unfortunate form of self-denial. It seems that a great number of people are frightened at what a happy demeanor would look like to other people, including coworkers, clients, and employers. After all, they assume, "Someone who is relaxed (or happy) must not be a hard worker." The logic goes something like this: If they looked happy, others might assume they were satisfied with the status quo and therefore lacking the necessary motivation to excel in their work or go the extra mile. They certainly couldn't survive in a competitive environment.

I'm often hired to speak to corporations around the country on stress reduction and happier living. On a number of occasions, the person who invited me to speak has asked me, in a nervous tone, whether I would help the employees become so happy that they would "lose their edge." I'm not kidding!

In reality, it's the other way around. It's nonsense to believe that a relaxed, happy person necessarily lacks motivation. On the contrary, happy people are almost always the ones who love what they do. It's been shown again and again that people who love what they do are highly motivated by their own enthusiasm to continually better themselves and their performance. They are good listeners and have a sharp learning curve. In addition, happy workers are highly creative, charismatic, easy to be around, and good team players.

Unhappy people, on the other hand, are often held back by their own misery or stress, which distracts them from success. Rigid, stressed-out people are a drag to be around and difficult to work with. They are the ones who lack motivation because they are so consumed with their own problems, lack of time, and stress. Unhappy people often feel victimized by others and their working conditions. It's difficult for them to be solution-oriented because everything is seen as someone else's fault. In addition, they are usually poor team players because they are often self-centered and preoccupied with their own issues. They are defensive and, almost always, poor listeners. If they are successful, it's despite their unhappiness, not because of it. In fact, if an unhappy, stressed-out person can learn to become happier, he or she will become even more successful.

I felt this strategy would be an excellent way to introduce this book because one of my goals is to convince you that *it's okay to be happy, kind, patient, more relaxed and forgiving.* It's to your advantage, personally and professionally. You won't lose your edge, nor will you be "walked on." I can assure you that you won't become apathetic, uncaring or unmotivated. To the contrary, you'll feel more inspired, creative, and driven to make an even greater contribution than you do right now. You'll see solutions and opportunities where others see problems. Likewise, rather than being discouraged by setbacks or failures, you'll bounce back quickly and resiliently. You will have increased energy, you'll be able to work "in the eye of the storm," and, because you'll be so level-headed, you'll be the one who is looked to when tough decisions need to be made. You will rise to the top.

If you dare to be happy, your life will begin to change immediately. Your life and your work will take on greater significance and will be experienced as an extraordinary adventure. You'll be loved by others and, without a doubt, you'll be sweating the small stuff far less often at work.

2.

BECOME LESS CONTROLLING

When I talk about being "controlling," I'm referring to unhealthy attempts to manipulate the behavior of others, having the need to control your environment, insisting on having things be "just so" in order to feel secure, and becoming immobilized, defensive or anxious when other people don't behave to your specifications—the way you think they should be. To be controlling means you are preoccupied with the actions of others and how those actions affect you. To put it in the context of this book, people who are controlling "sweat the behavior" of others when it doesn't match their own expectations.

I've made several observations about people who are controlling; two in particular. First, there are too many of them. For whatever reason, there seems to be a national trend toward controlling behavior. Secondly, the trait of being controlling is highly stressful—both to the controller and to those who are being controlled. If you want a more peaceful life, it's essential you become less controlling.

One of the most extreme examples of controlling behavior I've heard of involved, of all things, paper clips! A lawyer at a top-flight law firm had a penchant for certain things to be done in certain ways—not only "big picture" things, but very minuscule things as well. This fellow liked to use copper-colored paper clips instead of the silver ones his firm provided (what could be more important than that?). So he had his secretary buy his own private supply for him each week (and didn't even reimburse her). If something came to his desk with the wrong kind of clip, he'd fly into a rage. He became known in the office as "the paper clip king."

It probably won't come as a big surprise that this guy was almost always behind on his paperwork, and his work for his clients suffered. All the time he spent getting angry over petty things slowed him down. The paper clips were only one aspect of his controlling behavior—he had rules and regulations about everything from how his coffee was served (in a special china cup and saucer) to the order in which he was introduced in meetings. Ultimately, his controlling behavior turned off one too many of his clients, and he was let go from the firm.

This is a very unusual and extreme example, yet if you examine your own behavior, you may find areas that you are trying to control that are futile or just plain silly. I encourage you to take a look.

A person who is controlling carries with him a great deal of stress because, not only does he (or she) have to be concerned with his own choices and behavior, but in addition, he insists that others think and behave in certain ways as well. While occasionally we can influence another person, we certainly can't force him to be a certain way. To someone who is controlling, this is highly frustrating.

Obviously, in business, there are many times you want to have a meeting of the minds, or you need others to see things as you do. You have to sell yourself and your ideas to those you work with. In certain instances, you must exert your opinions, influence, even power to get something done. There are times you must insist on getting your way or think of clever and creative ways to get others to think differently. That's all part of business. And that's absolutely not what I'm referring to here.

We're not talking about healthy, normal attempts to come to a meeting of the minds or balancing points of view. We're also not talking about not caring about the behavior of others—of course you care. Rather, we're discussing the ways that insistence, singular thinking, rigidity, and the need to control translates into pain and stress.

What hurts the controlling person is what goes on inside—his feelings and emotions. The key element seems to be a lack of willingness to allow other people to fully be themselves, to give them space to be who they are, and to respect—really respect—the fact that people think differently. Deep down, a controlling person doesn't want other people to be themselves, but rather the image of who they want them to be. But people aren't an image of who we want them to be—they are who they are. So, if you're tied to an imagined image, you're going to feel frustrated and impotent a great deal of the time. A controlling person assumes that he knows what's best, and by golly, he's going to make other people see the folly of their ways. Within the need to control, there's an inherent lack of respect for the opinions and ways of others.

The only way to become less controlling is to see the advantages of doing so. You have to see that you can still get your way when it's necessary, yet you will be less personally invested. In other words, less will be riding on other people being, thinking, or behaving in a certain way. This will translate into a far less stressful way of being in the world. When you can make allowances in your mind for the fact that other people see life differently than you do, you'll experience far less internal struggle.

In addition, as you become less controlling, you'll be a lot easier to be around. You can probably guess that most people don't like to be controlled. It's a turnoff. It creates resentment and adversarial relationships.

As you let go of your need to be so controlling, people will be more inclined to help you; they will want to see you succeed. When people feel accepted for who they are rather than judged for who you think they should be, they will admire and respect you like never before.

3.

ELIMINATE THE
RAT RACE MENTALITY

I often hear people conversing about being stuck "in the rat race" as if they were discussing the weather—in a very casual, matter-of-fact manner. The assumption seems to be, "There's no escaping it—it's just a fact of life for everyone."

One of the problems with this mentality is that the label "rat race" implies, among other things, assumptions like, "I'm in a hurry, get out of my way, there's never enough time, there's not enough to go around, it's a dog-eat-dog world," and so forth. It sets you up to be frightened, impatient, and annoyed by constantly reinforcing and validating a self-defeating belief. You'll notice that most people who describe themselves as being "in the rat race" will indeed be hyper and easily bothered. It's important to note, however, that there are other people with the same types of jobs, pressures, responsibilities, and schedules who experience and describe their work in a much more peaceful and interesting way. Yet, they are every bit as effective and productive as their more nervous and agitated counterparts.

It's always refreshing for me to meet people who, despite being part of the corporate, commuting, and/or working world, have made the decision to not buy into this frenetic and destructive label. They refuse to box themselves in by the way they describe their experience. Instead, they live in a more accepting way, constantly on the lookout for a positive take on their experience.

So much of our daily work life exists in our own mind, dependent upon what aspects we focus on and how we characterize our experience. In other words, when we describe our day, we might feel very justified in saying, "Oh God, it was awful. I was stuck in horrible traffic with millions of other angry people. I spent my day in boring meetings, always scrambling a few minutes behind. There were arguments and almost constant conflict to deal with. What a bunch of jerks!"

The identical day might be thought of differently. You might describe it like this: "I drove to work and spent much of my day meeting with people. It was a challenge, but I did my best to stay as long as possible at one meeting without being late for the next one. The art of my work is bringing together people who, on the surface, don't seem to be able to get along very well. It's a good thing I'm there to help."

Can you feel the difference? And it's not a matter of one description being "realistic and accurate" and the other being wishful thinking. The truth is, both are absolutely accurate. It all depends on the well-being of the person doing the thinking. The same dynamic applies to whatever you happen to do for a living or how you spend your time. You can always make the argument, "I'm stuck in the rat race," or you can find another way to think about it.

You can begin to eliminate the rat race mentality and, in the process, become a calmer person and create a more interesting life, by deciding to stop discussing it with others—and by recharacterizing your day and your responsibilities in a healthier way. As your mind is focused in a more positive direction, and as you're looking for the gifts of your day instead of the hassles, you'll begin to notice aspects of your work life that may have been invisible to you. You'll actually see things differently. Everywhere you look, you'll see opportunities for personal and spiritual growth. You'll see more solutions and fewer problems, as well as plenty of ways to enhance and maximize your experience. I hope you'll consider eliminating the rate race mentality—your work will be a lot more rewarding if you do.

4.

DON'T DRAMATIZE
THE DEADLINES

Many of us work under the constant demands of tight deadlines. Authors are no exception to this rule. But have you ever stopped to think about how much mental and emotional emphasis we put on our deadlines? And have you ever wondered what negative consequences are attached to such emphasis? If not, I encourage you to give these questions some careful consideration.

It's true that deadlines are a fact of life. Yet a lot of this type of stress comes not so much from the deadline itself, but from all the thinking about it, wondering whether or not we will make it, feeling sorry for ourselves, complaining and, perhaps most of all, commiserating with others.

Recently, I was in an office waiting for an appointment. The person I was to meet with had been delayed in traffic. I was trying to read, but became fascinated by a conversation between two co-workers in the office. They were complaining among themselves about the unfair tight deadline they were on. Apparently, they had less than two hours to complete some type of report. Whatever it was, it was to be turned in by noon that same day.

I sat there, listening in amazement, as the two of them spent almost an entire hour complaining about how ridiculous it was to be put through this. They had not taken the first step toward the completion of their goal! Finally, about a minute before the person I was to meet finally arrived, one of them said in a frantic tone, "God, we'd better get started. It's due in an hour."

I realize that this is an extreme example, and few of us would waste time in as dramatic a manner as this. However, it does illustrate the point that the deadline itself isn't always the sole factor in the creation of stress. Ultimately, these two people seemed to realize that they could get the job done—even in one hour. So you have to wonder how different their experience could have been had they calmly taken a deep breath and worked together as quickly and efficiently as possible.

It's been my experience that complaining about deadlines—even if the complaints are justified—takes an enormous amount of mental energy and, more important to deadlines, time! The turmoil you go through commiserating with others or simply within your own head is rarely worth it. The added obsessive thinking about the deadline creates its own internal anxiety.

I know that deadlines can create quite a bit of stress and that sometimes it doesn't seem fair. However, working toward your goal without the interference of negative mental energy makes any job more manageable. See if you can notice how often you tend to worry, fret, or complain about deadlines. Then, try to catch yourself in the act of doing so. When you do, gently remind yourself that your energy would be better spent elsewhere. Who knows, perhaps you can ultimately make peace with deadlines altogether.

5.

HAVE SOME "NO PHONE"
TIME AT WORK

If you're like me, the telephone is a mixed bag of goods. On one hand, it's a lifesaver and obviously critical to most people. Without it, work would be impossible. On the other hand, depending on what you do for a living, the telephone can be one of the most distracting and stressful aspects of your work. Sometimes it seems as if we're always on the phone. And, if we're on the phone, it's impossible to get any other type of work done. This can create anxiety and resentment toward the people who are calling us.

I was once in the office of a manager when the phone rang. Immediately, he bellowed, "That darn phone never stops ringing." He then proceeded to pick it up and engage in a fifteen-minute conversation while I waited. When he finally hung up, he looked exhausted and frustrated. He apologized as the phone rang once again. He later confessed that he was having a great deal of trouble completing his tasks because of the volume of calls he was responding to. At some point I asked him, "Have you ever considered having a certain period of time when you simply don't answer the phone?" He looked at me with a puzzled look on his face and said, "As a matter of fact, no." It turned out that this simple suggestion helped him not only to relax, but to get more work done as well. Like many people, he didn't need hours of uninterrupted time, but he did need some! Because he was the one returning many of the calls instead of responding to them, he was able, in many instances, to cut the length of the return call. He would say things like, "Hi Joan, I've only got two minutes, but I wanted to get back to you."

Obviously, we depend on the phone, and are required to use it to varying degrees. If you're a receptionist, for example, or a telephone operator, or a salesperson, this strategy is going to have limited, if any practical relevance for you. However, for many others, it can be a real lifesaver. In my office, for example, if I didn't have any "no phone" time, I would be on the phone close to 100 percent of the day. The phone never seems to stop ringing. If I didn't have protective policies in place, I'd have very little time to write or work on other projects. I suspect the same may be true for many of you.

You can set this strategy in place in many different ways. I have certain times of the day when I turn off the ringer and don't take any calls other than ones that have been previously scheduled, or for real emergencies (which are extremely rare). This gives me some time to focus—without distraction—on what's most relevant to my work.

Many people, of course, are required to answer the phone as a company policy or as a part of their job, and these people must be a little more creative to implement this strategy. Perhaps you can arrive a little early and turn off the phone before your day "officially" begins, or do the same thing after work. I know one woman who decided to bring her lunch to work so that she could work at her desk during a time she was allowed to turn off the phone and let the voice mail answer it. She was able to negotiate an earlier quitting time so that her actual day wasn't longer, but she was then able to have a little more time to concentrate.

In certain instances, you might be able to convince your employer to allow you to experiment with this strategy—to see if you can get more done (and still return all the calls). Some calls that come in can be returned later, or after hours when you can answer specific questions by leaving messages on a voice mail. This may take a minute or two instead of engaging in a ten- or fifteen-minute conversation.

If you work at home (or if you ever need to get things done at home), this strategy works wonders and is often easier to put into place. You simply make the decision that for a specific period of time you will not answer the phone, thereby giving yourself the chance to get the things done that you need to do.

This is not a fool-proof strategy; there are often quirks to work out. For example, how do you handle emergencies or important personal calls? I have a separate line reserved for very close friends, family, and a select few people that I work with. Another possibility is to leave your pager number or an alternate phone number on your voice mail or answering machine that is specifically reserved for calls that truly can't wait. Most people will honor your "emergency only" request. One other possibility is that you can check your messages after each call, or on a frequent basis. That way, you can postpone the bulk of the calls until a better time, but still get right back to those people who absolutely can't wait.

I think you'll find that any hassles you must overcome to put this strategy into practice are, in most instances, well worth it. Let's face it. The work world is not going to accommodate us with fewer phone calls to respond to. I've found that I can get twice, even three times the amount of concentrated work done when I'm not distracted by the phone. Then, with all the time I have saved, I can almost always return my calls when everything else has been done.

6.

AVOID CORPORATE BRAGGING

One of the many things that I do professionally is travel around the country giving lectures to corporations and other groups on stress reduction, gaining happiness, and various ways to stop sweating the small stuff. At some of these functions, I'm asked to attend meetings, meals, and parties, either before or after my speaking engagement. And although I'm a fairly private person who enjoys being alone, particularly before I speak to a large group, I'd say that a vast majority of the people I've met are nice, thoughtful, talented, and well-meaning individuals.

I've noticed a destructive tendency, however, that seems to run through virtually every individual, corporation, and industry. That tendency is what I call "corporate bragging."

Corporate bragging is sharing with others how incredibly busy you are and how very hard you work—not just in passing, but rather as a central, focal point of conversation. It's almost as though we wear a badge of honor for being a person who is completely overwhelmed, deprived of sleep, and who has little, if any, personal life. I've heard hundreds of people discussing the number of hours they work, as well as the number of hours they don't get to sleep each night. I've heard people explain how exhaustion is a regular part of their life. They discuss the time they arrive at the office, and the number of months it's been since they had any real quality time with their spouse, children, or significant other, much less a vacation. I've heard people brag about not having time to go out on dates, about being so busy and frantic that they've forgotten to eat, and even a few people who have gone so far as to say they rarely have time to use the restroom.

Although corporate bragging is a catchy phrase, the tendency itself is certainly not limited to people working in the corporate world. Rather, it's a habit that seems to have taken hold over most people who work for a living—it's extremely pervasive.

Before I go on, let me assure you that I'm not minimizing how hard people work or how difficult and all-consuming work can be—I've been there too. The problem is that bragging about how busy you are reinforces, to yourself, how stressed out you are. It keeps you overly focused on the most negative aspects of your work. It becomes a self-fulfilling prophecy, keeping you caught up in your own business.

If you take a step back and think about it, you'll probably agree that corporate bragging is also a boring, nonproductive topic of conversation. I've observed many conversations centered around corporate bragging and I've yet to see a single person even slightly interested in hearing about someone else's busyness. Usually, the person listening (if you can call it that) is either waiting their turn to share about their own busyness, or they are looking around the room, paying little attention to what is being said. The truth is, "busyness" is old news—everyone else is already talking about it.

Think about it from the perspective of those to whom you are sharing. Unless I'm missing something, regardless of who you are or what you do for a living, it's not very interesting to hear about how busy or overwhelmed you are. In fact, it's really boring. Personally, I can't stand listening to people complain about it—and I try really hard to avoid it. Let's be realistic. Would you be interested in hearing about how busy I am? I hope not. I'd rather be around people who discuss interesting aspects of life—and I'm sure you would too.

So, no matter how you look at it, corporate bragging does no good. If you're too busy, you either need to cut back, or catch up. But talking about it to others only exacerbates your stress and makes you a less interesting person.

7.

MAKE THE BEST OF

THOSE BORING MEETINGS

I did a fairly comprehensive survey asking people what they liked least about work. Over and over again, people shared with me their distaste for all those meetings, especially the "boring" ones. Many people feel there are simply too many meetings to attend on a daily and weekly basis, and that many of them are entirely unnecessary.

Admittedly, due to the nature of my work, I'm not required to attend as many meetings as some people. However, I have developed a strategy regarding meetings that has helped me a great deal. And those who have tried it have reported back a similar result.

I've found two secrets to making virtually any meeting interesting and as productive as it can possibly be. The first thing I do is use the meeting to practice being "present moment oriented." In other words, I attempt to absorb myself in the meeting—not allowing my mind to wander. This deliberate attempt to be focused allows me to get as much value out of the experience as possible. After all, I'm there anyway. I can spend the time wishing I were somewhere else—or I can think about what I'll be doing later. Or, I can practice being truly present, a really good listener. This helps me be highly responsive to whatever is being discussed. That way, if there is something I can contribute, I'll be able to do so.

Since I've been doing this, I've found that the meetings I attend are far more interesting. Additional insights come to mind, and I feel as though I have more to offer. I've also noticed an increased sense of respect from others. They may even not be consciously aware of it, but it seems that when those present in a meeting sense that you are truly listening, they want to listen to you as well. There is a powerful sense of well-deserved trust that comes across when you are truly present. People are drawn to your energy and presence.

The second commitment I have made regarding meetings is to tell myself that I'm going to learn something new from each meeting. So, I listen intently to what is being said, trying to hear something I don't already know. In other words, rather than comparing what I'm hearing to what I already believe—or agreeing or disagreeing in my mind to what is being said—I'm searching for new wisdom, a new insight, or a new way of doing something. I've found that when my intent is to learn, I almost always do learn. Instead of thinking to myself, "Yeah, yeah, I already know this stuff," I try to clear my mind and allow myself to have a beginner's mind.

The results have been quite impressive and significant. My learning curve has dramatically increased, and meetings have become fun again. I've learned to make the best of it. The way I look at it is this: I'm in the meeting anyway. Why not spend the time in a productive, healthy way, practicing valuable emotional skills instead of wishing I were someone else? To do so makes my work life more interesting and effective.

8.

STOP ANTICIPATING TIREDNESS

Recently, I was on a flight from San Francisco to Chicago when I overheard one of the silliest conversations imaginable. It demonstrates a critical yet common mistake that many people seem to make on an ongoing basis. The conversation, which must have lasted at least half of an hour, centered around how tired each of these two people were going to be—tomorrow and all week!

It was as if each person was trying to convince the other, and perhaps themselves, how many hours and how hard they were working, how few hours of sleep they were going to get, and, most of all, how tired they were going to be. I wasn't quite sure if they were bragging or complaining, but one thing was certain, they were appearing more and more tired the longer the conversation continued.

They each said things like, "Boy, am I going to be tired tomorrow," "I don't know how I'm going to make it through the rest of the week," and "I'm only going to get three hours of sleep tonight." They told stories of late nights, lack of sleep, uncomfortable hotel beds, and early morning meetings. They anticipated feeling exhausted, and I'm sure they were going to be correct in their assumption. Their voices were heavy, as if the lack of sleep they were going to get was already affecting them. I actually felt myself getting tired just listening to part of the conversation!

The problem with anticipating tiredness in this way, or in any way, is that it clearly reinforces the tiredness. It rivets your attention to the number of hours you are sleeping and how tired you are going to be. Then, when you wake up, you're likely do it again by reminding yourself how few hours it has been since your head hit the pillow. Who knows what really happens, but seems to me that anticipating tiredness must send a message to your brain *reminding* you to feel and act tired because that is the way you have programmed yourself to respond.

Clearly, everyone needs a certain degree of rest. I've read a few articles suggesting that many, if not most, of us don't get enough sleep. And if you're tired, the best possible solution would probably be to try to get more sleep. But in those instances when it's not possible to do so, the worst thing you can do, in my estimation, is to convince yourself, in advance, that you are going to be exhausted. I've found that the best strategy is to get as much sleep as I possibly can and be grateful for whatever amount that might be.

Because I travel a great deal for speaking engagements and promotional events, there are times when I get as few as three or four hours of sleep, occasionally even less. I have noticed, however, that if I simply forget about it—absolutely avoid the tendency to keep track—I'm far more rested with the sleep I do get. Then as soon as I can, I take a nap, and all is usually well. One thing I try never to do is to discuss my lack of sleep with other people. I've learned that when I do, I always feel more tired as a result.

I've noticed this habit of anticipating tiredness creep into the conversations of many people (don't feel bad, I've done it plenty of times in the past). If you are someone who does this, see if you can avoid the tendency as much as possible. If you do, you may find yourself feeling less tired. It seems reasonable to assume that, if you aren't as tired, you probably won't be sweating the small stuff as much at work.

26

9.

DON'T SWEAT

THE BUREAUCRACY

I can't imagine that there are very many people who work for a living who don't have to deal with at least some form of bureaucracy. After all, there are local, state, and federal agencies, insurance companies, Social Security, Medicare, the post office, the Department of Motor Vehicles, city hall, payroll procedures, business licenses, permits required, regulatory agencies, and, of course, the IRS—to name just a few. Most industries seem to have their own agencies to deal with—education, medical, pharmaceutical, food and beverage, the airlines and other forms of transportation, the building industry, the environment, and all the rest.

You can, of course, spend your entire lifetime complaining about bureaucracy, wishing it would disappear, and fighting every step of the way. You can struggle, engage in negative dialogue, play out wars in your head, and drive yourself crazy. In the end, however, you're still going to have to deal with bureaucracy. My suggestion is to stop sweating it and, in fact, strive to make peace with bureaucracy. This is something that can be done.

Joe has a small business with six employees. He received a notice from his state tax agency verifying the closing of his business. The problem was—it wasn't closed! When he would call or write to clear the matter up, he was told again and again that he must be mistaken—the business was officially closed. It took six months, but the problem was eventually resolved.

The key to the resolution of this issue was Joe's lack of panic. He told me, "Statistically, sooner or later something like this was bound to happen." Rather than panic or go crazy, he kept his cool and maintained his perspective.

Let me make myself perfectly clear. I'm not suggesting that you roll over and become a victim of bureaucracy—or that you think of being caught in ridiculous bureaucratic loops as acceptable. Nor am I suggesting that you smile when confronted with one of those "from a different planet" conclusions that some bureaucrats seem to come up with. What I *am* suggesting is that you find a way to maximize your efficiency when you must deal with bureaucracy, do the very best that you can with it, make suggestions on ways to improve the system, and then detach yourself from the craziness.

When dealing with bureaucracy, it's important to take this attitude: "I know there is a solution here and I know this will be resolved." There are certainly indescribable exceptions where there is such a mess that there doesn't seem to be a way out but, luckily, in a vast majority of the cases, a resolution is eventually achieved if you are patient, persistent and don't worry about it. Develop a sense of humor and, if possible, see if you can accept the fact that rules and regulations do have a place in our society. We have just allowed it to become a little out of control.

This past year I've been trapped in two unbelievable bureaucratic webs—one with the Department of Motor Vehicles and one with a city agency dealing with a home-related project. In both scenarios, for a brief period of time, logic and common sense were removed from the picture. I found myself wondering what planet I was on! Yet, to the best of my knowledge, both situations have resolved themselves.

There is a bright spot. There are people within the bureaucracy that don't fit the mold—people who are flexible and who are trying to be of service. When you must deal with bureaucracy, try to find these people— they are out there. In both of my recent adventures, I was helped by wonderful, caring people who stepped out of the mess long enough to help me. And you know what else? Most people who work for a bureaucracy are just as frustrated as you and I. For the most part, they are really nice people who are, to some degree, trapped in a role.

Keep in mind that people who work for the IRS have to pay taxes— and most people who work for the Department of Motor Vehicles probably drive a car. They are just like the rest of us; none are exempt from dealing with bureaucracy. So the lesson is this: The more you are able to keep your bearings and composure, and have some perspective, the more likely it is that you will find one of these nice people to help you. Getting frustrated only makes matters worse. It brings out the worst in bureaucrats and encourages them to turn to the rule book rather than find a real solution.

I know this is a tough issue—it is for me too. Yet our options aren't good. I've thought about this issue a great deal and have come to the conclusion that it's not worth it to become frustrated. Far better to stop sweating the bureaucracy.

10.

REMEMBER THE PHRASE,

"BEING DEAD IS BAD

FOR BUSINESS"

Several years ago my father was involved in a wonderful organization called BENZ, which stands for Business Executives for National Security. One of their missions was to educate business professionals about the absurdity of the nuclear arms race, both the financial burdens as well as the outright dangers to all of us. One of my favorite sayings that came out of BENZ was, "Being dead is bad for business." In a humorous way, they were emphasizing the obvious—if we blow ourselves up, none of us will prosper!

I'll bet you can guess where I'm going with this one. You can, of course, easily extend this clever metaphor to the way we treat ourselves—particularly in the areas of our personal health. The saying holds true however you look at it: Being dead is bad for business.

Remembering this really helps to keep things in perspective. For example, when you find yourself saying things like, "I don't have time to exercise," what you really should be saying is, "I don't have time *not* to exercise." If you lose your health and sense of well-being, you won't make it to work at all. In the long run, it takes far less time to take care of yourself than it does to lose your ability to function well.

Jim was a partner for a large New York law firm. Although he loved his family as much as anyone I've ever met, he was burning the candle at both ends. He left early and came home late. He traveled a great deal and was under constant stress. His children were growing up and he was missing most of it. He lacked sleep and exercise. He said to me, "Richard, this pace is going to kill me." To make matters worse, there didn't seem to be any light at the end of the tunnel. The more valuable he became to the firm, the more demands were made of his time.

At some point, it all became too much. After a great deal of personal reflection, he came to the conclusion that, as important as his work was to him, it wasn't worth dying for, nor was it worth missing the opportunity to watch his own children grow up. He decided a change was in order. He quit the firm and opened his own practice. I've never seen a more magnificent transformation. Not too long ago, he said to me, "I've never been happier. Business is better than ever and, for the first time, I'm able to spend a considerable amount of time with Julie and the kids." Although he still works very hard, he has created a sense of balance that works well for him. There's little question that, had he continued on his earlier path, his health and happiness would have continued to deteriorate. It seems that he literally decided that being dead would be bad for business!

Obviously, not everyone can make such a dramatic and risky change, but doesn't it make sense to eat well, exercise, get plenty of rest, think positively, have regular physical checkups, and partake in other healthy habits? In addition to the obvious problems associated with ignoring these commonsense health habits, you can see that it's also a horrible waste of time in the long run. Each cold or flu costs you days of productive work time. Who knows how many years of time you will save by simply taking care of yourself?

By remembering that "being dead is bad for business," you'll probably begin taking better care of yourself—physically and emotionally. You'll feel better, be happier, and probably live longer. You can let go of your fear that you'll fall behind because, in fact, you'll be more productive and have a longer, happier career. So keep yourself alive and healthy. It's good for business.

11.

MAKE THE BEST OF
CORPORATE TRAVEL

For many business professionals, mandatory travel is somewhat rare, if not nonexistent. Yet those of us who must travel, especially a great deal, know very well the hassles associated with frequent travel. Rushing around, delays and cancellations, long periods of time in closed-in spaces, never-ending impatient crowds, safety fears associated with flying, living out of suitcases, time-zone changes, sleep problems, hotel food, and many other factors, are simply a necessary evil.

There is probably no satisfactory solution to the ongoing demands of frequent travel. It is, in fact, draining. There are several things we can do, however, to make each journey as pleasant as it can possibly be.

To begin with, I suggest you become much friendlier to the flight attendants on your flights. I've been told dozens of times that I'm the friendliest passenger a flight attendant has "ever seen." This is a bit disturbing to me because, as a rule, I really don't enjoy flying and am probably at my *least* friendliest while on an airplane. What this tells me is that most of us are dreadfully impatient when we travel. Try to remember that flight attendants not only have to fly to earn their living, but they must try to keep you and me safe and comfortable, as well.

I've found that when I go out of my way to be kind, say thank you, and be appreciative and friendly, the time goes by much quicker and my flights are much more pleasant. When I'm friendly, the flight attendants are usually friendly, as well. They go out of their way to make my flight as pleasant as possible, and, I might be imagining it, but I think the other passengers seem to lighten up, too.

Do the same thing while waiting in ticket lines. You'll be amazed at how much nicer you are treated when you are nice first! I've been "mysteriously" bumped up to business or first class while holding an economy ticket—and given preferential seating (or a seat on a completely booked flight) on several occasions, simply because I was apparently the only passenger waiting in line who wasn't complaining or giving the ticket agents a bad time. While traveling on business, compassion and patience pay huge dividends.

Then there are the more obvious things. Try not to overeat on planes. Once in a while, I even skip my meal, and I'm always glad I did. If you must drink alcohol, try to keep it to a minimum. When you eat and drink too much on planes (and almost everyone I travel with does), it makes you feel groggy and listless. It makes your recovery much more difficult, and makes it harder to keep your weight under control.

Bring not just one, but several good books. While on planes, your mood can do strange things. It's a good time to read a book you might not normally think of reading. Use the flight time to try something different: a novel, for example, or a mystery. Or I've met people who have learned a foreign language while flying. They purchase an audio-cassette program, close their eyes, relax, and learn. I've been told that 100,000 miles later, they can speak French or Spanish!

Of course, you can always use the time to work. I'd guess that at least one-fourth of my writing for this book (ironically, not this section), was done on an airplane. Not in all cases, but almost always, there's a way to get some time-consuming, or as in my case, creative work done on planes. As I mentioned, I don't really like to fly. However, I've actually gotten to the point where I look forward to the work I *know* I'll get done on airplanes.

When you arrive at your destination, try to take advantage of whatever situation you are in. Have you ever wanted to learn to meditate or take up yoga? If so, what better place than in the solitude of a lonely and quiet hotel room? Have work to catch up on? Great, it's quiet and nondistracting. Try to get some exercise, even if it's in the room. Or, take a walk before your meetings or when you are done in the evening. I've found that hotel rooms are great places to catch up with old friends. I rarely, if ever, have time to make calls from home or the office. But occasionally in hotel rooms, I can sit in a comfortable chair and call an old friend.

I guess my bottom line is this: Make the best of it. Be creative. Invest in yourself. Take advantage of your situation. Rather than complain about your travel, try to make something of it. Someday, when you look back on your career, you will probably say one of two things. Either you'll say, "Gosh, I had to travel a lot and it was a nightmare." Or, you'll say, "Gosh, I had to travel a lot for work, but it was okay. I did everything I could to make the best of it." Either way, the travel will be over. The difference won't be in the number of days you traveled, or to what cities. Nor will it be in the number of frequent-flyer miles you accumulate. The difference will be in your attitude, nothing more. So, the next time you travel for business, make the best of it—and have a nice flight.

12.

LIGHT A CANDLE INSTEAD OF
CURSING THE DARKNESS

This is a strategy for better living that I have heard mentioned for many years. And while I sometimes forget to implement this wisdom, I try whenever possible to keep it in mind. It's extremely simple and reliable, yet often completely overlooked. As the title suggests, this strategy involves taking positive, solution-oriented steps (however small) toward improving a situation instead of complaining about what's wrong. It means being more a part of the solution rather than a reminder or reinforcement of the problem. I've found that work is the ideal environment to practice this philosophy.

While we're working, it's easy to fall into the trap of spending our time and energy taking note and complaining about the wrongs of the world—the way things are, the economy, negative people, industry changes, greed, lack of compassion, bureaucracy, and so forth. After all, if we are looking for verification that the world is full of problems, we don't have to look far to prove our assumptions.

If you take a careful look, you'll notice that in most cases, commiserating with others about the problems at work, or thinking excessively about them only serves to increase your own level of stress, thus making it even more difficult to do anything about the very things that are bothering you. As we focus on the problem and discuss it with others, it can reinforce our belief that life is difficult and stressful, which, of course, it can be. When we focus too much on what's wrong, it reminds us of other things we disapprove of or wish were different, which can lead us toward feelings of discouragement and being overwhelmed.

It's interesting, however, to notice that in many instances you cannot only make a dent in a problem, but actually reduce your own stress level in the process by simply choosing to "light a candle." Simply put, this means making a suggestion or taking a positive step toward improving a source of stress. It means putting increased emphasis on a potential solution and less emphasis on "cursing" the problem.

For example, suppose gossip or talking behind others' backs is a problem where you work. Rather than remaining resentful or frustrated that this bad habit exists, see if you can make a tiny dent in the problem. Gather together a few of your friends and gently bring the issue to the table. But rather than accusing anyone, focus on your own contribution. Confess that you have been as guilty as anyone else in indulging in occasional gossip, and state that you're going to make a genuine effort not to do so. Invite others to join you. Make your invitation lighthearted and unthreatening. Focus on the positive benefits of decreased gossip—nicer feelings toward one another, not having to worry so much about what others are saying about you, less stress, and so forth. In many cases, the people you work with will jump at the opportunity to join you—simply because you have taken the first step. Even if they don't, you will have taken a positive step toward the reduction of a nasty corporate habit. Either way, you win!

I met Sarah in the Department of Motor Vehicles. She was the most helpful employee I've ever seen in the role she was performing. In her line, which was moving quickly, people were smiling and leaving satisfied. She was friendly, courteous, and efficient. I couldn't resist asking her what her secret was. Here is what she said: "I spent several years putting customers off with the excuse, 'That's not my department.' The truth was, at least half the time, I knew the answer to the questions being asked, and in most cases could have been much more helpful. Virtually everyone in line was either mad at me or disgusted by my bureaucratic attitude. At some point I became fed up with my own sourpuss behavior and decided to change. Now, whenever possible, I help people out instead of putting them off and forcing them to wait in a different line. Everything has changed; most people appreciate me now. I feel better about myself, and my job is a lot more fun."

See how easy it is to light a candle?

13.

JOIN MY NEW CLUB, "TGIT"

Until now, the business world was primarily made of two clubs. The most popular club, by far, was the "TGIF" club, or "Thank God It's Friday." To be a member of this club, your primary focus is on the weekend. Members think about, anticipate, and look forward to Fridays so that they can get away from their work. Most members are highly stressed because only two days of the week are considered "good days." Even Sunday is considered a stressful day because the next day they have to go back to work.

The other business club is substantially smaller, yet in some ways the members are more dedicated to the club. This one is called "TGIM," or "Thank God It's Monday." These members are usually workaholics who can't stand weekends because they are away from work! Members of this club are also highly stressed because while there are generally five days of the week to be preoccupied with work, there is always that darn weekend that gets in the way! The most difficult day of the week is usually Friday, because it often means the member won't be able to get back to work for a few days. They may try to work on weekends, but the demands of family get in the way. Needless to say, members of both clubs think that members of the "other club" are completely nuts!

I invite you to join an alternate club. My hope is that together, we can eventually achieve a 100 percent membership. In fact, I'd love to put the other two clubs out of business altogether! This new club is called

"TGIT," or "Thank God It's Today." Members of this club are happy seven days a week because they understand that every day is unique, and each brings with it different gifts. Members of this club are grateful to be alive; they rejoice in their many blessings and expect each day to be full of wonder, surprise, and opportunity.

There are no qualifications necessary to join the "TGIT" club, other than the desire to have a higher quality of life and the desire to appreciate rather than dread each day. Members of this club understand that it's useless to wish any day were different. They know that Mondays don't care if you like them or not—they simply go on being Mondays. Likewise, Fridays will come around every seventh day, whether you wish it were Friday or not. It's up to each of us to make every day as special as it can be. No amount of wishing will make the slightest bit of difference.

As simple as it seems, the desire to maintain a membership in this club can make a substantial difference in the attitude you carry with you at work, and in fact in all of life. Just think: If you wake up every day of the week with an attitude of, "I'm glad today is today. I'm going to make this day as positive and wonderful as I possibly can," you may be surprised at how much less stressed you'll be. This simple shift of attitude goes a long, long way toward a more positive experience of life and work.

14.

DON'T SWEAT
THE DEMANDING BOSS

I'd estimate that a large percentage of adults that I know are either working for, or have worked for, a demanding boss. Like deadlines, taxes, and budgets, demanding bosses seem to be a fact of life for many working people. Even if you don't technically work "for" someone else, you may have demanding people that you work with or who pay your bills, or demanding customers you must attempt to please.

Like everything else, there are two ways to deal with demanding bosses. We can, like most do, complain about them, talk behind their backs, wish they would go away, secretly plot against them in our minds, wish them ill will, and feel forever stressed about the situation. Or we can take a different path and try (hard as it is) to stay focused on the positive aspects of the demanding party.

This was a particularly difficult concept for me to embrace, as I've always hated it when I feel pushed to perform. However, after dealing with many, many pushy people in my career, I've come to realize some important things.

The first "saving grace" I realized about demanding people is that, generally speaking, they are demanding to everyone. In other words, it's not personal. Before I recognized this to be the case, I would assume, as many do, that Mr. or Mrs. Demanding was "out to get me." I took their demanding demeanor personally and felt pressured. I would then compound the problem by thinking about his or her hidden motives, making a case within my own head as to why I had "a right to be angry." I would even go home at night and complain to poor Kris, who had already heard my story many times before.

All this began to change as I began to see a hint of innocence in the demanding party. In other words, I began to see that, in a very real sense, he or she really couldn't help it—they were stuck in the role of being demanding. This didn't change my preference for working with less-demanding people, but it did make it easier to accept when I had to.

I was working on a book a number of years ago when I was forced to work with a very demanding editor. I was having a difficult time with all the criticism and pushing, when a friend of mine asked me a very important question. She said, "Has it ever occurred to you that the most demanding people are often the ones who push you out of your comfort zone and help you rise to a new level of competence?" Until that moment, it hadn't occurred to me that this was true. As I look back at my career, I now realize that it was often the case that demanding people were the ones who brought out the best in me. Everything—from my writing style, to my ability to use a computer and adjust to technology, to my ability to speak in public—was greatly enhanced by my connection to demanding, even abrasive people.

Suzanne worked for someone who could only be described as "a real jerk." She described him as "a person who was demanding for no other reason than to be demanding." He seemed to feel a perverse sense of power when he was ordering people around.

Other than Suzanne, everyone in the office was either frightened or resentful of this demanding boss. For some reason, she had the wisdom to see through his huge ego and obnoxious behavior. Whenever possible, she tried to see the humor in her situation and instead of hating him, to see if there were things she might learn from his skills rather than focusing on his flaws. Her learning curve was sharp. It wasn't too long before her ability to stay cool in a hostile environment was noticed by her boss's employer, and she was promoted to a more interesting position in a different department.

The realization that there are two sides to demanding people—positive and negative—has made my entire life, especially my work life, a whole lot easier. Whereas before I would become defensive and dread the process, I now approach demanding people in an entirely new way. I'm open to what they may have to teach me, and I don't take their behavior personally. What has happened is quite remarkable. Because I'm so much less adversarial and defensive than I used to be, the "demanding" people I meet and work with seem to be a lot easier to be around. I now realize that my overreaction to demanding people had a lot to do with how difficult they were for me to deal with. As is so often the case, as I have grown and have been willing to open my mind to my own contribution to my problems, I have been rewarded with an easier life. I'm not advocating demanding behavior, as I still see it as a negative and abrasive personality trait. However, I have learned to take it in stride and see it as "small stuff." Perhaps the same can happen to you.

15.

REMEMBER TO ACKNOWLEDGE

I can't think of a single person who doesn't love and appreciate being acknowledged. On the flip side, most people either resent, or at least feel slighted by not being acknowledged. This being the case, this one seems like a "no-brainer."

You can acknowledge others in many ways. When someone calls you, acknowledge the call. When they send you something, remember to say thank you, or take the time to write a note. When someone does a good job, say so. When they apologize, acknowledge that too. It's especially important to acknowledge acts of kindness—doing so reinforces the act and encourages more of the same. We all benefit.

Almost everyone loves to be acknowledged. We love to have our phone calls returned, to be told we are doing a great job, to be thanked for working so hard, to have our creativity appreciated, to be reminded that we are special.

Approximately fifty people report to Dennis, who runs a large department in an insurance company. Dennis was in the habit of taking everyone for granted. His exact words to me were, "My philosophy used to be that people were lucky to have a job. I felt that if someone was doing a good job, their reward was one more paycheck." I encouraged him to think in a more loving, generous way and to expand his definition of acknowledgment. It took some time, but he was able to do so, genuinely and graciously.

As he looks back, he can hardly believe how he used to behave. He told me, "Everyone who worked for me was frightened and insecure, and no one felt appreciated. Today, I try to always remember to acknowledge a job well done. I can sense an enormous difference. People are lighter, happier, less defensive and more loyal than before. It will probably take more time, but I feel like people are starting to forgive me. I've learned that I need my employees as much as they need me."

We should acknowledge others, not simply to get something in return, but because it's the right thing to do—because it makes them feel good. I have to tell you, however, that in this case, "doing the right thing" really does come back to help you. It's difficult to quantify, but I'm certain that acknowledgment has played a critical role in my own success as a professional and as a human being. I've written hundreds of thank-you letters and made thousands of phone calls simply to acknowledge the acts of others. I know that I drop the ball every once in a while and that things do fall between the cracks, but my intention is to acknowledge everyone, when it's appropriate. Time and time again I've been praised and thanked for being "the only person who took the time to acknowledge."

People remember acknowledgment and they appreciate it. When you need a favor, or advice, the fact that you have previously taken the time to acknowledge someone often comes back to help you. It makes others want to help you and to see you succeed. Also, people who have been acknowledged genuinely and with love are very forgiving. They will see beyond your mistakes and failures and forgive you freely. Needless to say, all of this makes your life easier and far less stressful. So think about it. Does someone in your work life deserve some sort of acknowledgment? If so, what's holding you up?

16.

DON'T KEEP PEOPLE WAITING

One of the ways I attempt to keep my own stress under control is to avoid, whenever possible, the bad habit of keeping other people waiting. Time is precious to everyone. I've observed that almost everyone feels that one of their most valued commodities is their time. This being the case, one of the ultimate slaps and most surefire ways to annoy someone is to keep them waiting. While most people are somewhat forgiving, keeping them waiting is a sign of disrespect and a lack of acknowledgment. The subtle message is, "My time is more important than yours." Consider the magnitude of this suggestion. Do you feel that anyone else's time is more precious than yours? I doubt it. Doesn't it make sense then that everyone else feels the same way?

Deep down, we all know that noone likes to be kept waiting. Therefore, it's highly stressful to keep other people waiting because you know you are disappointing someone. In the back of your mind, you know darn well the person is looking at his watch, wondering where you are and why you are late. You may be keeping him from personal or professional commitments and that could make him angry or resentful.

There are obviously exceptions to the rule—times when factors beyond your control prevent you from being on time. Things happen to all of us, and noone has a perfect record. Truthfully, however, a vast majority of the time, being late is preventable. But instead of planning ahead, allowing a little extra time, or making allowances for unexpected problems, we wait just a little too long, or don't allow quite enough time—so we end up late. We then compound the problem by making excuses like "traffic was horrible," when, in reality, traffic is virtually always horrible. The problem wasn't traffic—but the fact that we didn't factor enough time in our schedule for the traffic. It's likely the case that, even if traffic was horrible, or you got off to a late start, or whatever the excuse, the other person isn't going to be interested or impressed. It may not be fair, but sometimes your work and other positive traits will be over-shadowed by the fact that you were late.

I wouldn't underestimate the negative impact of making someone wait. It drives some people crazy. And, even if they don't express their frustration to you directly, it can show up in other ways—not taking you as seriously, avoiding you when possible, being disrespectful, choosing to spend their time with others instead of you, showing up late to your future appointments, as well as an assortment of other forms of retalia-tion.

Even if you were somehow able to discount the effects of your show-ing up late, it still creates an enormous amount of stress in your life in other ways. When you're late, you're scrambling. You're in a hurry, behind schedule. It's difficult to be present-moment-oriented because you're concerned about whatever it is you're running late for. Your mind is filled up with stressful thoughts like, "What might happen?" or "I've done it again." Or you might be hard on yourself, wondering, "Why do I always have to run late?"

When you're on time, however, you avoid all this stress and then some. They may not express it, but the people you work with will appre-ciate the fact that you're not late. They won't have any reason to be mad at you or to think you don't respect their time. They won't be talking behind your back, and you won't get the reputation as the person who is always late. You'll stop rushing and, because you won't be so hurried, you'll relax a little bit and have slightly more time to reflect.

Some of my very best ideas have come to mind between appointments, when I've had a few minutes to be quiet, when I wasn't in a hurry. I've thought up solutions to problems, as well as ideas for a book or a speech that was coming up. It's clear to me that had I been rushing around, running late, it's likely the ideas would have been buried in the frazzle. I've met a number of people who confess that they used to keep people waiting—and who have seen their lives change for the better by implementing this very simple and courteous strategy. Perhaps it can help you as well.

17.

CREATE A BRIDGE BETWEEN
YOUR SPIRITUALITY
AND YOUR WORK

When I've suggested that spirituality become a more integral part of a person's life, I've often heard the reply, "I'd love for that to happen but I'm just too busy. I have to go to work." If that sounds familiar, this strategy may be helpful.

To create a bridge between your spirituality and your work means that you take the essence of who you are and what you believe into your daily work life. You dismantle the dichotomy that so often exists between your spiritual life and that which you do for a living. It means that if kindness, patience, honesty, and generosity are spiritual qualities that you believe in, you make every effort to practice those qualities at work. You treat people with kindness and respect. If someone is late or makes a mistake, you try to be patient. Even if it's your job or appropriate to reprimand someone, you do so from a place of love and respect. You are as generous as you can be—with your time, money, ideas, and love.

In a way, work is a perfect environment to practice your spirituality. In a given day, you have so many opportunities to practice patience, acts of kindness, and forgiveness. You have time to think loving thoughts, smile, embrace others, and practice gratitude. You can practice being nondefensive and a better listener. You can try to be compassionate, particularly with difficult or abrasive people. You can practice your spirituality in virtually everything that you do. It can be found in the way you greet people and deal with conflict. You can exhibit it in the way you sell a product or service—or the way you balance ethics with profit. It's literally everywhere.

Grace is a literary (book and related projects) agent. She is someone who, in my opinion, has created this bridge very well. In part, she describes her spiritual philosophy as one of "non-violence, integrity, and a love of all creatures." I have never seen an instance where she didn't "walk her talk." She turns down books and other potential projects when they conflict with her values, even when she is turning away guaranteed money. I've seen her walk away from an offer when questionable ethics were involved. She has told me, on more than one occasion, "I'd never sell myself short just to make money. I'm always able to look myself proudly in the mirror and know that I'm a person who can be trusted." I know she feels good about herself, as well she should. I'm proud to know her, as she is the type of person I admire and love to be around.

There's something really comforting about creating this spiritual bridge. It reminds you of a higher purpose. It puts your problems and concerns into a broader context. It helps you grow from your difficult experiences rather than become hopeless or overwhelmed by them. Even if you have to do something terribly difficult such as firing someone, for example, you do so while remembering your humanity. Or even if you are fired or dealt some other tremendous "blow" or hardship, there is a part of you that knows there is a reason. Having this faith helps you get through difficult times. It gives you confidence in a bigger picture. It doesn't mean that difficult times become easy—just a little more manageable.

One of the nicest things that happens to people as they create a bridge between their spirituality and their work is that "small stuff" really *does* begin to seem like small stuff. Invariably, the same things that used to drive you crazy won't seem at all significant. You'll be able to take things in stride, move forward, and stay focused. So, in a roundabout way, becoming more spiritual at work is going to help you become even more successful than you already are. I can't think of anything more important than creating a bridge between your spirituality and your work. Can you?

18.

BRIGHTEN UP YOUR
WORKING ENVIRONMENT

I wish I could include a photograph of my office in this book. It's bright, inviting, friendly looking, and peaceful. In fact, it's so happiness-oriented that it's almost impossible to get depressed while you're in it. Most people who visit fall in love with it and claim they almost always feel better when they leave. Yet I can assure you that my office is not fancy, and is certainly not expensively decorated.

There are tropical fish swimming in a tank, photographs of my wife and children, and several beautiful pictures that they drew for me. The pictures are in frames and are changed and updated every few months. The ones that are replaced are never thrown away, but put in a scrapbook that is proudly displayed. Every week I bring new freshly cut flowers to the office and put them in water. They are beautiful and smell terrific. My bookshelf is filled with many of my favorite books, and I look out on a birdfeeder that is heavily used. My kids have even been nice enough to share a few of their Beanie Babies with me, and they sit proudly on a shelf keeping me company. My favorite is a purple hippo named Happy.

I know that most people don't have the luxury or permission to turn their office into a "happiness headquarters." I also know that my office, while appropriate for me, would not be appropriate for or even preferred by many others. That's all well and good. However, when I enter the working environment of many people, my immediate thought is, "No wonder this person feels so stressed-out." Many offices, cubicles, work stations, home offices, and other working environments are downright depressing. They're bland, boring, dark, and lack any creativity whatsoever. Many are completely void of any signs of life, happiness, gratitude, relationships, or nature.

Brightening up your working environment will not rid you of all your stress, nor is it the most important thing you can do to stop sweating the small stuff at work. However, you do spend an enormous amount of time where you work. Why not take a tiny bit of time, energy, and money and brighten it up, even a little? When I moved into my office, the carpet was thin, ugly, and dark. For a few hundred dollars, I bought a beautiful new carpet that really looks nice and feels good to walk on. If I'm in the same office for even five years, that amounts to a few cents per day. I believe I'm the only person in my entire office building to have invested in myself in this way. Sometimes it's interesting how little we value ourselves.

If you aren't able to do it yourself, perhaps you can ask someone to help you—a spouse, a friend, a coworker, even a child! You might be surprised at how easy it is. Try a few pictures, a brighter rug, inspirational books, freshly cut flowers, goldfish, signs of nature, or some combination. You'd be amazed at what a drawing from a child can do to lift your spirits. If you don't have kids, maybe someone you work with would be kind enough to share one with you. Even if you work in your car or drive a truck, there are little things you can do to make your environment a nicer place to be.

I once heard the brilliant comedian Steve Martin joking about how difficult it is to feel depressed while you're playing the banjo. He was singing about death and sorrow. As he strummed the strings, it was obvious that he was right. There's something about that particular sound that is inconsistent with sadness and grief—it sounds too happy. To some extent, the same is true of your working environment. It's really nice to walk in and feel good about where you are going to spend your day. Make it bright, cheery and friendly, and it's pretty hard to walk in and not feel the same way.

19.

TAKE YOUR BREAKS

One of the worst habits I developed early on in my career was my failure to take adequate breaks. I'm a little embarrassed to admit it, but I felt they were a waste of time. I assumed that by skipping my breaks unless it was absolutely necessary, I'd be able to save a great deal of time and get more done—I'd have an edge. I'd work through lunch and rarely take breaks throughout the day.

In recent years, I've learned that a failure to take regular breaks is an enormous mistake that not only wears you down over time, but actually makes you less productive. While you may not even feel it at the time, slowly but surely your frustration will sneak up on you. You'll become less patient and attentive, and your concentration and listening skills will suffer. I believe that the cumulative effects, over time, are also significant. You'll burn out much more quickly, and your creativity and insights will slowly fade away.

It can be subtle, but when I pay careful attention to what's going on inside myself, I can tell that the same things that don't get to me very much when I'm well-rested and take my breaks somehow start to annoy me a little when I don't. I'll be a little less patient and lose a little of my enthusiasm. I start to sweat the small stuff—a little more than before. It seems to me that, while everyone certainly has a different rhythm and different capacities to work without breaks, there is something nourishing and healing to the spirit that occurs when you take a few minutes for yourself, whether or not you feel you need it.

Your breaks don't have to be disruptive or last very long. Usually, all you need is a few minutes to clear your head, take some deep breaths, stretch your arms, or get some air. When you take this time—every hour, or so—you'll return to your work more enthusiastic, focused, and ready to go. It's almost as though you push a "reset button" and you provide yourself with a fresh start. Often after taking a short break, my wisdom and creativity are enhanced, and I'm able to produce some of my best results.

Like most people, occasionally I forget to take my breaks. I'll sit for hours in essentially the same position writing a chapter or working on a project. Eventually when I get up, I feel stiff and tired. Then it hits me: "I forgot to take a break." There have been exceptions, but usually when I look back on my work, I'll be able to tell it wasn't my best effort.

This strategy reinforces the idea that more isn't always better. I feel that by working a few less minutes each hour, I'll work smarter, more efficiently, and actually get more work accomplished. And because of all the energy I'm saving on a day-to-day basis, I may even add a few years to the life of my career.

I suppose it's time to practice what I preach. I'll close this section by telling you that I'm going to take a short break. Perhaps this would be a good time for you to take one as well.

20.

DON'T TAKE THE 20/80
RULE PERSONALLY

According to the 20/80 "rule," it's allegedly the case that in the workplace, 20 percent of the people do approximately 80 percent of the work. When I'm in a cynical mood, it sometimes seems that this ratio is grossly understated!

It's often the case that people who are highly productive or who have an intense work ethic don't understand why everyone else isn't just like them. It can be frustrating for these people to observe, work with, or in some cases, even be in the presence of people whom they perceive to be less productive than they should be—people who appear to get less done than they could. For some reason, they take it personally and allow it to bother them.

I've observed that many "overachievers" don't even see themselves as achievers—but rather as ordinary people who simply do what it takes to succeed or get the job done. They honestly don't understand why everyone isn't just like them. I once knew a super-achieving man who insisted, "I'm not an overachiever. It's just that most people are underachievers." I knew him well enough to know that he wasn't intentionally being arrogant. Rather, he was sharing with me the way he really saw the world. He honestly felt that most people don't work hard enough and almost no one lives up to their full potential. If you really believed this to be true, you can imagine how frustrated and irritated you would be most of the time. You'd be programmed to see everything that wasn't getting done, or that could or should be done differently. You would see the world in terms of its deficiencies.

You may not have such an extreme vision (I certainly don't), but you too may see the world from highly productive, efficient eyes. If so, it may be hard to accept (or understand) that other people have different priorities, work ethics, comfort levels, gifts, abilities, and mind-sets. People see things from entirely different perspectives and work at vastly different speeds. Remember, different people also define productivity in very different ways.

An easy way to come to peace with this productivity issue is to pay less attention to what other people *aren't* doing, and put more emphasis on what you get out of your own level of productivity—financially, energetically, emotionally, even spiritually. In other words, it's helpful to admit that you prefer to be a highly productive individual—it's your choice. And along with this choice comes certain benefits. You may feel better about yourself than if you were less productive, or feel that you are fulfilling your mission or living up to your potential. Perhaps you make more money, or enjoy your work more than you would if you were less productive. You may have a more financially secure future, or an increased likelihood of opening certain doors for yourself. Or you may alleviate anxiety by getting a certain amount of work done each day. In other words, you have a number of payoffs that are driving you. Therefore, you are not a victim of those people who make different choices, or who, for whatever reason, aren't as productive as you, at least according to your standards.

To put this issue into perspective, it's helpful to think about your own

work ethic, preferred pace of work, and overall ability to get things done. Ask yourself these questions: "Do I base my productivity choices on what others think I should be doing?" "Am I attempting to frustrate and irritate others by the pace of my work?" Of course not. Your choices are the result of your own rhythm, preferred pace of work, and desired results. Although you may be required to perform at a certain level, your overall productivity level stems from your own decisions and perceived payoffs.

The same is true for everyone else. It's not personal—it's not about you or me. Each person decides from within him or herself how much work is appropriate, all things considered. Everyone must weigh the pros and cons, consider the tradeoffs, and decide how hard they are going to work—and how productive they are going to be.

You may depend on other people—colleagues, coworkers, subcontractors, employees—to adhere to certain standards and levels of productivity. I certainly do. I'm not suggesting that you ease up or that you lower your standards. Instead, I'm suggesting that there's a way to look at varying levels of productivity in a healthy and productive way that can keep you from getting so upset and from taking it personally. I've found that when I'm able to maintain my perspective, and keep my own stress level under control, it's easy for me to bring out the absolute best in people without making them feel defensive or resentful.

I encourage you to examine your own subtle demands and expectations that others work the way you do. Once you accept the fact that it's not personal, you'll probably be able to lighten up enough to appreciate the differences in people and the way they choose to work. If so, you're going to feel more peaceful and relaxed.

21.

MAKE A LIST OF YOUR
PERSONAL PRIORITIES

I'll warn you in advance that this strategy can be humbling, but ultimately very helpful. It involves taking a careful look at those personal
things that you feel are most important to you. Once you decide what
they are, write them down on a sheet of paper and put the list away for a
week or two.

For example, you might create a list that looks something like this:
1. pleasure reading, 2. exercise, 3. volunteering my time, 4. spending time
with my family or close friends, 5. meditation, 6. spending time in nature,
7. getting organized, 8. writing in my journal, 9. trying something new,
10. eating healthily, 11. traveling.

Here's the hard part: after some time has gone by, take out your list
and read it to yourself. Now, think back honestly over the past week or
so, back to the time you wrote the list. How have you spent your time,
other than the time you were working? If your actions over the past few
weeks were consistent with your list, congratulations! You are in a tiny
minority, and my only suggestion is to encourage you to keep it up. My
guess is that you are fairly satisfied in your life, and that satisfaction spills
over into your work life.

If, however, you look at your list and realize (as I did the first time I
did this exercise) that a staggering percentage of your time was spent

doing other things, then you've got work to do. If you're like most people, you probably got little or no exercise, didn't get around to volunteering, and spent all your time inside. To varying degrees, we ignore that which we insist is more important in favor of things that seem pressing or are simply more convenient. Unfortunately, life isn't going to suddenly accommodate us with fewer demands or reward us with the time we wish we had to do these important things. If we don't line up our behavior with our priorities, it will never happen.

A friend of mine taught me a powerful lesson that I always try to remember. He said, "In reality, you vote with your actions, not your words." This means that while I can tell you that my friends and family are important to me, I can write well-intended lists, and I can even become defensive in my well-thought-out excuses, ultimately, the measure of what's most important to me is how I spend my time and energy.

To put it bluntly, if I spend my free time washing my car, drinking in bars, and watching TV, then presumably my car, alcohol, and my TV are what's most important to me.

This isn't to say there is anything wrong with these activities—it's just important to admit to yourself that this is how you've been spending your time. It's also not to say that there aren't times when watching TV, even washing the car, is the most important thing to you at that moment. Again, that's fine. What I'm referring to here are your patterns of behavior, the way you spend most of your time.

You can see why this exercise is potentially so important to the quality of your life. When you're busy and working hard, tired and overwhelmed, it's easy to postpone or overlook your true priorities. You can get so lost in your routine and busyness that you end up doing few or none of the things that, deep down, you know would nourish you. You tell yourself things like, "This is a particularly busy time," or "I'll get to it later," but you never get around to it. This lack of satisfaction translates into frustration at work and elsewhere.

Once you open your eyes to the pattern, however, it's fairly easy to change. You can begin to make minor adjustments. You can read a few minutes before you go to sleep, get up a little earlier to exercise, meditate, or read. And so on. Remember, you're the one who wrote the list of priorities. You certainly have the power to implement them. I encourage you to write your list today—it really can create a whole new beginning.

22.

USE EFFECTIVE LISTENING AS
A STRESS-REDUCING TOOL

I've written about various aspects of listening in most of my previous books. The reason I return to listening so often is that, in my opinion, it's one of the most important ingredients for success in virtually all aspects of life—personal and professional. Unfortunately, for many of us, it's also one of our greatest weaknesses. Yet the slightest improvement in our listening skills can pay enormous dividends in the way of better relationships, enhanced performance, and yes, even stress reduction!

Take a moment to reflect on your own listening skills at work. Do you truly listen to your colleagues? Do you let them finish their thoughts before you take your turn? Do you sometimes finish sentences for other people? In meetings, are you patient and responsive—or are you impatient and reactive? Do you allow words from others to sink in, or do you assume you know what the person is trying to say, so you jump in? Simply asking yourself these and related questions can be enormously helpful. Most people I've asked (I'm in this category too), admit that, at least some of the time, their listening skills could use a little improvement.

There are a variety of reasons why effective listening is an excellent stress-reducing technique. First of all, people who listen well are highly respected and sought after. Truly great listeners are so rare that when you are around one, it feels good, it makes you feel special. Since effective listeners are loved by the people they work with (and the people they live with), they avoid many of the most common stressful aspects of work—backstabbing, resentment, sabotage, and ill feelings. Good listeners are easy to be around, so, quite naturally, you want to reach out and help them. Therefore, when you become a better listener, there will probably be plenty of people in your corner to offer assistance. People tend to be loyal to good listeners because they feel acknowledged and respected.

Effective listening helps you to understand what people are saying the first time they say it, thus allowing you to avoid a great number of mistakes and misinterpretations which, as you know, can be very stressful. If you ask people what frustrates them and makes them angry, many will tell you that "not being listened to" is right near the top of their lists. So, being more attentive to what others are saying also helps you avoid many, if not most, interpersonal conflicts. Finally, effective listening is an enormous time-saver because it helps you eliminate sloppy mistakes. Instructions as well as concerns from others become crystal clear, thus helping fend off unnecessary, time-consuming errors.

This is one of those powerful strategies that can generate immediate and significant results. You may have to work at it a little but if you do, it will be well worth it. The people you work with may not be able to put their finger on exactly what it is that you're doing differently, but they will notice a difference in how they feel when they are around you, or when they are speaking to you. And, in addition to being more liked and admired, you'll find yourself becoming calmer and more peaceful as well.

23.

MAKE FRIENDS WITH
YOUR RECEPTIONIST

Not too long ago I was in San Francisco in a reception lounge, waiting for my lunch partner. I was lucky enough to be a witness to the following chain of events which were so to the point of this book, I immediately knew I would like to share them with you.

A man walked in and barked out, in an unfriendly and demanding tone, "Any messages?" The female receptionist looked up and smiled. In a pleasant tone she answered, "No, sir." He responded in a nasty, almost threatening manner, "Just be sure to call me when my twelve-thirty appointment arrives. Got it?" He stormed down the hall.

No more than a minute later, a woman entered the room who apparently also wanted to know if she had any messages. She smiled, said "hello," and asked the receptionist if she was having a nice day. The receptionist smiled back and thanked the woman for asking. She then proceeded to hand the woman a stack of messages and shared with her some additional information which I could not hear. They laughed together a few times before the woman thanked the receptionist and walked down the hall.

It's always shocked me when I've seen someone who isn't friendly to the receptionist or who takes him or her for granted. It seems like such an obviously short-sided business decision. Over the years I've asked many receptionists whether or not they treat everyone in the office equally. Most of the time I receive a response such as, "You're kidding, right?" Indeed, it seems that receptionists have a great deal of power—and being friendly to them can make your life a lot easier. Not only does being nice to your receptionist all but ensure a friendly hello and someone to trade smiles with a few times a day, but in addition, your receptionist can do a great many intangible things for you—protect your privacy and screen calls, remind you of important events, alert you to potential problems, help you prioritize and pace yourself, and on and on.

I've seen both ends of the spectrum. I've seen receptionists protect people they work with from a variety of unnecessary hassles, even save them from major mistakes. I once saw a receptionist run down the hall and all the way down the street to remind someone of a meeting she was sure the person was going to forget. I later asked the person who was chased to tell me what had happened. He verified that the receptionist had been his "hero." He went so far as to claim that she may have even saved his job. When I asked this receptionist about their rapport, she informed me that they weren't really friends, but that he was an extremely nice person. I asked her if that had anything to do with her willingness to run down the street in the hot sun to remind him of a meeting. She just smiled and said, "You get right to the point, don't you?"

Sadly, the opposite can occur when a receptionist feels taken for granted or resentful of someone. I've heard stories of receptionists who have mysteriously "lost" messages, or who have failed to remind someone of a meeting, because it was inconvenient to do so.

Obviously, there are plenty of great receptionists who are able to set aside their personal feelings and do what is best, most if not all of the time. But think about this issue from the perspective of the receptionist. He or she might answer the phone, respond to the messages for a relatively large number of people, and have a number of other important responsibilities. Some of the people they work with are really nice, most are moderately so, and a few are jerks. Isn't it obvious that being friendly to your receptionist is in your best interest? Aside from the fact that it's their job, what possible motivation does a receptionist have to go the extra mile, or do something they aren't officially being paid to do, if you aren't nice to them—or at very least respectful?

In no way am I suggesting that you make friends with your receptionist just to get something in return. Primarily, you want to do so simply because it's a nice thing to do and because it will brighten the workday for both of you. After all, your receptionist is someone you see on a daily basis. But aside from that, it's just good business and it takes so little time or effort. My suggestion is to think of your receptionist as a key partner in your life. Treat them as if you truly value them—as you should. Be kind, genuine, patient, and courteous. Thank them when they do something for you—even if it's part of their job. Can you imagine the stress and other possible consequences of missing just one of those important phone calls—or a single important message? It's your receptionist who prevents that from happening. Wouldn't it seem wise to include your receptionist on your holiday shopping list? Incidentally, the same principle applies to many other roles as well, in different ways—the janitor, housecleaner, managers, cook, and so on.

I think you'll find that making friends with your receptionist is a wise thing to do. It's a great way to brighten your day-to-day work life, as well as an effective way to make your life a little less stressful. If you haven't already done so, I encourage you to give it a try.

24.

REMEMBER THE MOTTO,

"YOU CATCH MORE FLIES

WITH HONEY"

When I see someone badgering another person, acting aggressively or intimidating someone, pushing their weight around, or being mean-spirited or manipulative, I feel like reminding them that, in the long run, you really do catch more flies with honey. Simply put, it pays to be nice! Sure, there are times when being pushy or aggressive will assist you in getting your way—you can scare or intimidate certain people some of the time. But I believe that this type of aggressive attitude and behavior almost always comes back to haunt you.

When you are kind, loving, and patient—when you are fair, a good listener, and when you genuinely care about others—your attitude comes across in all you do. As a result, people love to be around you and will be comfortable and trusting in your presence. They side with you, share their secrets of success, and want to assist you in any way they can. Very simply, they delight in your success. When you are gentle, people are drawn to you like "flies to honey." They forgive you easily when you make a mistake and are willing to give you the benefit of the doubt. When they talk about you behind your back, their comments will be positive and upbeat. You will have a notable reputation.

It's unfortunate, but the opposite is also true. When you're difficult or demanding, your positive qualities are often overlooked, disregarded, or forgotten. In addition, you create a great deal of stress for yourself with an adversarial, aggressive attitude. You'll be looking over your shoulder wondering who, if anyone, is on your side. When you're pushy, you actually push people away. But when you're gentle and kind, people are drawn to your energy and sincerity.

I acknowledge that the "bottom line" is important and must be taken into consideration. That being said, I often make business decisions based not so much on cost, quality, or how much I'm being paid, as much as I do on how nice or pleasant someone is to work with. I've always felt that if I follow my heart and surround myself with great people, my experiences will be generally positive. I'll develop a healthy reputation with people who will like me, and my business decisions and relationships will develop and flourish into successful ventures. So far, my assumptions have been extremely accurate.

I've met a number of people who have said something like, "I'll never hire that person again." When I've asked, "Weren't you happy with his work?" they will usually say, "Absolutely. That's not it at all. It's just that he is so difficult to work with."

Chelsea is a hard-working, driven, and talented woman who works in retail. However, she is also very generous and kind. One of the many difficult aspects of retail work can be the long hours, particularly during weekends and holidays. Often, employees compete for time off and are very protective of the most sacred holidays.

When Chelsea began her career she decided that, despite what many people believe about being "walked on," gentleness and kindness were usually the most effective ways to behave. In her efforts to be kind, she was often willing to take someone else's shift so that they could spend time with family over an important holiday.

One day, Chelsea was given the extraordinary "once in a lifetime" opportunity to travel through Europe for two exciting months. In her position, however, it wasn't possible to take an extended trip without losing her job, unless she could somehow find a way to cover her extended time off. She had worked hard to achieve her position, and didn't want to "start over."

Much to her delight, her reputation allowed her to take the trip *and* keep her job. Her fellow employees jumped at the opportunity to come to her rescue. With tears in her eyes, she described it as "the most incredible, unselfish act by a group of people she had ever seen at work."

I think it's important to consider this strategy even if you feel you are a relatively gentle person. Most of us—certainly I include myself—have a long way to go. We might be doing okay, but, without even realizing it, still push others around from time to time, act a little arrogant, try to guilt them into doing certain things, or use other tools of manipulation to get our way. When we reflect on the practical, real-life importance of being gentle and patient, we can become even more so. I'd like to believe that, on an intuitive level, most people already know that you catch more flies with honey. Nevertheless, I think it's a good reminder for all of us.

25.

AVOID THE PHRASE,
"I HAVE TO GO TO WORK"

I'm going to suggest a strategy that has to do with six of the most common words in the English language: "I have to go to work."

Before I continue, let me assure you that I'm aware that in all probability, it's absolutely true that you do "have to" go to work. Nevertheless, these particular words carry with them some really negative baggage that, I believe, is self-destructive.

Other than your thoughts, your words are your primary entry point into your experience. They paint a picture of your expectation and pave the way toward your experience. When you "have" to do something, it implies that it's not a choice—that you'd rather be somewhere else, doing something different. This, in turn, implies that your heart isn't fully into what you are doing, which makes living up to your potential extremely difficult and enjoying your experience near impossible. So, when you say, "I have to go to work," you are in a subtle way setting yourself up for a bad day. This doesn't mean you'll always have a bad day—but it certainly increases the likelihood.

Beyond that, however, there is a more subtle negative message you send to yourself and to others. It seems that deep down, what you're really saying is, "I don't like my work. I'm not capable of choosing work that I enjoy." What a horrible message to say to yourself (or to someone else) about something you spend most of your time doing! Think about it. If you really loved your work, why would you be saying, "I have to go to work"? Do you say, "I have to start my weekend now"? Wouldn't it make more sense to be saying, "I get to go to work," or "I'm off to earn my livelihood," or "I'm off to another day," or something even simpler like, "I'm off to work," without the attached negativity? I'm not suggesting you jump for joy or yell out, "Yippee, I get to go to work," but can't you come up with something just a little more upbeat to begin your day? Wouldn't you be just a little prouder of yourself? And don't you think it would be more pleasant for others to hear these more positive words? When I leave for work in the morning, for example, I don't want to send the message to my children, however subtle, that "work is a bummer and here I go again." Yuck!

I think you're going to be surprised at what may happen if you choose to implement this strategy. When you take this strategy to heart, as you habitually mumble "I have to go to work" in your typical grouchy mode, you begin to catch yourself doing so. This makes you smile or laugh at yourself because you now see how ridiculous it is. Then, as you rephrase your statement to something slightly more positive, it seems to send a subtle reminder to your brain that your expectation is that you're going to have a good day. Wouldn't you agree that, more often than not, your expectations tend to come true? When you expect to have a bad experience, you usually do. And when you expect to have a good one, you very seldom disappoint yourself.

If nothing else, I hope you'll at least ask yourself the question, "What possible value could these words have to the overall experience of my work day?" Keep in mind that most people spend a minimum of eight hours a day, five days a week, working. It's something you're going to do regardless of how you choose to verbalize it to yourself and to others. Why not get yourself off to a good start by avoiding the tendency to bad-mouth what you are about to do?

·

26.

BE AWARE OF THE
POTENTIALLY STRESSFUL
EFFECTS OF YOUR PROMISES

It wasn't until a few years ago that I began to realize how often I made subtle promises to people during the course of a given day—and how often I regretted doing so. It was surprising to discover that my need to make promises was playing a key role in my feelings of stress. Once I saw how I was contributing to my own feelings of being overwhelmed, it was relatively easy to make some minor adjustments in my behavior and reduce the overall stress in my work life.

Think about some of the promises we make to others that may not even seem like promises, or that we make semi-unconsciously. Statements like, "I'll call you later today," "I'll stop by your office," "I'll send you a copy of my book next week," "I'd be happy to pick that up for you," or, "Call me if you ever need me to take your shift." In a more subtle way, even innocent comments like, "No problem," can get you into trouble because this can be perceived as an offer to do something that, deep down, you may not really want or be able to do. In fact, you have just allowed that person to ask you to do even more for her because you told her it's not a problem.

I used to engage in this habit virtually every day. Someone would ask me to do something simple like, "Can you send me a copy of that article you were talking about?" I'd automatically say, "Sure, no problem." I'd even write myself a note so I wouldn't forget. However, by the end of the day or week, I'd have an entire page of promises that now needed to be delivered. I'd often regret making so many promises. Sometimes I'd even feel resentful. I was so busy trying to deliver on my promises, I'd often be short of time or forced to hurry on things I really needed to do.

If you're at all like me, you probably try really hard to keep your promises. Obviously, the more promises you make, the more pressure you have to keep them. At some point, if you make enough promises, it's almost inevitable that you'll feel stressed out in your attempts to keep everyone happy.

Let me be very clear about something. I'm not suggesting you stop making promises, or that many promises aren't necessary or important. Many are. What I'm suggesting is that a certain percentage of your promises (maybe even a small percentage) probably don't need to be made in the first place. And if they're not made, you will have less pressure to keep them! I know, for example, that I've often told my publisher, "I promise to get this to you by this time next week," when the truth is, they weren't expecting a promise—only my best effort. But now that the promise has been made, I'm almost forced to do whatever is necessary to stick to my word. Had I not made the promise, but instead simply done the best I could, there would have been less pressure on me. This is pretty subtle stuff, and no one thing is likely to create all that much stress, but cumulatively it really adds up.

I have learned to evaluate each request that is made to me and each offer that I make to others. For example, if I'm asked for that copy of an article that I mentioned earlier, I may offer to send it—or I might suggest an alternate way for the person making the request to obtain it. Sometimes it's appropriate to make a promise, and other times it's not.

I've also learned to make slightly fewer unsolicited offers to do things for people. In other words, rather than saying, "Hey, I'll send you a copy of that book we were discussing," as is my tendency, I sometimes resist making the offer out loud. That way, I can (and often do) still go ahead and send the book if I still feel like it later and have the time to do so, but I'm not obligated.

There are two major advantages to paying attention to the effect of your promises. First, it will save you a great deal of time and energy. Some of the promises you make are unnecessary and unappreciated. Others, you simply don't have the time to keep. One of the most precious assets we have is our time. In fact, a lack of time is one of the most consistent complaints that people share with me about their work. Everyone seems to agree that there's rarely enough time to get everything done. When you make fewer promises, you'll have more time to do that which is most relevant to you.

The other advantage to making fewer promises is that the promises you do make will mean more to you and to the people you are promising. You'll take extra care to attend to those promises that mean the most to you and those you love. If you are burdened by too many promises, it's easy to lose sight of what's most important. You usually end up breaking promises to those you love most. However, with less on your plate, you can keep things in perspective and keep your priorities straight. I won't *promise* this strategy is going to help you—but I suspect that it probably will.

27.

EXAMINE YOUR RITUALS AND
HABITS (AND BE WILLING TO
CHANGE SOME OF THEM)

When you work for a living, it's very easy to get into certain habits—some good, some not so good; some out of necessity, some out of default; some just because everyone else seems to be doing so; and some simply because you've "always done it that way." Many of these habits become so much a part of us that we never seem to question, much less change them. Often we'll begin a habit and continue it for our entire career.

Taking a close look at some of these habits and rituals, and being willing to change a few of them, can pay huge dividends in the quality of your life. Our habits are often enormous sources of stress in and of themselves. Because they create so much stress (with or without our knowledge), they can make the rest of our life seem even more stressful than it already does.

Here are a few common habits and rituals, among hundreds of possibilities. Some of these may sound familiar, others may not: You may be in the habit of not allowing yourself enough time to get ready before work, and are always in a hurry. You may be in the habit of eating a large lunch, yet complain of not having any time to exercise or always feeling tired in the afternoon. Perhaps you commute in your car—but have other options like a train or bus, which would be cheaper and would allow you to read or relax. Maybe you drink too much caffeine and feel nervous and agitated a great deal of the time. Perhaps you head for a bar after work for a few drinks, or have wine or other alcohol as part of your ritual at home. Maybe you're a little grumpy or argumentative in the morning instead of being friendly to the people you work with, which makes them hesitant to be helpful or creates unnecessary resentment. Maybe you spend too much time reading the newspaper, yet rarely allow time for your favorite book. Perhaps you go to bed too late in the evening—or too early. Or that late night snack that is supposed to be a form of relaxation may be interfering with the quality of your sleep. Only you know which, if any, habits are making your life more difficult.

You can see that any one of these habits has the potential to create a great deal of stress in your life—making your day harder and encouraging you to sweat the small stuff at work. That being the case, the willingness to examine your habits can almost always be a helpful exercise.

Let's explore, very briefly, how changing a few of the above examples might help reduce the stress in your life. Despite the apparent simplicity, they are powerful changes to make. Instead of saying to yourself, "I could never do that," open your mind and imagine making a change!

Often the difference between a stressful day and one that is satisfying or manageable is simply a question of whether or not you're in a constant hurry, particularly first thing in the morning. Getting up an hour earlier, or simply beginning the process of getting ready a little earlier, can make a world of difference.

I've known many people who have substituted a one-hour walk for their usual midday meal. Their lives have been transformed by this single decision. They have lost weight and became much healthier. They feel better and have far more energy. They are saving money on lunch and investing that money in their future. They often meet friends for their walk, thus turning it into a social hour. They feel more relaxed and calmer than at any point in their entire lives.

Many people who drink regularly feel sluggish and grumpy the next day. Quitting, or even cutting back, can make you feel better than you've ever thought possible. You may sleep better and have tons of extra energy during the day. You'll probably lose weight and spend less money as well, as alcohol is certainly an expensive habit. Most people who cut back their alcohol consumption feel that they are more patient and that their relationships improve as well.

If you commute in your car, you may have other options. I know people who have made the decision to take the train (or other types of transportation) instead of their car, and have benefited greatly by doing so. Instead of gripping the wheel and feeling frustrated, they use the time to read or listen to tapes. They nap, meditate, think, or simply relax.

Obviously, these are only a small handful of potential changes you might consider. Everyone is different, and we all have different habits that get in the way of our happiness. While I have no idea which habits you may want to change, I'm relatively certain you can think of at least one. Give it a try. What have you got to lose—except perhaps a little stress?

28.

STAY FOCUSED IN THE NOW

Much has been written about the magical quality of "being in the moment." I believe, however, that this is one of those evergreen bits of wisdom that you can never quite get enough of. As you train your attention to be more focused in this moment, you will notice some remarkable benefits occurring in your work life. You'll be far less stressed-out and hurried, more efficient, and easier to be with. You'll also enjoy your work more than ever before, become a much better listener, and will sharpen your learning curve.

So often, our attention wanders off into the future. We think (and worry) about many things all at once—deadlines and potential problems, what we're going to do this weekend, reactions to our work. We anticipate objections and hassles and things that are likely to go wrong. We often convince ourselves how difficult something is going to be, well in advance of the actual event.

Or our attention is drawn to the past—we regret a mistake we made last week, or an argument we had this morning. We sometimes fret about "last quarter's poor earnings," or relive a painful or embarrassing event. And whether it's in the future or the past, we usually find a way to imagine the worst. A great deal of this mental activity is about things in the future that may or may not ever happen. And even if they do, the anticipation of it is usually worse that the actual event, and is rarely helpful. Or it's about past activities that are over and done with; things that may have actually happened, but that we no longer have any control over.

All of this mental activity is happening, of course, while we are supposedly working. But how effective are we, really, when our minds are practically everywhere except right here?

I've done it both ways—worked while my mind is spinning every which way and while my mind is very focused—and I can tell you with absolute certainty that a focused mind is more relaxed, creative, and efficient than one that is scattered. I'd say that one of my greatest strengths is my ability (that is still in progress) to stay focused on one thing at a time. Whether I'm on the phone with someone or with them in person, I'm usually able to be "right there" with them without being distracted by other things. This allows me to really hear and understand what is being said.

I try to do the same thing when I'm writing. Short of an actual emergency, I'm completely absorbed in what I'm working on. This allows all of my available attention and energy to be directed to one single activity— an ideal environment for creativity and effective work. I've found that a single hour of truly focused work is at least equal in productivity to a full day of distraction. The same is true when I'm speaking to a group. One of the things I've worked really hard to achieve is the ability to be with a group of people without ever wishing I were somewhere else. In other words, if I'm in Chicago, I'm not thinking about tomorrow's engagement in Cleveland. I believe this present-moment orientation has made me a far more effective speaker and has allowed me to work very hard and travel a great deal without feeling overly exhausted.

This quality of "being in the moment" has far more to do with what's going on in your mind than on what's going on in your office. There will always be external distractions—phone calls, interruptions, appointments, and so forth. The key element is how quickly you can bring your attention back to what you are doing, going from one thing to the next and back again.

Even more than increased effectiveness, however, the greatest benefit of being fully present is that your work will become much more enjoyable. There is something truly magical about getting completely absorbed in what you are doing. It increases your satisfaction immensely. I'm sure you're going to enjoy this one.

29.

BE CAREFUL WHAT
YOU ASK FOR

M any of us spend a great deal of time wishing things were different. We dream of a "better job," more responsibility, less of this, and more of that. Sometimes, the things we spend our energy longing for actually do (or would) improve the quality of our life. Other times, however, the very things we wish for are hardly worth the tradeoffs, or the effort. For this reason, I suggest you be really careful what you ask for.

The purpose of this strategy isn't to encourage you to stop dreaming of, or working toward, a better life, but to remind you that sometimes your life is pretty darn good exactly the way it is. My goal here is to remind you to carefully think through what it is you think you want, because you just might end up getting it, which is often more than you bargained for—more frustration, more grief, more travel, more responsibility, more conflict, more demands on your time, and so forth. When you think in these terms, it often helps you reconnect with your gratitude and realize that perhaps things aren't as bad as we sometimes make them out to be.

I've met plenty of people who spent years focused on how much better their lives were going to be when certain things occurred—i.e., when they were finally promoted to various positions—so much so that they took for granted the good parts of the position they already had. In other words, they were so focused on what was wrong with their careers that they failed to enjoy and appreciate the gifts they were enjoying all along.

For example, a man I knew dreamed of a job he felt would be "so much better" within the same company he was working with. He lobbied for that job for quite some time, constantly complaining about his current position. It wasn't until he finally secured that job that he realized the major tradeoffs that were involved. It was true that he had a bit more prestige and a slightly better salary, yet he was now forced to travel several days a week, often much more often than that. He missed his three kids terribly and started missing important events—soccer games, music performances, teacher conferences, and other special dates. In addition, his relationship with his wife became strained as their relatively peaceful routine was set aside for the alleged "better life." He was also forced to scale way back on his much-loved exercise routine due to his busier, less flexible schedule.

A woman I knew worked hard to convince her boss that she deserved to telecommute instead of coming into the office. She succeeded. The problem was, she never realized (until a month later) that, despite the dreaded traffic, she actually loved coming into the city each day. This was her chance to be with friends at lunch and after work. It was her social structure, her chance to be with people. She also missed lunches at local cafes, her favorite music that she listened to on her way to work, and other taken-for-granted simple pleasures. After a while, she began to feel trapped in her own home.

Other people crave power or fame. Only after they achieve it do they realize that the lack of any real privacy is a real drag. Instead of anonymity, which most of us take for granted, people are now looking over their shoulders. They are often exposed to more criticism and closer scrutiny.

I want to emphasize that I'm not taking a negative stance on any of these tradeoffs. Often, making more money is crucial, and outweighs any other consideration you might have. For many people, traffic is almost unbearable and would be worth avoiding at almost any price. Some people love the spotlight and the increased visibility. The important point here isn't the specifics, or any sort of value judgment, but the recognition of the relevance of asking yourself the important questions—"What am I really asking for, and why?"

When thinking about your job or career, it's important to consider what's right and good about your work in addition to focusing on what might be better. Feeling satisfied or being happy doesn't mean you aren't still working hard to make your career as successful as possible. You can have both—happiness and drive—without sacrificing your sanity.

Keep in mind that more responsibility might be a great thing, but it could very well lead to less personal freedom, privacy, and so forth. Similarly, a better paying position might make you feel more financially secure and it might be worth it—but you may give up other things that you haven't yet considered, or that you simply take for granted. It's all just food for thought. Remember, be careful what you ask for, because you might just get it—and more.

30.

ABSORB THE SPEED BUMPS
OF YOUR DAY

A metaphor I've found helpful in my own life is that of a speed bump. Rather than labeling the issues that come up during a typical work day as problems, I think of them as speed bumps. An actual speed bump, as you know, is a low bump in a road designed to get your attention and slow you down. Depending on how you approach and deal with the bump, it can be a miserable, uncomfortable, even damaging experience, or it can simply be a temporary slow down—no big deal.

If you step on the gas, speed up, and tighten the wheel, for example, you'll hit the bump with a loud thump! Your car may be damaged, you'll make a great deal of noise, and you can even injure yourself. In addition, you'll add unnecessary wear and tear to your car, and you'll look foolish and obnoxious to other people. If, however, you approach the bump softly and wisely, you'll be over it in no time. You'll suffer no adverse effects, and your car will be completely unaffected. Let's face it. Either way, you're likely to get over the bump. How you (and your car) feel once you get over it, however, is an entirely different issue.

If you ski or ride bikes, you already know how this works. If you tighten up your body, it's difficult to absorb the bump. Your form will be terrible and you may even fall. The bump will seem bigger than it really is.

Problems can be looked at in a similar light. You can be annoyed by them, think about how unfair and awful they are, complain about them and commiserate with others. You can remind yourself, over and over again, how difficult life is and how this problem is yet another justification for why you "have a right" to be upset! You can tighten up. Unfortunately, this is the way many people approach their problems.

When you think of your problems as speed bumps, however, they begin to look very different. You'll begin to expect a number of speed bumps to present themselves during a typical day. Like riding a bike, bumps are simply a part of the experience. You can fight and resist, or you can relax and accept. As a problem shows up during your day, you can begin to say to yourself, "Ah, here's another one." Then, like the ski mogul or bump on your bike ride, you begin to relax into it, thereby absorbing the shock, making it seem less significant. Then you can calmly decide what action or decision is likely to get you over this hurdle in the most effective, graceful manner. Like skiing, the calmer and more relaxed you remain, the easier it is to maneuver.

Thinking of problems as speed bumps encourages you to say things like, "I wonder what the best way to get through this one might be?" There is a healthy element of detachment involved, where you're looking at the problem objectively rather than reactively, looking for the path of least resistance. In other words, you assume there is an answer; you just need to find out what it is. This is in sharp contrast to seeing such concerns as problems, where it's tempting to think in terms of emergencies.

If you think about your work life, you'll probably agree that in one way or another, you do manage to get through a vast majority of the problems you are confronted with. If you didn't, you probably wouldn't last long in whatever it is you are doing. That being the case, where is the logic in panicking and in treating each problem like a major disaster?

My guess is that if you experiment with this one—simply thinking and labeling your problems as speed bumps instead of problems—you're going to be pleasantly surprised at how much more manageable your day is going to seem. After all, problems can be really tough, but almost anyone can maneuver over a speed bump.

31.

HAVE A FAVORITE
BUSINESS CHARITY

Sometimes the best way to understand something of value is to study its absence. This is one of those times. Realistically, if you don't have a favorite business charity, how much of your business profit is going to go to charity? Five percent, two percent, zero? Who knows? We do know one thing for sure. In business, there's always going to be something to spend your money on. So, if you wait until everything else is taken care of, your business may never get around to giving.

Whether individually or through a business, there are so many good reasons to give to charity—need, satisfaction, compassion, desire to be of service, giving back, securing our future, embracing others, spiritual nourishment, and yes, even to get a tax deduction. Having a favorite business charity, however, provides you with even more reasons to give. It gives your business a service-oriented focus and goal. Rather than some abstraction or last-minute tax planning, you know exactly—month to month—how much money your business is sharing. It's quite satisfying. It's also an added incentive to do well. In other words, if your business pledges 5 percent of its net profits to charity, it means that the more money your business makes, the more money goes to those in need. This action makes your business a role model of how a company should operate. It makes you stand out because you're doing the right thing.

Whenever you stand out in a positive way, with sincere intentions, it can only come back to help you.

Having a favorite business charity has an intangible benefit to your business as well. It creates a feeling of team work, a coming together for a valuable accomplishment and a shared goal. It gives everyone involved in your business a feeling of satisfaction, the sense that your business is making a positive impact, not just for the employees, shareholders, and consumers, but for outside causes as well. It encourages people to think in terms of giving and sharing, which tends to make them do more of it outside the workplace as well. All of this good will and emphasis on sharing helps to create a more harmonious and gentle working environment. Giving makes everyone feel good about themselves and their efforts. This, in turn, helps people relax, maintain perspective, and stop sweating the small stuff.

If you own your own business, this strategy is easy to implement. You just start doing it. If you work for a small business, it can be relatively simple as well. You make your case to the owner or to the appropriate person. If you work for a large company, however, it can be a different story. In a large firm, there can be a silent assumption that "someone else will take care of it" or a feeling that no one would be willing to listen to your suggestion. And while that's a possibility, it's certainly worth a try. I've met a number of corporate leaders. My experience is that, for the most part, they're just like the rest of us. They have a heart and at least some degree of compassion. Most people enjoy giving. Don't make the mistake of assuming that your employer wouldn't be willing to have a favorite business charity. My guess is that most employers would love to contribute, and probably already do in other ways. Many would welcome this suggestion from you—even thank you. And if you give it your very best shot and you can't make it happen, that's okay too. You can implement a similar strategy in your personal life.

Can you imagine the cumulative impact on society if every small business and corporation would share 5 or 10 percent of their profits with those in need? Pretty amazing to think about it. Someday, as you look back on your career, you'll probably be proud of many things. If you participate in giving to charity, this will be near the top of your list. By encouraging your business to take action, to create a favorite business charity, you will have made an important contribution to the world. Thank you for doing your part.

32.

NEVER, EVER BACKSTAB

I was attending a corporate function prior to being a guest speaker when a young man approached me and introduced himself. He seemed nice enough until he launched into his backstabbing mode.

He moaned and complained about his boss and many other people he worked with. Within ten minutes, I became an expert on the "dirt" in his company. If I were to believe his version of the story, his entire firm was completely screwed up—except, of course, for himself.

The sad part of it was that I don't even think he was aware that he was doing it—it seemed to be a part of his ordinary conversation. Apparently, backstabbing was something that he was in the habit of doing.

Unfortunately, this man is not alone in this tendency. As someone who travels to diverse groups of people in different parts of the country, I'm sorry to report that backstabbing is alive and well. Perhaps one of the reasons it's so prevalent is that too few of us consider the consequences.

There are two very good reasons never again to backstab. First of all, it sounds terrible and makes you look really bad. When I hear someone slamming someone behind his back, it says nothing about the person they are referring to, but it does say a great deal about their own need to be judgmental. To me, someone who slams a person behind his back is disingenuous or two-faced. I doubt very much that the man I'm referring to in the above example said the things to his coworkers that he said to me. In other words, he would put on a smile and say nice things to them but, behind their backs, he would act in a completely different way. To me that's not fair play, and it's a poor reflection on oneself.

But aside from being a mean-spirited and unfair thing to do that makes you look bad, it's important to realize that backstabbing creates other problems for you as well. It causes stress, anxiety, and other negative feelings.

The next time you hear someone backstabbing someone else, try to imagine how the offending person actually feels—beneath the confident, secure appearance. How does it feel to say nasty, offensive, and negative things about someone else who isn't even there to defend themselves? Obviously, that's a loaded question—but the answer is so obvious that it's almost embarrassing to discuss. I know that when I have backstabbed in the past, my words have left me with an uncomfortable feeling. I remember asking myself the question, "How could you stoop so low?" You simply can't win. You may get a moment or two of relief from getting something off your chest, but you have to live with your words for the rest of the day—and longer.

Backstabbing also causes anxiety. The man I was talking to was sure to speak in a quiet voice—he didn't want to be heard. Wouldn't it be easier and less stressful to speak kindly about others, in a respectful tone? When you do, you don't have to worry whether or not someone will overhear your conversation or share your backstabbing stories with others—perhaps with the person you're attacking behind his back. Indeed, when you backstab, the pressure's on—you're on guard, now forced to protect your secret. It's not worth the price!

Finally, it's absolutely predictable that if you backstab someone, you will lose the respect and trust of the people you are sharing with. Remember, most of the people you're sharing with are your friends or colleagues. It's important to realize that, even if they appear to enjoy what you are saying, and even if they too are participating in the gossip, there will always be a part of them that knows that you are capable of backstabbing. They've seen it firsthand. It's inevitable that they will ask themselves the question, "If he will talk behind someone else's back, wouldn't he be capable of doing the same thing to me? What's more, they know that the answer is yes.

One of the nicest compliments I ever received was when someone with whom I have a great deal of contact said to me, "I've never heard you say a mean thing about anyone." Unfortunately, as I mentioned above, I have said mean things about others behind their backs, and I'm not proud of it. However, I took this compliment to heart because I'm doing my best to avoid backstabbing at all costs.

No one bats 100 percent. An occasional comment or the sharing of feelings probably isn't going to cause you great stress or ruin your reputation. But, all things being equal, it's a really good idea to put backstabbing out to pasture, forever.

33.

ACCEPT THE FACT THAT, EVERY ONCE IN A WHILE, YOU'RE GOING TO HAVE A REALLY BAD DAY

Recently, I had one of those bad days that, in retrospect, was absolutely hilarious. It seemed that everything that could go wrong did. Here are a few highlights: I was asked to fly to a different state to give a talk to a large group of people. To be honest, I really didn't want to go because I had just returned home from a series of trips and was missing my family a great deal. I was tired, jet-lagged, and behind in my work. Although I already had plans, I was informed by my publisher that this was a very important event and that the group would really appreciate my being there, so, I agreed to go.

On the way to the airport, I was caught in one of the worst traffic jams I've ever experienced—a normally forty-five-minute drive took well over two hours. I compounded the problem by spilling coffee all over my shirt.

When I arrived at the airport, the plane was late and my seat had been given to someone else, leaving me crammed in the middle seat. This is difficult for me because not only am I a very tall person who is claustrophobic, but I also do quite a bit of writing on airplanes. (In fact, I'm writing this strategy en route from Miami to San Francisco.) Because the plane was late, I missed my connection in Chicago and had to wait many hours to catch the last flight that evening. While I was reading in the Chicago airport, a woman tripped over someone's suitcase and spilled her sticky soft drink directly in my open briefcase. While she was apologizing, the rest of her drink spilled on my book! My speaking notes, ideas for this book, as well as my airline tickets, bills, photos of my children, and many other things were essentially ruined.

When I finally arrived at my destination, I was exhausted, but it was almost time to "wake up." So, with no sleep, I took a shower and went downstairs. My instructions were to meet my escort to the event in the hotel lobby at a certain time, but she never showed up! I called the convention center where I was to speak, and was informed that they wouldn't allow me in without my escort, due to some strange security issues they were having. I was told, once again, to stay where I was and to wait for my ride. You've probably guessed by now that I missed the event. Essentially, I "stood up" 2,000 people who were expecting me to speak. It was clearly "one of those days."

As is often the case, it really wasn't anyone's fault—just a comedy of errors, bad luck, and poor communication.

Disaster, right? An emergency? Time to panic? Hardly. The way I look at it is this: Why should I be exempt from the rest of the human race? Let's face it. We all have really bad days every once in a while. It must have been my turn. It had been a long time since I had experienced a work-related day like that. In fact, until that day, I'd never missed a scheduled speaking event for any reason. I guess it was inevitable.

This isn't a crass, apathetic, I-don't-care attitude. To the contrary, probably like you, I do my absolute best and often go to great lengths to ensure a punctual arrival. I take great pride in an almost perfect record of noncancellations of events and, when I do arrive, I do the very best I can to speak to the concerns of my audience. Yet we're all human. Beyond giving 100 percent, I don't know what can be done. Do you know something I don't?

I've found that it's helpful to accept the fact that every once in a while, it's going to happen to you too. It may not be a speaking engagement, but it will be something. This doesn't mean you like it; only that you make peace with this inevitable fact of life. This way, instead of being surprised and frustrated, wondering "how can this be happening to me," you can learn to make allowances in your attitude for this (hopefully) occasional nightmare. When you leave room in your heart for human error and tricks of nature, it allows you to keep your sense of humor, to not take yourself or your role too seriously, and to make the best of a bad situation. It also allows you to be forgiving of others who also make innocent mistakes on occasion and have bad days of their own.

As is usually the case, when you keep your cool instead of panicking, most everyone else will rise to the occasion as well. In this particular instance, I ended up spending the day with several truly delightful and talented people. We were able to salvage the meeting by doing a book-signing instead. Although we had obviously hoped for a different type of day, we made the best of the day we had, and ended up laughing together and having a lot of fun. The world didn't stop spinning simply because Richard Carlson had a mishap.

You can look at situations like this (and so many others) as horrible and frustrating—or you can look for a silver lining. And even if you can't find any silver linings, you can at least laugh at yourself and the way the universe sometimes works and make the best of it. My suggestion is simple: Accept the fact that every once in a while, you're going to have a really bad day. So what else is new?

34.

RECOGNIZE PATTERNS
OF BEHAVIOR

No matter where you work or what you do, becoming an expert in recognizing patterns of behavior can help you reduce the stress in your
life by eliminating many of your unnecessary interpersonal conflicts. It
will also help you to keep your perspective by being less surprised when
"stuff happens." When you learn to recognize patterns of behavior, you'll
be able to detect problems before they have a chance to get out of hand,
nip certain arguments in the bud, and prevent hassles that might otherwise manifest themselves.

If you take a careful look at the people you work with, you'll probably agree that most people (you and I too) have a tendency to repeat patterns and engage in habitual reactions. In other words, we tend to be
bothered by the same things, irritated by the same sets of circumstances,
argue over the same sets of facts, and act defensively toward certain types
of behavior. Indeed, for most of us, our reactions to life, particularly stress,
are fairly predictable.

This being the case, it's enormously helpful to take careful note of the
people you work with—and recognize any negative or destructive patterns of behavior that are likely to repeat themselves. You might notice,
for example, that if you take on or challenge a member of your team, he
will become defensive and tend to argue. This doesn't mean it's never

appropriate to challenge him—there will certainly be times when it is. What it means is that when you recognize, with relative certainty, what's going to happen if you engage in certain types of interactions, you might determine that it's not worth getting into. In this way, you can avoid unnecessary conflict and spend your time and energy in more efficient ways. In order to be able to do this, of course, you'll have to take an honest look at your own patterns of behavior. Perhaps you're the one who starts some of the arguments, or you are a willing participant once they get going.

Maybe there is someone in your office who is virtually incapable of completing a project on time—he's always a day or two late. He's always got a great and legitimate-sounding excuse, yet the end result is always the same—he's late. By being aware of the pattern and the virtual certainty with which it occurs, you may be able to protect yourself, or at least be less frustrated by it. You can attempt to avoid participating in projects with him where on-time performance is a must. If working with him can't be avoided, you can try to build in some extra time, or get off to an early start, knowing full well what is likely to occur. And in a worst-case scenario, you will probably be less stressed out by his lateness because you already knew it was going to happen.

Perhaps someone else you work with gets argumentative when she feels criticized. If you recognize this particular pattern of behavior, you might think twice before offering habitual advice that she is likely to receive as criticism. Again, if it's necessary and appropriate to criticize or offer advice, that's a completely different story. What I'm referring to here is the daily, habitual types of comments that lead to hard feelings and unnecessary conflict.

Maybe a friend or coworker is someone who loves to gossip. By recognizing this pattern of behavior, you can avoid a great deal of potential grief and stop rumors before they have a chance to start. You begin to realize that if you share a story with her, she *is* going to share that story with others. It doesn't matter whether you ask her not to—or that she promises that she won't—or that her intentions are pure. This doesn't mean she's a bad person, only that her pattern is that she can't help but gossip. If you recognize the pattern, you have an enormous edge. You can bite your tongue and keep your secrets to yourself when you are with her, unless you really don't mind her sharing them with others. And if you make the decision to go ahead and tell her something, don't get upset when others discover your secret. It was predictable. It's part of the pattern.

I could go on and on. A person who is cheap is almost always cheap. Someone who gets jealous usually does so on a consistent basis. Someone else who steals the glory does so whenever the opportunity presents itself. A person who is dishonest tends to be dishonest whenever it seems to suit his needs. Someone who is hypersensitive will likely feel criticized, regardless of how gentle you attempt to be. An individual who is consistently late will probably show up late even though you've asked her not to—and so forth. Once you witness the pattern, whatever it is, it's a bit self-destructive to feed into it.

By recognizing patterns of behavior, you are in the driver's seat at work. This type of reflective wisdom allows you to better choose what to say and what not to say; who to spend time with and who to avoid, when possible. It helps you make the decision "not to go certain places" with certain people. Starting today, take a careful look at the patterns of behavior where you work. You'll be less stressed-out very soon.

35.

LOWER YOUR EXPECTATIONS

I was sharing this idea with a large group of people when someone in the back of the room raised his hand and said, "What kind of an optimist are you, suggesting that we lower our expectations?" His question was a valid one and, in fact, you might be wondering the same thing.

It's a delicate question to answer because, on one hand, you absolutely want to have high expectations and to expect that things will work out well. You want to believe that success is inevitable, and that your experiences will generally be positive. And with hard work and some really good luck, many (perhaps even most) of these expectations may indeed come true.

On the other hand, when you expect too much from life, when you are unrealisitc and demanding, you set yourself up for disappointment and a great deal of unnecessary grief. You'll probably also alienate at least some of the people you work with, because most people don't appreciate being held to unrealistic expectations. Your expectation is that the events in your life will evolve in a certain predictable way, and that people will behave according to your plans. When they don't, which is often the case, you end up stressed-out and miserable.

Often simply lowering your expectations, even slightly, can make your day (and your life) seem a whole lot easier. You can create an emotional environment for yourself whereby, when things do work out well, rather than taking them for granted, you'll be pleasantly surprised and grateful. And when your expectations don't go according to plan, it won't devastate you. Lowering your expectations helps to keep you from being so surprised when you bump into hassles and "stuff" to deal with. Instead of reacting negatively, you'll be able to say, "Oh well, I'll take care of it." Keeping your composure allows you to deal with the irritant or solve the problem, and be done with it.

Life just isn't neat and trouble-free. People make mistakes, and we all have bad days. Sometimes people are rude or insensitive. No job is entirely secure, and no matter how much money you make, it probably doesn't seem like enough. Phone lines and computers occasionally break down, along with everything else.

When I met Melissa, she worked for a software development company. She described it as her first "real job." She was young and driven, and had exceptionally high expectations. The problem was, many of her expectations weren't being met. She wasn't being treated with the degree of respect she wanted (or expected), and her ideas weren't being taken seriously. She felt under-appreciated and taken for granted. She was frustrated and burned-out.

I suggested she lower her expectations and consider thinking of her job in a new way. Rather than expecting her job to be all things to her, I asked if she might see it as a stepping stone to bigger and better things later on. She took the suggestion to heart, and her world began to change for the better. Without the mental distraction regarding what needs *weren't* being met, she was able to focus on the most essential aspects of her work. Her learning curve accelerated, and her stress level dropped.

About a year later, I received a nice voice mail message from Melissa letting me know how helpful it had been to lower her expectations.

Specifically she said, "I don't know why I made such a big deal about everything. Obviously, every job has tradeoffs to deal with. I guess I've learned to have a little more perspective and to take things in stride." She must have been doing something right, as she has been promoted twice since the last time I spoke to her.

Many people confuse expectations with standards of excellence. Please understand that I'm not suggesting that you lower your standards or accept poor performance as okay. Nor am I saying you shouldn't hold people accountable. What I'm referring to is making room in your heart for bad moods, mistakes, errors, and glitches. Instead of spending so much time being annoyed about the way things unfold, you will be able to take most of it in stride. Life and its many challenges won't get to you as much. This will conserve your energy and, ultimately, make you more productive.

Make no mistake: You'll still want to do everything possible to put the odds in your favor—work hard, plan ahead, do your part, be creative, prepare well, solicit the help of others, be a team player. However, no matter how hard you try, life still isn't always going to go as planned. One of the best ways to deal with this inevitability is to stop expecting it to be otherwise. So ease off your expectations a little, and see how much nicer your life can be. You won't be disappointed.

36.

PAT YOURSELF
ON THE BACK

For most of us, there are times when we feel underappreciated, as if no one understands how hard we work and how much we are trying. One of my favorite pieces of advice has always been to praise often and tell people how much you appreciate them. You'll find bits of this advice scattered throughout this book. There are times, however, when no one seems to be applying that advice toward us, when no one seems to be appreciating us.

At times, it's important to stop what you are doing and pat yourself on the back. Take a few moments to reflect on what you've been doing and on the nature of your intentions and actions. Mentally review your accomplishments. Think about how hard you work and how much you are contributing to your goals, and to the people you are working with.

As simple as this sounds, it really helps! I've done this many times, and have found that it puts things in perspective. Sometimes it reminds me of how busy I have become, which gives me compassion for everyone else who is busy. I can recognize why people sometimes forget or are unable to be appreciative—they are absorbed in their own work and their own lives.

Sometimes we get going so fast that we forget to pause and reflect. When we take a moment, however, we can regain our perspective and realize that we are making a valuable contribution to ourselves, our families, the people and business we work with, and humanity. Recognizing your contribution from within yourself is actually more powerful and satisfying than hearing it from others. In fact, in order to feel good about yourself and your efforts, you must be able to compliment yourself and recognize and acknowledge your contribution from within.

Almost everyone loves to be patted on the back by others. It feels good. However, when it's not happening, don't let it get you down or adversely affect your attitude. Praise from others is never a certainty, and making it a condition of your happiness is a really bad idea. What you can do is praise yourself and pat yourself on the back. Be honest and genuine regarding your compliments. If you're doing a good job, say so. If you're working long hours, give yourself some credit. If you're making life a little better for even one person, or making any type of contribution to society, then the world is a better place because of you. You deserve to be recognized. If you'll actually take the time to do so, I think you'll find this exercise is well worth the effort.

37.

BECOME LESS
SELF-ABSORBED

To me, there are very few human qualities less appealing than someone who is highly self-absorbed. A person who falls into this category takes him or herself extremely seriously. They love to listen to themselves speak, and value their own time—but no one else's. They are usually quite selfish with their time, love, and money, in addition to lacking compassion for those less fortunate. They are arrogant and come across as pompous and self-righteous. Self-absorbed individuals see others and often treat others as instruments or objects to get something they want. They usually see only one point of view—their own. They are right, and everyone else is wrong, unless, of course, you agree with them.

People who are self-absorbed can be rude, insensitive to the feelings of others, and primarily interested in themselves—their own wants, needs, and desires. They tend to see people in a hierarchical manner. In other words, they see certain people as being beneath them and, as such, they see them as less important than they are. Finally, self-absorbed people are poor listeners because, quite frankly, they aren't very interested in other people beyond a superficial level.

Obviously, I'm painting a worst-case scenario picture. Very few people are quite this bad. I paint this picture, however, because I believe it's important to be fully aware of what type of person you absolutely never, under any set of circumstances, want to become. This encourages you to be certain that none of these ugly characteristics ever creep into your life, and if they do, that you act quickly to move in a different direction.

Don't confuse self-esteem with self-absorption. The two are completely unrelated. In fact, you could say that the two are virtually opposite in nature. A person with high self-esteem loves others and feels good about herself. Because she already has what she needs in an emotional sense (feeling positive about herself), her natural instinct is to reach out to others in an unselfish way. She's extremely interested in hearing what other people have to say and in learning from them. She's very compassionate, always looking for ways to be of service or ways to be kind and generous. She is humble and treats everyone with respect and kindness.

There are many excellent reasons to become less self-absorbed. To begin with, as you can see by the picture I have painted, being self-absorbed is an ugly human quality. Beyond that, being self-absorbed is highly stressful. In fact, self-absorbed people sweat the small stuff as much, or more, than any other group of people—everything bothers or frustrates them. It seems that nothing is ever good enough.

For instance, self-absorbed people often have very poor learning curves. Since they don't listen well and aren't interested in other people, they don't have the advantage of learning from them. In addition, self-absorption comes across loud and clear to others, making them extremely resistant to wanting to be supportive or of any significant help. It's difficult to cheer on an arrogant person. In fact, it's tempting to want to see them fail.

For these reasons and so many more, it's a good idea to check in with yourself and make an honest assessment of your own level of self-absorption. Judge for yourself. If you feel you've drifted in that direction, then perhaps it's time to make a mental adjustment. If you do, everyone will benefit. You'll be more inspiring to others and, ultimately, you'll experience an easier and more fulfilled life.

38.

DON'T BE TRAPPED BY
GOLDEN HANDCUFFS

From the first time I heard the expression "golden handcuffs," it has had a profound impact on my perspective and on many of the lifestyle choices that I have made in my life. I've known a great number of people who have been trapped by these mental cuffs. My goal in writing this strategy is to see if I can help prevent this from happening to you or to someone you love or care about. Or, if you find you are already "cuffed," perhaps I can give you a nudge toward a potential solution.

The term "golden handcuffs" means that you voluntarily live at, or very close to the edge of your current means (or, in many cases, well above). It means that, in effect, you trap yourself into keeping a job or career (or moving in a career direction), and/or working too many hours because, while you may enjoy the benefits of, and completely rely on, a certain level of income, you may not enjoy (or you may even resent) what is required of you to earn that level of income. In other words, the rewards of your income are overshadowed by the stress of maintaining your lifestyle.

You may feel you don't have time for a life outside of work and wish that you could. Or, you may get precious little time to be with your friends, children, spouse, or other loved ones, or you may feel you spend too much time on the road as well as other difficult sacrifices. To have golden handcuffs means that you have knowingly or unknowingly chosen to trade certain aspects of the quality of your life (time, hobbies, relationships, solitude) in exchange for driving a certain type of car, living in a certain type of home, and enjoying certain material comforts and privileges. We get used to a certain lifestyle and can't imagine doing with less.

Pay particular attention to my use of the word "voluntarily" in my description of this problem. Obviously, this strategy doesn't apply to people who are living "on the edge" or barely surviving, spending every dollar earned on actual necessities. Instead, it applies in those instances where there is at least some degree of choice involved in your lifestyle. When you carefully and honestly examine your situation, you may find that you have more choices than you previously imagined. And, before you skip to the next strategy, read on! Because even if you're not trapped right now due to your current income, it's still important to be aware of this tendency so that you can avoid it later on in your career or if your circumstances change.

Some important questions to ask include: Did the seductive advertisement for that great new car convince you that you've "earned" the privilege of driving it? Are the high payments really worth it? Were those new clothes that were supposed to make you feel good about yourself worth working overtime to get? Is it really an honor to carry all those credit cards and, despite being able to purchase something practically anytime your heart desires, to be saddled with debt? Is a three-bedroom apartment that you can't quite afford really better than a two bedroom that is much less expensive? Might camping be as much fun as a hotel? Do the kids absolutely have to attend private school? Do you need two phone lines? Are restaurants always better than a bag lunch or a quiet picnic? Would taking public transportation or joining a car pool to work, thereby saving money on parking, gas, and road tolls, really be much of a sacrifice? Do you need so much stuff? Is more always better?

By most standards, Mark was a very successful businessman. He had been "climbing the corporate ladder" working for the same company for more than twenty years. He held an important, challenging position, enjoyed a large salary and benefits package, and was highly respected. He lived in a nice home, drove an expensive car, and his children went to a top private school. As the years went by, however, Mark became less interested in his career and longed to try something different. He loved nature and dreamed of a new career focused on helping the environment.

The problem was, Mark lived over his head. As he lost interest in his career, he found himself spending greater amounts of money in an attempt to fill up his empty feelings. He bought a new truck, an expensive boat and various other recreational toys. He rationalized his spending by assuming certain salary and bonus increases in future years. It got so bad that he was spending "future income" three and four years down the road. He had effectively trapped himself because in order to afford his lifestyle and continue to pay his ever-increasing bills, he was now forced to remain at the same job because of the relatively high salary. His options had disappeared and his dream would have to wait.

While it can be difficult to accept, there is, for many people, an effective way to deal with golden handcuffs. You can, in many cases, choose to lower your standard of living (that's right—lower), spend less money, consume less, and simplify your life. I know that this suggestion goes against the "American way" of ever-increasing wants and desires, and the seemingly universal tendency to want to increase our standard of living. Yet, if you think about it for a minute, this one simple suggestion could make your life much easier and less stressful.

I guess we all need to ask ourselves, are we really lowering our lifestyle if we are less stressed and worried? Would our standard of living be lessened if we were able to create more time for ourselves and for the people we love? Are we really worse off if we are genuinely easing our financial pressures and concerns, and perhaps even carving out a little more time to enjoy our lives?

I'm not arguing against achievement, material comforts, or the desire to improve the quality of your life. I believe in your right to be all you can be, and to have all that you deserve. I acknowledge that spending less money and living beneath your means can involve tough choices and trade-offs. Remember, however, that my goal in writing this book is to help you feel less stressed and to help you sweat the small stuff less often in your work life. One thing I am absolutely certain of is this: It's really difficult not to be sweating the small stuff if you are trapped by golden handcuffs.

I'm not suggesting that everyone who makes a good living needs to sell their home and move to a smaller home in the country; or that you should trade in your job that you've worked so hard for, in exchange for something less strenuous; or that you accept less income as a viable alternative. I am, however, suggesting that golden handcuffs can be a tremendous and painful source of stress and, if you take them off, your life can become a great deal easier. So, take a careful look at your lifestyle and decide for yourself if this strategy is for you. It can be difficult to face, but for many people, the freedom they will feel is well worth it.

39.

GET REALLY COMFORTABLE
WITH USING VOICE MAIL

I always chuckle when someone says to me, "Gee, you leave really long voice mail messages." While it's true that I sometimes do so, it's a potentially stressful mistake to think of them as "long." The truth is, even the longest voice mail messages, if they are even remotely effective, are huge time-savers and excellent communication skills.

In most instances, the longest voice mail message you can leave is around three minutes. In those three minutes, you can leave very detailed, specific information, and respond carefully and accurately to specific questions or concerns, all the while allowing the other person the luxury of reflecting on your comments, hearing them several times, if necessary, and listening at their leisure. Voice mail messages are an excellent way to explain a point of view with the luxury of being uninterrupted. It's also a great chance for someone to listen to a message without familiar knee-jerk reactions such as defensiveness, or making a decision, or jumping to conclusions before hearing all the facts.

Obviously, I don't know your phone habits, but if they're anything like mine, it would be unheard of to have a personal phone call that lasts less than six or seven minutes, usually much longer. Most person-to-person calls include at least a few minutes of "How are you doing?" as well as other assorted distractions that are removed from the real bottom-line point of your call. I'd estimate that, even when my intention is to keep my conversation short, the average length of time per call is easily ten minutes.

As writing partners, my dear friend Benjamin and I put together four entire anthologies, including *Handbook for the Soul and Handbook for the Heart*, using voice mail more than 90 percent of the time. We live three hundred miles apart, and it was such an effective way of communicating that it made our job fun and easy. Since each of us had full-time jobs, we were able to leave thoughts and ideas on each other's voice mail during our breaks in the day. We would check our voice mail and/or leave messages at lunchtime, as well as early in the morning and late at night. We've discussed the issue many times and both agree that, had we chosen to communicate in person the bulk of the time rather than by voice mail, it's probable that none of the books would have ever been written. It simply would have been too difficult to coordinate our busy schedule and make the time for lengthy brain-storming sessions.

Some of you may think that by making this suggestion, I'm somehow unfriendly or don't enjoy personal conversations. Not true. As long as I have the time, and as long as the use of voice mail isn't more suited to the goals of my phone call, I love to talk to the people I work with. But see, that's part of the problem. Once I'm engaged in a conversation, I get so interested in what we're talking about that it's difficult for me to get off the phone. There are many times when a personal chat is preferred, and other times when voice mail is a perfect answer. And, certainly, I'm not suggesting that voice mail should replace any interactions you have regarding matters of the heart.

I'm not a voice mail salesperson and know it's not the perfect answer in all scenarios. It is, however, a real time-saver and an excellent way to communicate in certain situations. Many people already love voice mail and for you, this strategy may be a bit unnecessary. If that's the case, perhaps you can share this strategy with someone you feel it may benefit. But if you've had any sort of aversion to using voice mail, or if you're one of those people who complain about "long messages," I encourage you to rethink your position. By utilizing voice mail a little more often in your work-related calls, you can save tons of time and become even more effective in certain types of communication.

40.

STOP WISHING YOU WERE
SOMEWHERE ELSE

If you reflect on the insidious tendency to be wishing you were somewhere else, you may agree that it's a silly, even self-destructive thing to do. Before you jump up and say, "Wait a minute, I don't do that," let me explain what I mean.

There are many ways that we spend time wishing we were somewhere else. We'll be at work and wish we were home. Or during the middle of the week we might be wishing it were Friday. Sometimes we wish we were doing something else with our careers. We wish we had different responsibilities or could spend our time with different people. We wish our boss were different, or our employees. We wish our working environment were different or that we had a different kind of commute. We wish our industry were different, or that our competition would respond differently, or that our circumstances would change. This list could obviously go on. The problem is, these wishes aren't reality, but rather, they are thoughts of a different reality.

If you're not careful, you can begin to wish your life away, always wishing you were somewhere other than where you actually are. But you're not somewhere else. Rather, you're right here. This is reality. One of my favorite quotes is, "Life is what's happening while we're busy making other plans." A slightly different version might be, "Life is what's happening while we're wishing we were somewhere else." When you are wishing you were somewhere else, it's almost as though you are one step removed from life rather than actually being in it, open to life exactly as it is.

From a practical standpoint, it's very difficult to be focused and effective when your mind is preoccupied with where it would rather be. In fact, the two are a contradiction in terms. Your concentration suffers because there is a lack of engagement, a lack of zeroing in on what's truly significant. In addition, it's virtually impossible to enjoy yourself and what you are doing when you're focused more on where you'd rather be than where you actually are. Think about the things you enjoy most. In all cases, they are activities where you are completely absorbed in the moment, really focused on what you're doing. In the absence of the focus, the joy you experience is diminished. How much fun is it to read a good novel when you're thinking about something else?

But here's where this bit of wisdom gets a little tricky. When you're not getting any pleasure out of your work, it's easy to say, "Of course I'd rather be somewhere else, I'm not enjoying myself." But step back for a moment and take a closer look at what's contributing to the lack of enjoyment. The question is what comes first—a lack of enjoyment, or a mind that is focused elsewhere? Not all but at least some of the time, the boredom or lack of satisfaction we feel is caused not by our careers or by how we are spending our time, but by the lack of focus in our thinking. The fact that you're thinking about where you'd rather be is literally sapping the joy out of what you're doing.

I think you'll be pleasantly surprised, even shocked, if you make the decision to spend less time wishing you were somewhere else and more time focused on what you're actually doing. You may regain your spark and enthusiasm for your work, and in doing so, begin to have more fun. Plus, because you'll be more focused, you'll be more creative and productive as well.

Obviously, I'm not suggesting that it's not appropriate or important to plan for the future or dream. Nor am I saying you shouldn't make changes when you are drawn to do so. These are wonderful things to do and are very often appropriate. However, when you become more immersed in what you are doing instead of what you'd rather be doing, both the nature of your dreams as well as your planned course of action will begin to change. If you have a dream, the path to get there will become clear and obvious. Instead of being distracted by your conflicting and worried thoughts, you'll have a clear mind loaded with wisdom. Good luck on this one. I think you're going to find yourself enjoying your work more than you ever thought possible.

41.

ASK YOURSELF THE QUESTION,
"AM I MAKING THE ABSOLUTE
BEST OF THIS MOMENT?"

To me, one of the most important questions you can ask yourself is, "Am I making the absolute best of this moment?" Think about it. If you were to make the most of this particular moment, and then do the same in all future moments, life would have a magical way of working itself out. You would be effective and productive and, most important, it would be very difficult for things to bug you.

So often we spend our moments wishing they were different, complaining, whining, commiserating, or feeling sorry for ourselves. But when we get right down to it, spending our moments in this manner is not only a waste of time, it's absolutely counterproductive! By using this exercise, however, you may notice an almost immediate change.

Whenever you are feeling overwhelmed or stressed at work, ask yourself the question, "What am I doing with this moment?" Are you thinking about something stressful? Are you reminding yourself, once again, how incredibly busy you are? Are you justifying in your mind your "right to be upset"? Are you reinforcing a negative belief? Or are you using the present moment to its fullest advantage? Is your attitude and thinking pointed in a positive direction? Are you being solution-oriented?

I started practicing this strategy several years ago and have discovered something truly remarkable. It seems that in most instances when I'm feeling negative, overwhelmed, or pessimistic, I can improve my state of mind by checking in with this question. I guess I shouldn't be surprised that when I'm feeling overwhelmed, I'm spending my present moment thinking about all the things that I'm overwhelmed by, rather than spending it doing the best I can or coming up with the best plan of attack.

In reading this strategy, you can probably sense that when you don't make the absolute best out of this moment, you'll be a sitting duck to sweat the small stuff! You'll be thinking about all the things that bug you and all that's wrong with your life. Fortunately, the reverse is also true. When you're making the best of this moment, it's unlikely that you'll be sweating the small stuff because you'll be focused on solutions and enjoyment instead of problems and concerns.

42.

STOP SCRAMBLING

For many people, there are essentially only two speeds—fast and faster. It seems that, most of the time, we are scrambling around, moving very quickly, doing three or four things at once. Often we are only paying partial attention or half listening to the people we are working with. Our minds are cluttered and overly busy.

Perhaps the reason so many of us spend so much time scrambling is that we fear falling behind or losing our edge. Our competitors, and everyone else around us, seem to be moving so fast that we feel we must do the same.

It's important to note that, in this hyper, frenetic state of mind, our concentration suffers. We waste precious energy and have a tendency to make mistakes. When we're scrambling, it's difficult to determine what's truly most relevant because we are so preoccupied with getting everything done. Because we are moving so quickly, it's easy to get stressed out, nervous, and agitated. And because we are so "on edge," things get on our nerves easily and often. When we are scrambling, it's really easy to sweat the small stuff.

As an experiment, see if you can make a conscious effort to slow down—both your thinking and your actions. If you do, I think you'll be pleasantly surprised to discover that, despite the slower speed, you'll become more relaxed and far more effective. The reason this happens is that you'll regain your composure and be able to see the bigger picture.

Your stress level will drop dramatically and it will even seem like you have more time. Your thinking and listening skills will become sharper and more honed. You'll be able to anticipate problems rather than finding yourself in the middle of them so often.

I'd estimate that I operate at about half the speed I did ten years ago. However, I get about twice as much work accomplished! It's actually quite remarkable how much you can do when you're calm and collected. And perhaps even more importantly, you enjoy what you are doing far more than when you're rushing around. I fully acknowledge the need to be productive, and I realize how much work there is to do. However, ironic as it may seem, it's often the case that you'll get more done in less time when you stop scrambling so much.

43.

BECOME AWARE OF
YOUR WISDOM

I don't know anyone who questions the value of analytical thinking when it comes to being a success in whatever you do. But there is another type of intelligence, other than the use of your analytical mind, that is every bit as important—wisdom. Wisdom not only provides you with creative, appropriate ideas, perspective, common sense, and an excellent sense of direction, it also makes your life easier and less stressful. This is true because, unlike the use of your analytical mind which can be effortful and clouded by doubt, wisdom is derived from a sense of confidence, a sense of knowing which direction or course of action you should take, as well as a sense of inner confidence when making decisions, creating ideas, or solving a problem.

When you use your analytical mind, it's as if you are trying hard, actively pursuing your thinking. It requires effort. Analytical thinking involves filling your head with data, sorting, figuring, calculating, comparing, and wondering.

Wisdom, on the other hand, involves quieting or emptying the mind. When you access your wisdom, it's as if instead of actively pursuing your thoughts, you instead allow your thoughts to come to you. When wisdom is present, it's almost as though wise, clever and appropriate thoughts bubble up to the surface as if out of nowhere. Using your wisdom makes your life infinitely easier.

Have you ever struggled to find an answer? You think and think, rack your brain, and analyze the data. You go over and over the same sets of facts, yet nothing seems to happen. When you think in this manner, you often feel insecure, frightened, and quite stressed. You're easily bothered because you're trying so hard to figure everything out. You're trying hard, exerting effort, and tiring easily. There's a part of you that isn't sure you'll be able to find an answer. This is clearly a time when you have a tendency to sweat the small stuff.

Then for whatever reason you stop thinking—you quiet your mind—you forget about whatever is occupying your mind and, like magic, an answer appears. And not just any answer, a perfect answer! This is wisdom in action.

You can learn to access your wisdom by the simple recognition that often it's an appropriate use of the mind. You need to start trusting yourself enough to know that when you need an answer or an idea, quieting your mind—instead of filling it with data—may provide the best possible answer or solution. Accessing wisdom requires little more than the confidence in knowing that when you quiet your mind, your mind isn't turned off. Just like a back burner of a stove slowly cooking a pot of delicious home-made soup, your mind often works best when it's not operating at high speed.

Carol works as a property manager for a large apartment complex in Texas. It's her job to implement creative ideas to keep her existing tenants happy and to draw new prospective clients to the property. She shared with me her unique way of creating ideas. In her words, "Almost everyone in property management seems to think in exactly the same way—boring and predictable. I think it's because they think inside the box. I've discovered that it's better to think outside the box—to think differently. If I tell myself I want a new idea, however simple or weird it might be, the best thing I can do is clear my mind, stop trying so hard, and go jogging. Then, like magic, some idea will pop into my mind. Over the years I've had hundreds of simple, creative ideas that set my properties apart from the others. Little things that make a big difference; everything from our own community vegetable garden to our video checkout library. I've learned to trust my passive thinking as much or more than my analytical thought process. It's a lot more relaxing and more effective too."

I asked Carol how effective her ideas had been. She responded by saying, "I'm proud to say we have zero vacancy and a one-year waiting list."

The next time you find yourself mentally struggling, try quieting down your mind as a means of accessing your wisdom. You may be surprised at how quickly and easily the answer you need will come to you. With practice, you can learn to integrate wisdom into your daily life. It will be natural and effortless. Your wisdom is a powerful tool. Learn to trust it and, without question, you'll be a less-stressed and more effective person.

44.

REALIZE THE POWER

OF RAPPORT

Rapport is a subject that is often overlooked, yet it's critical to success. The ability to establish rapport contributes to a more relaxed way of being. It helps you establish trusting, long-term relationships based on mutual honesty and integrity. It helps you become a better "people person," a better negotiator, and an overall smarter and wiser businessperson. Rapport assists you in bringing out the best in yourself as well as in other people, and prevents others from acting defensively in your presence. In addition, the necessary ingredients of establishing rapport are identical to those that help you become a kinder, more patient, and relaxed person. So, you might think of establishing rapport as a form of self-therapy, a way to help you grow—personally, professionally, and spiritually.

Many of us have a tendency to dive in too quickly, push too hard, or ask for what we want from someone before we establish the necessary rapport. In most cases, this overzealous or ambitious attempt to get something from someone will backfire. It's a turn-off. You will have acted prematurely, and lack the vital connection necessary to optimize your goals.

When you lack a sense of rapport with someone, the problem can be difficult to describe. It may be that you lack a connection or a sense of trust. For whatever reason, you just don't click. Without rapport, you can come across as demanding, unrealistic, condescending, or arrogant. Sometimes you can't quite put your finger on what's wrong—but something is missing.

Many people do understand the need for rapport when they first meet someone. In other words, it's obvious that in order to sell someone something, or ask them to do something, it's necessary that they feel okay about you. The more subtle implication of rapport, however, exists after the first meeting. It's important to know that rapport is not necessarily something that you establish once and then lasts forever. Instead, it's necessary to reconnect with people on an ongoing basis, to check in with others to be sure you're in synch.

The best way to establish rapport with someone is to assume that you don't have it. In other words, don't take for granted that simply because you know someone or that because you've done business with them before, your rapport is intact. Instead, take the time to reconnect. Be more interested in listening than in speaking. Be highly respectful and courteous. Demonstrate your sincerity and your genuine concern. Ask questions and be patient. The key to rapport is to make the person you are with (or speaking to) feel as though he or she is the most important person in your life at that moment. You want to be so present with them—so genuine that they feel special. You can't fake this type of sincerity; you have to be real.

Dan assumed it was "a done deal." He had skillfully convinced his new client to purchase a large life insurance policy over the phone. Dan had never bothered with small talk with Walter, his client, but he had done his homework and knew his product well. There was no question in his mind that the product was in Walter's best interest. Walter knew that he was under-insured and had made the decision to purchase the policy. The two of them agreed to meet over lunch and sign the papers.

The moment they sat down, Dan pulled out the application and handed Walter a pen. Suddenly, something didn't feel quite right. Walter became uneasy, hesitant, and began to have second thoughts. Shortly thereafter, he stood up and announced to Dan that he was going to have to "think about it a little longer" before making his final decision. Needless to say, Dan lost the deal. He had minimized the power of rapport. Had he bothered to get to know Walter better, his client would have felt more comfortable with him and probably wouldn't have backed out.

Once genuine rapport is established, the rest of the interaction goes much more smoothly. I know people who, when I see them, somehow always take the time to reestablish their rapport with me. They ask me how I'm doing and actually wait to hear my answer before they go on or ask me to do something for them. They don't seem rushed or preoccupied with other things. Instead, they are right there with me, treating me as if I really mattered. These are the people I want to do business with. These are the people I want to be around.

If you take the time and energy to establish rapport with others, your life will begin to change immediately. You'll have a better connection with people, which will create more nourishing interactions—personally and professionally. You will be trusted, loved, and admired, and you will become far more effective when dealing with others.

45.

RECOVER QUICKLY

There's no question about it: There will be times when you make mistakes, sometimes big ones. There will be times when you overreact, offend someone, overlook the obvious, butt in when you're not wanted, slip up, say something you shouldn't have (put your foot in your mouth), and so forth. I've yet to meet a person who is exempt from these oh-so-human facts of life. So, perhaps the most important question isn't so much whether or not you will mess up, but rather how quickly you can recover when you do.

We can turn a relatively minor setback or mistake into a much bigger deal by overanalyzing our actions (or someone else's), or being too hard on ourselves. Or we say something wrong and can't let go of it, or we become defensive of our actions and refuse to apologize.

I remember an incident that occurred a few years ago where I was taking credit for something that, in retrospect, I could see didn't really belong to me. For whatever reason, I was acting more defensive and stubborn than I usually do. As a result, the person who felt slighted by me became angry and hurt. Other people became involved, and a great deal of energy was wasted. I was sharing my story with a friend of mine who said, "Richard, it seems to me you were really stealing her glory." He explained his rationale, which made a great deal of sense. I felt embarrassed and a little stupid. Later that day, I called the person to offer my sincere apology which, to my relief, was gratefully accepted. It turned out that all she really wanted was a simple acknowledgment for her actions and an apology from me. Had I done so earlier, recovered more quickly, a great deal of frustration and wasted energy could have been avoided.

That incident, and others like it, have helped me to learn how to recover from my mistakes much more quickly than before. There are still times that I overreact, get too defensive, fail to express my appreciation, say something I wish I hadn't, as well as many other day-to-day mistakes. The difference, however, seems to be that more often than not, I'm able to see my mistakes, admit to them, and move on—I recover quickly. The result seems to be that when someone I'm working with offers a suggestion, or some type of constructive criticism, rather than feeling defensive or struggling to point out how I'm right and they are wrong, I try to keep an open mind and remain receptive to growth. And you know what? In most cases, the person making the suggestion has at very least a grain of truth or some wisdom in their position. The trick seems to be the willingness to forgive yourself—and others—for being human and for making mistakes. Once you recognize the truth of the old adage, "To err is human, to forgive is divine," you create the emotional climate to recover from practically any mistake and move on.

I'm finding that by recovering more quickly, I'm learning from others as well as from my mistakes and, as a result, my work life has become substantially less stressful. If you reflect on this strategy, I'll bet the same can be true for you as well.

46.

ENCOURAGE COMPANY
STRESS-BUSTERS

Several years ago, I was speaking to a gentleman who was really upset that the company he worked for didn't do anything to relieve the stress in the office. He felt that the company executives were "selfish, uncaring people who didn't give a hoot about their overworked employees."

I asked the man, "If you were in charge, what changes would you make?" He had obviously given the matter quite some thought because he quickly responded by saying, "If it were up to me, I'd allow employees to dress casually and have shorter days on Fridays, I'd open a company gym, provide child care, and provide regular massages for everyone." "Wow," I replied, "that would be great. What did they say when you proposed these changes?" There was a long silence before he finally admitted that he had never so much as mentioned these ideas!

This person, like probably millions of other people, assumed that his employers knew that they should be doing these things. He also assumed the worst about the people running the show—that they were monsters and that they didn't care about the health and well-being of their employees. He was wrong.

I was touched by a phone call I received on my voice mail by the same man about six months later. He said that, after he made the request, he was shocked by the positive response. Several people, including his boss, had said to him, "Why didn't I think of that?" and "Great idea." He said that not all, but some of the ideas had actually been implemented, and that several ideas from other people were being seriously considered and looked into.

It's certainly not always true, but often it's the case that employers really do care about their people in the organization. It's also very often the case that the reason nothing is happening in the way of stress-reducing efforts is that no one is suggesting any changes. There is always plenty of complaining and wishing that things were different, but rarely someone who is willing to bring the ideas to the table in a logical, well-thought-out manner.

Even if you can't convince your employer to make any changes, it's often stress-reducing to hear their side of the story. The changes you'd like to see may be impossible, yet you might discover that there are people in your company—people just like you—who do care about your stress level and would like very much to do something about it. Knowing this is the case can be richly rewarding and can make you feel better about the company you work for. And in those rare instances when it appears that no one really does care, well, at least you can know that you did everything you possibly could to make a change.

I have a friend who works for a giant company in New York. She asked if it would be possible for her to work four days at home and continue to come into the office on Wednesdays so that she could move away from the city and spend more time with her son. The company agreed. She feels wonderful about the company she works with, and does an absolutely excellent job for them. Everyone wins.

Other companies, after being asked, implement casual Fridays, company work-out rooms, or other employee perks designed to make life around the office a little less stressful. A company I was familiar with many years ago had a bunch of vacation homes and would allow employees to sign up and use the homes at no charge. The same company had soft drink machines that didn't require the user to insert any money, and interesting guest speakers who would come and speak to the employees. I could go on and on.

Not all companies are open-minded, and you certainly wouldn't want to feel defeated if you can't pull it off, but it's almost always worth the effort to propose changes that would make employees feel less stressed. If enough people want the changes and if they are known to management and decision makers, who knows what may happen?

Keep in mind that happy employees who don't feel overstressed are usually more productive, less adversarial, and more loyal. They are also less likely to quit or feel bitter toward their employer than those who feel stressed-out and unappreciated. Sometimes if you can gently remind your employer of these facts, it really can make a difference. I hope it can happen for you.

47.

GIVE UP YOUR FEAR OF
SPEAKING TO GROUPS

I used to be absolutely petrified of speaking in front of any type of group. In fact, I was so scared that I actually fainted (twice) in high school while attempting to do so.

But I'm not alone. I've heard that public speaking is the number one fear in America. It seems that speaking to groups is even more frightening to people than air travel, bankruptcy, even death!

Just for fun, I ran this strategy by a respected friend of mine to see whether or not he understood why I would include this specific strategy in a book on becoming less stressed at work. His specific response was, "I know that speaking in public is a huge fear, but how would becoming less frightened to do so help you sweat the small stuff less at work?"

It's a fair question, but I have the answer.

A fear as big as this one doesn't exist in a vacuum. In other words, it doesn't show up only on those occasions when you are called on to speak in front of a group. Instead, the stress associated with speaking in front of others looms over you, perhaps very subtly, if there is any chance whatsoever that you will ever need to speak in front of people. Whether you may be required to give a presentation, a sales pitch, the results of a report or study, an all-out speech, or simply share an idea with others, the stress factor is the same—enormous—if you're scared.

Another factor to consider is this: If you're frightened of speaking to groups, even a little bit, you may avoid doing things that could greatly benefit your career, give you a promotion or more responsibility, or an advancement of some kind. Before I overcame my fear of speaking, I remember making many decisions based on the likelihood that I may or may not have to speak. Getting over this fear helped me to relax about my work so that I could focus on other things. It made my work life easier and far less stressful. There is no question that overcoming this fear has also helped me to become more successful as an author. Had I not done so, I doubt very much that I would be writing books, because writing books requires promoting them, often in front of huge groups of people.

If you have any fear whatsoever, I urge you to consider this suggestion very carefully. Once you get over the fear you experience, you will be less stressed and more easygoing in your work life. This will help you be more creative and solution-oriented because the distraction of this fear will be gone forever. Because you'll be less on edge, you'll be sweating the small stuff less and less.

The way to get over this fear is to put yourself in situations where you are required to speak to groups. You can start really small—even one or two others is a great place to start. There are classes you can take, coaches who can help you, books to read, and tapes to listen to. There are a variety of methods and strategies to look into. In the end, however, you'll have to take the first step and get in front of people. If you do, I think you'll find, as I have, that if you get over this common fear, you'll be richly rewarded in terms of the quality of your work and, indeed, the quality of your life.

48.

AVOID COMMENTS THAT ARE LIKELY TO LEAD TO GOSSIP OR UNWANTED CHATTER

This is a real eye-opener strategy that has helped me a great deal in my own life. It's proven to be a real time-saver, and has helped me to see how often I innocently contribute to my own stress.

If you're like most people, there are times when you make innocent, fairly benign comments to others about a variety of things. You'll say things like, "Did you hear about John?", "Have you heard about so and so?", or "Did you know that?" Sometimes you initiate the conversation. Other times you keep a conversation going without realizing that you're doing so. You'll embellish someone else's comments, share a story or example, get into too much detail, or ask one too many questions. Then, if you're like me, you'll wonder why you spend so much time on the phone and why you can't seem to get enough work done.

On the surface, this may not seem like a really big deal until you consider how much time and energy you spend engaged in conversations that may not be entirely relevant, or may not be happening at an ideal time. Think about how often you feel stressed for time or energy. How often do you look back on your day and wish you could have had just thirty more minutes to get something done or simply catch up? Or think about how often you're in a hurry to complete something.

If you take a careful look at how you actually spend your time, you may come to the same conclusion that I did: that there are many instances when I'm engaged in unimportant conversations, in person or on the phone, when I honestly don't have the time or energy to be doing so. As you might suspect, this tendency can contribute to your overall feelings of stress at work. This habit can leave you unnecessarily short of time, or force you to be in a constant rush. Unless you become aware of this tendency, it's easy to blame the world and the people you talk to during the day for your feeling overwhelmed, when in fact, you may have played a significant role in the problem.

Obviously there are many times when you want to be engaged in conversation with friends or coworkers, and that's perfectly fine and healthy. The trick is to be aware of when you are conversing out of habit rather than by choice. The slightest shift in your awareness in this tendency can pay tremendous dividends in the quality of your work life.

I used to think that all the time I spent talking about other people and discussing somewhat trivial things was entirely beyond my control. What I have learned is that this is only partially true. The truth is, only some of it is beyond my control. The rest of it, I have learned, I create all by myself with my own innocent comments and questions. I have learned that it's possible to shorten my conversations while remaining polite and respectful. I've also learned to avoid asking certain types of questions that I know are likely to lead to lengthy or unnecessary conversation unless I truly want to be talking *and* I have the time. The results have been spectacular. Even though I'm busier than ever before, I feel like I have even more time. What's more, when I do take the time to converse with others, I do so knowing that it's a good time to be talking.

This is a very powerful strategy because even if you add only an hour or so a week to your work life by virtue of biting your tongue, that's one extra hour of much-needed time that you didn't have before. That one hour can sometimes make the difference between a stressful week and a peaceful one. I'm not suggesting you become antisocial or rude, only that you be careful of what and how much you say—when what you say is likely to lead to further, perhaps unwanted conversation. You'll be amazed at the power of this strategy.

49.

SEE BEYOND THE ROLES

It's almost inevitable that you will (at least on occasion), have a tendency to see people as their role instead of remembering the person behind the role. In other words, it's tempting to forget that a businessperson (or anyone performing a job or a task)—whatever he or she happens to do—isn't really a businessperson, but a special, unique human being who happens to be doing business (or performing a task) in some capacity. A baker has a life of her own, her own stories and dramas to deal with. The flight attendant is tired and can't wait to get home. The person pumping your gasoline has a family, insecurities, and problems of his own. The corporate executive probably argues with her husband and has plenty of problems unknown to the rest of us. Your secretary loves her friends and children as much as you do, and feels the same frustrations as everyone else. Whether it's your staff or your boss, it's all the same. We're all in this together.

This problem of seeing others as their role is reinforced in so many ways. How often is our first question, "What do you do?" Or how often do we describe someone as "an accountant," or "a lawyer," as if the role is really who that person is? Some of this is probably inevitable, but we can, if we choose, begin to shift the way we see and label others and in doing so make our life so much more pleasant.

I recently heard a story about a woman's boss who was so locked into roles that he actually put his pencils in his out-box for his secretary to sharpen! It would have taken him a few seconds to do it himself, but in his mind it was her role and "By God, she was going to do it." He was either oblivious, or simply didn't care how this made her feel.

When you see people as human beings first—their role second—the people you are in contact with sense your deeper perspective. In other words, they see you in a different light as well. They often treat you better, listen to you, and make allowances for you that others don't enjoy. When you see beyond the roles that people perform, you also open the door for much richer, nourishing, and more genuine interactions. You get to know people, those close to you and those you merely come into contact with. People will like you and trust you. They will often go to great lengths to help you. Time and time again, people in stores, airports, and taxis have been super helpful to me simply because I treated them as a human being first.

My guess is, had the man in my above example treated his secretary more as a fellow person and less as her role, she would have probably sharpened the silly pencils anyway. As it was, however, the way he handled it made her feel like dirt and she ended up quitting the job. Sadly, she had been an excellent secretary. One small consolation was that the boss later realized how badly he had treated her. Hopefully, he learned his lesson.

One of the places I shop has some of the warmest, friendliest people I've ever met. Yet to this day, I often observe other customers treating them almost like objects—not really mean or disrespectful, but like they weren't even there, as if there isn't a person behind the counter who smiles and enjoys their children and their time off just like everyone else. As if he or she is a checker and *only* a checker, put here on earth to serve them and take their money. I observe people moving through the line, never looking up, never smiling, never saying hello. You've probably seen the same dynamic at your local store, as well as in restaurants, airports, taxis, buses, hotels, retail outlets, and every other place you can imagine.

This strategy is simple and easy to put into practice. You don't have to become best friends or even social with everyone you meet, or for that matter, anyone you meet or work with. It's not about that. Neither do you have to forget that roles are a part of life. If someone works for you, obviously it's appropriate that they treat you in a certain way.

My suggestion is simply to remember that each person is special, and is so much more than what they do. Each person you meet has feelings— sadness, joy, fears, and all the rest. Simply knowing this and keeping it in mind can transform your life in some simple yet powerful ways. You can brighten other people's days merely by smiling and making eye contact. You can contribute to making the world a nicer, friendlier place for others and for yourself.

50.

AVOID THE TENDENCY TO PUT
A COST ON PERSONAL THINGS

One of the stressful habits that many of us get into at work is that we tend to put a cost on too many things. In other words, we calculate in our minds the cost of what we are doing or owning—when we could be doing or owning something else. Obviously, there are times when this is enormously helpful, such as when we spend time watching television or organizing our desk when we could be spending that same time working on the report that is due tomorrow morning. In this case, it might be helpful to remind yourself that, in effect, that television program is carrying with it an enormous cost—perhaps even your job.

I remember when Kris and I bought a one-fifth interest in a sailboat. The only problem was that during the next two years we only stepped on that boat once—and even then it was for a picnic with our best friends, not for a sail. In this case, it was helpful for Kris and me to realize that our picnic had, in effect, cost us over two thousand dollars! Oh well, at least we had a lot of fun on the picnic.

There are other times, however, when it's important that we not put a price tag on what we are doing. I've known quite a number of people, for example, who rarely take days off to spend time relaxing or doing something just for fun because the "cost is too high." They make the mistake of calculating what they could be earning during the days, or even hours, they are away. Even on those rare occasions when they do get away, they find it difficult to relax because they are so preoccupied with what they could be doing instead, or with what they might be missing. They will say or think things like, "If I were seeing clients (or earning) at a rate of fifty dollars an hour, I could be making four hundred dollars today. I shouldn't be here." And while they are technically correct in their arithmetic, they are effectively eliminating any possibility for a calm, inwardly rich life—because in order to achieve a less-stressed life, you must value and prioritize your need for recreation, fun, quiet, and family at least some of the time. So, even if your earning capacity is much less than the above example, there still has to be some limit on how out-of-balance you allow yourself to become.

One of my fondest memories growing up was one day that my dad helped me move from one apartment to another. It was during the week, and my dad simply took the day off. Looking back, it was a time when my father was busier than ever before. He was running a giant company and was dealing with some very complex issues. His time was extremely in demand and valuable. I remember thinking I was being financially clever when I said to him, "Dad, this is probably the costliest move ever made," referring to the fact that he could have easily hired a few people to help me at a tiny fraction of the actual cost of his being there with me. Doing so would have been far less stressful, much cheaper, and a lot easier on his back. Without even thinking about it he looked at me and said, "Rich, you can't put a price tag on spending time with your son. There's nothing in the world I'd rather be doing than spending time with you." Those words have stuck with me for almost twenty years, and will do so for the rest of my life. I probably don't have to tell you that my dad's comment meant more to me that all of the thousands of hours he spent in the office "for his family." It made me feel special, important, and valued. It also reminded him that his life was more than "another stressful day at the office."

If you want to reduce the stress in your life and be a happier person, I have found it to be useful to look at certain issues without attaching a price to them—spending time alone, with someone you love, or with your children. When you take time doing things that nourish you, or spending time with people you love, it reduces the stress you feel in all aspects of your life, including work. When you know that, no matter what, certain parts of your life simply aren't for sale—at any price—it reminds you that your life is precious and, furthermore, it belongs to you.

Go ahead and allow yourself to do some things just for you. Take some time for yourself—take a regular walk, visit nature, read more books, learn to meditate, get a massage, listen to music, go camping, spend more time with your loved ones or alone—but do something. And when you do, don't spend your time thinking about how you could be more productive. My guess is that if you learn to value your personal life and your true priorities, you'll discover that life will seem easier than before. You'll be surprised by the number of good ideas that will pop into your mind when you allow yourself to have fun—without calculating the cost.

51.

WHEN YOU SOLICIT ADVICE,
CONSIDER TAKING IT

One of the most interesting interpersonal dynamics that I've been able to observe is the tendency that many people have to share something that is bothering them, yet completely ignore the advice they receive in response. The reason I find this so interesting is because, as I have listened to conversations over the years, I've been impressed over and over again by a great deal of the creative advice I have heard. So often, it would appear as though the advice being given would solve the problem at hand, easily and quickly. In fact, there have been plenty of times that I've heard ideas designed for other people that were completely dismissed by the person to whom it was intended—that I've taken as a means of improving my life!

Obviously, there are times when we share a concern simply because we want to vent or because we simply want someone to listen to us. But there are other times when we are genuinely confused about what to do and actively seek advice, such as when we say, "I wish I knew what to do," or "Do you have any ideas?" Yet when a friend, spouse, coworker, or someone else offers a suggestion, our immediate response is to tune it out, or in some way dismiss it.

I don't know exactly why so many of us tend to dismiss the advice we receive. Perhaps we are embarrassed that we need help or we hear things we don't want to hear. Maybe we are too proud to admit that a friend or family member knows something we don't. Sometimes the advice we receive requires effort or a change in lifestyle. There are probably many other factors as well.

I'm the first to admit that I do many things wrong. But one of the qualities I'm most proud of—and am certain has helped me a great deal in both my personal and professional life—is my ability to really listen to advice, and in many instances, take it. I'm absolutely willing to admit that I don't have all the answers I need to make my life as effective and peaceful as possible. Usually, however, someone else can offer a suggestion that can help me. Not only do I often benefit from the advice I receive, but the person offering it to me is thrilled that I'm actually willing to listen and even *take* the advice. People have suggested that I talk too much—and they were right. I've been told I needed to become a better listener—and I did. People have suggested that I take a certain course or try a certain diet, and I have. And it really helped. Over and over again, I've asked people to share with me any blind spots they see in my attitude or behavior. As long as I remain receptive and nondefensive, I can almost always learn something. And sometimes, one simple suggestion can make a world of difference.

The trick is to be willing to admit that other people can see things about us (or our circumstances) that we may be too close to or too personally involved with to see ourselves. So, while you probably won't want to accept all the advice that comes your way, you may want to become just a little more open to some of it. My guess is, if you do, your life is going to be a whole lot easier.

52.

TAKE ADVANTAGE OF
YOUR COMMUTE

I was talking to an executive of a fairly large corporation who was complaining to me about his "nasty commute," which took almost an hour and a half each way. "Wow," I said, "that's too bad, but at least you're able to read some good books." His response shocked me. He said in a dead serious tone, "What are you talking about? I don't have any time to read." At first I thought he was kidding. Once I realized he wasn't, I said, "You mean you don't listen to audio tapes of books while you're in the car?" He shook his head no. "What do you do for those three hours each day?" His answer was a little uncertain; he didn't seem to really know how his commuting time was spent. I gather that he spent those three hours a day being mad at the traffic and feeling sorry for himself. I'm sure he spent a little time listening to the news and perhaps making a few phone calls on his cell phone, but for the most part, he just sat there wishing things were different. Keep in mind that this is a highly educated, extremely successful businessman. I wonder what he would think about any of his employees who wasted three hours a day, without even knowing what they were doing.

Assuming he works fifty weeks a year, he spends 750 hours a year driving to and from work. That's a staggering amount of time for anyone to waste, especially when there is such a great alternative.

Not all, but many great books are now available on audio tape. If your commute is long enough, you can listen to the entire book while driving to and from work. You can see how incredibly valuable your driving commute time can be, should you decide to look at it that way. I love audio books. With two small children, a hectic work schedule, lots of travel, and a ton of outside interests, I don't have nearly the time to read that I wish I did. But audio tapes have solved that problem. My daily commute isn't very long, but I do take advantage of the time I have to drive, as well as the traffic jams I get stuck in. Living in the San Francisco Bay Area, I get plenty of them! During these times, I listen to all sorts of great books—novels, self-help, and all the rest.

If you're one of the millions of people who must commute to work or who regularly gets stuck in traffic, rejoice! You now know of a way to take advantage of that commute. (And if you take a bus or train, you can either listen to audio books or read a book.) You might even want to start an "audio book club" with some of your friends. Four or five of you could purchase a few tapes and take turns listening to them. You'll get hours of listening enjoyment for very little cost. Give it a try. When you get home from work, instead of complaining about your commute, you'll be able to discuss the latest book you've listened to.

53.

LET GO OF BATTLES
THAT CANNOT BE WON

One of the major contributing factors to self-created stress is the tendency that most of us have to hold on to battles that we have virtually no chance of winning. For whatever reason, we keep alive unnecessary arguments and conflicts, we insist on being right, or we try to get someone to change when there is almost no possibility that we will succeed. We bump up against stone walls, but instead of backing off and taking the path of least resistance, we keep right on struggling.

Suppose you're driving to work when some aggressive driver starts to tailgate you. You get annoyed and bothered. You focus your attention in the mirror. If you get mad enough, you might even slow down or tap your brakes just to retaliate. You think to yourself how awful the world has become and how road rage is a sad fact of life.

Even though your assessment of this driver may be correct, this is clearly a battle that you cannot win. By participating in the battle, the best that can happen is that you'll end up frustrated. At worst, you may even contribute to the cause of an accident. It's not worth it because either way you lose. By recognizing that this is a battle not worth fighting, you can calmly move to a different lane and allow the driver to go on and have his accident somewhere else. Period, end of subject. Let go of it, and go on with your day.

An arrogant and chauvinistic male CPA was arguing with two bright female colleagues. They were questioning his conclusion regarding a complex tax issue, and he wasn't interested in listening. They provided what appeared to be conclusive proof of their position, including supportive documentation and precedence. Despite his lack of evidence to support his position, he brushed them off and discounted their data. Officially, he was the decision maker and, as far as he was concerned, the case was closed.

The fact of the matter was, in this instance, *his* reputation was officially on the line, not theirs. They were trying to do him a favor and save him the embarrassment of a mistake and the hassle of correcting it later on down the road. Furthermore, his error wasn't intentional, nor was it significant. The truth was, they had done everything they could do. It was clear that this was a battle they were not going to win—there was nothing they could do to change his mind. They could spend the next week complaining to each other and feeling frustrated—or they could let it go and stay focused on their own integrity and excellent work.

Luckily, the two women had learned not to become overly dramatic over relatively small things. You might say they had learned not to sweat the small stuff—which this clearly was an example of. Keep in mind that, had the stakes been higher, or had the issue involved integrity or a significant amount of money, they may have decided to take their efforts to a new level. But, in this instance, it clearly wasn't worth the hassle. Their decision had nothing to do with apathy; both women were real pros. It was simply a matter of having the wisdom to know how to choose their battles carefully.

Obviously, if something legitimate or terribly important is at stake, you may have to prove your position and it will be worth the trouble. Most of the time, however, that's not where daily frustration stems from. In fact, most of us handle the "big stuff" pretty well. The stress you feel often comes from fighting those "no chance of winning" battles where the outcome is practically irrelevant anyway.

Perhaps you're frustrated by the complaining of a coworker. You may spend countless hours and a great deal of energy attempting to share with her why she shouldn't be so upset. But try as you might, she just keeps on complaining. For every valuable insight you share with her, she comes back with yet another, "Yeah, but . . ." and never, ever takes your advice. If you're frustrated by this type of typical interaction, it's because you're fighting a battle that can't be won. She's probably going to be complaining for the rest of her life. Your involvement, caring, ideas, and insights have zero effect. Does this mean you should stop caring? Of course not. It simply means you can dismiss the idea that you are ever going to convince her to stop complaining. Case closed. You can wish her well and be there for her as a friend, but if you want less stress in your life you're going to have to let go of the battle.

We fight these silly battles (and so many others) sometimes out of stubbornness or out of our own need to prove ourselves, other times out of pure habit, and sometimes simply because we haven't thought through exactly what it is we are hoping to accomplish or where our efforts are likely to lead. Whatever the reason, however, this tendency is a serious mistake if your goal is to stop sweating the small stuff. The great football coach Vince Lombardi was known to have said, "When you're doing something wrong, doing it more intensely isn't going to help." I couldn't say it any better.

I'm certain that one of the major reasons I'm a happy person is that I'm usually able to differentiate between a battle worth fighting and one that is better left alone. I've always felt that my personal sense of well-being is far more important than any need I might have to prove myself or participate in an irrelevant argument. That way I can save my love and energy for truly important things. I hope you'll take this strategy to heart because I know it can help you stop sweating the small stuff at work.

54.

THINK OF STRESS AND
FRUSTRATION AS DISTRACTIONS
TO YOUR SUCCESS

I couldn't tell you how often I've been asked the question, "Don't you think you need to be stressed and harried to be successful?" I've yet to meet anyone who can convince me that the answer to this question is "Yes."

Many people assume that stress and success are linked in the same way that glue sticks to paper. The assumption is, "There's a huge price to pay in order to achieve your dreams, and enormous stress is an inevitable and essential part of the process." People think of their stress as a source of motivation. Consequently, people are not only looking for verification of stress in their work life, but even more to the point, they begin to assume that stress is a valuable emotion to have, something they actually need to stay motivated and to keep their edge. Thus, they begin to look and behave in very stressful ways—they become short-tempered and poor listeners. They don't allow adequate time between appointments, therefore assuring the need to scramble and feel rushed. They become nervous and agitated. They lose their perspective and wisdom. They rush out the door in the morning and complain about how busy they are when they finally return home after work. In short, they sweat the small stuff—big time!

The problem is, if you assume that stress is a positive and necessary factor, you're going to create—knowingly or unknowingly—a great deal more of it. If, however, you can begin to think of stress as a distraction that is actually interfering with your goals and dreams, you can begin to rid yourself of a great deal of it.

Stress is, in fact, a distraction. It interferes with clear and logical thinking. It makes wisdom, insights, and creativity more difficult to bring forth. Stress is also exhausting, robbing you of valuable and precious energy—both physical and emotional. Finally, stress is an enormous source of relationship problems. The more stressed-out you are, the more quick-tempered you become. You lose your ability to stay focused, and your listening skills are affected. You lose your compassion and sense of humor.

I acknowledge that some degree of stress is inevitable. And certainly, becoming successful in whatever you do can be difficult and demanding. However, thinking of stress as valuable makes matters worse, not better. Looked at in this way, it's easy to see that stress isn't something you want to think of in a positive light. Far from being your primary source of motivation, stress has a way of defeating your spirit and energy. And contrary to the notion that stress helps you keep your edge, it actually gives that edge to your competitors.

My suggestion is this: When you begin sweating the small stuff at work, and when you begin to feel stressed-out, gently remind yourself that, while work may be difficult, the stressful feelings you are experiencing aren't helping and certainly aren't worth defending. In doing so, you may begin to notice the some of the stress that you've always assumed was necessary will begin to fade away. If so, you'll experience the success that comes from seeing stress as a distraction, instead of as an ally.

55.

ACCEPT THE FACT THAT THERE'S ALMOST ALWAYS GOING TO BE SOMEONE MAD AT YOU

This is a difficult concept to accept, particularly if, like me, you are a "people pleaser," or worse still, an approval seeker. Yet I've found that if you don't make peace with this virtual inevitability, it guarantees that you will spend a great deal of time struggling with one of the unfortunate realities of life—disappointment.

The fact that someone is virtually always going to be mad or at least disappointed in you is inevitable because while you're busy trying to please one person, you're often disappointing someone else. Even if your intentions are entirely pure and positive, you simply can't be in two places at one time. So, if two or more people want, need or expect something from you—and you can't do it all—someone is going to be left disappointed. When you have dozens, even hundreds of demands on your time, and requests being fired at you from all different directions, a certain number of balls are going to be dropped. Mistakes are going to be made.

Your boss or client needs you to do something—the only problem is, your child or spouse needs you too at the same time. You're a waitress at a busy restaurant and every table seems anxious—you're doing the very best you can, but customers are still mad. Four people asked you to call them before five o'clock. Whoops, the second call took much longer than anticipated. The two who didn't receive calls are probably going to be upset. If you hurried the call you were on, you risked upsetting that person. Either way, someone's left upset. Or you go the extra mile to do an excellent job on one project—but only have time to do an adequate job on another project. Again, you let someone down. You forget someone's birthday. Even though you remembered nineteen other birthdays, you still managed to upset one person. And so it goes.

You can try and try—you can put all the odds in your favor, you can make allowances for contingencies and mix-ups, but there are still going to be errors. And when errors happen, or when you prove that you're human; when you're overcommitted, need some time to yourself, forget a promise, meeting, or commitment; then someone is going to be hurt, upset, mad, or disappointed. In my heart, I know that I try as hard as any human being can try—and I can tell you there is no way around it (at least I haven't found one)! Here's a personal example.

For a period of time, I was blessed in receiving in excess of three hundred letters a week from readers. A good number of these letters asked for a personal response, and in my view, each person deserved one. After all, someone who takes their time and effort to write a kind letter is, to me, quite special. To this day, I appreciate every letter I have ever received—many bring tears to my eyes. But it can also be frustrating because like almost everyone else, my problem is that there are only so many hours in a day and, again like everyone else, I have to juggle many different responsibilities and commitments.

I have a hectic travel schedule and tight writing deadlines. I have numerous speaking engagements to prepare and deliver on an ongoing basis, promotional commitments, and dozens of other requests for my time each and every day. Most importantly, I have a family that I love very much and wish to spend time with, as well as a few close friends.

To put it in perspective, if I were to spend even ten minutes apiece on all the letters I receive, it would take virtually all of my time. In any event, you certainly wouldn't be reading this book today because there would have been no time to write it. What can I do? I hired a responsive person to help me answer my mail. Each week, she helps me choose as many letters as possible to answer personally, and she responds to the rest. Her letters are kind, thoughtful, and respectful. For a while, I thought I had solved my dilemma.

Not! Although a vast majority of people understand my predicament, there is always a small percentage of people who are disappointed, and a few who are enraged that I didn't have the courtesy to write them myself. Again, the problem is you really can't please everyone, no matter how hard you try. It's no different for me than it is for you.

When you make peace with this fact of life, a huge weight is lifted off your shoulders. Obviously you would never intentionally hurt or disappoint someone. In fact, most of us will do everything within our power not to— yet it's still going to happen. And when you know it's inevitable, your gut reaction to the disappointment is going to be much more peaceful. Rather than becoming upset, defensive, or guilty, you'll maintain your bearings and remain compassionate. You'll understand that there's simply nothing you can do—other than your best. You didn't intend for it to happen, you did everything you knew how to prevent it, yet it happened. And it will happen again. It's time to let it go. And in letting go, you will find peace.

56.

DON'T LET YOUR OWN THOUGHTS
STRESS YOU OUT

I'm often asked the question, "What is the single most important thing a person can do to stop sweating the small stuff?" I must confess that I do not know for sure what that single secret would be. I can tell you, however, that way up there on my list would be my suggestion of not allowing your own thoughts to stress you out.

Think about how often we all have conversations in the privacy of our own minds. It happens, practically nonstop, all day long, every day of our lives. We're in the car thinking about something—a deadline, an argument, a potential conflict, a mistake, a worry, whatever. Or we're at the office or in the shower, doing the very same thing—and it all seems so real.

When we are thinking, however, it's easy to lose sight of the fact that we think thoughts, not reality. Let me explain. It may seem strange, but most of us have a tendency to forget that we're thinking because it's something that we're always doing—like breathing. But until I mentioned breathing, you weren't really consciously aware that you were breathing—were you? Thinking works in a similar way. Because it's such a part of us, we tend to give enormous significance and take very seriously most of the thoughts that drift through our minds. We begin to treat our thoughts as if they were the real thing, allowing them to stress us out.

If you reflect on this idea, you'll probably be able to see the practical implications. When you have a thought, that's all it is—a thought. Thoughts certainly don't have the power or authority to stress you out without your conscious or unconscious consent. Thoughts are just images and ideas in your mind. They are like dreams—only you're awake while you're having them. But with waking thoughts, you get to decide how seriously you are going to take them.

For example, you might have a series of thoughts while driving to work: "Oh gosh, today is going to be really horrible. I've got six meetings and must finish those two reports by noon. I dread seeing Jane. I just know she's still going to be angry about the disagreement we had yesterday."

At this point, essentially only one of two things can happen. You will either take the thoughts seriously, start feeling worried, think about them some more, analyze how difficult your life has become, feel sorry for yourself, and so forth. Or if you recognize what has just happened, if you are consciously aware that you've just had a mini "thought attack," you can simply remind yourself that all that has occurred is yet another series of thoughts has traveled through your mind. You're not even at work yet—you're still driving in the car!

This doesn't mean that your day is going to be trouble-free or that you're pretending all is well and good. But think of how illogical it is to be having a bad day at work before your day officially begins. It's ludicrous—but that's precisely what most of us do all day long. We have thought after thought after thought. Yet we forget that it's thought. We treat it as real.

If you can change this way of relating to your thinking, you're going to be pleasantly surprised at how quickly and dramatically you will be able to reduce the stress in your work life. The next time you find yourself having a "thought attack," see if you can catch yourself. Then say something gentle to yourself like, "Whoops, there I go again," as a way of reminding yourself that you're taking your own thoughts a little too seriously. I hope you'll take this strategy to heart—it will make a world of difference.

57.

MAKE ALLOWANCES FOR
INCOMPETENCE

Like so many things, incompetence seems to be represented by a bell-shaped curve. There is always going to be a small percentage of people who are near the top, most people will fall somewhere near the middle, and a few will lie toward the bottom. In most professions (other than those where only highly competent people are considered qualified), it's just the way life seems to pan out. A few people in each field will be really good, most will be sort of average, and there will always be a few that make you wonder how in the world they manage to make a living.

It's interesting, however, that so many people don't seem to understand this dynamic or, if they do, they certainly don't exhibit any compassion or common sense in their reaction to it. Despite the fact that incompetence is an obvious and unavoidable fact of life, it's as though people are surprised, take it personally, feel imposed upon, and react harshly to it. Many people complain about incompetence, are bothered by it, discuss its rampant trend with others, and spend valuable time and energy hoping and wishing it would go away. I've seen people so upset about obvious incompetence that I thought they might have a heart attack or a nervous breakdown. Instead of seeing it as a necessary evil, they get all worked up, often compound the problem with their harsh reaction, and bang their head against the wall in frustration. In the end, nothing was accomplished except that the frustrated person had an emotional meltdown and made himself look bad.

One of my favorite television shows is the comedy "Mad About You." The brilliant comedian Lisa Kudrow plays the part of an almost unimaginably incompetent waitress in a cafe. I assumed her role was non-duplicable until recently when I was in a restaurant in Chicago. My waitress was so bad that, for a moment, I thought I was being "set up" with a hidden camera to see if I would sweat the small stuff. As far as I could tell, she managed to get every single order completely messed up. I ordered a vegetarian sandwich and ended up with rare roast beef. The customer next to me ordered a milk shake and ended up with a bottle of beer which was quickly spilled on his expensive looking shirt. It went on and on, each table seemingly worse than the next. After a while, it actually became amusing. When the check arrived, she had charged me for the roast beef, the other man's beer, and a T-shirt with the restaurant's logo!

Another story comes from someone I met who works in a real estate office. In addition to selling homes, she helps coordinate her clients with the various professionals who put the deal together—lenders, inspectors and appraisers. She told me of an appraiser she had worked with (twice) who had also worked with many of her colleagues. This appraiser was in her words, "beyond belief." His job was to appraise the market value of the home being sold to be sure the loan was a reasonable risk for the lender. Apparently, he was in the habit of appraising homes for up to twice their actual value. She was selling one home, for example, that was worth approximately $150,000 that he appraised for $300,000. The almost identical home next door sold for $150,000. She claimed that this was his standard operating procedure—he would toss out all rational and standard appraisal methods and rely on his "instinct." His incompetence must have worked out pretty well for the buyers—but imagine the risk the lenders were taking with home appraisals that had no relationship to reality.

The most unbelievable part of this story is that, allegedly, this appraiser has managed to stay in business for more than ten years! Despite a lengthy pattern of blatant incompetence, he continues to be hired by lenders who depend on his judgment to protect their loans.

In no way am I saying it's pleasant to deal with incompetence, but if you want to avoid feeling so irritated, it's important that you stop being so surprised and caught off guard by it. It's helpful to understand that some degree of incompetence is about as predictable as an occasional rainy day—even if you live in California, as I do. Sooner or later, it's bound to happen. So, instead of saying, "I can't believe my eyes," or something similar, keep in mind that it's bound to occur every once in a while—it's inevitable. This acceptance of the way things really are will probably allow you to say (or think) something like, "Of course it's going to be like this from time to time." You'll be able to keep your perspective and remember that, a vast majority of the time, it's not personally directed at you. Rather than focusing on the most dramatic and extreme examples to validate your belief in rampant incompetence, see if you can recognize and appreciate the fact that most people do really well, most of the time. With a little practice and patience, you'll cease being so upset over things you have very little control over.

I'm not suggesting that you should put up with or advocate incompetence, or that, if you're an employer, you shouldn't replace incompetent employees with harder-working, more qualified people. These are totally different issues. What I'm saying is that, regardless of who you are or what you do, you are going to run into (and have to deal with) at least some amount of incompetence in your work life. Why not learn to take it in stride, and not let it bother you so much?

By simply making allowances in your mind for something that is going to happen anyway, you'll be able to dramatically improve the quality of your life. I know that dealing with incompetence can be frustrating—especially when the stakes are high. I can virtually guarantee you, however, that losing your cool isn't going to help very much.

The next time you run into incompetence, even if it's flagrant, see if you can make the best of it, rectify the situation if possible, and then go on with your day. Let it go. Rather than turning the incompetence into front page news in your mind, see if you can turn it into just another minor story. If you do, you'll be free from yet another of life's sources of frustration.

58.

DON'T BE TOO QUICK
TO COMMENT

It's hard to quantify exactly how helpful this strategy has been in my own work life because often the results are subtle or speculative. I can say for sure, however, that it's been a significant and powerful tool. Learning to be less quick to comment has saved me from engaging in a great deal of unnecessary or untimely conversation. Without question, it's also saved me time, energy, and probably more than a few arguments.

Many of us are quick to comment on practically anything. We'll gladly comment on someone else's comment, their opinion, or a mistake that we perceive may have been made. We will offer our own opinion, comment on a policy, a pattern of behavior, or a personal gripe. Often we just want to get something off our chests. Sometimes when we're mad or frustrated, we'll blurt something out—an expression of the way we are feeling, or a defensive jab. We'll comment on the way someone looks, behaves, or seems to think. Sometimes our comments are critical in nature, other times they are complimentary or engaging. Often we'll share our vision, a belief, a potential solution, a prejudice, or a simple observation.

Obviously, there are times when other people ask that we comment or share our point of view. And a great deal of the time we are simply being responsive to the moment, and our comments are absolutely appropriate. In fact, this is probably the case a vast majority of the time. Most of our comments are probably useful, helpful, necessary, or simply entertaining. Sometimes our input can help solve a problem, come up with a solution, a better way of doing something, or contribute in some meaningful way. Terrific. Keep commenting.

Invariably, however, some of our comments are at best unnecessary and at worst counterproductive. They arise out of habit, a knee-jerk reaction, or some unexplained need we have to comment. Some of these comments lead to arguments, hurt feelings, or confusion. These are the ones that you want to avoid making, if possible.

Recently, a woman I met shared with me the following example. She had been working all day long and was just about to leave her office. She said she was dreaming of spending the evening alone—having a hot bath and curling up with a good book before bed. She saw a few coworkers down the hall and she walked over to say good night.

The others were discussing a heated issue that, in a practical sense, had little or no affect on her. No one even asked her opinion. Yet she had an idea she decided to share with the group. She said, "Do you know what you should do?" You can probably guess the rest of this story. Immediately, she was engaged in the conversation, and because she was the one who brought up the idea, it would have been inappropriate for her to leave. She spent the next hour and a half explaining and defending her position. In the end, there was no resolution. She went home exhausted, too tired to read. She had been looking forward to a peaceful evening. Instead, she ended up getting home late with a lot on her mind, feeling resentful and confused.

While the details are always a little different, there are hundreds, maybe even thousands of ways that most of us do something similar on a regular basis. This woman did nothing wrong; her only intention was to be helpful and friendly. Yet her simple, harmless comment led to a stressful free-for-all that wore her out. Are there times when it's appropriate to engage in this type of conversation? Of course there are. Yet her goal was to spend a quiet evening alone.

On many occasions, I've done essentially the same thing. For example, I'll be finishing a phone conversation and, at the very last second without thinking, I'll say "What ever happened to such and such?" My question will encourage the person I'm speaking with to launch into a detailed discussion and I'll be on the phone an extra twenty minutes. Meanwhile, someone else is waiting for me to return their call and now I'm running late. Isn't it obvious that, in instances such as these, I'm contributing to my own stress?

Occasionally, we'll blurt out a comment that has longer-term implications. I once heard a woman in a small office yell out to one of her coworkers, "You are the worst listener I've ever met. I hate talking to you." Had she been less quick to comment, she may have been able to reflect on a slightly less adversarial and more effective way to share her feelings.

The question is, how much stress could you avoid by simply learning to bite your tongue when it's in your best interest to do so? I've met more than a few people who claim that this simple change in habit has greatly contributed to a more peaceful life. They now say fewer things that they regret later by reflecting with wisdom before they speak. This is a fairly simple idea to implement into your life. For the most part, it involves nothing more than a gentle pause before you speak—just enough time to allow your wisdom to tell you whether what you are about to say is in your best interest. Give it a try. You may save yourself a great deal of grief.

59.

LET GO OF

"PERSONALITY CLASHES"

Invariably, as people share with me their list of gripes about their work, the subject of "personality clashes" is brought to my attention. People say things like, "I simply can't get along with certain types of people," and "Some personalities just don't match mine." The assumption is often made that certain personality types just don't mix—shy people can't get along with outgoing people, or sensitive individuals can't work well with more aggressive people, to name just a few. This is unfortunate because rarely can we pick and choose the types of personalities we work with. Instead, we usually get what we get. If we can't rise above the stereotypical assumptions regarding who can and can't work well together, we're out of luck, doomed to a life of frustration.

While it's easy to understand why some people make these assumptions, in reality there's no such thing as a personality clash. If there were, then our generalities would always apply—and they obviously do not. I've met tons of supposedly mismatched colleagues who are super team players and who love to work together. I'll bet you have too.

"I understand what you're saying, but my personality clashes are more specific and serious," I've been told by numerous employees. "For example, I can get along with some opinionated people, but not others. Sometimes two people just don't jell, and there is nothing you can do about it." While this can sometimes seem to be the case, to roll over and give in to the acrimonious feeling is self-defeating and, I believe, unnecessary.

Like everyone else, I prefer to work with certain types of people over others. For example, generally speaking, I'd prefer not to work with pushy people or those who are very hyperactive. I've found, however, that with some gentle effort on my part, along with some heightened perspective, I can usually work well with practically anyone, regardless of their personality type. The trick, I believe, lies in the word "gentle." It's critical to understand that our typical "roll up your sleeves and try hard" approach doesn't work very well when our goal is to overcome a difference in personality. In fact, the harder you try or the more you force the issue, the more it's going to seem that you're swimming upstream.

What works well for me is to think in terms of getting along as part of my job description. In other words, I attempt to take responsibility for making the relationship work; I put the ball in my own court. Rather than writing off the relationship (or my experience of the working relationship) as doomed for failure or frustration, I see if I can rise to the occasion and accept the challenge. Instead of seeing myself as good and the other person as flawed, I humorously label each of us as "characters," each playing a different role. I keep my spirit light and my sense of humor intact. Gently, I try to let go of my insistence that other people see life or behave the way I do. Almost without fail, this opens my heart and broadens my perspective.

Amy and Jan are fourth grade teachers at the same elementary school. I was told that the teachers were supposed to be working together to create a consistent curriculum for the students. The problem was, they couldn't stand each other and were constantly criticizing each other's teaching style. Apparently, both women felt they had an irreconcilable personality clash. In addition to a great deal of backstabbing and passive-aggressive jabs, the two of them engaged in a verbal confrontation in front of the parents at a parents and teachers meeting. Amy accused Jan of being "so undisciplined and detail-oriented that her students wouldn't be prepared for fifth grade level studies the following year." Jan barked back that Amy was "not only incompetent, but that parents should know that she played favorites and had tougher standards for the kids she didn't like."

Their inability to respect their differences and dismiss their childlike personality clash petrified the parents, who became visibly upset. The remainder of the school year was filled with stress, anger, and worry for the parents of the students, and self-created (and well-deserved) embarrassment for the two teachers. Instead of understanding that differences in personality and style can create a more interesting learning environment, the two of them took their differences personally and acted out their frustration. In this example, as in all others, no one wins.

Letting go of personality clashes in this way has made an enormous difference in my work life. I've been able to see that often it is to my advantage to work with people who are very different from me, and that ultimately it makes my work more interesting. I suggest you take a similar look at your own personality clashes. Letting them go will take a huge weight off your shoulders.

60.

DON'T GET STRESSED BY
THE PREDICTABLE

In many industries there are certain standard procedures or problems that are, to a large degree, predictable. The first few times they happen, or if you're caught off guard, it's understandable that they can create some anxiety or stress. However, once you factor them into your awareness, and you can predict how events are typically played out, it's silly to be annoyed and upset. Yet I find that many people continue to feel bothered and stressed, even after they see how the game is played. They continue to get upset, angry, and complain about a pattern that is predictable. To me, this is self-induced stress in its purest form.

I've had several fairly relaxed friends who are, or who have been, flight attendants for major airlines. Although they themselves are usually the type of people who take life in stride, they have shared with me some interesting stories about colleagues who fall apart (luckily without the passengers being aware) over absolutely predictable parts of their job.

One woman gets completely stressed out every time her flight is delayed. She calls her husband to complain about her stressful job, and shares her frustration with her friends (who have already heard the story hundreds of times). Rather than saying to herself, "Of course there are going to be occasional delays," she tortures herself by reacting to the predictable.

Another flight attendant (this one a male) gets super angry whenever he runs into a rude or unappreciative passenger. He's obviously bright enough to understand that this is bound to happen every once in a while (or probably more often than that). Yet, every time it happens, he goes crazy and feels compelled to share his anger with others. All he does is stir up the other flight attendants by getting them focused on the few disrespectful people instead of the vast majority who are quite pleasant.

I met an accountant who gets annoyed every March and April because his hours are increased and he can't leave the office at 5:00. He jumps up and down and complains about how "unfair" it is, even though it's absolutely predictable. It would seem to me that virtually *all* accountants who prepare income tax returns for a living would be the busiest during tax season. What am I missing?

I met a police officer who took it personally when people would drive faster than the speed limit. He would get frustrated and dish out harsh lectures, apparently forgetting that it was his job to catch people speeding to create safer roads. Again, this is a predictable part of his work. I've spoken to a number of other police officers who simply take this part of their job in stride—because they know it's coming, it's predictable. Most of them say, "Sure, we have to issue a citation, but why in the world would I get stressed out over it?"

Before you say, "Those are silly examples," or "I'd never get upset over something like that," take a careful look at your own industry. It's always easier to see why someone else shouldn't be upset than it is to admit that you, too, can make a bigger deal out of something than is really necessary. I admit I've made this mistake myself on more than one occasion, and perhaps you have too. By seeing certain aspects of your profession as predictable, you can alleviate a great deal of frustration.

Although the specific details and hassles are different in each industry and while many of the predictable events don't appear to make much sense, I've seen a similar pattern in many fields. In some industries, for example, there are built-in delays. You'll be waiting on suppliers, orders, or someone or something else in order to do your job, so it will always *seem* like you're running late and in an enormous hurry. And while it's true you have to wait until the last minute to get everything you need, it's entirely predictable and consistent—you know it's going to happen. Therefore, if you can make the necessary allowances in your mind for the inevitable, you won't have to feel the pressure. Instead, you learn to take it in stride. This doesn't mean you don't care. Obviously, it's necessary and appropriate to do your best job and work as quickly and efficiently as possible. To be surprised and resentful that you're constantly waiting for others is foolish.

In other fields (perhaps most of them), there is always more work to be done than time to do it. If you look around, you'll notice that everyone is in the same boat—it's set up that way. Work is designed to land on your desk slightly quicker than you're able to complete it. If you examine this tendency, you'll notice that it's absolutely predictable. If you worked twice as fast as you currently do, nothing would change in the sense of getting it all done. As you work faster and more efficiently, you'll notice that magically more work will appear. Again, this doesn't mean your work isn't demanding or that you shouldn't work hard and do your absolute best. It just means that you don't have to lose sleep over the fact that it's never going to be completely done—because it isn't.

As you see these and other work-related tendencies in their proper "predictable" perspective, you can eliminate a great deal of stress. You can make allowances in your mind, attitude, and behavior for that which you know is going to happen anyway. You can breathe easier and, perhaps, learn to relax a little more. I hope this added perspective is as helpful to you as it has been to me.

61.

STOP PROCRASTINATING

Recently I received a frantic phone call from an accountant that demonstrates one of the most widely used excuses for being late. She used the familiar statement, "It was really complicated and took a great deal of time." If you take a deep breath and a step back, I think you'll agree with me that, in a way, this is a ridiculous excuse that creates unnecessary grief for both the person being late, as well as the person who has to wait. All it really does is ensure that you'll continue to be late, as well as encourage you to feel victimized by a shortage of time.

Every project takes a certain amount of time. This is true whether it's a tax form, other paperwork, a report, the building of a house, or the writing of a book. And, although factors that are well beyond our control and completely unpredictable do come into play, the truth is, in a vast majority of cases, you can make a *reasonable* estimate of the amount of time you will need to complete the task even if you have to factor in some extra time for unknown elements.

For example, the accountant I'm referring to was well aware that there was some measure of complexity to her task and that she would have to factor the degree of difficulty into her time schedule. She also had the advantage, as the rest of us do, of knowing the exact date that Uncle Sam demands the complete return! Why then did she wait so long to begin? And why did she use the "really complicated" excuse instead of simply admitting that she waited too long to get started? It would have taken her exactly the same number of hours to complete the project, whether she had started a month earlier or had she waited even longer.

Many of us do the very same thing in our work as well as in our personal lives. I know plenty of people who are virtually *always* late, whether it's to pick up the kids in their car pool, sit down before church starts on Sunday, or prepare food for dinner guests. The interesting part of this tendency isn't the fact that they are always running late, but the excuses that are used: "I had to pick up three kids," "I had to make two stops before work," "It's tough to get everything done before I run out the door," "Having dinner guests is more work for me."

Again, I'm not denying that it is tough to get everything done—it is—but in all of these examples, you are working with absolutely known variables. You know exactly how many kids you have, how long it takes to get them ready and to get them where they need to be. You know how long it takes to drive to work, and that there will almost certainly be traffic to contend with. You are absolutely aware of the fact that having dinner guests can be a lot of work, and that it takes a certain amount of extra time to prepare dinner and get everything ready. When we use the "I didn't have enough time" excuse we are fooling ourselves, thus virtually guaranteeing that we will make the identical mistake next time.

To get over this tendency requires humility. The only solution is to admit that, in most instances, you do have the time, but you must start a little earlier and make whatever allowances are necessary to ensure that you won't be in a mad rush. So, if you're constantly running five minutes late, or thirty minutes late, and this is creating stress in your life and stress for other people, you need to make a real effort to start five minutes earlier, or thirty minutes earlier, on a consistent basis.

My deadline for completing this book was September 1 of last year. I had known that this was my deadline for over six months. I had been given plenty of time. Do you think it would have been a good idea for me to wait until July 15 to begin? Of course not. This would have created a great deal of unnecessary stress for myself and for my publisher. I would have been rushed, and wouldn't have been able to do my best job. Yet this is precisely what many people do in their work. They wait too long to begin, then complain about how much else they had going on.

Think of how much less stress would be in your life if you would simply begin your tasks a little earlier. Then rather than rushing from one project to the next, you'd have plenty of time. Rather than gripping the wheel and swerving your way from lane to lane to the airport or office, you'd arrive with a few minutes to spare. Rather than having the parents of the kids in your carpool angry and frustrated at you some, if not most of the time, you'd develop a reputation as a reliable and conscientious friend.

This is one of the simplest suggestions I've made in any of my books, yet in some ways it's one of the most important. Once you get in the habit of starting a little earlier, a great deal of your daily stress, at least that portion that you have some degree of control over, will fade away.

62.

CONFRONT GENTLY

It's hard to imagine working for a living without at least some degree of confrontation. After all, we live in a world of conflicting interests, desires, and preferences. We have different standards and expectations. A job that is considered well done and complete to one person may be woefully inadequate to another. Something that you consider to be an emergency or absolutely critical may seem almost irrelevant to someone else, or at least unworthy of their time. There are so many issues and people to deal with that an occasional confrontation seems inevitable. At times, you may have to confront someone in order to achieve a desired result, clarify an intention, shake someone up, make things happen, resolve a conflict, break out of a rut, or improve communication.

While confrontations may be inevitable, they don't necessarily have to seem like a war or lead to hurt or angry feelings, stress, or disappointment. Instead, it's possible to confront someone (or be confronted) in a gentle, effective way that leads not only to your desired result, but also in a way that brings the two of you closer together personally or professionally.

It seems to me that most people are too aggressive and defensive during confrontations. They lose their humanity and their humility. They approach the issue in a hostile way, as if they are right and the other person is wrong. It's "me against you," or "I'm going to teach you." The assumption seems to be that confrontations are by definition confrontational, and that being aggressive is the best approach.

179

If you're too aggressive, however, you're going to seem adversarial to others, thus encouraging them to become defensive. The people you confront will see you as difficult, as if you are the enemy. When people are defensive, they become poor listeners, incredibly stubborn, and seldom change their point of view or see their contribution to a problem. They don't feel respected and they lose their respect for you. So, if you are confronting someone in an aggressive way, chances are you're going to run into a brick wall.

The key to effective confrontation is to be firm yet gentle and respectful. Approach the confrontation with the assumption that there is a solution and that you will be able to work things out. Rather than assessing blame and assuming fault, try to see the innocence in yourself as well as in the other person. Rather than using phrases that are almost guaranteed to elicit a defensive response such as: "You've made a big mistake and we need to talk," try instead to say things with a little more humility, something like, "I'm a little confused about something—can you help me out?"

More important than the words you use, however, are your feelings. It's not always possible, but when it is, try to avoid confrontations when you're angry or stressed out. It's always best to wait a little while until you get your perspective, or until your mood rises. Keep in mind that most people are reasonable, respectful, and willing to listen when dealing with a calm, collected person who is speaking honestly from his heart.

When you approach your confrontations in a gentle manner, it not only produces more effective results, but it keeps your own stress level down as well. In other words, a gentle spirit is a relaxed spirit, even when it has to do something that is normally considered difficult. There is something very comforting about knowing that you're going to keep your cool regardless of what you must do. In addition, you'll have fewer battles to fight, and those that you do have will be shorter and less severe. You'll receive more cooperation and respect from others and, perhaps most importantly, your own thoughts and feelings will be much nicer.

The next time you confront someone, for whatever reason, I hope you'll consider doing it a little more gently. If you'd like for your life to seem less like a battle, this is an excellent place to start.

63.

REMEMBER THE THREE R'S

If I asked you what I meant by the Three R's, many of you would probably guess, "Reading, writing, and arithmetic." I've developed my
own three R's, however, that I feel are equally important, especially if
you want to learn to be a less reactive, happier person. The three R's
I'm referring to are: "Responsive, receptive, and reasonable."

"Responsive" means acting appropriately to the issue at hand. Rather
than being driven and controlled by habitual, knee-jerk reactions, being
responsive means having the ability to maintain perspective and to
choose the best possible alternative or course of action, given your
unique situation. Because they are able to see the entire picture so well,
responsive individuals are able to factor into every equation all the variables, instead of being limited to their usual way of doing things. They
are willing to change direction, if necessary, and admit their mistakes
when appropriate.

For example, it's common for a builder to run into unexpected
changes in the original plans—unknown soil conditions, a shortage of
capital, or unforeseen design problems. A reactive builder will panic,
overreact and become difficult to work with. A good builder will take the
changes in stride, be responsive to the changes, rise to the occasion and
get the job done.

"Receptive" implies being open to ideas and suggestions. It means
you are inclined and willing to receive whatever it is that you need at that

moment—data, creativity, a new idea, or whatever. It's the opposite of being closed-minded and stubborn. People who are receptive are willing to have a "beginner's mind," the willingness to learn, even if they are considered the expert. Because they are not defensive, these people have sharp learning curves and are almost always the ones who come up with the best ideas. They are fun to work with and are great team players because they think "outside the box" and consider differing points of view.

A retired CEO that I know is one of the most receptive individuals I've ever had the privilege of knowing. He was a business leader who was willing to listen to everyone—and who would frequently take the advice of his employees. Rather than stubbornly insisting that his answers were always the best, he would take his ego out of the picture and nondefensively reflect on the suggestions to determine the best possible course of action. He told me, "It made my job so much easier. By being genuinely receptive to suggestions and ideas, rather than shutting them off, I had the advantage of hundreds of brilliant minds working together—rather than having to rely on my tiny little mind."

"Reasonable" suggests the ability to see things fairly, without the self-serving justification that so often clouds our vision. It's the ability to see your own contribution to a problem and the willingness to listen to and learn from other points of view. Being reasonable includes the ability to put yourself in the shoes of others, being able to see the bigger picture, and to maintain perspective. People who are reasonable are well liked and highly respected. Because they are willing to listen, others pay close attention to what they have to say, as well. Reasonable people rarely have enemies, and their conflicts are kept to an absolute minimum. They are able to see beyond their own desires and needs, which makes them compassionate and helpful to others.

If you can strive to be responsive, receptive, and reasonable, my guess is that most everything else will fall into place and take care of itself.

64.

GET OUT OF THE
GRUMBLE MODE

Grumble, grumble, grumble. A great big sourpuss. Someone who takes himself, others, and everything else too seriously. The primary focus is on problems, always critical, frowning, angry, defensive, hurried, frustrated, and stressed. Someone who is waiting for life to get better, for things to be different. Is this you?

Now, use your imagination and zoom forward ten years, twenty, thirty. Are you still blessed with the gift of life? If not, you missed the point, and it's too late to do anything about it. While you're in the midst of your career, while there are problems to deal with, it seems as if life is going to last forever. Yet deep down we all know that in reality, life slips away too quickly. You had your chance to experience and explore life and its many facets—the beauty as well as the hassles. But in a way, you took it for granted. You spent your time grumbling, wishing life was different.

If, on the other hand, you are still lucky enough to be alive years down the road, looking back, are you happy that you were so serious and grouchy for all those years? If you could do it all again—if you could live your life over— are there things you'd do differently? Would you be a different person with a different attitude? Would you have more perspective?

If you knew right now what you're going to know then, would you take it all so seriously? Would you grumble so much?

We all get too serious at times. Perhaps it's human nature. Yet there's an enormous difference between someone who gets serious from time to time, and someone else who is constantly in the grumble mode. The good news is, it's never too late to change. In fact, once you see how ridiculous it is, you can change quickly.

A grumbler will blame life for his sour attitude. He will validate his negativity by pointing to the problems and hassles that he must face. He will justify his position by pointing out the injustices of life and the flaws of others. He hasn't a clue that his vision of life stems from his own thoughts and beliefs.

Charles Schulz has always been one of my favorite cartoonists. In one scene, Charlie Brown's head is hanging and he's slouching his shoulders. While frowning, he explains to Linus that if you want to be depressed, it's important to stand in this posture. He goes on to explain that if he were to stand up straight, lift his head and shoulders, and smile, he wouldn't be able to remain depressed.

In the same way, a grouch can begin to feel better by recognizing the absurdity of a negative attitude. Ideally, to cure yourself of this, you'll want to experience a major insight—a feeling of "I can't believe I was really that way." In order to shift from grumble mode to a less serious nature, you'll need to get a sense of humor—the ability to look back at the way you used to be, and chuckle.

The world has become too serious. If you're part of this sad trend, it's time to change. Life is really short. It's too important to take so seriously.

65.

GET IT OVER WITH

Sometimes it's helpful to be reminded of the obvious—especially when it involves something that is frightening, unpleasant, or uncomfortable. As you undoubtedly already know, it's easy to look at your list of things to do and avoid, procrastinate, postpone, or even conveniently forget that which you least want to do. Somehow you find a way to save the worst for last.

I've created a habit for myself that has undoubtedly saved me thousands of hours of unnecessary stressful or worrisome thinking. The habit I'm referring to involves attending to the most difficult or uncomfortable parts of my day first, before anything else; getting them out of the way.

For example, I may have to resolve a conflict, make a difficult phone call, deal with a sensitive issue, engage in a confrontation, turn someone down or disappoint them, or something else that I wish I didn't have to do. I've made a commitment to myself that, whenever possible and practical, I make that phone call first—before anything else. I get it over with! That way, I avoid all the stress that would have been inevitable had I waited. But even more than that, I find that I'm usually more effective in dealing with the situation because I'm fresher and more alert. I haven't spent the day dreading or rehearsing my conversation. This makes me more responsive to the moment, a key element in solving most problems effectively and gracefully.

187

Without question, saving the most uncomfortable parts of your day for last is an extremely stressful thing to do. After all, it's not going to go away—so it's hanging over your head. Even if you're not consciously thinking or worrying about whatever it is you have to do (which you probably are), you're still aware of it. It's looming. The longer you wait, the more likely you are to blow it out of proportion, imagine the worst, and get yourself all worked up. While all this mental activity is going on, you remain tense and stressed, which of course, causes you to sweat practically everything that comes your way. On a more subtle level, this fear and anxiety that you are feeling is a distraction to your concentration. This affects your performance, judgment, and perspective.

The simple solution is to dive in and get it over with, whatever "it" happens to be. You'll breathe a sigh of relief when it's over and done with. You can then get on with the rest of your day.

I'm sure there are exceptions, but I've yet to experience a single scenario where I've regretted this decision. I know for sure that this strategy has helped me to keep calmer and, overall, happier while I'm engaged in my work. My only concern in sharing this strategy with you is now whenever I call someone first thing in the morning (assuming they have read this book), they might assume we have an issue to resolve.

66.

DON'T LIVE IN AN
IMAGINED FUTURE

If you want to be a happier, less-stressed person, there is no better place to start than with becoming aware of what I like to call "anticipatory thinking," or an imagined future. Essentially, this type of thinking involves imagining how much better your life will be when certain conditions are met—or how awful, stressful, or difficult something is going to be at some point down the road. Typical anticipatory thinking sounds something like this: "I can't wait to get that promotion, then I'll feel important." "My life will be so much better when my 401K is fully funded." "Life will be so much simpler when I can afford an assistant." "This job is only a stepping stone to a better life." "These next few years will be really tough, but after that I'll be cruising." You get so carried away by your own thoughts that you remove yourself from the actual present moments of your life, thereby postponing the act of living effectively and joyfully.

There are other, more short-term forms of this type of thinking as well: "The next few days are going to be unbearable," "Boy, am I going to be tired tomorrow," "I just know my meeting is going to be a disaster," "I know my boss and I are going to argue again the next time we meet," "I'm dreading training that new employee." There are endless variations of this stressful tendency. The details are usually different, but the result is the same—stress!

189

"I used to worry so much about my upcoming annual reviews," said Janet, a comptroller at an auto parts manufacturer. "Finally I decided I had to break my habit. My worry was eating me up and draining my energy. I realized that only once in fifteen years had I been given a negative review—and even then, nothing bad happened. What's the point of worry anyway? What we worry about rarely happens, and even when it does, the worry doesn't help."

Gary, a restaurant manager, described himself as a "world-class worrywart." Every night, he anticipated the worst—hostile or dissatisfied customers, stolen food, contaminated meat, an empty room—"You name it, I worried about it." At the time, he considered himself somewhat wise, as if his anticipatory thinking would head off certain negative events. After many years of anticipating the worst, however, he concluded that, in reality, the opposite was true. He began to see that his worrisome thinking would, in some cases, create problems that weren't really there. To quote Gary, "I would work myself up into a lather and get really upset. Then, because I was anticipating the worst and expecting everyone to make mistakes, I'd be unforgiving of really minor things—a waitress would mix up an order and I'd chew her out. She would become so upset and worried that she'd start making much more serious mistakes. Looking back, most of it was my own fault."

Obviously, some planning, anticipating, and looking forward to future events and accomplishments are an important and necessary part of success. You need to know where you'd like to go in order to get there. However, most of us take this planning far too seriously and engage in futuristic thinking far too often. We sacrifice the actual moments of life in exchange for moments that exist only in our imaginations. An imagined future may or may not ever come true.

Sometimes people ask me, "Isn't it exhausting and unbearable being on a promotional tour—a new city every single day, living out of a suitcase for weeks at a time?" I admit that occasionally I do get really tired, and sometimes I even complain about it, but in reality it's a lot of fun as long as I take it one event at a time. If I spend a great deal of time and energy, however, thinking about how many interviews I have tomorrow, my next ten public appearances, or tonight's long airplane flight, it's predictable that I'll be exhausted and overwhelmed. Whenever we focus too much on all there is to do instead of simply doing what we can in this moment, we will feel the stress associated with such thinking.

The solution for all of us is identical. Whether you're dreading tomorrow's meeting, or next week's deadline, the trick is to observe your own thoughts caught up in the negative expectations and imagined horrors of the future. Once you make the connection between your own thoughts and your stressful feelings, you'll be able to step back and recognize that if you can rein in your thoughts, bringing them back to what you are actually doing—right now—you'll have far more control over your stress level.

67.

MAKE SOMEONE ELSE
FEEL GOOD

After years of working in the stress reduction field, teaching people to be happier, I'm still amazed that some of the most effective methods of reducing one's stress and of improving one's life are actually the simplest. One of the first real-life lessons my parents taught me when I was a child is perhaps the most basic of all: If you want to feel good about yourself, make someone else feel good! It really is that simple. Perhaps it is because this idea is so simple that we sometimes forget to do it.

I've attempted to implement this bit of wisdom into my work life for as long as I can remember. I'd say that the results are nearly perfect. It seems that anytime I go out of my way to make someone else feel good, it ends up brightening my day and making myself feel better as well. It reminds me that so often the nicest things in life aren't "things." Instead, they are the feelings that accompany acts of kindness and nice gestures. It's clear to me that "what goes around, does indeed come around."

Whether it's remembering a birthday with a thoughtful card, taking the time to write a note of congratulations for a job well done, a written or verbal compliment, a friendly phone call, an unasked-for favor, a bouquet of flowers, a note of encouragement, or any number of other possibilities, making someone else feel good—however you do it—is almost always a good idea.

Acts of kindness and good will are inherently wonderful. There's an old saying: "Giving is its own reward." This is certainly true. Your reward for being kind and making someone else feel good are the warm, positive feelings that invariably accompany your efforts. So, starting today, think of someone you'd like to make feel better and enjoy your rewards.

68.

COMPETE FROM THE HEART

Competition is a fact of life. To pretend that it doesn't exist or that you should avoid it all costs would be ridiculous. I've always loved to compete. As a child I was the fastest runner at school and the number one tennis player in Northern California in my age group. I was a high school All-American Athlete and went on to receive a college scholarship in tennis, where I played in the number one position and became the youngest captain in my team's history. I've run three marathons, one of them in three hours.

As an adult, my love of competition has continued, not only in sports, but in business as well. I love to negotiate, buy low, and sell high. I'm proud to be creative, and I'd like to believe I have a flair for marketing. The publishing world is fiercely competitive. I love to see my books doing well, and it's fun to get a standing ovation after a speech. I could certainly make the argument that if I didn't compete well, I wouldn't be helping very many people. So it's important that I compete.

I tell you these things because I've spoken to many people who assume that I'm too relaxed to compete, which is not true. I don't want to give the impression, as I suggest you compete from the heart, that you can't compete effectively if you are a gentle person and become less attached to winning. You can have it all. You can be a winner and financially successful, have fun, compete hard, but never lose your perspective of what's most important—enjoying yourself, giving back, and taking it all in stride.

To compete from the heart means that you compete less from a desperate or neurotic need to achieve and more out of a love for what you do. Competing is its own reward. You are completely immersed in the process, absorbed in the present moments of the activity—the business deal, the sale, the negotiation, interaction, or whatever. When you compete from your heart, the process itself provides the satisfaction; winning is secondary. When looked at in this healthier way, your business life becomes so much easier. You play hard—and then let go. You bounce back almost instantly. You're resilient. You're a good sport. By not being so attached to a specific outcome (winning), you conserve energy and see hidden opportunities. You learn from your mistakes and losses. You move forward. Isn't it obvious that this not-so-attached attitude is in your best interest?

It's been said, "Winning isn't everything, it's the only thing." To me, this is utter nonsense. This philosophy stems from the fear that if you aren't consumed with winning, you never will win. I can tell you that I'm not consumed with winning—never have been, never will be—yet I've won many awards, contests, and first-place finishes. I've also done well financially and made some wise investments. But none of my competitive accomplishments would mean anything to me if they weren't from the heart—if I became so carried away with the competition and outcome that I forgot my humanity. So, to me, the "Winning is everything" motto is grossly inaccurate.

"Maybe it's just because I'm older now, but ever since I turned fifty,

I've become much softer," says Mary, a television producer. "Looking back, I realize how incredibly harsh I was, and how unnecessarily mean-spirited I could be. I'd reject people and their ideas as if they were disposable diapers. People must have hated me. It's weird—but now, I'm just as discriminating and picky as before, but when I have to reject someone, I do so with compassion, without making them feel worse than they already do. I like myself better now, too."

Ed worked for a bio-technology company for five years. Part of his job was to consolidate, cut costs and help his company become "lean." He told me something so awful I almost didn't believe him. "I hate to admit it, but I used to get a thrill out of firing people. I didn't think of myself as a horrible person or anything like that, but cutting costs meant more to me than the effects it had on the people involved. That's how I measured my effectiveness, and that's how I was judged. The fact that these people were scared and didn't know what to do, or that they had three children to support and rent to pay, had no effect on me whatsoever. Then, one day it happened to me! Out of the blue, I was fired, or 'let go' as they put it. I'm sure many people were happy and thought I deserved it. I suppose I did, but I can tell you that, painful as it was, it was probably the best thing that ever happened to me—it opened my eyes to my compassion. I'll never treat people like that again."

Beyond the inaccuracy of this fearful attitude are the social implications. Competing only to win creates poor losers and poor winners. Psychological message: Unless you win, you must feel terrible. This sends a harmful message to kids and feeds into a sense of self-importance that is not only unhealthy, but ugly. How about this message instead:

Give it your very best effort, compete hard, enjoy every moment—and, if you should lose, be happy anyway. This is competing from the heart.

To compete from the heart is a gift, not only to yourself but to those to whom you are a role model and to the world at large. When you compete in this healthier, more loving way, you get the best of both worlds—achievement and perspective.

69.

BACK OFF WHEN YOU
DON'T KNOW WHAT TO DO

Without question, this is one of the most important mental techniques I have ever learned. In fact, it's become more of a way of life than a simple technique. It's made me more productive and, what's more, it's definitely helped me to sweat the small stuff less often at work.

It's tempting, when you don't know what to do, when you don't have an immediate answer, to try to force the issue. You try harder, think faster, attempt to figure things out, and struggle to come up with something. You give it your best shot.

At least that's what most of us assume. The problem is, it usually isn't your "best shot."

It seems ironic, yet often the most powerful and productive thing to do when you don't have an immediate answer to a problem is to gently back off of your thinking, consciously ease up, let go, and extend less effort. Doing so frees your mind and allows your innate intelligence and wisdom to come into play. Put another way, when you feel pressured and stressed, your wisdom is obstructed. But, as you ease off your thinking, it's free to surface and help you. Ideas will come to you.

Most of us have had the experience of (metaphorically) banging our head against a wall, struggling to make a decision or solve a problem. It's so complicated and difficult you simply don't know what to do. There doesn't appear to be any good solution. You're so frustrated that essentially you give up. A few minutes (or hours) later, you're doing something unrelated to your concern. You're thinking about something else when, out of the blue, an answer pops into your head. But not just any answer— a really good one. "That's it!" you rejoice.

This process isn't a matter of good luck. The truth is, our minds are more creative, solution-oriented, clever, and receptive to new answers when we aren't trying so hard—when we relax. This is difficult to accept because it seems important to work hard. And, of course, it is important to work hard. It's just that it's not always to your advantage to think so hard. We mistakenly believe that when we relax, our minds stop working. This is far from true. When we quiet the mind, it's still working—only in a different way.

When your mind is active, full speed ahead, it tends to spin and churn. An over-active mind often goes over the same set of facts again and again, encouraging you to think "inside the box." Your thinking becomes repetitive and habitual because it's going over that which it already knows or believes to be true. Because you're working so hard, you use a great deal of energy, creating unnecessary stress and anxiety. You can probably guess that an overactive mind is the perfect environment for sweating the small stuff.

Somewhere in all the churning of an overactive mind, your wisdom and common sense are lost. These invisible, usually overlooked qualities get buried in a sea of activity and you fail to see the obvious. I know it seems strange that less effort is better, but it's really true. I hope you'll give this strategy a try because I'm virtually certain that it can help your work life become a great deal easier.

70.

ADMIT THAT IT'S YOUR CHOICE

This can be a difficult strategy to embrace. So many people resist it, yet if you can embrace it, your life can begin to change—immediately. You will begin to feel more empowered, less victimized, and as if you have more control of your life. Not a bad set of rewards for a simple admission of the truth.

The admission I'm referring to is your choice of career and the accompanying hassles. You must admit that, despite the problems, limitations, obstacles, long hours, difficult coworkers, political aspects, sacrifices you make, and all the rest, that you are doing what you are doing because you have made the choice to do so.

"Wait a minute," I've been told so many times, "I'm doing what I'm doing, not by choice, but because I have to. I have no choice." I know it can seem that way. Yet if you think through this issue in a reflective way, you'll begin to see that in reality it really is your choice.

When I suggest that you admit that your job or career is your choice, I'm not saying that your problems are necessarily your fault, or that it's realistic that you make other choices. What I am suggesting is that ultimately, all things considered (including necessity, lifestyle choices, income needs, and the possibility of losing your job or even your home), you've made the decision to do what you're doing. You have weighed the options, considered your alternatives, studied the consequences, and, after all is said and done, you've decided that your best alternative is to do exactly what you are doing.

Chris, who works for a large advertising firm, resented this suggestion. In a bitter tone of voice, he told me, "That's absolutely ridiculous. I'm not choosing to work twelve hours a day on these stupid campaigns; I'm forced to. If I didn't work so hard, I'd be blackballed as lazy and go nowhere in this business or in the entire industry."

Can you see what a corner this man had painted himself into? Despite being a bright, up-and-coming advertising account executive, he felt trapped and resentful, a victim of "the way things have to be." He felt absolutely out of the loop when it came to taking any responsibility for his career choices and how hard he was working. The problem is, when you feel trapped and as if you aren't making your own choices, you feel like a victim.

Despite his objections, Chris had decided that it was worth it to work twelve hours a day. His decision was that, all things considered, he'd rather stay in his current position than go through the hassles, risk, and fear of looking for another job, making less money, losing his prestige, missing out on his chance to advance his career, and so forth. I can't tell you if his decision was a good one or not, but isn't it obvious that this was his choice?

Megan, a single mother, had a full-time job as a nurse, but dreamed of becoming a hospital administrator. When I met her at a book signing, she confessed to having spent the previous eight years convincing herself that she was a victim. Frequently, she would tell others, "I'd love to pursue my dream but it's impossible—look at my life."

Despite the very real difficulties she was facing, her greatest obstacle was her unwillingness to admit that her profession was her choice, as was her decision to stay right where she was. She had access to a good school, the grades to be admitted, and some good friends who would help her out with her daughter. None of that mattered, however, because she was a single mom.

The way she described her transformation, one of her friends had convinced her to stop blaming her circumstances. Somehow, she listened, and had the humility to make the change.

The way she put it, "The moment I admitted that *I* was the choice-maker, everything fell into place. I was able to enroll in the part-time night school program, and I'm already a third of the way through. It's frightening to think about how much I was getting in my own way. I realized that I may be a single mom for the rest of my life."

From time to time, most of us fall into the trap of believing that our circumstances are entirely beyond our control. Taking responsibility for your choices, however, takes you out of any "poor me" thinking and into an empowering, "I'm in charge of my own life" mind-set. I hope you'll reflect on this strategy because I'm confident that if you do, you'll feel less stressed and significantly more successful.

71.

BEFORE BECOMING DEFENSIVE,
TAKE NOTE OF WHAT
IS BEING SAID

This is a stress-reducing trick I learned many years ago. Essentially, all that this strategy involves is making the decision to step back, breathe, relax, and genuinely listen before you react or feel defensive. That's it. This simple commitment will help keep you from becoming defensive.

Reacting in a defensive manner usually involves a knee-jerk or instantaneous reaction to something that is being said. Someone makes a comment and you feel hurt. Someone deals you some constructive criticism and you feel the need to defend yourself, your work, your honor, or your point of view. Then after reacting defensively, you continue to think about what was said or what was done. You may even reply with some form of criticism of your own, or get into some kind of power struggle or argument, which usually only serves to escalate the situation.

Suppose your boss takes a quick look at something you've spent months working on. You've poured your best efforts and many late nights into the project. You're proud of your work and expect that others will be too. Your boss, however, says something less than kind. She obviously doesn't appreciate what went into your efforts, nor is she impressed. Her comment is something to the effect of "Couldn't you have done this differently?"

Most people are annoyed if not angered or hurt by this type of insensitive comment. And in case you've not noticed, many people therefore feel hurt and defensive a great deal of the time. It would be nice if everyone were kind regarding their reactions to us and our work, but unfortunately, that's not the world we live in.

If you implement this strategy into your reactions, you would in effect create a buffer or space between the comment and your defensive reaction—time for you to gather your composure and perspective. Does the comment make sense? Is there an element of truth in it? Can you learn something here? Or is the person simply being a jerk? The more honestly you can assess the situation, the more helpful it will be.

While it's not always easy, it sure pays huge dividends to take careful note of what is being said—before becoming defensive. If you do, you'll find yourself becoming less defensive on a regular basis.

72.

COMPLETE AS MANY
TASKS AS POSSIBLE

I don't think most people realize how stressful it can be to have multiple incomplete tasks hanging over your head. Just in case you are one of these people, let me assure you, it is stressful. I like to call this the "almost finished syndrome." It has always intrigued me because often, it would be relatively easy to simply bear down and complete something—not almost complete something, but really complete it 100 percent, and get it out of the way.

On many occasions, I've hired people for everything from a building or repair project around the house to an editing job at work. The person I've hired has been competent, creative, hard-working, skilled and motivated. Yet for some strange reason, they won't quite finish the job. Sure, they almost finish—sometimes they are about 99 percent done, but that last remaining bit seems to hang over their heads (and mine too). Often the last 1 percent takes as long as the first 99 percent.

When you absolutely finish a project, several good things happen. First, you enjoy the nice feeling of a sense of completion. It feels good knowing you've set out to do something and it's done, it's out of the way. Completion allows you to move forward without the distraction of having things hanging over your head.

Beyond the obvious, however, is the respect you feel for yourself and the respect you secure from others when you complete something. You said you were going to do something, and you did it—all of it. You send the message to others that "I am a person of my word," "You can trust me," and "I am reliable." And you affirm the message to yourself: "I am competent and trustworthy." This makes people want to help you—and want to refer business to you and want you to succeed.

Whether you are working for a corporation or a customer, it's undeniable that people will be irritated at you if you don't complete your tasks as agreed. Further, they will be on your back, complaining to you and about you. How can this be worth the stress it so obviously creates? Wouldn't it be easier to simply plan ahead and do whatever is necessary to get the job done—all the way done?

This is an easy habit to break. Take an honest look at your own tendencies. If you are someone who often almost finishes something, take note of the tendency and commit yourself to that last final completion. You can do it—and when you do, your life is going to seem so much easier.

73.

SPEND TEN MINUTES A DAY

DOING ABSOLUTELY NOTHING

I'll bet you're already thinking, "I could never do that," "He doesn't understand how busy I am," or "What a waste of time." If so, I'm happy to tell you that you're off base on all counts. The truth is, I absolutely understand how busy you must be, and I'm certain beyond any doubt that ten minutes of doing absolutely nothing can be the most productive ten minutes of your entire day.

It's precisely because you're so busy that spending ten minutes a day doing nothing is such a great idea. For most of us, a typical workday is sort of like a horse race—the moment we're out of bed, the race has begun. We start out fast and increase our speed as the day goes on. We rush around doing things, being productive, solving problems, and checking items off our ever-so-important "to do" list. It's really no wonder we're sweating the small stuff. Collectively, we're so busy that when the slightest glitch occurs or when something goes wrong, we fall apart and feel frustrated.

Spending a few minutes doing nothing, sitting still, embracing the silence helps prevent you from falling apart. It gives you a chance to regain your perspective and to access a quiet part of your brain where your wisdom and common sense exist. When you sit still and do nothing, it allows your mind the opportunity to sort things out and settle down. It turns what usually looks like chaos into a more manageable moment and provides your mind with a chance to rest and regroup. Ideas and solutions will pop into your head that would never have done so in a frenetic state of mind. When you're finished doing nothing or sitting still, it will often seem like life is coming at you a little slower, which makes everything seem a whole lot easier and less stressful.

One of the most successful CEOs that I've ever met does just this. Every day, regardless of how busy he is, he picks a time to enjoy his few minutes of quiet. He realizes that the busier he is, the more it's needed. He jokingly told me, "My quiet time has made me realize how much idle chatter runs through my mind, mostly nonsense. Clearly, all that noise gets in the way of my being able to see right to the heart of the matter. A few minutes of doing nothing usually cuts through the clutter."

Clearly, there are times when we are trying too hard or moving too fast. This is the ideal time to put on the brakes and quiet down. At first glance, this concept may seem counterproductive. Yet one of the most powerful and sure ways to achieve even more success in your life is to do absolutely nothing for a few minutes a day. You won't believe what you discover.

74.

LEARN TO DELEGATE

For obvious reasons, learning to be a better delegator can make your life easier. When you allow others to help you, when you put your faith in them and trust them, it frees you up to do what you do best.

I've found, however, that many people—even very high-achieving, talented and successful people—are often very poor delegators. The feeling is, "I might as well do it myself—I can do it better than anyone else." There are several major problems with this attitude. First of all, no one can do all things or be two places at once. Sooner or later, the magnitude of responsibility will catch up with you. Because you're so scattered, you'll be doing a lot of things, but the quality of your work will suffer. Learning to delegate helps to solve this problem by keeping you focused on what you're most qualified to do and that which you enjoy doing. In addition, when you don't delegate properly, you aren't allowing others the privilege of showing you what they can do. So, in a way, it's a little selfish.

Jennifer is a mortgage broker in a busy downtown office. Ironically, one of her biggest problems may have been that she was talented and highly competent at practically everything! She felt so secure about her ability to accomplish tasks, that she had become frightened at delegating almost any authority or responsibility. Whether it was making phone calls, negotiating with lenders, communicating with clients, or filling out paperwork, she was involved and on top of it all.

For a while, she managed to juggle things pretty well. As the years went by, however, and her time became more in demand, her unwillingness to delegate responsibility began to catch up with her. She was making more mistakes and becoming increasingly frustrated, forgetful, and stressed out. The people she worked with claimed she had become more short-tempered and arrogant.

At a seminar designed to help her prioritize more effectively, it became obvious to her that her greatest professional weakness was her unwillingness to delegate and share responsibility. She learned the obvious—-that no one can do everything indefinitely, and keep doing it well.

As she began to delegate responsibility—little things as well as those more important—she began to see light at the end of the tunnel. Her mind calmed down, and she began to relax. She could see more clearly where her talent could be used and where her time was best spent. She told me, "I'm back to my old self again."

Often it not only helps you but someone else when you delegate at work. When you ask for help, share responsibility, or delegate authority, you are often giving someone a chance to show you, or someone else, what they can do. In the publishing world, a senior editor might allow an associate editor to do some editing on a particular book, even though it's one of her favorite authors. This not only frees the senior editor's time, it also gives the associate editor a chance to show what she can do—so that she can enhance her career. My friends in the legal and corporate worlds say it works in the same way. Partners in law firms delegate a great deal of work to younger lawyers. Managers of corporations do the same to their less-experienced coworkers. I know that a cynic will say, "The only reason people delegate is to shove off the tough and dirty work on others." And, yes, there are plenty of people who look at it that way—but you don't have to. The point is, there are good reasons—in addition to selfish ones—to practice delegation.

I've seen flight attendants who are masters at delegation. Somehow they are able to get everyone working as a team, so that everyone's job is a bit easier. I've seen others who insist on doing everything themselves. They are the ones who seem the most stressed, and who make the passengers wait the longest. I've seen great chefs delegate certain chores—chopping, for instance—not because they don't like to do it, but because it allows them to focus on other aspects of food preparation that they excel at.

Whether you work in a restaurant, office, airport, retail outlet, or practically anywhere else, learning to delegate can and will make your life a bit easier. Obviously, there are select professions and positions that don't lend themselves well to delegation. For a good number of people, there's no way to say, "Here, you do it." If you fall into this category, perhaps you can practice at home. Can your spouse or roommate help you? Can you delegate certain chores to your kids? Might it be a good idea to hire someone to clean your home, change your oil, or something else that is time-consuming? If you think about your specific circumstances, you'll probably be able to think of at least a few ways to become a better delegator. If you do, you'll free up some time and make your life easier.

75.

STRENGTHEN YOUR PRESENCE

Whether you sell hot dogs to the public or work for IBM, strengthening your presence will make your experience of work more effective and enjoyable. It will enhance your rapport and connection with others, sharpen your concentration, and dissolve your stress.

Presence is a magical quality that is difficult to define. In fact, it's easier to describe its absence. In other words, you can usually tell in an instant the difference between someone who has it—and someone who doesn't. A person with powerful presence is said to be charismatic and magnanimous—people are drawn to his or her energy.

Having a strong presence does not necessarily mean you are outgoing, although it might. It's more a matter of being centered in yourself, comfortable with who you are, and completely absorbed in the moment. When you have a strong presence, the people you are with sense that you are truly "right there" with them, fully present. Your mind isn't drifting somewhere else. Instead, you are focused on what's going on and you are truly listening to what is being said. All of your energy is focused on the person who is talking to you.

So much of the stress that we experience has to do with our minds being in too many places at the same time. We are doing one thing, yet preoccupied with a dozen others. We're distracted by our own thoughts, concerns, and worries. Being present eases our stress because our minds are drawn back to this particular moment, fully attentive to the task at hand. We begin to operate at an optimal mental pace with near-perfect concentration. Although we are working smarter and more effectively, we become calmer and more relaxed.

Our stress is further reduced because of the increased enjoyment we experience. It's difficult to experience genuine satisfaction when your mind is too busy, scattered here and there, thinking about three or four things at once. Yet when your mind is focused, when you are fully present and engaged, your world comes alive. Everyday, ordinary experiences are seen in a new light. In many instances, they begin to appear quite extraordinary. Think about your hobbies. There's nothing inherently exhilarating about bird watching, knitting, or tinkering with your car. However, when you are fully present, these activities and so many others come alive—they become genuine sources of satisfaction. When you are fully present, something as simple as reading a book can become, for the moment, the most intriguing part of your life. You become lost in the story. Yet when you lack focus, that same book can seem boring and insignificant.

When you have presence with others, they are drawn to you. They relax around you and become undefensive. They enjoy your company and feel your sincerity; they feel important when they are with you. They want to do business with you and see you succeed. They are highly cooperative and rarely adversarial. They respect your boundaries and your wishes, and listen to what you have to say. Presence makes every interaction you have more interesting, since every conversation is a potential source of joy. In the absence of presence, all of this disappears. Interactions become habitual, lifeless, and boring.

Sometimes you meet someone and think to yourself, "There is something special about that person. I can't quite put my finger on it, but something is there." So often that "something" is presence.

The way to strengthen your presence is to understand its value. Make an ongoing effort to stop your mind from wandering. When you are with someone, be *with* them. When your mind wanders, gently bring it back. When you are doing something, don't be thinking about something else. Try to have more presence, see it as a worthwhile goal, and it will appear in your life. Once you experience its value—and feel the effects—there will be no turning back. You'll be hooked.

76.

LEARN TO SAY NO
WITHOUT GUILT

One of the ways that many of us get ourselves into trouble is that we commit to too many things; we fail to say no. We say, "Sure, I'll do it," or "No problem, I'll take care of it," when deep down, we know we don't really want to, or that we already have too much on our plates.

The problem with always saying yes is two-fold. First, the end result is almost always feeling overwhelmed, stressed and tired. There is simply a point when enough is enough, a point of diminishing return when our attitude, spirit, even our productivity begins to suffer. Our work suffers, as does our personal and family life. By saying yes too often, we begin to feel victimized and resentful that we have so much to do. Because we tend to feel guilty when we say no, it's often difficult to see that *we* were the ones who got ourselves into this mess by failing to say no more often.

The second major problem with failing to say no when it's appropriate to do so is that you end up with a slightly disingenuous attitude. In other words, you are doing things you really don't want to be doing or shouldn't be doing—but you are acting, on the surface, as if everything is just fine. For example, you'll agree to perform a task or switch shifts with a coworker by saying, "Oh, it's all right," when what you really need is a day off to yourself. Then because you don't get your much-needed rest, you feel victimized by your overwhelming schedule or angry that so many people ask favors of you! Again, you played a key role in the creation of your own stress, but you believe the stress is caused by outside forces, or that it's inevitable.

Saying no without guilt is not selfish—it's a protective necessity. If someone said to you, "Can I have the air you breathe?" you'd probably question their sanity. You certainly wouldn't feel guilty saying no. Yet if someone says, "Can I ask you to do something for me that will push you over the edge and make you feel stressed out and resentful?", there are many times that you'll agree either out of habit, obligation, or simply guilt. Sure, the person probably didn't phrase the request like that, but in reality, that's what is being asked of you.

Obviously there are many times that we can't say no, and many other times when it's in our best interest to say yes or that we simply want to say yes. Terrific! The trick is to use our wisdom, instead of old knee-jerk reactions, to decide when to say yes and when to say no. The key is to be reflective and to ask yourself, "All things considered—e.g., the feelings and needs of the person making the request, the need to say yes, and most importantly my own sanity, is it in my best interest to say yes, or is it okay to refuse? I think you'll discover that, put in this perspective, there are probably many instances when it's perfectly fine to say no.

77.

TAKE YOUR NEXT
VACATION AT HOME

This is a strategy I began using a number of years ago. To be honest, the first few times I gave it a try, I felt sure I was going to be giving up something—fun, relaxation, "my big chance to get away"—and that I would end up disappointed. However, I can honestly say that every time I have stayed home for my vacation, I'm really glad I did. Never once have I regretted my decision.

Vacations are something most people look forward to. They are usually wonderful, well-deserved, and almost always needed. However, a vacation which is ideally designed to be relaxing, rejuvenating, and energizing can at times bring on more stress than it eliminates. Here's a scenario. You finally get a week off. You have a great trip planned, yet you still have to do all that's necessary to leave. You rush to pack and to get all the loose ends and assorted details attended to. You're exhausted. It feels like you haven't had a chance to sit still for weeks. Yet here you are, running to catch another airplane, or rushing out the door to avoid traffic. In a way it seems like you're *speeding up so that you can slow down*. You want to get the most out of your vacation, so you won't be back until late next Sunday night—so you can start work again early the next day. Even before you leave, you know it's going to be tough coming back.

Part of you can't wait to leave because you know you're going to have a great time and get away from your normal routine—but the other part would love the chance to piddle around the house, curl up with a great book, start that yoga or exercise program, or maybe take a couple of simple, but relaxing day trips closer to home. But all that will have to wait because you're going on vacation.

Unfortunately, that other part of you—the part that would love to turn off the phone, play with the kids, clean the closet, avoid crowds, read a book, jog or walk through a local park, plant a garden—rarely, if ever, gets a chance to be nurtured. Your normal life keeps you way too busy, or you're on vacation away from home.

Kris and I had a great home based vacation several years ago. We agreed that work was off limits—even for one minute during the week. No work-related phone calls would be made or returned—just like we were on vacation. As far as we (and everyone else) were concerned, we *were* on vacation. We turned the ringer on the phone to the "off" position.

We hired a baby-sitter (the kids' favorite person, to make it fun for them) to play with the kids every morning for a few hours while we went jogging together, did yoga, or went out to breakfast. We did several little home projects we had wanted to do for years. We worked in the garden. We sat in the sun and read. It was heavenly. In the afternoons, we did something really fun as a family—hiking, swimming, or hide-and-seek. One day, we hired a massage therapist to give us back-to-back massages, and every night we had different take-out for dinner. We had someone come to the house and help us with the cleaning and laundry—just like being at a hotel. We saw several great movies and we slept in every day. It was like having nine Sundays back to back at a great hotel—at a tiny fraction of the cost!

The kids had a blast, and so did we. We felt as if we finally had the chance to really enjoy our home as a family. The kids were able to see their parents not rushed, at home. (What a concept!) I was more relaxed and rested than I ever remember being after going away for a vacation. And it was so much easier, not only to plan, but to get back into the swing of things once I was back—no travel delays, no lost bags, no jet lag, and no exhaustion from traveling with kids. Because we thought of it as a vacation, we lived like royalty that week—massages, restaurants, a house cleaner, take-out—yet we spent a fraction of what we would have spent flying or even driving to some exotic vacation or fancy hotel. But more than all of that, it was truly special. We realized we work so hard to have a home and to care for it—yet it's so rare that we get to enjoy it without being in a hurry.

I'm not advocating replacing all traditional vacations. I love to go away, and I suspect you do too. I can tell you, however, that this is a great way to relax, as well as a chance to do things you almost never get to do at or close to home, while spending very little money. As I look at my calendar, I can see that we have another one of these home vacations coming up soon. I can hardly wait.

78.

DON'T LET NEGATIVE COWORKERS
GET YOU DOWN

Regardless of where you work or what you do for a living, it's almost inevitable that you're going to have to deal with your share of negative people. Some of these people are going to have bad attitudes, others may be cynical or passive-aggressive, and some are probably going to be downright angry.

Learning to deal with negative people is a real art form, but I can tell you with absolute certainty that it's well worth the effort. Consider your options. If you don't learn the secrets of dealing effectively with negativity, then certainly there will be times when these people will bring you down with them. Their negativity will rub off on you, and you'll end up discouraged, frustrated, or even depressed. If you don't do what's necessary to deal gracefully with negative people, you may yourself end up cynical and negative.

You can get to a point where negative people rarely, if ever, bring you down. I believe that the best place to start is by increasing your level of compassion. It's critical to see the innocence, to understand that when someone is negative, they are unfulfilled or in some way unhappy. In most cases, they are not doing it on purpose. Like you, they would prefer to experience contentment and joy. They just don't know how.

Enthusiasm is our most natural state of being. In other words, it's

220

natural to feel inspired, positive, creative, interested, and uplifted by the work that we choose to do. When this quality is lacking, something is wrong. So, when someone regularly expresses negativity, there is almost certainly something missing in that person's life. Their negative attitude and behavior are stemming from a sense of lack, a sense that something is wrong or out of place.

One of the reasons negativity tends to bring us down is that we take it personally or we feel that we are in some way responsible. When viewed with compassion, however, it's easy to see that negativity is usually not directed at us, even if it appears to be. Nor is it our fault.

Try to imagine (or remember) how horrible it feels to be negative and to lack enthusiasm. When you do, it will become clear that if a negative person felt that he or she had any realistic alternatives, they wouldn't be acting negatively. They certainly aren't doing it on purpose or for the fun of it.

Usually, only one of two possibilities will result when two people communicate or work together. Either the more negative person will lower the spirits of the more positive person, or the more positive person will somehow lift the spirits of the other. Your best chance of distancing yourself from the effects of negativity is to remain enthusiastic yourself, therefore being part of the solution rather than contributing to the problem. Instead of focusing on how hard it is to be around a negative person, or over-analyzing the reasons why the person is the way he is, try instead to be genuinely enthusiastic about your work and about your life in general. In all likelihood, you will have a significant effect on the negative people you work with. But, even if you don't, you'll be assured of being less adversely affected.

79.

MAKE THE BEST OF A
"NONCREATIVE" POSITION

I felt compelled to include this strategy because I've spoken to so many people over the years, who either complain about their "non-creative" position or yearn for a more interesting job.

Yet actually, you have a choice regarding any job that you might consider to be noncreative. You can dread each day, count the minutes, remind yourself again and again how boring your job is, complain and whine and wish it were different. Or, you can remind yourself, "It is what it is," and go ahead and make the best of it. You can smile, be enthusiastic, and have a positive attitude. You can find ways to make the job as interesting as it can possibly be. You'll be at work for the same number of hours, either way. In a year's time, you will likely have worked 2,000 hours, perhaps even more.

Once in a while I'll meet someone who will say, "Oh yeah, you haven't seen my job," meaning of course, that this advice doesn't apply in all situations. I beg to differ. In reality, you always have the choice to make the best of it or not.

There's a story I love about two bricklayers who were interviewed by a reporter. The reporter asked the first worker how he spent his day. He replied in a resentful tone, "I spend hours in the hot sun picking up these stupid bricks and putting them on top of each other. Leave me alone."

The reporter turned to the second worker and asked the same question. His response was quite different. He said in a grateful, enthusiastic tone, "I take these simple bricks and turn them into beautiful structures. Without people like me, there would be no buildings and no economy." The moral of the story is, of course, that both workers are correct— depending on how you look at it. I've met toll-takers who have told me that their job isn't to take money from people, but to see how many people they can make smile. I've seen popcorn and candy salespeople who entertain their customers as much as the professional ballplayers, always smiling and always evincing an uplifting attitude.

I've found that those people who approach their job in this positive way are almost always the ones who enjoy their work the most—and usually the ones who move quickly up the ladder if that is what they choose to do. Their attitude is lighthearted and relaxing to themselves, and inspiring and contagious to others.

Customers love these types of people, as do coworkers. They tend to use their lunch and other breaks to study, learn new things, or reflect on their dreams and how they are going to achieve them. They never feel victimized, almost always seek advice from experts, and are willing to listen to those who know the ropes. In every sense of the word, they understand that "it is what it is," and they definitely make the best of it. If you've gotten in the habit of thinking only certain jobs and careers can be fun, give it some more thought. When you make the best of it, almost anything can be "creative."

80.

STAY CLOSE

TO YOUR CENTER

Being centered lies at the heart of a satisfying, productive, and effective life. It's a quality that most people admire and many aspire to. It's a quality I have attempted to nurture for as long as I can remember, and it remains one of my top priorities. There's no question in my mind that any success and happiness I have achieved is a direct result of this quality. And as I look back on my life, it's clear that most of my troubles, failures, and major mistakes have been the result of losing my center and getting off-balance.

Your center is a calm, inspired feeling. When you're centered, you have the sense that you're flowing, on target, and in the groove. You have the feeling that you're on track, that you'll be able to work things out, solve your problems, and get your work done. Despite any apparent difficulties, you feel confident, enthusiastic, and in control. You're able to remain calm and collected in the eye of the storm. Even though you're not exerting tremendous effort, you have a healthy flow of thoughts that are organized and creative. Little things don't bug you.

On the other hand, when you're off-center, you are filled with frightened, scattered, agitated, and other stressful feelings. You tend to panic and assume the worst. You feel pressured and off-balance, as if there's not enough time. Being off-center brings with it feelings of being bothered and frenetic. There is a lack of concentration, and you're out of the flow. You're distracted, stressed, and more prone to making mistakes. Virtually everything bugs you.

You can think of your center as home base, your most natural way of being. Your center is built into your psyche in the same way that an ideal temperature is built into your body. In both cases, you can get off track, but your natural instinct is to return home. Because this is your most natural state of mind, there is nothing you have to do to get there. Rather, it's more a matter of knowing what not to do. In other words, in the absence of a busy, distracted mind, this is the state of mind you would be in most of the time, the feeling you would keep coming back to. Therefore, to return to your center, all you have to do is let go of your stressful thinking, and clear your mind. The rest takes care of itself.

Staying close to your center isn't as difficult as you might imagine. It involves paying attention to your feelings and gently bringing yourself back when you start to drift away. For example, you might be working on a project when your attention starts to drift forward in anticipation of your impending deadline. You begin to imagine the various responses to your work. You think to yourself, "I'll bet she won't approve of or appreciate what I've done."

If you pay attention to the feelings that accompany these thoughts, you'll probably notice yourself beginning to get tense and stressed. In moments like these, you're moving away from your center toward inner chaos and stress.

You're at an important fork in the road. If you continue with your train of thought, it's likely that you will continue to feel agitated, pressured, and maybe even resentful. If you observe what's happening, however, you'll notice that you can choose to back off your thinking for the moment in order to regain your bearings and get back closer to your center.

Built into your center is the wisdom you need to put all odds in your favor and to do everything possible to achieve your goals. In other words, the fact that you're not getting hysterical doesn't mean you're not going to meet your deadline and do a superb job. To the contrary, because you're centered and focused, you'll do a better job in far less time.

There's no question that staying close to your center is in your best interest. I encourage you to explore this idea, work with it, and enjoy the rewards.

81.

FORGIVE YOURSELF;

YOU'RE HUMAN

Earlier I mentioned the quote, "To err is human, to forgive divine." You might as well insert the word "yourself" into this all-so-true observation about being human. Let's face it. We are human, and to be human means you're going to make errors, at least some of the time. You're going to make plenty of mistakes, mess up from time to time, lose your way, forget things, lose your temper, say things you shouldn't have, and all the rest. I've never understood why this simple fact of life—our tendency to make mistakes— is so surprising or disappointing to people. I certainly don't understand why it's such a big deal.

To me, one of the saddest mistakes we make is a lack of forgiveness, especially to ourselves. We constantly remind ourselves of our flaws and previous mistakes. We anticipate future mistakes. We're highly critical of ourselves, frequently disappointed, and ruthless in our self-judgment. We badger and blame ourselves, and often we're our own worst enemy.

It seems to me that to be unforgiving of yourself is foolish and ridiculous. Life didn't come with a fool-proof manual. Most of us are doing the best that we can—really. But we're not perfect. The truth is, we're a work-in-progress. We learn from our mistakes and from stumbling. The best any of us can do, in any given moment, is to call it as we see it, to give it our best shot. None of us, however, certainly not I, have mastered life.

I'm sure that one of the reasons I'm a happy person is that I'm very forgiving of my mistakes. Someone recently asked me how I learned to be so kind to myself. My response was, "Because I've made so many mistakes, I've had lots of practice." She laughed, but it's actually true—I have had lots of practice! I can assure you, however, that my mistakes are not intentional. I truly do the best that I can. My work ethic as well as my standard of excellence is as high as most people's. So my forgiving attitude toward myself has nothing to do with any sort of apathy or a lowering of standards. It's more a matter of being realistic. Like almost everyone else, I have a great number of responsibilities. In fact, it usually seems like I'm juggling ten or twenty balls in the air simultaneously. So, to assume I'll never make mistakes is absurd.

Can you sense how framing mistakes in this more realistic way gets you off the hook? In other words, when you make a mistake—even a stupid one—this more philosophic outlook allows you to keep your perspective and sense of humor instead of beating yourself up. Instead of saying to yourself, "What an idiot," you'll be able to say, "More proof that I'm human."

Jack is a broker for a large financial institution. About a decade ago, a client specifically asked him to invest his life savings in a little stock called Intel! Jack, conservative by nature, convinced his client that it's never a good idea to invest in individual stocks, even at his client's relatively young age of 45. Jack felt it would be a better idea to put all the money in mutual funds.

Obviously, in this specific instance, Jack's advice cost his client a fortune. Jack had given the same advice to a number of other people, and he became despondent and self-destructive. He lost his self-confidence and eventually changed careers. All this because he simply couldn't forgive himself. His friends, colleagues, even his clients, tried to convince him that his judgment and rationale at the time were solid—and that, by most standards, his clients had all done exceptionally well. He should be proud. When someone is unforgiving of himself, however, logic isn't usually received with an open mind.

Luckily, at some point, he hooked up with a good therapist who taught him the obvious—that everything is much clearer in hindsight and that noone has a crystal ball. Eventually, he was able to forgive himself and return to the career he had loved—financial planning.

Obviously, some mistakes are big. An air-traffic control mistake or one wrong move by a surgeon can be deadly. A vast majority of the mistakes we make, however, are not life or death; they are nothing more than "small stuff" disguised as "big stuff." It's true that even small mistakes can cause inconvenience, conflict, or extra work—and, as in the previous example, can be expensive—but what else is new? When did life suddenly become convenient or trouble-free?

While no one enjoys making mistakes, there is something very freeing about learning to accept them—really accept them—as an unavoidable part of life. When we do, we can forgive ourselves, thus erasing all the stress that usually results from badgering ourselves. So my suggestion is simple. Forgive yourself; you're human.

82.

PUT YOUR MIND
IN NEUTRAL

One of the first observations I made when I learned to meditate was that my life seemed to calm down. Although I had the same number of things to do, the same responsibilities, and identical problems to deal with, I felt as if I had more time, which made my work life become easier and more enjoyable. I was still surrounded by chaos, but not as adversely affected by it.

While meditation isn't for everyone, there is a reasonable substitute that can be of tremendous help to anyone wishing to become calmer, less reactive, and more peaceful. It involves learning to put your mind in neutral, which you might think of as a form of "active meditation." In other words, unlike some forms of traditional meditation where you sit down, close your eyes, and focus on your breath, active meditation is something you can incorporate into your daily life. The truth is, there are select times you already engage in this process but because it doesn't seem like much, you probably disregard it as insignificant. Therefore, you never learn to use its power.

Essentially, putting your mind in neutral means clearing your mind of focused thinking. Rather than actively thinking, your mind is in a more passive or relaxed state. When your mind is in neutral, your experience of thought is effortless, yet completely responsive to whatever is happening in the moment. Great teachers, for example, or public speakers, will often describe "being on" or "being in the zone" as those times when their thinking is very relaxed, when they aren't forcing the issue.

My best writing is always produced when my mind is in neutral, when I'm not "trying." As I clear my mind, it's almost as though the writing is done for me. Rather than actively pursuing ideas, the thoughts I need and the best ways to express them come to me or "through me." You may notice that when you suddenly remember an important phone number, a person's name, or a forgotten combination, or when you suddenly have an idea that solves a problem, or when you remember where you put your keys, it's your usually relaxed "neutral thinking" that provides the insight or sudden surge of memory. You'll have a "That's it!" moment. At times like these, the harder you try, the less is achieved. It's this effortless quality that is so critical and helpful. Once you start trying or focusing your thinking, you put yourself back into your more normal or analytical thinking.

The reason most people don't consciously use neutral thinking is because they don't recognize its power, or necessarily even consider it to be a form of thinking—but it is. It's taken for granted, seldom used, and almost always overlooked. However, although it's relaxing and de-stressing, it's also very powerful. When your mind is in neutral, thoughts seem to come to you as if out of the blue. New ideas and insights become a way of life because your mind, when it's relaxed, becomes open and receptive to your wisdom and unique greatness.

Obviously, there are times when it's inappropriate or impractical to put your mind in neutral. When your task requires focused concentration, or when you're learning something brand new, it's often in your best interest to think in a more traditional, analytical mode. You'll be amazed, however, at how powerful this process really is—and how much easier your life can become when you learn to incorporate neutral thinking into your daily life. Whenever you feel highly stressed or as though you're expending too much mental energy, it's a good idea to check in with yourself and decide if a little neutral thinking might be just what you need. You can use neutral thinking as a stress-reducing tool, as a way to relax, or as a way to bring forth greater creativity. The applications are virtually unlimited.

To put your mind in neutral is surprisingly simple. You can only be in one mode of thinking or the other—neutral or active. Like a walkie-talkie, you are either on "talk" or "listen," but never both at the same time. So, as you let go or back off of your analytical thinking, your mind automatically shifts into neutral. Once you accept neutral as a viable form of thinking, the rest is easy. I hope you'll experiment with backing off your thinking and quieting your mind. Soon you'll be more relaxed than you could have ever imagined.

83.

MARVEL AT HOW OFTEN
THINGS GO RIGHT

If you were to eavesdrop on a typical conversation and if you took what you heard to heart, it would be easy to believe that almost nothing ever goes right! The focus of many conversations is limited to, or at least slanted toward, the problems of the day, the ills of society, the obstacles, injustices, and the hassles of work. The emphasis is almost always on the negative or on what's wrong. There's a great deal of discussion of what's wrong with other people, coworkers, customers, investors, clients, and everyone else. The working environment is criticized, and nothing is ever quite good enough.

But have you ever, even once, stopped to marvel at just how often things go right? It's amazing. Literally thousands of events—work related and otherwise—go right every single day, without a glitch. Everything from the vast majority of phone calls that are returned and reservations that are honored, to travel and food safety, dependency on various forms of technology, roofs that don't leak, the competency of coworkers, the interdependence of schedules, right down to the fact that most people are friendly—so much goes right. And for the most part, we take it all for granted. For whatever reasons, we choose to focus on the few exceptions. Perhaps we believe that more will go right if we focus on what's wrong. Conversely, many people are frightened that if they were to become more accepting of imperfection, then more things would end up going wrong—which isn't true.

I fly quite a bit and hear a great deal of complaining about air travel. And it's true that I've had a few horrible experiences pertaining to delays, canceled flights, lost or missing baggage, overbooking, misplaced reservations, and other hassles. However, the percentage of the time that I get where I need to go either on time or nearly on time is astonishing. Given the enormous amount of traffic volume, tight schedules, weather conditions, and dependency on technology, this is truly remarkable. For example, I can wake up in Northern California and before dinner, I'm safely in New York City, baggage in hand—most of the time. I suspect that similar percentages of good fortune are true for most business travelers.

Yet have you ever heard anyone complimenting the airlines? I'm sure that if you have, it's been the exception, rather than the norm. In the midst of a delay, we're far more inclined to become angry and frustrated, maybe even take it personally, than we are to keep in mind that everyone involved is doing the very best he or she can, and that occasional delays are inevitable. The same lack of perspective seems to be true with so many aspects of daily business. A huge percentage of people are friendly, helpful, and courteous. What you hear about, however, are the tiny percentage of people who are rude, insensitive or incompetent. A person may have a dozen tasks to complete in a day. Eleven of them went smoothly; the other one is discussed over dinner.

I'm not going to discount the fact that there are problems to deal with; there most certainly are. Likewise, most of us must face our share of hassles, disappointments, incompetence, and rejection. It's all part of working for a living. It seems that we've become so accustomed to things going smoothly, however, that we expect near-perfection. When we don't get it, we go crazy.

I think it's wise to keep at least a little bit of perspective. When I remind myself of how often things actually go right, it really helps me deal with those things that don't. It allows me to make allowances for the fact that "stuff happens," people make errors, Mother Nature does her thing, and things do sometimes go wrong. What else is new? When I focus on how often things go right, it opens my eyes to the bigger picture and keeps me from sweating the small stuff. I think the same will be true for you as well.

84.

MAKE PEACE WITH CHAOS

One of my favorite "to the point" quotes is from Wallace Stegner. It has helped me immensely in my efforts to keep things in perspective. It reads, "Chaos is the law of nature. Order is the dream of man." Reminding myself of these words has brought me great comfort during times of extreme stress and disorder, as well as in my daily work life. They have given me perspective when I have needed it most.

Indeed, chaos is the law of nature. It's everywhere you look. People are coming and going, trends come and go, there are unlimited conflicting interests and desires, and change is constant and inevitable. Phones are ringing, demands and requests are being made of you, and piles of paper are always on your desk. Even though you try to be fair, you sometimes end up being a hero to one person and someone else's enemy—without even knowing why. A plan unfolds, another falls apart. One person gets a promotion and is thrilled; someone else is laid off, devastated and angry. You try to help, but only make matters worse. People are confused, frustrated, and stressed-out. Just when you think you're about to get on top of things, you catch a cold!

Despite this undeniable law of nature, human beings would love to have at least some degree of order. We would love to be able to keep things the same, predict our future, keep a perfect balance, and know the answers. But no one can make perfect sense of chaos because it doesn't really make any sense—it just exists. Indeed, no matter how hard you try, chaos is right beside you.

There is something magical that happens to you, however, when you surrender to chaos—when you make peace with it. By easing up on your need to control your environment or predict certain outcomes, you're able to learn to work within an environment of chaos without being as affected by it. You begin to experience chaos with a degree of equanimity, with a sense of humor and perspective.

The trick seems to lie in the willingness to embrace rather than struggle against the chaos. In other words, surrendering to the way things really are instead of insisting that things be a certain way. We must come to peace with the fact that chaos is a law of nature—just like gravity. The quality of surrender allows you to look at chaos in a new way. Rather than being caught off-guard and annoyed when you see it, you'll be able to say, "There it is again." You'll acknowledge it and respect the fact that it exists, but not be defeated by it. Rather than fighting against it, you'll be able to choose the path of least resistance.

Allison works evenings in a hospital emergency room. I asked her what chaos meant to her. "Sometimes, every minute is like a nightmare. Someone is rushed in who has been shot—side by side with someone who has been involved in a serious auto accident. Sometimes we have to prioritize that which shouldn't have to be prioritized. People are in pain. There is panic, disorder, concern and tears. Who are you supposed to help first when everyone wants and needs you, all at the same time? We have policies, of course, but they don't always apply or seem fair. It often seems that I'm being yelled at by someone, and rarely is there time to catch my breath. But, despite all the chaos, I've learned to keep my cool—at least most of the time. You have to, or you'd go crazy and, more importantly, the patients' care would suffer." Her description helped me to put that which I perceive as chaos into better perspective.

To a lesser extent than Allison, I have learned to accept chaos as an inevitable part of life. I still don't like it, and I do everything I can to avoid it and keep it to a minimum. Yet, by surrendering to it, I've made peace with the fact that chaos is inevitable. Life isn't as predictable, as organized, or as hassle-free as I would prefer. Instead, it's just the way it is.

I've accepted this, and the results have been astonishing. Many of the same potentially frustrating things happen in my day-to-day life—unreturned phone calls, lost mail, miscalculations, mistakes, overcommitments, deadlines, disapproval, and all the rest. The difference, however, is in the way they affect me, or more accurately, the way they *don't* affect me. Many things that used to drive me crazy are now seen for what they are—just another part of the chaos. I've found that there are enough challenges in life to contend with, without also fighting and struggling against things that can't be controlled or avoided. Chaos is on top of this list. Perhaps you, too, can open your heart to chaos and accept it for what it is. If you do, you'll notice far fewer things getting to you.

85.

PREVENT BURNOUT

Work-related burnout is an enormous, disruptive, and often expensive problem for millions of people. To put it bluntly, people get sick of and fed up with their jobs and crave a better, different, or more satisfying life. Obviously, there's no way to guarantee the prevention of burnout, but there are things you can do to put the odds in your favor.

The keys seem to be balance and growth. If you talk to people who aren't burned out, you'll discover that most of them strive to have a balanced life and to be growth-oriented. This means that while they work hard, compete well, strive for excellence, and have very specific, often lofty goals, they nevertheless insist on having a life outside of work—they enjoy and spend time with their families and friends, they exercise or enjoy hobbies, they value their free time, and strive to make a contribution to their community apart from their work. In addition, people who avoid burnout are constantly attempting to better themselves and to grow, not just professionally, but spiritually and emotionally as well. They attend workshops or classes, they learn new things, and are open-minded. They strive to overcome their own blind spots. They have a fascination with learning and a zest for life. They are curious and enjoy listening to others.

Those who avoid burnout do so with their uplifting, positive attitude. They have outside interests and take advantage of their time away from work. Their interest in and ability to focus on aspects of life other than work keeps their spirits nourished and their lives relatively content. Doesn't it make sense that if a person was fulfilled and satisfied outside of work, he would carry that sense of freshness and wonder into his work life?

When all you do is work, even if it's satisfying, burnout will be the end result. You're too invested in one thing. You become stagnant, predictable, habitual, even boring. Think about it. What would happen if you only ate one food, over and over again, day after day, year after year? It wouldn't matter if it was your favorite food or not—you'd get sick of it. Or what if you watched the same episode of your favorite television show again and again? Boring!

Andrew worked for the same mid-sized company for fifteen years before he caught a major case of burnout. Outside of work, he had no life to speak of—no exercise or outside activities, very few friends (and almost no time spent with them), no pets, and no real hobbies. Because his whole world was his job, he assumed that his job was the source of his burnout. He didn't know what to do. Eventually, he became so frustrated, he resigned.

He didn't have the financial luxury of *not* working for too long, so, within a month or so, he was forced to start looking for a new job. During his month off, however, he tried some new things for the first time—and loved them. He read a few books, took some regular walks, and even enrolled in a yoga class. "I not only had fun but met some really nice and interesting people too," he told me. For the first time in his life, he was having fun. His enthusiasm returned, his burnout disappeared and his perspective was enhanced.

Because he felt so much better, he called his old boss and explained what had happened. Luckily for Andrew, his company hadn't found an adequate replacement and they offered him his old job back—which he accepted with gratitude. He realized that there was nothing wrong with his career, but that his life lacked balance. He made the commitment to keep doing the things he now knew he enjoyed and, in fact, to try even more things as time went on.

This is a strategy that some (really busy) people try to dismiss with the old excuse, "I don't have time to have a life." Unfortunately, this is a narrow, shallow, and extremely short-term way of looking at your life and your career. The truth is for most people, if you don't "get a life," you will end up with a major case of burnout. You're playing with fire—it's only a matter of time. So, you have to ask yourself, "Is it smarter for me (i.e., better business) to continue my lopsided, out-of-balance lifestyle, or might it be better to reserve even a little time for some other things—regular reading, exercise, meditation, an evening with friends, time alone or with family, a course on how to have a positive attitude, or some hobby?"

Even if you're a full-fledged workaholic, or if you are by circumstances forced to work excessive hours, it's a great idea to at least think of balance as a desirable goal. But hard as it can be, you must back up your good intentions with action.

A good place to start is to evaluate your priorities apart from work. If you had to pick, what would be most important? Would it be to volunteer some time or learn to meditate? Is it your spiritual life that's most important? Would it be to schedule a regular date with your partner, child or friend? Or might it be to exercise on a regular basis—or something else entirely? Whatever it is, take a look at your calendar and begin to carve out the time. Anything is better than nothing.

I remember when I began running on a regular basis. The only realistic time for me to do it was early in the morning, well before sunrise. So that's when I did it. Some health clubs are open twenty-four hours a day. Where there is a will, there's a way. Perhaps you can volunteer some time on the weekends, as I used to do for the Big Brothers of America program, or set aside thirty minutes each evening to relax in the bathtub and read a great novel.

Most people take a lunch break. You can spend this time watching a soap opera in the lunch room or learning to meditate. It's your choice. If you work five days a week, a year from now you will have had 260 lunch breaks. In that time alone, you could be well on your way to speaking a foreign language, being in better physical condition, becoming semiproficient in yoga, or many other worthwhile ventures. Whatever it is that you love to do, it will be worth it, and it will help you create a more balanced, growth-oriented life. It's inconceivable that you wouldn't feel better about life and about yourself by creating some balance. And as an added bonus, you'll prevent burnout. It really is that simple.

86.

EXPERIENCE A MAGICAL
TRANSFORMATION

If you're looking for a way to jolt yourself out of being stuck or to give yourself a fresh start, this strategy may help. A magical transformation is like a new beginning. It involves extricating yourself from an old, worn-out way of thinking or behaving, and replacing it with a more positive alternative. The transformation itself occurs out of the blue, often when you least expect it. In a way, the experience is like learning to ride a bike. One minute you can't do it—and the next you can.

Magical transformations can occur in many ways and might be the result of any number of issues you are facing. It might involve giving up a destructive habit or addiction, or it might be a matter of recognizing a self-defeating pattern of behavior or attitude and somehow seeing how to change it.

The easiest way to experience a transformation is to mentally review your most negative traits and habits, the ones you know you'd like to change, and to make a mental note that you'd like to see it differently. If you drink too much, for example, you might wish to experience a magical transformation and become a nondrinker. If you're always running late, you may wish to become a person who gives himself a little extra time. If you tend to be impatient, perhaps you'd like to become someone who is known for her patience. I was once sitting with a man who, in the midst of our conversation, had the sudden realization that he was virtually always critical. It was as if he saw it for the first time. I remember him saying, "I can't believe I've always been that way." From one extreme to another, magical transformations contribute to a changed life. It's as if you have a sudden shift upward in your level of understanding. They seem to occur most often shortly after you tell yourself you'd like to see things in a new way.

These positive transformations are life changing, not only because of your isolated shift in perspective, but also because they reinforce your resiliency, your ability to bounce back and change. Someone who is habitually frenetic who becomes genuinely calm tucks away this transformation into his memory. Then whenever he feels discouraged, he remembers this experience as validation of his strength and his ability to make changes. Once you experience a magical transformation, your sense of confidence in yourself will be enhanced.

I've had a number of these transformations during my lifetime, and I hope to have many more. One, in particular, stands out in my mind.

Like most people, I was very sensitive to criticism. When someone would make a suggestion or criticize me in some way, I would feel attacked. Usually, I would act or at least feel defensive. I would defend my ground and my actions.

About fifteen years ago I had an instant change of heart, or magical transformation. I was standing in my kitchen with my back turned when some heavy criticism was thrown in my direction. My initial instinct was to coil up and defend myself. My thoughts began to spin and churn, as they had always done before. But for some reason, I recognized my own mental contribution to the problem and, for the first time in my life, I realized that I had a genuine choice in how I was going to respond and in fact, how I was going to feel.

I could see myself as the thinker of my own thoughts. In other words, I recognized that although the critical comment was directed at me, it was now in my court, and only my own thinking could keep the experience alive in my mind. Without my consent, the comment had no power! The metaphor that came to me was that of a check—it's not worth anything unless it's signed. In the same way, in order to feel hurt by criticism, I have to take the bait.

For the first time in my life I was able to dismiss the comment and go on with my day—no hurt feelings, defensive behavior, or retaliation. I wasn't pretending that it didn't hurt—it really didn't. The comment was made and I let it go. I had experienced my first magical transformation and to this day, I'm seldom bothered by criticism. Obviously, my experience is only one out of an unlimited number of possibilities. Yours will be unique.

Experiencing a magical transformation involves recognizing that you do, indeed, have a choice. I wanted to share this story and this strategy because so often, once you are aware that magical transformations are possible, you begin to look for them in your own life. When you're frustrated, for example, you might find yourself saying something like, "I know it's possible to see this (or experience this) differently." And often, this awareness or even hope that there is another way of experiencing your conflict, dilemma, or problem opens the door for it to occur. I hope that by opening to the possibility, you too will have a magical transformation.

87.

AVOID "IF ONLY, THEN" THINKING

I first began reflecting on this idea more than twenty years ago. It has always struck me how often many of us fall into this tendency, or mental habit, that virtually guarantees a great deal of stress and a lack of satisfaction. As I have reflected on this concept, and as I have engaged in this habit less often in my own life, I've found that my stress level is substantially lower than it once was. I have also noticed that I truly enjoy virtually everything that I do that is related to my work. In the process, I have also become more effective. I hope that you can realize the same types of benefits by becoming more familiar with this concept and by putting it into practice in your own life.

Just as it sounds, "if only, then" thinking refers to the oh-so-common tendency to fill your head with thoughts designed to convince yourself that "if only" certain conditions were met—then you'd be happy (or satisfied, or less stressed, or peaceful, or whatever). It's a form of longing, or imagining that if things were different, boy-oh-boy would things be great! Here are a few examples of what could be a very long list: "If only I made more money, then I'd feel secure," "If only I received more attention or credit, then I'd feel good," "If only he (or she) were different, I'd have a better life," "If only I could go on a certain vacation, then I could relax," "If only I could make some headway on this in-basket, then I'd spend some time with the kids," " If only I could live in a larger home, then I'd feel satisfied." You get the picture.

In order to see the flaw in "if only, then" thinking, all you need to do is think back to a few of the thousands of times you told yourself essentially the same thing, and ended up getting exactly what you wanted, and you still weren't satisfied. Or if you were, it didn't last for long! You convinced yourself that if only you could get that new car, you'd feel great. But a day or two after getting it, the thrill was gone. You told yourself that a new relationship would fulfill your every need, yet when you found that "perfect person," you inevitably found that you struggled with him (or her) too. You make more money than you used to, yet despite telling yourself how secure you'd feel when you did, you still worry and want even more.

This type of thinking is destructive to the human spirit because longing to be somewhere else, or to be doing something else, or to have different circumstances is almost by definition stressful. It's almost like saying, "I'm going to put my happiness on hold. I'll be happy later, once things change." How often do you forget to appreciate the life you already have because you are too busy thinking about how grateful you will be somewhere down the road? It's almost impossible to be content when you're focused on future plans because your mind isn't engaged in the moment, but focused elsewhere.

Obviously, I'm not suggesting that you don't have to know where you're going or that it's not important to have a plan. You probably do, and it is. Neither am I saying you don't have to work hard to achieve your goals. You do. What I'm talking about here is the tendency to discredit or under-acknowledge the life you have now at the expense of some imagined future. So, whether you're an entrepreneur, work for someone else, or are climbing the corporate ladder, don't forget to enjoy and absorb yourself in every step along the way. Keep in mind that happiness is a journey, not a destination. My dad used to say to me, "If you start out at the bottom, enjoy it while you can. Because if you do, you won't be there for long." What I've found is that his words of wisdom are true in whatever you do for a living. When you are fully engaged and make the best of what you are doing, you will bring out the best in yourself.

My advice is simple. Go ahead and be all you can be, dream your dreams, and have a plan. But never forget that the secret to satisfaction isn't getting to some imagined destination, but in enjoying the ride along the way.

88.

ELIMINATE THE WORRY FACTOR

Those of you who are familiar with my work may be aware that because it's such a destructive force in the lives of so many people, worry is one of my favorite subjects to tackle. In fact, my entire book *Don't Worry, Make Money* is dedicated to overcoming this often insidious tendency. In it, I make the connection between less worry and more success.

For our purposes here, there are several additional reasons to eliminate worry from your life. First and foremost, it's highly stressful. Think about how you feel when you're worried. It's all-consuming and energy-draining. It encourages you to focus on problems and on how difficult your life has become. When you worry, you are on edge and tense. Therefore you tend to be easily bothered or irrationally upset—the perfect conditions for sweating the small stuff.

When you worry, it's more difficult to concentrate and focus your efforts. Rather than being completely absorbed in your work, your mind tends to wander toward an uncertain future or a mistake-ridden past. You anticipate trouble, whether it's realistic or not—and you review past mistakes as a way to justify your concerns.

For example, you might be worried about an upcoming review of your work by your employer. Rather than giving your job your undivided attention, you spend the week prior to your review thinking and worrying about the possible consequences. You remember the negative highlights of your last job review. Your mind drifts and your thinking is scattered.

Instead of being as highly productive and efficient as you usually are, your work suffers and you become more insecure. Obviously, this insecurity and the accompanying less-than-ideal performance will be noticed by your employer and possibly reflected in your review. It's a vicious cycle that begins with worry.

Worry is also contagious. When you worry, it either suggests or reinforces the idea (to others) that there is something legitimate to worry about. It spreads a negative message and a feeling of fear. This feeds into an overly cautious, sometimes even paranoid working environment. When people are frightened, it sets the stage for selfish and narcissistic behavior where self-protection is the first priority.

Ellen, an ex-big-time worrier, manages a large florist. She told me she used to worry all the time, especially about large events such as weddings. She told me of one specific example when she finally realized she had to change.

She and three others were preparing for a large wedding. To date, this was one of their largest orders, and she was worrying more than usual. She feared she had written the order down incorrectly and she felt certain that there was no way they would have the complete order done in time. She just knew something major was going to go wrong. She was rushing around, visibly shaken, when she finally realized that the others were doing the exact same thing. They were making obvious mistakes, knocking over vases, cutting in the wrong places and every other mistake a florist might make. Ellen told me, "It was so bad, I just had to laugh out loud." It was obvious that her nervousness and sense of worry was indeed contagious—and that everyone around her had caught it, too. Ellen took her colleagues out for a coffee break, where everyone loosened up and relaxed. When they got back to the shop, they proceeded with their normal efficiency, not getting overly stressed about the order—and the arrangements came out perfectly.

A powerful, internal shift begins to take place as you lose your respect for worry. A new type of trust develops within yourself. In a very practical way, you begin to trust that in the absence of worry, you'll know exactly what to do and you'll know how to go about it.

An ideal example of this process exists in the field of public speaking. You can spend years worrying and telling yourself how hard it is to speak to large groups of people. You can anticipate the worst and play it out in your mind. And every time you try, you're even more convinced because your fear is validated by your negative experience.

Yet many speakers will tell you, as I will now, that you won't stop worrying by having good experiences—as much as you will have good experiences by letting go of worry. It's one of those "put the cart before the horse" issues. In other words, when you decide to throw caution to the wind and set your worry aside, you'll miraculously discover that speaking to a group is not all that different from speaking to a single person. In the absence of worry, you'll know what to say and you'll be responsive to the subject matter and the needs of the group. The same internal process occurs regardless of what you do for a living—get rid of the interference of worry, and your wisdom will surface.

Please understand that when I say "throw caution to the wind," I don't mean you stop caring, or that you become indifferent to the outcome. I'm merely suggesting that you become aware of how credible and competent you are when you let go of the interfering and distracting aspects of worry. I encourage you to see for yourself how brilliant and resourceful you can be when you let go of worry. As this happens, your life will begin to seem easier and less stressful.

89.

ASK FOR WHAT YOU WANT, BUT
DON'T INSIST ON GETTING IT

There's an old saying: "If you don't ask for what you want, you're not going to get it." And while this isn't always the case, from a certain perspective it does make a great deal of sense. After all, if your boss doesn't know you want a raise or that you feel you deserve one, you can't really blame her for not extending the offer. Or if you'd like to have lunch with someone or pick their brain for ideas, chances are, it probably won't happen if you don't ask. If you're selling something, it's usually a good idea to ask for the sale—you certainly increase the odds.

The only problem with the "be willing to ask" philosophy is that it doesn't take into consideration the large percentage of the time that you don't get something, even when you do ask or when you feel you deserve it. So, the old saying, if taken literally, can create some frustration.

Any potential frustration, however, can be prevented by including a lack of insistence upon your desired result. In other words, it's terrific, courageous, and important to ask for what you want, but if you're attached to the outcome, you could be in for a long and ongoing series of disappointments in your life. You'll only be happy when you get exactly what you want and when life accommodates you with your preferences. Once you detach from the outcome, however, you'll win either way. You'll either get what you want—or you'll be okay with the fact that you didn't.

The key to becoming less attached to the outcomes of your requests is to depersonalize them. In other words, try to see that more often than not, being turned down has very little to do with you. For example, if you ask for a raise, your request may or may not be possible, depending on factors other than you—your company's budget, the implications to other workers, rules within the department, and so forth. Similarly, if you ask for a sale, you're more likely to get it. However, it's obviously the case that your customer may not want or be able to afford what you're selling.

Dennis, an accountant who worked for a grocery chain, loved his job except for one thing—the location of his office. His office was upstairs in the middle of the building. He told me, "It wasn't too bad, but it had no window. I felt I would work better if I had natural light." The problem was, there were only a few offices that had windows.

Dennis decided to act. He asked his boss what it would take to ever be allowed to change offices. He told him, gently, that he loved and appreciated his job, but that he has a tendency to get a little claustro-phobic. He made it clear that it wasn't a "deal breaker," but that he would surely appreciate it if could be worked out. A week or two later, he wrote a thank-you note to his boss for listening to his concern and for taking it into consideration. The letter wasn't written with any edge or demands—just a simple note.

When I last spoke to Dennis, he still hadn't been moved. He did say, however, that he felt fine about it. He had done everything he could. The good news was that his boss had brought it up on several occasions and had said that, should something open up, he *would* get the new office. Dennis felt confident that, eventually, he would indeed have a window. I loved his story because it shows how it's possible to not get what you want (at least right away), and still feel good about it. It demonstrates the wisdom of asking for what you want—but not always insisting on it.

I've written or called hundreds of people during my career who have never written back or returned my call. I've learned that people are often overwhelmed and overcommitted, and therefore unable or unwilling to help me. Instead of feeling defeated, I try to focus instead on how grateful I am that many other people have returned my calls or answered my letters. I've learned that if it's in the cards, it happens. If not, that's okay too. The key to success is to keep trying, stay out there, but to detach from the outcome.

Sometimes it's helpful to put yourself in the shoes of the person you are asking. Many years ago, I wanted to get in to see a certain professional and was told that I couldn't because he wasn't taking any new clients. I persisted, but never succeeded. Finally, I spoke to the receptionist in an impatient tone and said, "Look, I really need to see him. Isn't there anything you can do?" She responded to me in a very calm and respectful manner. Her words were, "I'm truly sorry, Mr. Carlson, but the doctor has a three-year waiting list. He works six days a week, twelve hours a day, and hasn't had a vacation in over five years. He's doing the best he can, but he too would like to have a life." His schedule put my own busyness into better perspective.

When you're willing to ask for what you want but don't insist on getting it, there are some potential hidden benefits as well. For example, you sometimes bring out the compassion and generosity in others. Several years ago I arrived in Atlanta very late one evening. Despite having a confirmed reservation, the hotel was overbooked and was turning people away. The man in front of me was enraged and became very threatening.

He insisted on getting his way—but there were no rooms. He stormed out, defeated and angry. He was totally oblivious and insensitive to the fact that it wasn't the receptionist's fault. It wasn't personal.

I walked up to the receptionist and in a gentle voice I said, "I understand your predicament and don't blame you a bit. These things happen. I would appreciate it so much if you would help me. I know you don't have any rooms here, but could you help me find another hotel, close by?" I thought it was wise to ask—as long as I didn't insist. (I had just been reminded of how much good the insisting does.)

She was very nice and apologetic. Remarkably, she said she had some great news. She had completely overlooked the fact that one of the guests had to leave in an emergency and wouldn't be back. It turned out to be the largest and most expensive suite in the hotel! Because I had been so patient, she gave it to me at the lower rate.

The question is, why didn't she remember this empty room and give it to the angry man in front of me? He was there before I was, and seemed a lot more desperate for the room. I think the answer is pretty obvious. His insistence pushed her away and may have even contributed to her "forgetfulness." When I was talking to her, however, she relaxed and felt less pressure. Her memory returned and I ended up getting a few hours of much-needed sleep. So be sure to ask for what you want, but don't insist on getting it.

90.

REMEMBER THE WHOLE STORY

I predict that if you experiment with this strategy, you'll begin to realize that in most cases, your life isn't quite as bad as you can sometimes make it out to be. This in turn will heighten your perspective and enjoyment surrounding your work, and help you relax and reduce your stress.

As you probably know, it's extremely seductive, when sharing with others about your workday, to focus primarily on the negative. A fairly typical response to the question, "How was your day?" is, "I had a really tough one." If you elaborate, it's likely that you'll focus on how little time you had, your nightmare commute, the tough issues and conflicts, problems, difficult people, hassles, your sense of hurry and being rushed, negative coworkers, all the things that went wrong, and your demanding boss. And to a certain degree, you're probably right on the mark. For most people, a typical workday is really tough and often downright exhausting. But is this negative assessment the whole story—or is it only part of it? Are you recharacterizing your day the way it actually was—or are you being selective in what you choose to remember and discuss?

I encourage you to be completely honest with yourself as you ponder the following questions about your latest workday: On your way to work, did you stop for a bagel and coffee? Did you take a lunch break? If so, who were you with? Was it enjoyable? How was the food? Did you have any stimulating conversations during the day? Any new insights? Did you have a chance to express your creativity? Did you see any pretty sights or nature—a waterfall in your courtyard, trees and flowers, birds or animals? Did you hear any good jokes today? Did anyone give you a compliment? Did you listen to any good music in the car or perhaps an interesting talk show? Did your in-basket get any smaller? Did you resolve any conflicts? Are you being paid?

I'm not trying to get you to become unrealistically happy. As I mentioned above, I'm well aware that work can be (and often is) difficult. Yet let's not forget that if you answered any of the questions above with a positive response, your day was brighter than a vast majority of the world's population. This doesn't mean you should pretend that you had a wonderful day—yet isn't it easy to take the nice parts of your day completely for granted? We treat them as if they never happened, as if we had no perks, simple pleasures, or conveniences. Indeed, when you examine the above questions, it becomes clear that, for most of us, our day is not entirely negative—or even close to it. If this is the case, why do we describe it as such?

I think there are several reasons. First of all, many of us want to either impress others with our busyness or difficult life, or we are seeking sympathy. Rarely will you hear either spouse say to each other after a long day at work, "I had a terrific day. Lots of things went right." The fear is that to do so (even if it were true) might be seen as a weakness—as if your life were too easy. I know for a fact that some men complain to their wives about how difficult their workday is, in part, because they don't want to be expected to do too much once they get home!

In addition, most of us want to be appreciated and respected for how hard we work. By sharing all that went right during the day, the fear is that we might lose some of that appreciation or respect, and be taken for granted.

But more than all of that, focusing on the negative is just a bad habit—plain and simple. Complaining is contagious, and everyone seems to do it. So, unless you make a conscious effort to do less of it, you're probably going to continue for as long as you are working.

Since I began focusing more on the best parts of my day, my eyes have been opened to a whole new world. I've become increasingly aware that there are all sorts of interesting and enjoyable aspects to my day that were virtually invisible to me prior to this shift in focus. I no longer take for granted those stimulating conversations, interesting challenges, personal contact with friends and others. Perhaps most of all, my appreciation has been heightened. Because of this, I find myself less bothered and annoyed by the hassles and all the "small stuff" that I must deal with on a daily basis. I'm sure the same will be true for you.

91.

TAP INTO YOUR SECRET

STRESS-BUSTER

Many years ago I was home one night scrambling to finish a work-related project that was due the next day. I was uptight, stressed, hurried, and agitated. In those days, it seemed like I was always nervous about something.

A friend of mine who was considerably calmer and wiser was visiting from out of town. In his customary casual style, he looked at me very compassionately and said, "Richard, are you breathing?" Shocked and a little annoyed by what I believed to be a superficial question, I replied, "Of course I'm breathing, aren't you?"

He went on to explain that in his experience, most adults breathe too shallowly and do not get enough air into their lungs. He put his hand on my chest and showed me what I was doing (or wasn't doing). It was one of the most surprising moments of my life. I realized that I was breathing so superficially, it was almost as if I weren't breathing at all!

To my great surprise, as I began to take slightly deeper breaths, I felt instantly better. My body seemed to relax and my thinking became clearer. As I have become more practiced and a little better at taking deeper breaths, I've also noticed that I have more energy and, perhaps more than anything else, I almost never feel panicked the way I used to.

I'm not an expert in this area, but I have learned to breathe more deeply over the years. And although I can't prove it, I know in my heart that doing so has played a significant role in my own journey of becoming a less-stressed person. I'll bet that if you put a tiny bit of attention on the way you breathe, you may decide that it's in your best interest to learn to breathe a little deeper. In fact, you may be shocked at how quickly you can make an improvement in the way you feel and in the quality of your life.

The idea of breathing a little deeper makes sense if you think about it. After all, if you're really scared to do something, but you have to do it, what do you do? You may not even be aware of it, but you probably take a really deep breath. Have you ever seen a professional basketball player right before he or she shoots an important, pressure-packed free-throw? In most instances, the athlete takes a long, deep breath before taking the shot. What I'm suggesting in this strategy is that you incorporate deeper breathing into your everyday work life. Rather than waiting until you feel desperate to take a deep breath, why not instead take deeper breaths as a regular practice?

If you think about it, it's somewhat obvious. We're all rushing around like little bees, getting all sorts of things done. Yet if you aren't getting enough air in your lungs, is it any wonder most of us feel so panicked so much of the time? Taken to an extreme, it's as if we're suffocating. If you've ever been under water just a little too long, you know how paranoid and frightened you can become. In a way, when we aren't breathing deeply enough, it's as if we're all spending our workdays underwater—at least some of the time. True, we aren't going to drown, but we may pay an enormous price in terms of self-created stress.

Check in with your breath. How deep is your inhalation? Notice what happens when you consciously breathe just a little deeper. If you're like me, you'll instantly feel more relaxed and less stressed. When you're getting enough air, the world seems a little less crazy and things are brought into perspective. Life seems to move at a more manageable pace and many of those everyday annoyances don't seem to bother us quite as much. In a nutshell, you're less likely to sweat the small stuff if your body is getting enough air!

I think of my breathing as my own secret weapon that I can use against stress at any time. It's simple, produces quick and significant results, and is completely private. No one other than myself ever has to know that I'm breathing a little deeper in an attempt to relax. I hope you'll add this "weapon" to your arsenal against the stress in your work life. It's certainly helped me, and I'll bet it will help you too.

92.

SPEAK TO OTHERS WITH
LOVE AND RESPECT

Not too long ago, I was being interviewed by an extraordinary person who, off the air, shared with me a simple yet life-shaping story that he said contributed to his gentle, kind manner. I asked him if I could share his story and he said that I could.

Some twenty years ago, this man had bought a brand-new car with an area in the back that would accommodate his large, furry dog. Not too long after purchasing the car, he had it washed in an upscale, expensive car wash. Afterward, however, he noticed that the back portion of the car was still filled with dog hair. Because he had paid so much money for the wash, he felt ripped off and became upset.

He complained to the staff, but to no avail. They insisted that their policy was to "not vacuum the trunk." Apparently, they considered his "dog space" to be a trunk and therefore refused to do the extra work. When it became apparent that his complaining wasn't going to help, he demanded to see the manger.

He spent the next five minutes yelling at and chewing out the manager of the car wash in what he described as a harsh, obnoxious and arrogant tone. When he had finished his rampage, the manager looked him in the eye and in a gentle, undefensive tone, asked the man if he were finished. He said that he was.

The manager then told the customer in a calm, unthreatening tone that he would go ahead and vacuum the car himself until every dog hair was gone. Then, in a compassionate but firm voice, he said, "I have to ask you, sir. What makes you think you have the right to speak to me or anyone in that harsh, demanding manner?"

He was stunned and embarrassed, realizing that nothing gave him that right. He told me that he has spent the last twenty years trying to live up to what he learned that day—remembering that everyone deserves to be treated with respect, even if he is justifiably angry or disappointed. It was interesting to speak to this man because I was certain that he really had learned something that day, in of all places—a car wash! It was difficult to imagine that this person had ever been rude or insensitive to another human being. He was gentle, sincere, kind, and centered, a real pleasure to be around and, incidentally, one of the top people in his field.

When I observe others who are rude, demanding, or insensitive to a flight attendant, a stranger, waitress, grocery clerk, or whomever, I often ask myself the same question that the car wash manager asked the man in my story: "What gives this person the right to speak like this?" I still don't know the answer to this question—do you? Sometimes people believe that if someone is doing his job, he ought to put up with snobby customers or an arrogant boss. It's always seemed to me, however, that if someone is doing his job, and I'm one of the beneficiaries of their performance, that's all the more reason to speak to him with gratitude and respect. But even beyond what's right and wrong, it's just smart business to speak to others with love and respect.

If you're looking for ways to make your life less stressful, this is one of the keys.

93.

DON'T GO THERE

This is one of my favorite popular expressions. I have no idea where it came from, but I believe that it has some very important implications for all of us. It certainly does for me.

"Don't go there" is an expression that essentially means you know that if you continue on a certain path—thinking in a certain way, arguing, inquiring, discussing, behaving, or whatever—it's going to lead to a predictable, negative result, guaranteed. So, very simply, don't do it! Stop. Don't continue.

For example, you might be asking someone at work a series of personal questions and notice that he is getting increasingly defensive and angry. If there is no actual reason you need the answers to your questions, this might qualify for the "don't go there" wisdom. To continue with your questions virtually guarantees that you will create problems for yourself now or down the road. You'll have a new enemy, or at least someone who is mad at you. Why continue? The same idea applies to so many interpersonal issues. Often, we know deep down what's going to happen if we say certain things to certain people. Sometimes it's best to just "not go there."

Suppose you're feeling sorry for yourself and completely overwhelmed. You're thinking about quitting your job and about how horrible your life has become. Here, the "don't go there" expression would mean "stop thinking along these lines." To continue only guarantees that you're going to feel even worse. What's the point? Wouldn't it be wiser to wait until later, when you feel better, to analyze your life? Why go on when you know the result is going to be pain?

I once had a friend who was about to have an affair. He asked me what I thought. My exact words to him were, "Don't go there." For whatever reason, he didn't, and he and his wife were able to improve their marriage.

For some reason, the simplicity of this expression carries a great deal of power. It's so straightforward that it's capable of stopping you in your tracks, or at least helping you to see the futility of certain thoughts or acts. It can provide the necessary wisdom and perspective to change direction or avoid certain mistakes. So, when you say it to yourself, or when someone says it to you, you're able to take the advice seriously.

I've witnessed many instances where this simple idea could have saved a person's job, prevented an argument, or a great deal of unnecessary stress. Suppose someone is angry at his boss and decides to tell him off while he is still angry. A good friend could have said, "Don't go there." He may have thought twice. Or one of those ridiculous "I'm determined to be right" arguments is just getting started. This same advice could have provided the wisdom to simply allow the other person to be right, thereby saving the trouble and stress of the argument, and leaving time for a peaceful lunch. So often, going down a negative path leads to a series of stressful and destructive actions. If you can nip the problem in the bud early by using these simple words, you can prevent a great deal of stress.

I'd be willing to bet that you can think of many applications of this expression in your life. There are many instances where as simplistic as it may seem, "not going there" is really solid advice.

94.

REMEMBER TO APPRECIATE
THE PEOPLE YOU WORK WITH

One of the most consistent complaints of working people in virtually all industries is that they either feel completely unappreciated, or at the very least under-appreciated. There seems to be an unspoken assumption that workers are lucky to have jobs—and the fact that they have jobs is appreciation enough. Any demands, expectations, or even hopes of verbal or behavioral appreciation is often treated as trivial or unnecessary.

The problem is, people need and deserve to feel appreciated. People who feel appreciated are happier, less-stressed, and more loyal than those who feel taken for granted. Overall, they are harder workers and are excellent team players. They quit less often, show up on time, get along with others, exhibit abundant creativity, and strive for excellence. Conversely, people who are (or even feel) unappreciated often feel resentful and lose their enthusiasm for their work. They can become apathetic and lazy. They are easily bothered, and certainly are no fun to be around or work with. Perhaps most of all, people who feel unappreciated have a tendency to sweat the small stuff.

Unfortunately, I can't create a strategy for feeling appreciated, only one for remembering to appreciate. However, I think you'll discover that, in a way, the two are very closely related. In fact, it has been my experience that the more committed I have become to remembering to appreciate those I work with, the better I have felt about myself. And as an added bonus, those I work with seem to appreciate me much more than ever. In this instance, it really does seem that what goes around comes around.

Even if someone is "just doing her job," it's critical that she feels appreciated. My suggestion is to go out of your way to make sure those you work with know that you genuinely appreciate them. Praise often. Dish out compliments. If it's at all possible and appropriate, send a card, e-mail, or handwritten note. Make a phone call or, even better, look the person in the eye and tell them how much you appreciate them. On occasion if you can do it, and again when appropriate, send a small gift or token of your appreciation. Make your appreciation known. Do all of this often.

For example, even if it's the job of the mailroom guy to bring your mail, thank him when he drops it off. Notice his reaction and notice the way it makes you feel too. Thank the person at the copy shop for copying your papers. So what if it's "her job." Likewise, send an occasional card to thank someone you do business with for using your service. It will always come back to you, several times over. And, even if it didn't, it would still be worth it. Make sure your secretary and/or staff is aware that you value their work and their presence in your life. Make a point of thanking them.

Several times a year, I put a thank-you note outside with our normal garbage delivery and, inside the card, I include a small tip for the garbage collector, who does an extraordinary job. Not only does he wave to me on those occasions when he sees me jogging early in the morning, but he's always happy to take extra trash to the dump.

By remembering to appreciate the people you work with, your business relationships will be enhanced and, as importantly, you'll be actively making everyone's day a little brighter—including your own.

When you dish out a dose of appreciation, take note of how you feel. In all likelihood, you'll feel peaceful and satisfied, like you're on target and headed in the right direction. Offering genuine appreciation is quite stress-relieving. It feels good, not only to the person receiving the appreciation, but to the giver as well. It feels good to know that you're helping another person feel acknowledged. It's also nice to know that you're helping that person bring out the best in themselves.

I remember a time when I was having some difficulty with a person I was working with. I felt she wasn't meeting my professional expectations, and the two of us were engaged in what seemed like petty arguments. Then it dawned on me that, in reality, she was really working hard and probably felt taken for granted. I decided to start over and try a new strategy. Instead of continuing to let her know of my dissatisfaction, I started thinking of the things that she was doing right. I listed her strengths, of which there were many, and I wrote her a thank you note. My compliments were genuine and from the heart. About a week later, I received a beautiful thank you note where she also pointed out how easy, for the most part, I was to work with. As an added bonus, I noticed an almost immediate improvement in those areas that I had felt needed work. With almost no effort and certainly no struggle, I had turned our relationship around and we were back on track.

It's important to know that I didn't issue the thank-you note in an attempt to manipulate her. I did so because I realized that she was feeling under-appreciated. And I was right. As soon as she felt appreciated and knew that it was genuine, she was able to move forward.

It's certainly not always the case that you will receive such immediate and positive feedback. I've been involved in many instances where I felt I was doing a good job being appreciative, yet didn't feel any reciprocal efforts coming back. But you know what? It doesn't matter. Regardless of whether you get anything in return, deep down it feels good and it's the right thing to do. The worst that can happen is that you make someone else feel good. I can't think of very many things that feel better than offering genuine appreciation toward those you work with.

95.

DON'T SWEAT YOUR CRITICS

To be honest, if I became upset or immobilized by my critics, I can guarantee you that you wouldn't be reading this book today. The truth is, critics are a fact of life, and criticism is something all of us must face. In fact, the only way to avoid criticism is to live an isolated life where people aren't exposed to your work, personality, or behavior. Sometimes the criticism we receive is valuable, even helpful. Other times, it's utter nonsense. Either way, learning to see criticism as "small stuff" is incredibly useful in our efforts to live a life of reduced stress.

For as long as I can remember, my goal was to spread joy to as many people as possible. I've spent my career trying to help people become more relaxed and patient, to appreciate life, and to sweat the small stuff less often. Yet despite my good intentions and my love for people, I've been criticized for being everything from a Pollyanna, to simplistic, naive, and unrealistic. I've even had a few people accuse me of attempting to harm people with my message of cheer! For as long as I can remember, a certain percentage of people have told me, "You couldn't possibly be that happy," or "Your life must be easier than mine." There's just no way around it. Someone is always going to have an objection to something you are doing.

If you think about it, a landslide political victory would be one where the winner received 60 percent of the vote. That means that even in a convincing win, 40 percent of the people will be wishing the winner had lost!

Realizing this somewhat startling statistic has helped me to keep the criticism directed at me in its proper perspective. No one is important enough, good enough, or well-intentioned enough to escape their share of criticism.

I asked a fellow author who is extremely calm and nonreactive how he handles bad reviews and criticism. He told me, "I always try to see if there is a grain of truth in what is being said. Quite honestly, there often is. In these instances, I try to learn what I can, and then let go of it. Very often my greatest growth comes directly after a dose of criticism. On the other hand, I've learned that if there's nothing to the criticism, it will simply fade away. The worst thing to do is take it personally and become defensive."

Everyone is entitled to their opinion. We will always run into people who have differing points of view and who see life very differently from the way we do. When this becomes okay with you, criticism won't have the same hold on you that it once did. Remember, the same thing that one person loves will irritate someone else. Something you find funny, I might think of as boring, or vice versa. No matter how hard any of us try, no matter how positive our intentions, there will always be someone there to criticize us. Welcome to the human race. When you make the decision to stop sweating your critics, your ego and self-image won't be hurt any more, and your work life will seem a great deal less stressful.

96.

REDUCE YOUR
SELF-INDUCED STRESS

An insightful colleague of mine with a great sense of humor had a terrific idea for a T-shirt. He was going to call it something like "The Shirt to Take Away Your Stress." He was going to offer a 100 percent guarantee that while you were wearing the shirt, you would never feel any stress—other than that which you create from within your own head!

Obviously, his premise was that all of your stress originates from the way that you think, therefore he would never have to return any money. I wouldn't go quite that far, but his point is well taken. To me, if someone breaks into your home and points a gun to your head—that's real stress. Or if your child is sick, you're fired from your job, or there's a fire in your home, or any of thousands of other real-life scenarios occur, there is good reason to feel stressed.

That being said, however, it's clear that a significant percentage of the stress we feel does indeed originate from within us—from the way we think and hold on to things. Most of us use our thinking as ammunition against ourselves many times a day, without even knowing it. We think like victims or we think ourselves into a corner. We blow things out of proportion and make a big deal out of little things. We overanalyze our lives and exaggerate our responsibilities. We sweat the small stuff. We engage in "thought attacks" and mentally rehearse problems, concerns, and outcomes that may or may not manifest themselves. We engage in negative speculation and attach motives to the behavior of others. We live not in the moment, but in anticipation of future moments.

Or we wallow in the past. We fill our minds with angry, overwhelmed, and stressful thoughts, and all the while wonder why we are so unhappy. We have a series of negative, pessimistic thoughts and take them all very seriously. And for the most part, we are completely unaware that we're doing any of this—nor are we aware of how destructive we are being. Instead, our tendency is to blame the world, our circumstances, and other people for the stress that we feel.

Imagine what would happen to the quality of your life if you were to eliminate or even reduce the self-induced portion of your stress. Because so much of our stress and unhappiness comes from the way that we think, you'd be among the happiest people on earth—without changing a single thing in your life. Why not give it a try?

The hardest part of dealing with self-induced stress is to have the humility to admit that it is, indeed, self-induced. It's much easier to say, "I'm stressed because of the way my life is set up" than it is to say, "I'm stressed because of the way I think." Nevertheless, if you insist on validating and reinforcing how difficult your life is, it's going to be very difficult to change the way you feel. Once you see your part, however, you have the power to change.

Once you can admit that, at least to some degree, you are your own worst enemy, the rest is pretty easy. You can begin by paying attention to your own thoughts—and remembering that you are the one thinking them. When a negative or self-defeating thought runs through your mind, you have the capacity to say, "There's another one," or something similar to acknowledge the fact that your thinking is getting in your own way. You can then gently dismiss the negative thought from your mind, not taking it so seriously. In this way, one by one, you can virtually eliminate negativity from your life. Again, the trick is to see that it's *you* doing it to *you*.

The only lasting way to reduce your stress is to break the habit of thinking in self-defeating ways. More specifically, the solution involves taking your own thoughts—particularly the negative ones— a little less seriously. Remember that they are just thoughts, and be willing to pay less attention to or even dismiss those that are bringing you down or getting in your way.

Start by observing your thoughts. Are you practicing optimism and good mental health? Are you keeping your perspective and sense of humor? Or do you allow your thinking to get the best of you? Do you take your thinking too seriously? If so, this is the place to start. Remember, it's far easier to shift your thinking than it is to shift the ways of the world. By reducing your self-induced stress, you'll be making great strides in your efforts to feel more relaxed and calm.

97.

BECOME AWARE OF
THE THOUGHT FACTOR

Becoming aware of "the thought factor" is without question one of the most important ingredients in learning to stop sweating the small stuff at work—and elsewhere. In order to become a calmer, gentler, and less reactive person, it's essential to understand that your experience of life is created from the inside out—not the other way around, as it so often seems.

My good friend and coauthor of *Slowing Down to the Speed of Life,* Joe Bailey, was involved in an interesting experiment designed to demonstrate this critical point. He interviewed dozens of drivers during rush hour traffic who were on a busy freeway on-ramp in Minneapolis.

The assumption is often made that traffic is one of those irritations that everyone resents. It's often included on stress tests designed to quantify how stressed-out you must be. At best, traffic is tolerated; at worst, it's cause for road rage. Joe's goal, however, was to teach people that, in fact, our thinking, not the traffic itself, is ultimately responsible for the feelings that are experienced in traffic. He was trying to show that we do, indeed, have a choice in how we experience traffic and that we are not victims of traffic—or anything else.

The responses to being stuck in horrible traffic were as varied as the types of cars being driven. As you might expect, a certain percentage of drivers were incensed, red-faced, and completely bothered. Some yelled and cursed at Joe and the camera. Others were accepting and relaxed. Some of them used the time to listen to audio tapes or talk on the phone. And believe it or not, a few actually reported that being in traffic was their favorite time of the day—it was the only time they had to be completely alone. In traffic, they could slow down and relax. No one could bother them or ask them to do anything.

Remember, a vast majority of these people had just finished work. All of them were probably tired. They were in the same traffic jam, delayed for the same amount of time. No one was given any advantages—the circumstances were essentially identical for all. So, if the traffic were actually responsible for our negative reactions, then it would logically follow that the traffic would affect everyone in the same way. It doesn't.

This experiment shows us that our experience of life does, in fact, come from our own thinking and perception. If you carefully consider what I'm suggesting here, you'll see some powerful implications. It means that you really do have a choice in how you respond—not only in traffic, but also in all those other situations that are almost always associated with misery and stress.

If you're in a traffic jam, for example, and can admit to yourself and recognize that your inner experience is being dictated by your thinking (not the traffic), it changes the entire nature of your experience. It reminds you that a shift in your thinking can result in a shift in your stress level. Rather than insisting that life accommodate you with fewer demands and hassles, you can learn to stay relatively unaffected and relaxed in spite of it all. I'm not suggesting that it's always going to be easy. It won't. However, you can see that with this knowledge comes hope. Even when you're really frustrated, it reminds you that it's possible to see the situation differently. Without a doubt, you'll get through it easier than before.

There are certain cause-and-effect relationships in life. If you jump off a fifty-story building, for example, you're not going to live. If you put your hand on a burning stove, it's going to hurt. If you put a giant cork at the bottom of a lake, it's going to rise to the surface. These are laws of nature.

Most of us, however, treat everyday events—traffic, hard work, conflict, mistakes, deadlines, being criticized, and so forth—with a similar cause-and-effect relationship. We assume that these events must cause stress and grief in the same way that fire causes a burn. Events like traffic are assumed to cause upset. Being criticized is supposed to make you feel defensive. Making a mistake is going to lower your spirits, and so forth. The reason we make these erroneous assumptions is because we think the traffic or other stressor is causing our stress, while in actuality it does not.

Understanding this concept can open the door to a whole new way of looking at life and the minor irritations and hassles we all must face. We can't often change our immediate circumstances—but we always have the ability to change our thoughts and attitudes. I hope you'll reflect on this strategy and embrace its compelling logic. Becoming aware of the thought factor will change your life.

98.

EASE OFF YOUR EGO

The goal of this book has been to help you become less stressed at work and to assist you in your efforts to stop sweating the small stuff. I can't think of too many factors that contribute more to our stress, anxiety, and frustration than a large ego. Therefore, easing off your ego is one of the most leveraged efforts you can make to reduce the stress at work.

I think of the ego as that part of us that needs to stand out and be special. And while each one of us is certainly special and unique in our own way, our ego has the need to prove this to everyone. The ego is that part of us that brags, exaggerates, criticizes, and judges others (as well as ourselves). The ego is very self-centered, as if it needs to yell out, "Look at me!" Because the ego is so self-preoccupied and selfish, it encourages us to lose our compassion for and interest in others. Its sole commitment is to maintain itself.

In addition to the obvious drawbacks, the ego is an enormous source of stress. Think about how much energy and attentiveness it takes to prove yourself, show off, and defend your actions. Consider how stressful it is to compare yourself to others and to put yourself down. Think about how draining it is to constantly be keeping score of how you're doing and to be overly concerned with what others think about you. I get tired just thinking about it!

Easing off your ego is accomplished by intention. The first step is to have the desire to shrink your ego down to size and to see how destructive and stressful it can be. The rest is easy. All it takes is humility and patience. Begin paying attention to your thoughts and behavior. When you notice yourself in your "proving mode," gently remind yourself to back off. You can say something simple to yourself like, "Whoops, there I go again." Be sure to laugh at and be easy on yourself. Don't make letting go of your ego into yet another contest with yourself. It's not an emergency. Be patient and it will happen.

There is a lot to be gained by easing off your ego. First and foremost, you'll feel as though a huge burden has been lifted. As I mentioned, it takes a great deal of effort to be on guard and in the proving mode. Therefore, you'll have a great deal more energy and will become more lighthearted. In addition, as you ease off your ego, you'll become much more interested in other people. You'll become a better listener and a kinder, more generous person. This will translate into people liking you even more than they already do. As you let go of the need to impress others and simply be yourself, you'll end up getting more positive attention than ever before. You won't need it, but you'll get it.

I hope you'll give this strategy some careful consideration and gentle effort. If each of us can become more humble, sincere and generous, the world will be a much nicer place. And to top it off, none of us will be sweating the small stuff.

99.

REMEMBER,

SMALL STUFF HAPPENS

As we near the end of this book, I felt it would be helpful to remind you of a key point—small stuff happens. In other words, you could memorize this book, practice every strategy faithfully, and become an incredibly peaceful person. Yet despite all that, and no matter who you are, how successful you become, who your contacts are, or anything else, you're still going to have to deal with your share of "small stuff." Guaranteed. It's important to remind yourself of this fact—regularly—because it can be tempting to believe that your new wisdom and insights or a more positive attitude are somehow going to exempt you from the reality of daily hassles. The question isn't whether or not we will have to deal with such issues, but how we will approach them. With practice, the small stuff you will have to deal with won't seem like such a big deal. Instead, it will be seen as "small stuff."

Even to this day, when I get frustrated over the barrage of small stuff that I have to deal with, my dad reminds me of a quote that, perhaps, says it all: "Life is just one thing after another." How true! You get through one hassle, and another one is just around the corner. You resolve a conflict and inadvertently begin another. You solve a problem and, like magic, another one presents itself. One person is delighted at your performance and in pleasing him, you irritate someone else. Your plans fall through, an error is committed, your computer crashes. It's all part of life, and it's not going to change.

There's something incredibly peaceful in recognizing and surrendering to the fact that small stuff does happen, and that the nature of life is that it's full of conflicting choices, demands, desires, and expectations. It has always been that way and always will be. To assume otherwise creates pain and suffering. Once you stop demanding that life be different, however, the nature of the game changes and you regain control over your life. The same things that used to drive you crazy no longer do. What used to cause you grief, you now see with perspective. Rather than wasting your valuable energy banging your head against walls, you remain calm, deal with the issue as best you can, and move forward.

To the best of my knowledge, there is no magic pill that is going to make your experience of work perfect or trouble-free. I'm certain, however, that by enhancing your perspective and becoming a less reactive, calmer person, you can learn to take life in stride while bringing out the best in yourself. I hope this book has been helpful to you in your efforts to lighten up, enhance your perspective, and most of all, to stop sweating the small stuff.

100.

DON'T LIVE FOR RETIREMENT

Knowingly or unknowingly, many people practically live for retirement. They think about how wonderful life will be without the burden of daily work outside the home. Some people go so far as to count the years, months, even days before retirement. It's common for people to postpone joy, contentment, and satisfaction until "later." It's almost as though people are "putting in time" as if they were serving a sentence, patiently waiting for their freedom.

Admittedly, most people don't go quite this far. It's usually a bit more subtle than this. However, a staggering percentage of people expect that life down the road is going to be better than it is today. Frequently, daydreams as well as conversations with coworkers and friends make it clear that the expectation is that "someday" will be better than now—when you're retired, have more money, freedom, wisdom, time to travel, or whatever.

I'm passionate about this topic because it's clear to me that thinking in these "someday life will be better" terms is a guaranteed way to set yourself up for a long and tiring career. Rather than enjoying each day, being open to new challenges and opportunities, sharing your gifts with others, and being willing to learn from and become inspired by your work-related experiences, you choose instead to essentially put your life on hold, to go through the motions, get stuck in a rut, and, to one degree or another, feel sorry for yourself.

It's far better, I believe, to wake up each morning and remind yourself of the old adage, "Today is the first day of the rest of my life." Make the decision to honor your gift of life by giving today your best effort, regardless of what you happen to do for a living. See if you can keep perspective when others may not, inspire another person, or make a contribution, however small, to the life of someone else. Remind yourself that all days were created equal, that today is every bit as important as any future day after retirement.

Another important reason to avoid living for retirement is that doing so increases the likelihood that you'll be disappointed when it arrives. A strange thing happens when we postpone happiness until a later date. It's as though, in the meantime, we're rehearsing how to be unhappy. We become experts. When we tell ourselves we'll be happy later, what we're really saying is that our life isn't good enough right now. We have to wait until our circumstances are different. So we wait and wait. Thousands of times, over the course of many years, we remind ourselves, in the privacy of our own minds, that when things are different—someday down the road—we'll feel satisfied and happy. But for now, we'll have to make do.

Finally, the big day arrives—the first day of retirement. Yippee!

But here's the problem. As you probably know, old habits die hard. If you smoke or stutter, it's difficult to quit. If you're highly critical or defensive, it's hard to change. If you have bad eating and exercise habits, it takes enormous discipline to make a permanent shift. In the vast majority of cases, most people simply can't do it. It's too hard to change.

Why in the world do we assume that our thinking habits are any different? They're not. In fact, in some ways, learning to think differently is the most difficult habit of all to change. All of us have been trapped from time to time by our own thinking. We become accustomed to thinking in a certain way—so much so, we can't see it any other way.

If you spend years and years thinking that life isn't good enough right now—that something else is going to be better—it's ludicrous to believe that in a single moment when retirement becomes reality, you're going to somehow begin to think differently; that somehow life as it is is suddenly going to be good enough. No way. It's not going to happen. Instead, it's predictable that the opposite will happen. Your mind will continue to believe that something else will be better. You have a habit of seeing life this way, and it's not going to stop simply because your external life has shifted.

The way around this problem is to commit to being happy now—to make the absolute best of the job or career you have right now, to see it as an adventure, to be creative and insightful. Make this your habitual way of thinking about your job and of being in the world. Practice this type of healthy, optimistic thinking on a day-to-day, moment-to-moment basis. If you do, then when retirement arrives, whether it's a year from now or twenty years from now, you will know the secret of happiness: that there is no way to happiness; happiness *is* the way. It will be second nature to you.

So, go ahead and look forward to a fantastic retirement. Plan ahead and plan well. But do yourself a great big favor. Don't miss a single day along the way. I will conclude by saying that I hope this book has been helpful to you and that I send you my love, respect, and best wishes.

Treasure yourself,

Richard Carlson

DON'T SWEAT THE SMALL STUFF ABOUT MONEY

SPIRITUAL AND PRACTICAL WAYS
TO CREATE ABUNDANCE AND
MORE FUN IN YOUR LIFE

THIS BOOK IS DEDICATED TO

MY FATHER AND GOOD FRIEND, DON CARLSON,

WITHOUT WHOM NEITHER THIS BOOK, NOR ITS TITLE,

WOULD HAVE BEEN CREATED.

THANK YOU FOR YOUR LOVE, GENEROSITY, AND

CREATIVE IDEAS.

I LOVE YOU.

ACKNOWLEDGMENTS

A special, heartfelt thanks to Don Carlson and Marvin Levin, two very special, highly talented, and generous mentors. Your ideas and concepts were enormously helpful, not only in writing this book but throughout my entire life. I don't know where I'd be without you. Also, a great big thanks to Kenny Trout, Steve Smith, and all the folks at Excel Telecommunications who have taught my wife, Kris, and me both so much about what it takes to become successful. And a warm thank-you to Patti Breitman and Linda Michaels, who both help keep me on track in my career, and Leslie Wells, for her continued inspiration and brilliant ideas. Finally, thank you to my incredible family—Kris, Jazzy, and Kenna—for being so patient and supportive while I was writing this book. I love you all so much.

CONTENTS

*Indicates a new essay

INTRODUCTION

When the subject of money comes up, there's often stress in the air. Money is necessary, of course, but it's confusing to most of us. Most people feel they have too little of it; a few people have too much. Money causes rifts between friends as well as family members. Money breaks up marriages as well as lifelong friendships. I've heard that there are more arguments, fights, and disagreements about money than any other subject in the world!

People become greedy about money, and they become stubborn. Rarely does this topic bring out the best in someone; often it brings out the worst. Many people are foolish and wasteful with their money. Others become very controlling and uptight. To further complicate matters, money is often associated with power and prestige. Therefore, many people attach their self-esteem to their net worth and, in doing so, ruin their chance to have happy and peaceful lives.

More than anything, we worry and obsess about money. We wonder if we have enough now, and if we'll have enough later on. You turn on the radio to hear how the stock market is doing. You may even link your happiness to the market. When it's up, you're joyful; when it's down, you're miserable.

We have all sorts of questions about money. How should we use it? How much should we save? How much should we give away to charity, and how much to our children? Who gets our money when we die?

We have other concerns and gripes surrounding money as well. Most people think they pay too much in taxes and that taking care of their money is too complicated. Many feel "ripped off" when they think something

1

costs too much. Others feel insecure when someone else has more than they do, or guilty when they are the one with the most.

You'd think that when a person acquired a certain degree of wealth, they'd stop sweating about money, but usually the opposite occurs. Rather than feeling relief, most people with money become even more obsessed. Now, rather than worrying about getting money, they are worried about keeping it, protecting it, caring for it, and so forth. Then, the questions come up: "Are people trying to take advantage of me?" and "Does he only like me for my money?"

I've known people whose family business destroyed the entire family, even when the business was profitable. I've met others whose families have been torn apart fighting over the estate after their parents have died. I've known family members and good friends who sue one another over money disputes. I once witnessed a taxi driver reach back and almost kill an elderly man over a disagreement about a few dollars. It goes on and on.

I've been with many poor people, a great number of rich people, and a vast number of people in-between. In all honesty, I'd have to say that 99 percent of them, regardless of their financial statures, sweat the small stuff about money. Indeed, it's a universal tendency.

This book was originally published with the title *Don't Worry, Make Money*. With the benefit of hindsight, however, it's obvious that it should have been part of the "Don't Sweat" series all along. Because money is perhaps our greatest source of stress, it fits right in with the philosophy of learning to be less worried, stressed, annoyed, and irritated.

You can't (and probably don't want to) avoid the issues surrounding money, but you can learn to take it more in stride. And when you do, your entire life will become more relaxing and peaceful.

It's quite possible to achieve great wealth and success in your life, yet remain unaffected by it. It's possible to make wise and appropriate decisions

2

about money without excessive worry or grief. That's what this book is about: finding ways to create abundance and more fun without the stress that is usually associated with such intentions.

Learning to not sweat the small stuff about money won't take away all the monetary issues you have to deal with, but it sure will bring you more peace of mind. With added perspective, and perhaps a bit of humor, you'll be able to tend to your money wisely—make great choices and see things clearly without having fiscal issues take over your life.

If you've read any of my other "Don't Sweat" books, you know that I believe strongly in the potential of people. I believe we have the potential for great joy, compassion, and wisdom. And part of this potential is manifested when we learn to stop sweating the small stuff.

When you stop sweating the small stuff about money, everyone benefits. You'll feel better, and, what's more, you'll probably make more money, too. To me, it's pretty obvious that any success we enjoy is despite our worry, not because of it! Worry and excessive stress are distractions that keep us from our dreams and from our greatest potential. So as we discover ways to worry less, to "not sweat it," we ignite that capacity within us.

Even as importantly, others benefit, too. As we worry less about money, we are more willing to do things for others. We are more generous and charitable. Rather than postponing the giving of our time, energy, ideas, or money because of fear, we learn to give freely, from the heart. I've known many people who, after dropping some of their concerns about this issue, started donating money and volunteering their time for others. Their ability to "not sweat it" gave them the confidence to become more giving with their time and money.

Without the emotional burden of getting too uptight about money, you can use your energy in more constructive ways, doing the things that bring you the most joy. The strategies you are about to read were written

3

to help you banish worry from your life forever. Whether you want the confidence to pursue a new career or dream, the emotional freedom to ask others for help or for a raise, the ability to handle criticism or rejection, the confidence to take a risk, speak to a group, do more for your favorite charity, creatively and confidently market a service or product—or simply to become less uptight about money—this book will help you.

I'm grateful that you're going to take the time to read this book and hopeful that it will help you create an even better life. I send you my very best wishes.

1.

REMEMBER THAT THE JOURNEY OF A THOUSAND MILES BEGINS WITH A SINGLE STEP

I can vividly remember the first sentence I ever wrote in my very first book! It seems like a long time ago. Yet had I not written that first sentence, I wouldn't have finished that first book, or the second, and so on. And so it goes. Every journey, however long it may be, begins with a single step. But you *must* take that first step. Once you do, each step takes you closer and closer to your goal.

Sometimes, when you consider taking on a new venture—whether it's raising a child, writing a book, starting a new business, beginning a savings plan, or anything else—the task can seem overwhelming. It's as though you'll never be able to arrive at your final destination, as if the first step isn't going to help. When you look too far out toward the horizon, it can seem too difficult. You might even wonder where to begin.

The trick to success sounds very simplistic, because it *is* very simple: Just begin. Take a single step, followed by another, and then another. Don't look too far out into the future, and don't look too far back either. Stay centered in the present moment as best you can. If you follow this simple plan, you'll be amazed at what you can accomplish over time.

When I graduated from my Ph.D. program, my dear friend Marvin gave me, as a gift, the complete works of Carl Jung. That's twenty-six long volumes of material. In volume one was a note from Marvin worth sharing here. He wrote: "Becoming educated doesn't happen overnight! Education is a lifelong process that happens in short intervals. If you were to read only eight pages a day, for the next seven years, you would be one of the world's most knowledgeable experts on the work of Carl Jung, *and* you would get through every page!" Despite not being a huge fan of Jung, I have always appreciated my friend's message.

The same, of course, is true with all ventures. A wealthy friend of mine, worth many millions of dollars, remembers opening his first savings account with his wife over forty years ago with $10. They both laugh when they say, "It's amazing what a little time will do." Had they not decided to start somewhere, their incredible success would never have manifested itself.

Over and over again I hear people telling me about the book they are *going* to write, the savings account they are *about* to open, the business they are *going* to start, or the charity they are *planning* to help. But, in many instances, these plans and dreams keep getting put off until "the conditions are right." One of the most powerful messages I can share with you, one that I'm absolutely certain of, is this: In almost all cases, the conditions you are waiting for will *not* be significantly different next week or next year. Don't worry that the conditions have to be perfect. The truth is, you are *still* going to have to take that first step! If you take it now, instead of later, you'll be many steps closer to your dreams by this time next year. Congratulations, you've just taken the first step in the completion of this book!

2.

GIVE, GIVE, GIVE

Many of us have heard the expression "Giving is its own reward." And while this is certainly true, and more than reason enough to give, there's another aspect of giving that many fail to recognize. Giving is an energy that not only helps others but creates even more for the person who is doing the giving. This is a natural law that is true regardless of whether the person who is giving wants or even realizes what is occurring.

Money is "circulation." It needs to flow. When you are frightened, selfish, or when you hoard everything for yourself, you literally stop the circulation. You create "clogged pipes," making it difficult to keep money flowing back in your direction. Any success you have is despite your lack of giving, not because of it. The way to get the flow going again is to start giving. Be generous. Pay others well, tip your waitress that extra dollar. Support several charities. Give back. Watch what happens! Things will start popping up out of nowhere.

The same dynamic is true if you want to fill your life with love or anything else worthwhile. Giving and receiving are two sides of the same coin. If you want more love, or fun, or respect, or success, or anything else, the way to get it is simple: give it away. Don't worry about a thing. The universe knows what it's doing. Everything you give away will return, with interest!

3.

LEARN THE MAGIC OF NONATTACHMENT

Without realizing it, many of us confuse nonattachment with not caring. In actuality, the two are completely different. Not caring suggests apathy: "I couldn't care less. It doesn't matter to me." Nonattachment, on the other hand, means: "I'll do everything possible, I'll put the odds in my favor, I'll work hard and concentrate. I'll do my best to succeed. *But*, if I don't, that's okay, too."

Being attached to an outcome, holding on, takes an enormous amount of energy, not only during an effort but often after an effort is complete, after you've failed, or been let down, or were dealt a bad hand.

Being nonattached, however, creates emotional freedom. It means holding on tightly but letting go lightly. It suggests trying hard, really caring, but at the same time being completely willing to let go of the outcome.

Attachment creates fear that gets in your way: What if I lose? What if the deal doesn't go through? What if I'm rejected? What if, what if, what if. . .Your belief that everything must work out exactly as you want it to with no glitches creates enormous pressure. Everything rides on your success.

Nonattachment, on the other hand, works like magic. It allows you to have fun in your efforts, to enjoy the process. It helps you succeed at whatever you are doing by giving you the confidence you need. It takes the pressure off. You win regardless of the outcome. The act of *not* worrying helps you focus and stay on purpose. It helps you stay out of your own way. You know in your heart that, even if things don't work out the way you hope they will, everything will be all right. You'll be okay. You'll learn from the experience. You'll do better next time. This attitude of acceptance helps you move on to the next step in your path. Rather than being lost or immobilized in disappointment or regret, you simply move on—with confidence and joy.

4.

EXPERIENCE RELAXED PASSION

Most people would agree that having passion for one's work is a helpful, if not necessary, ingredient for success. Many of these same people, however, confuse useful passion with hyper or frenetic behavior.

Passion takes different forms. It can be the feeling of being driven to success, of rolling up your sleeves, or working long, hard hours. This "hyper" passion can be very exciting, even addicting. The problem with it, though, is that it drains your energy and can be very exhausting. It's generated from external sources, from tight deadlines and big deals. Because of the external nature of this type of passion, a tint of fear always goes along with it: "I love this as long as everything works out well." This type of passion also lends itself to boredom. The only time you're having fun is when there's something on the line, when something exciting is happening. The rest of the time can seem like a letdown. You spend your time waiting and looking for more excitement.

Another, calmer type of passion is what I like to call relaxed passion. This is a contained, "time-release" type of feeling that permeates everything you do. It brings joy and great success to virtually anything. Rather than being frenetic, this feeling is more like exhilaration and enthusiasm. It's a much calmer version of excitement. It can be described as excitement without the worry: "I love this simply because I'm absorbed in what I'm doing."

The way to bring forth this type of passion is to learn to keep your attention fully in the present moment. Try to do only one thing at any given moment and give that "one thing" your full and complete attention. If you're on the phone, stay focused, be "with" the person to whom you are speaking. Don't let your mind drift; be there. If your mind does wander, gently bring it back to the present moment.

Almost anything we do—preparing a report, speaking to a group, solving a problem, generating an idea, doing a difficult task, and so forth—is a potential source of relaxed passion. And it comes not from exciting, external ventures but from our own attention, our own thinking. Too many of us live in moments past or moments yet to be. When our mind is not right here, in this moment, we suck the joy out of an experience. You can bring passion back into your life and your business dealings by simply being more oriented in the present moment. Your focus and insight will be greatly enhanced, as will your ideas and creativity.

5.

BECOME A STRESS-STOPPER

There's little doubt in the minds of most business people I've met that, overall, stress interferes with the quality of business. People who are too stressed are reactive and frightened, and tend to make more mistakes than those who are calm. Stressed-out people blow problems out of proportion and fail to see solutions. Because they are moving so fast, they often spin their wheels, rushing around, repeating efforts as well as mistakes. Stressed-out people aren't very centered; therefore they have a difficult time seeing to the heart of the matter or being able to differentiate between what's really important and what's less significant. Because they are irritable and bothered, they tend to bring out the worst in others and often end up pushing people away—including customers, clients, and important prospects.

It makes sense, then, that if you want to maximize your chances for success and profit, when stress is present in your workplace and/or in your mind, you should do everything you can to prevent its spread. In other words, rather than get others all riled up and bothered and sharing all that's disturbing you, it's often best to keep it to yourself. Doing so can pay handsome dividends.

If I'm stressed out, that stress is going on inside my own head. For example, if I'm worried that I'm not going to be able to make my deadline, my thoughts about my deadline are the primary source of my stress. Or, if I've had to deal with an extremely difficult customer earlier in the day, my lingering thoughts about that person keep that stress alive in my mind.

Sometimes because it's therapeutic or even entertaining, other times out of pure habit, we feel compelled to share the details of our stressful thoughts with others around us, thereby encouraging them to get caught up in our dramas and/or to focus on other things they perceive to be stressful. We think about, commiserate, and emphasize the negative. As our coworkers become absorbed and focused on the stress, they reinforce and sometimes even exacerbate the stress we are feeling, creating a vicious circle that can be hard to break. It's hard to imagine anything less effective than an entire group of people upset, irritated, and stressed out!

When you make the conscious decision to become a stress-stopper, you'll find yourself nipping tons of stress—especially stress that is "small stuff"—in the bud. Your refusal to "spread the virus" not only prevents stress from escalating around the office or workplace, but actually reinforces to you that many of the things we get all worked up about are, in the scheme of things, pretty irrelevant. Plus, what you start to see is that much of what we stress or worry about never manifests itself anyway.

I was once driving to the airport with Kris and the kids, certain we were going to miss our flight. I must have mentioned my pessimistic prediction more than a dozen times. So, I got them all worried and concerned, too, and reinforced my own worry. When we ended up making the flight, I realized how silly it had been to draw them into it—there was no upside; only downside. Had I simply been a stress-stopper, I could have avoided getting the others in the car upset and frightened.

The idea of being a stress-stopper even applies to simple situations surrounding your finances at home. A friend told me that she was really frustrated by her and her husband's poor record keeping. In a stressed-out state of mind, she ranted and raged to her husband how horrible and disorganized everything was. She got him all worked up and concerned about their tax records, and he too became stressed and agitated. She later realized that it would have been far more effective and substantially less stressful for both of them had she simply kept her bearings, waited for a calmer time, and discussed some constructive organizing ideas with her husband.

Obviously, there are times when it's necessary or useful to share our stress with others—for example, when doing so will help solve a problem. Yet, if you're honest about it, I think you'll find that much of the time it's better and ultimately more effective to be a stress-stopper rather than a stress-spreader.

6.

PAY YOURSELF FIRST

On the surface, this is one of the least original ideas in this book. The idea of paying yourself first—before anyone else—is a concept that is often talked about. Most financial professionals realize that it's virtually impossible to accumulate great wealth without this type of discipline and wisdom. The idea is that, if you wait until everyone else is paid before you pay yourself, you'll never get around to it. There won't be anything left. Despite its importance, however, a very small percentage of people actually implement this strategy. The major reason: worry.

If you are worried about having enough, you never will! Fear will prevent you from taking the obvious steps that are needed to create abundance. Thus, one of the first and most important steps you need to take is to nip your worry in the bud.

From this moment on, make a commitment to yourself that you will ignore all thoughts of worry and pay yourself first—before *anyone* else. Every day, or week, or month—whatever is appropriate for you—write yourself a check. Invest in yourself. Trust in yourself. You will have enough for everything else.

You'll be surprised, but somehow, regardless of your income, there will always be enough left to pay your bills. You'll make invisible, wise adjustments in your spending habits. You'll make new choices. And in a very short amount of time, you'll get into the habit of always paying yourself first, saving or investing something for you. You'll watch your savings and net worth grow. As this happens, you'll see how destructive worry can be and how unnecessary it was all along. This will create even more confidence, which will translate into more discipline, creativity, and new ideas. You will find yourself in a new mind-set, creating wealth.

It's critical to realize that you won't stop worrying simply because your income rises. There are plenty of people with enormous incomes who worry all the time. The trick is to trust, without any doubt whatsoever, that the magic works in the other direction. You need to stop worrying, first, and *then* you'll do what it takes to create the abundance you deserve.

7.

DO GOOD WHILE DOING WELL

One of my favorite salad dressings is Paul Newman's Balsamic Vinaigrette. Near the top of the bottle are the words "Paul Newman donates all his profits, after taxes, from the sale of this product for educational and charitable purposes." What a great example of someone who does good while doing well!

Many celebrities and successful businessmen and women are doing similar things—mixing business ventures with charity and good causes. What a brilliant and wonderful thing to do—and everyone wins. The charities receive financial benefits and, in some cases, name recognition, while the businesspeople feel the joy of helping out while also earning goodwill in the marketplace. The customers, too, are the winners, because each purchase helps the selected cause(s). All things being equal, I'd much rather buy a product that was helping a great cause than one that wasn't.

There are countless examples of noncelebrities who are doing the very same thing. People everywhere are looking for, and finding, ways to combine business with good works. This is a relatively easy strategy to implement, regardless of what type of business you are in. In fact, I'll share with you a funny (and touching) story to demonstrate this fact.

I was discussing this topic at a book signing when a somewhat cynical gentleman commented, "Easy for you (Richard) to say." His point was that it would be easy to combine business efforts with good work for others if you were in a financial position to do so. Otherwise, it would be a huge burden. Before I even had a chance to respond, a little boy, no more than ten years old, stood up and said, "Do you want to know what I do?" "Sure," I said. "We'd all love to hear." "I keep track of my sales. After every hundred cups of lemonade I sell, I donate a whole pitcher to the retirement home down the street." The crowd loved it! Can you imagine how hard it would be to *not* buy lemonade from this young man?

If a ten-year-old's lemonade stand can be a vehicle to help others, why can't the rest of us contribute? Imagine how easy it would be to set something up in your business, however small, in order to help a great cause. Or, if you work for a business that isn't open to doing so, you can just as easily do it as an individual. You can donate a portion of your money, time, or energy. Whether you formalize it or not, there are thousands of ways to be helpful. You'll be amazed at how good you'll feel knowing you're making an actual difference. Your business efforts will have even more meaning to you, and, in fact, I believe you'll be less stressed as a result. I've found that people who consciously set out to be helpful to others are far less likely to sweat the small stuff. So again, everyone wins; especially you!

I often wonder what kind of world we'd live in if everyone looked at their work as an opportunity to be of help. If each of us does our own little part, we just may find out someday.

DON'T DEAL WITH PROBLEMS, TRANSCEND THEM

When I suggest that clients *not* work on problems, they often appear irritated, as if I'm telling them not to bathe or brush their teeth! This is because most people assume that the only way to solve problems is to work on, or struggle, with them. I have found, however, that focusing on problems is one of the key ways of keeping them alive—as well as preventing you from moving past them. Focusing on problems is also a key ingredient keeping people stuck in worry.

I can assure you that there is a way to get from where you are to where you want to be *without* focusing on problems. It's a natural, virtually effortless, yet far more effective alternative to the usual "roll up your sleeves and solve this problem" manner of dealing with issues.

Recently I knelt down to clean up some glass and a piece got stuck in my knee. I ended up at the urgent care center getting ten stitches. We all know that the worst thing I could possibly do to the healing process would be to poke or pick at my scab. A wiser method is to treat the wound gently, creating the best possible healing environment. Miraculously, the wound will heal all by itself.

Most problems can and should be dealt with in a similar manner. The thoughts we have around our various issues—business and otherwise—create and trigger emotional reactions. What usually happens is that we spend our time and energy dealing with these reactions instead of the actual issue. Simply put, when we are frightened, angry, or impatient, we lose our bearings and get in our own way. Instead of bringing out the best in ourselves and others, we bring out negativity and squeeze out creativity.

Deep down, we all know that for every problem there *is* a solution.

Many times, the solution is obvious to a dispassionate observer, which is the primary reason corporations as well as entrepreneurs hire outside consultants. Often, the reason we cannot see these obvious solutions is that we are trapped in our emotional reactions and habitual ways of seeing life.

The alternative to dealing head on with problems is to clear your mind instead of filling it with painful, confusing details. Quiet down, reflect, and listen. Allow your wisdom, that softer part of your thinking, to surface. More often than not, seemingly out of nowhere, you will have an insight, an answer to your problem. You may be shocked or even struggle with how easy this process is to implement. Nevertheless, the less you worry about your problems, the easier they will be to solve!

9.

LEARN ABOUT MOODS AND MONEY

Moods are one of those unavoidable, mysterious parts of life that must be dealt with by everyone. Our understanding of moods greatly affects not only our wisdom and perspective but our overall level of satisfaction as well. Generally speaking, when our mood is high, our spirits are up. When our mood is low, our spirits are down. Moods are like the weather, constantly changing.

The implications of moods as they relate to money are significant. When we are low, we think of our dissatisfactions more than when we feel good. We worry! We compare ourselves to others and convince ourselves that others are doing better than we are. We focus on our belief that making money is hard work. Perhaps we believe that there isn't enough money or opportunity to go around, or that people are selfish and out for themselves.

The fascinating thing about moods is that, to a large degree, we only believe these negative, fearful, and self-defeating thoughts when our mood is low. When our mood is high, we think very differently. We don't worry as much. Rather than believing that others are doing better than we are, or even spending energy comparing ourselves to them, we realize that we are all on different paths, doing the best we can. Instead of complaining that making money is hard work, we get a kick out of the entire process and see new ways to create abundance for ourselves and others. Rather than seeing limitations in the supply of money, we know that there is plenty to go around. Finally, instead of seeing people as selfish and out for themselves, we realize that most people are very generous and giving. And those who aren't have simply lost touch with their heart.

So what do you do? The trick is to be grateful when your mood is high and graceful when it is low. Try to keep in mind the effect your mood is having on the way you are thinking and feeling. Your understanding of moods allows you to keep your perspective and not take so seriously the thoughts you are having when you are low. Rather than believing in your negative and fearful perceptions, you can dismiss them as being mood-related.

The same dynamic applies to your creativity and your ability to create abundance. When you are in a low mood, don't make important business (or life) decisions. Don't force it. Your thinking and wisdom are not as sound as they will be in a higher state of mind.

Resist the temptation to worry about your moods. Moods are always changing, and yours could change at any moment. Simply realizing that you are stuck in a mood usually raises your spirits. Again, don't worry! As your mood rises, your capacity to create will unfold.

10.

CONSIDER THE POSSIBILITY THAT IF IT SOUNDS TOO GOOD TO BE TRUE, IT MIGHT NOT BE

The old adage "If it sounds too good to be true, it probably is" isn't always correct. In fact, the suspicion, cynicism, and doubt that are inherent in this belief can and do keep people from taking advantage of excellent opportunities.

Cynicism contradicts abundance. Cynics, critics, and doubters are clouded by their own destructive, self-defeating filters that say things like "That can't work," "That's impossible," or "It's too good to be true." These people are big-time worriers. They're concerned with what other people think, and they are stuck in doing things "the right way," the same way everyone else does them. These people have closed minds that are fixated on the status quo.

I was lucky enough to hear about a great stock from a good friend of mine. He told me and four others what he knew about it. Unfortunately for my other friends, they were true cynics. "Sure," they all said in a sarcastic tone, "I'll bet it's a great deal." They instantly dismissed the suggestion. I've learned, however, to keep an open mind. And while I would probably decide to buy less than one stock in every hundred that I hear about, I'm always willing to take a look. It took me less than an hour to do a little research on the stock, and I decided to buy some shares. Lo and behold, the stock doubled in less than a month. Lucky? Of course. But had I not been open-minded, I wouldn't have been in a position to be lucky!

If you think something is too good to be true, you'll be very hesitant to take a careful look at it, and you'll dismiss it as being superficial or too risky. What happens, however, if you're wrong? You'll miss out. Often there are great deals and wonderful opportunities that come your way. But to take advantage of them, you must be open, willing to take a look, learn something new, try something different. Obviously, this doesn't mean you jump into risky ventures or avoid careful consideration, but it does mean that sometimes you have to do something a little differently to do a little better, to have a little more.

Being a nonworrier doesn't guarantee success, but it sure makes it easier to spot great opportunities when they come your way. You'll be far more open to taking a look, to considering new options, new ways of doing things, marketing products or services, or taking an uncharacteristic risk. By becoming a less cynical, more open-minded nonworrier, you'll bring far more joy into your work and open the door to far more abundance in your business and career.

11.

HIRE UP

If you want to talk about a strategy that is 100 percent related to less worry, this is it. The concept of hiring up is critical to your success. Essentially, hiring up means you hire and work with people that are more qualified than you. That's right, *better* than you.

It won't come as a surprise to very many of you that the factor that prevents people from subscribing to this philosophy is fear. The fear that "I can be replaced" or "someone might be better than me."

Do you ever wonder why so many businesses operate as if no one knows what they're doing? Sometimes the answer is that no one really does know what they're doing. Take a typical small business that is based on fear. Picture the manager who is responsible for hiring the people she works with. If she's frightened of being replaced or overshadowed, she's likely to hire people who aren't quite as bright or competent as she is. In all likelihood, she won't even be aware of her hidden agenda to keep the business down, but that's precisely what she'll do. She was hired not so much for her expertise in running the business but for her efforts in *building* a successful business. But what she's doing is surrounding herself with people even less qualified than herself because she believes she'll look better. Businesses based on fear are doomed to failure.

People who are self-employed often fall into the same trap. "I can do this myself better than anyone else" is really a foolish statement based on fear. It's ridiculous to spend your time doing things that others can do better, because your time is better spent doing the things that you're really good at. The truth is, none of us are experts at everything, but most of us are good at something. A simple example would be that if you can consis-

27

tently earn $50 an hour doing whatever it is you do, then it makes more sense for you to keep doing it and to hire someone to do the time-consuming job of keeping your books and records. That way you don't waste valuable income-earning time—and you'll probably be better organized than if you'd done it yourself.

A very successful friend once joked that he couldn't afford "the luxury" of driving from San Francisco to the Pacific Northwest, despite the fact that airline fares were high at the time. He would much rather pay the airline to do what they do best—get him where he needs to be quickly—than spend twelve or more hours in the car missing out on untold opportunities for success and building his business.

As you let go of worry and "hire up," some magical things begin to happen. You begin to get out of your own way and allow success to unfold. One of the turning points in my career was when I realized that, although I believe I'm an excellent writer, I'm not always such a great editor. As I let go of the fear that an editor could change my essential message, I began to experiment with working with various editors. I started to "hire up." Guess what? They didn't change my message, they improved it. And to top it off, a good editor could clean up my writing in a fraction of the time that I spent struggling with it, giving me far more time to do what I do best.

As you let go of fear, you will find that you will be rewarded for your willingness to reach out. Rather than losing your job, you'll be praised for contributing to the success of your business. The truth is, if you can become one of the few people who operates not out of fear but out of a sincere willingness to do what's in the best interest of your business, you'll become an indispensable part of that company's success. And if for some strange and unlikely reason your good faith efforts are not appreciated and rewarded, you will know beyond any doubt that you aren't working in the best possible environment. Don't worry. When you're thinking in "hire up" terms, another, better opportunity is just around the corner.

A good definition of an entrepreneur is someone who can achieve predetermined goals through the efforts of himself and others. Why not raise the standards of those results by hiring up? The quality of your work will improve, and your profits will explode.

12.

DON'T WORRY ABOUT THE MARKET—INVEST IN IT

I believe that one of the closest things to a worry-free, wealth-building strategy is to invest, *long term*, in the stock market, preferably through your company 401K or, if you're self-employed, your SEP. Why? Because historically, to profit from this simple, well-known strategy, it doesn't matter in the short term if the market is going up or down. You win either way. There is absolutely nothing to worry about.

Once you commit to the "don't worry" attitude, you'll chuckle as you notice how many people worry, every day, unnecessarily, over which direction the market is moving. "What a relief, the market is having a good day" and "Oh no, the market is down" are frequent comments, but in reality, they have virtually no relevance if you are investing for the long term.

What is there to worry about? By implementing the "pay yourself first" strategy, by investing a predetermined percentage, such as 10 percent of your income to yourself (into high-quality, no-load mutual funds), you virtually guarantee that, over time, you'll amass a small fortune. You simply put the money in, month after month, and leave it there.

If the market is going up, your investment is worth more money. Congratulations, you win. But if the market is going down, your next investment will afford you the luxury of purchasing more shares of stock at a lower price. Congratulations, you win again!

To top off this worry-free, wealth-building strategy, you can get the federal and state governments to pitch in a third, or even more, of your total investment. By using a company retirement plan or self-employed SEP, you can deduct your contribution from your taxable income up to a certain maximum limit, saving you thousands of dollars and reducing the out-of-pocket costs of your investment. Your tax adviser, or even a knowledgeable friend, can probably show you how simple it is to accumulate wealth using this strategy and how to maximize the government's contribution toward your financial goals. The point here, however, is to show you that "don't worry" is not simply a cliché. There are many worry-free, practical approaches to building your fortune; this is simply one of the best. As always, your external success begins with your attitude toward life.

13.

BECOME LESS REACTIVE AND MORE RESPONSIVE

In business and in life, we have essentially two psychological modes that we are in most of the time: reactive and responsive. The reactive mode is the one that feels stressful. In it, we feel pressured and are quick to judge. We lose perspective and take things personally. We're annoyed, bothered, and frustrated.

Needless to say, our judgment and decision-making capacity is severely impaired when we are in a reactive state of mind. We make quick decisions that we often regret. We annoy other people and tend to bring out the worst in them. When an opportunity knocks, we are usually too overwhelmed or frustrated to see it. If we do see it, we're usually overly critical and negative.

The responsive mode, on the other hand, is our most relaxed state of mind. Being responsive suggests that we have our bearings. We see the bigger picture and take things less personally. Rather than being rigid and stubborn, we are flexible and calm. In the responsive mode, we are at our best. We bring out the best in others and solve problems gracefully. When an opportunity comes our way, our mind is open. We are receptive to abundance.

Once you are aware of these two drastically different modes of being, you will begin to notice which one you are in. You'll also notice the predictability of your behavior and feelings when you are in each mode. You'll observe yourself being irrational and negative in your reactive mode and calm and wise in your responsive state of mind.

Simply becoming aware of the different dynamics of your mind will open the door to tremendous changes in your life. You'll begin to notice when you fall into a reactive state of mind. You'll feel your own impatience. When this happens, simply say to yourself, "Whoops, there I go again" or something to this effect. Any type of simple acknowledgment will do the trick. You'll discover, as you notice and acknowledge your own reactivity, coupled with your understanding that, in all cases, it pays to be more responsive, you'll quickly come out of a reactive mode and fall into a more responsive state of mind.

A responsive state of mind is fertile ground for success. When your mind is clear and relaxed, you pave an open channel for abundance and joy. There is a direct and clear relationship between how much time you spend in a responsive state of mind and your own level of success. The more you are able to stay out of reactivity, the more opportunities will present themselves. Beginning right now, use the power of responsiveness to create your own success.

14.

WORK ON "KNOWING" INSTEAD OF "BELIEVING"

When you believe something, it's usually due to the fact that someone told you so—your parents, an instructor, a friend, a colleague, a partner, boss, or employee. You were influenced, often in a positive way, by what you were told. Consequently, your belief system was formed, altered, or solidified in some measurable way. For example, your parents may have attempted to convince you that holding a corporate job was more important, held more status, and had a more secure future than being a gardener. If you believed them, you would have factored this concept into your career decisions and the directions you followed. Every one of us has beliefs and there is certainly nothing wrong with this.

Knowing, on the other hand, is intrinsic in nature. When you know something, you feel it. You are certain. You may not always be able to explain or articulate why you feel the way you do, but something within you—wisdom, common sense, guidance, whatever—is providing you with needed answers and guiding you in a direction, as long as you listen.

For example, I always knew that I would be a teacher of some kind. I knew that my calling or role as an adult was to be sharing what I knew to be true through writing and speaking. This is difficult to explain because I believed I was an inadequate writer and was terribly frightened to speak in public. In fact, I nearly flunked high school English and had actually fainted while attempting to speak in front of a group! Perhaps the *only* thing I did right was listen to my inner voice—the source of knowing. It kept insisting that, despite appearances to the contrary, somehow I was going to teach. It took many years, but, as is always the case, knowing is more powerful than believing. Eventually I was guided in the direction I now call my career—writing, speaking, and teaching.

All of us have things that we know to be true about ourselves—dreams that we have, gifts we wish to share, unique talents we want to pursue. But all too often we bury these things we know with our own beliefs, and ultimately they become our limitations. Our beliefs convince us of things like: I can't do it, or It's for someone else, or It's not in my nature. Or they provide us with convenient excuses: I don't have time, or I never get any breaks, or My life isn't set up right.

The good news is that, the moment you decide that what you *know* is more important than what you have been taught to *believe*, you will have shifted gears in your quest for abundance. Success comes from within, not from without. It begins by listening to your inner calling and wisdom. What do you truly value and enjoy? What is your heart trying to tell you? Is there something that you have an inner need to pursue? These are the types of questions that will put you on your path toward greatness. Once on that path, you will discover your own unique way to make the path an enormous success and a great deal of fun. I've seen people turn hobbies into fortunes, change careers completely, start side businesses, or magically transform their existing career by changing their attitude. Over and over again, I have seen people turn dreams into realities through a simple shift in perspective. How this process unfolds is up to you. The path will be clear when you listen to your own inner voice.

15.

REMIND YOURSELF THAT YOUR LIFE BEGINS NOW

One of the most severely limiting beliefs that many of us have is that the person we were yesterday is the person we have to be today. This belief keeps us tied to our past mistakes, habits, and limitations. We somehow buy into the notion that history truly does repeat itself, that if we weren't successful yesterday, we certainly can't be successful today or tomorrow.

If you can see how ridiculous and self-defeating this belief is, you can make an instant shift toward success and fulfillment. All of us have unlimited potential and a clean slate in this moment—now. What prevents us from tapping into this potential is our own mental ties to the past. Letting go of your past is like taking a set of heavy chains from around your neck. It frees you to pursue your dreams and rise to your greatest potential.

I heard a wonderful story about the power of living in the present moment. It involves imagining that you are on a boat in the middle of the ocean. You are standing at the helm, heading due east, as you ask yourself three important questions: First, what is the wake? You turn back and observe the water behind the boat that is left behind. The wake is that water. It forms a shape *behind* the boat until it disappears into nothingness. Second, you ask yourself the question, Can the wake drive the boat? You quickly answer, "Of course not. That's preposterous." The wake has no power. Finally, you ask yourself, What then powers the boat? You think for a moment and come to the obvious conclusion. All of the power of the boat comes from the present-moment energy of the engine. That's it. There is nothing else.

The analogy to your own life is clear. Your present-moment energy is all you need. It's incredibly powerful and resourceful. The problem is, many of us don't use our present-moment energy to its fullest because we are constantly trying to use our "wake," that which is behind us, our past, to move us forward. But like the wake in the ocean, our past has no power. It is nothingness.

Our past has no power other than the power we give it. One of the most dynamic and significant changes you can make in your life is to make the commitment to drop all negative references to your past, to begin living now. Operate as if all the power in your life begins and ends in this moment. The positive energy you create may shock you. New doors and opportunities will open. As your past habits creep into your consciousness, simply acknowledge them and let them go. This is not a complicated process, and you can begin doing so immediately. Your past was important because it was needed to get you into the present. Your life, now, is a series of present moments to be experienced, one after another. Focus on what you can do today, right now in this moment, and you will have already begun to create the abundance that is your birthright.

16.

SURROUND YOURSELF WITH EXPERTS

Charles Givens, author of the phenomenally successful book *Wealth Without Risk*, has said, "If you want to learn about money, learn from someone who has a lot of it." So, many people surround themselves with "successful" people, "experts" on making money, and people who have a lot more money than they do. Yet they are intimidated by them, frightened that people who are more successful won't be willing to spend time or share their ideas with us. Nothing could be farther from the truth. The reality is, accomplished people love it when someone takes an interest in their success; they love to share their wisdom, good ideas, or business secrets. It makes them feel wanted and needed.

Two of my favorite people in the world each have a great deal of money. One is entirely self-made, the other comes from inherited wealth. Both are exceptionally willing to sit down and share ideas with me, or practically anyone else who asks them. The interesting thing, however, is that they both claim that very few people have the courage to ask to pick their brains for ideas. What a waste! I probably know, personally, over a hundred super-successful people, and I can't think of a single one whose door isn't almost always open for others. I've worked on projects with some very famous, successful people through some of my other books. When people ask me, "How in the world did you convince them to participate?," they are often shocked at the simplicity of my answer. I respond honestly by saying, "I just asked them." You'll be amazed at the number of people who are more than willing to help, whether it's the owner of a successful grocery store, a top-producing insurance salesperson, a well-known author, a physician, a lawyer, or an excellent teacher. Most want and are willing to offer advice. In fact, asking someone you admire and respect for their feedback and ideas is the greatest compliment you can offer them.

Not all, but most highly successful people (in any field) are available to help others. Usually, it's the people fighting to climb to the top who are the most frightened, insecure, or unwilling to offer guidance. If you do ask for help or advice and are turned down, you can bet that the next person you ask will be more than willing. If you want great advice and you want to avoid big mistakes, seek help. Surround yourself with winners. Don't get advice from Uncle Charley unless he, himself, is a successful person. Go straight to the top.

17.

BE AWARE OF WHAT YOU DON'T KNOW AND
WHAT YOU'RE NOT GOOD AT

My father used to tell me as he read my poorly written essays in school, "Richard, it's not important that you're not a great speller. It's really important, however, that you know that you're not a good speller. That way, when in doubt, you can use the dictionary." Boy, was he right! I have gotten more mileage out of this tiny piece of wisdom than perhaps any other.

My dad was absolutely correct, but not just about spelling. The same idea applies to virtually everything. In my work, for example, it's not critical that I'm an expert editor as long as I know my own weaknesses and limitations. I can hire someone to fill in where I'm weak. Similarly, I'm not a great coordinator for putting together all the details of a public lecture. No problem. I can hire someone who is. It's always smarter to do this and, in the long run, it's almost always less expensive and more profitable. The only time there would be a problem is if I didn't know that I wasn't good at something or if I was unwilling to admit it.

Chances are you're probably really good at certain things and really bad at others. So what? Why should you frustrate yourself and waste your time doing those things you struggle with? This doesn't mean you can't learn new skills or improve existing ones. It merely suggests that you spend the bulk of your time doing whatever it is you do best as well as that which is most important to your success. It's easy to get bogged down and defeated doing tasks you don't enjoy and aren't very good at. Certainly, many if not most of these tasks need to get done, but not necessarily by you.

41

What if you could spend an extra two or three hours a day focusing on that which you truly love and are genuinely good at? What would happen to your productivity, creativity, and bottom line? You'll never know for sure until you try, but I can assure you that, for me and for so many others I know, this simple idea has been an extremely profitable insight.

18.

BECOME AWARE OF THE PASSION FACTOR

As Marsha Sinetar's incredible best-seller reminds us, *Do What You Love, the Money Will Follow.* Perhaps the reason this book is so popular is that it reminds us of something we intuitively already know: When we are passionate about what we do, success will follow!

Passion for life and for our work is a critical element of success and abundance. Passion is a virtually unstoppable, attitudinal force that generates energy, creativity, and productivity. When you love what you do, it's difficult not to succeed. Your enthusiasm is obvious to everyone around you and contagious.

Part of the process of creating passion in your work is choosing work that you truly love. Doing so requires conscious choice, which often takes a great deal of courage. It can be frightening to change career directions or to try something new, irrespective of how much we may "want to." After all, most of us were indoctrinated into believing that walking a certain safe path was the way to achieve security.

Fear is a powerful, highly destructive force that prevents many of us from pursuing our dreams. However, if you take a careful look at most successful people, more often than not, they have faced very similar fears and conquered them. A client of mine once said, "I finally asked myself the question, Whose life is this anyway? and when I couldn't answer the question, I knew I had to make a change."

I have a story of my own that reinforces this strategy. Many years ago I was taking the safe route. Shortly after college, I began work for an M.B.A. (master's degree in business). The problem was, I couldn't stand it. I dreaded every class and knew I wasn't on my path, following my own dreams. Although it was extremely frightening to me, I decided to walk out and never return. I was determined to follow my bliss instead of my predetermined career path. It was one of the best, most important decisions of my life.

It's important to ask yourself: How safe is it *really*, spending your time doing something you don't enjoy? How well can you perform a task you dread? How creative and original is your thinking? How easy is it to go the extra mile and/or to do what's necessary to achieve greatness? The answers to each of these questions are clear: Without passion, your odds of success are minimal. You will either struggle in your career or burn out completely. But the opposite is just as true when passion for your work fills your heart. When you follow your heart, when you discover what is truly nourishing to your soul, an abundant, joyful life is just around the corner.

19.

DON'T LET SUCCESS GO TO YOUR HEAD

There's an alarming trend taking place: People who have had some degree of good fortune and success tend to lose their humility and become at least slightly arrogant. This is very unfortunate for many reasons. First, and most obviously, no one really wants to be around someone who is arrogant or self-absorbed. It's boring, and it's annoying! Arrogance implies a lack of gratitude. The assumption is, "I did this all by myself; it's all about me." Factors such as fortuitous timing, good luck, breaks, and so on are forgotten or disregarded.

In addition, when you allow success to go to your head, your stress levels skyrocket and your quality of life gradually disappears. People will stop liking you, and eventually, you'll stop liking yourself.

How often have you either known or heard about someone who "used to be" a really nice person? He or she was hardworking, ethical, compassionate, thoughtful, concerned about others, and blessed with a good sense of humor. Yet, shortly after being promoted, making a great deal of money, acquiring stock, or succeeding at something, the person became a real jerk. He became self-absorbed, overwhelmed, greedy, hard to please, and demanding.

In a way, it's ironic. Someone finally gets what he or she has always wanted—success—yet now he is rarely satisfied. In fact, he often becomes difficult and paranoid. People are constantly letting him down and nothing is good enough anymore: the house is too small, the car needs to be fancier, his temper fuse is shortened, perspective is lost, greed sets in, and more is always better. People who used to love to be around him can't stand him anymore. In fact, people start to hope that his good fortune will fail. Friendships slip away, obsessive busyness and a lack of time take over. Someone who was happy and relatively easy to please is now impossible to satisfy. I was once sitting next to a very wealthy man in his $100,000 car. He was so used to being perfectly comfortable that he became practically hysterical, complaining to the driver that the temperature in the car wasn't cool enough! I'm totally serious.

I've read articles about celebrities, athletes, and business people who have done really well—their talent, timing, hard work, luck, and all the rest of it kicked in at just the right time. And good for them. Yet, rather than being grateful and keeping a sense of perspective, they act put out, as if life isn't fair, or as if they are somehow better or more important than others simply because they're good at something and have enjoyed some success. It's exactly the opposite of the way it should be!

It's amazing, yet there are teachers in my own field—teachers of happiness—who are hard to please, who regularly send food back at restaurants, complain constantly about service, act rude to drivers and waitresses, and so forth.

The question is, "Why would anyone want to be like that?" To be so constantly disappointed and bothered by things is just another way of saying you are always sweating the small stuff—even the tiny stuff.

So, whether you've already made your fortune or are still working on it, try to see the absurdity and humor behind letting any type of success go to your head. Even if you've slipped in that direction, it's never too late to turn yourself around. You can have it all—tremendous success, good fortune, and a lifetime of abundance—and still be a thoughtful, kind, generous person. If you can do this, then you'll really have something, because not only will you be successful, you'll be happy as well!

20.

BE PREPARED TO WALK AWAY FROM A
NEGOTIATION—YOU CAN USUALLY GO BACK

Many people get less out of a negotiation than is otherwise possible because of fear—fear that if they don't accept the terms of the deal, as is, they sabotage the deal completely. While it's possible this could occur, it's far more likely that you will sabotage your success—both immediate and long term—if you are unwilling to walk away from a negotiation. If you believe in your product or service, in whatever it is that you bring to the table (your time, your expertise, etc.), you're virtually always better off if you're willing to walk away, to consider the option of starting over or bringing your business elsewhere. This doesn't mean that you *do* walk away; only that you're comfortable doing so. You're not attached, one way or the other.

This don't-worry attitude is applicable in most business situations. Let's consider one of the simplest examples, purchasing a home. Suppose you find a house that you truly love, and the asking price is $100,000. You believe, however, that to make this purchase wisely, you should pay no more than $90,000. The current owner seems stubborn. The problem is, you really love the house and don't want to jeopardize the deal.

Being "attached" to an outcome can cost you a great deal of money. If you feel it's in your best interest to pay no more than $90,000 for this house, the wisest financial and emotional decision you could make would be to offer the $90,000, be willing to walk away, and not worry about it! The simple act of not worrying about the outcome will, more often than not, come back to help you because the truth of the matter is, most people *are* worriers! And it is very likely that the person you are negotiating with is one of them. Although there are rare exceptions, the recipient of your offer will almost never slam the door on the deal at this point. He will, however, be forced into making a very important, quick decision—most likely a decision that *he* is worried about. He can, of course, turn you down, but if he's a worrier, he might not. After all, he's turning away a sure thing in exchange for an unknown future, something that worriers can't stand. He may come back with a counteroffer, but if he knows you're *not* a worrier, that you're perfectly willing to walk away, the counteroffer is likely to be much lower than if he senses your fear. This is pretty simple stuff. But the truth is, the reality of making money and wise decisions isn't very complicated. However, not many people understand the importance of a don't-worry attitude. If you do, you're one step ahead of the game.

A friend of mine is the shrewdest negotiator I have ever seen. He once walked into a car dealership and made an incredibly low-ball offer on a brand-new luxury car. This is exactly what he said: "Good afternoon, sir. I have a certified check in my hands in the amount of $35,250 for which I'd like to buy this particular automobile. I know you're going to have to ask your boss, so the offer is good for nine whole minutes—but not one second longer. I will not pay one penny more for the car, but the check is yours if you want to part with this car." As the visibly nervous salesperson started to respond, my friend calmly looked at his watch and said, "You have eight and one half minutes left before I walk out the door."

He got the car!

Obviously, few of us would have the nerve (or the means) or perhaps even the desire to do this. Yet the example does demonstrate the power of the willingness to walk away. Clearly, my friend's offer had to be in the ballpark for what the car was truly worth. The dealership certainly wasn't going to give the car away. But my friend had factored that into his strategy.

He did some research into the dealer's actual cost, and knew that if they took the deal, they would still make a tiny profit. But he also knew that his price would, in all likelihood, be lower than anyone else had paid for the same car. Since he wanted that particular car but wasn't attached to it, he couldn't lose either way. He knew that, in most cases, a salesman would have to spend a great deal of time with a potential customer before any sale would take place. In this instance, his total time involvement, other than the actual paperwork, was less than nine minutes. It just might be worth it to the dealership to make a quick, small profit rather than wait days, weeks, even months for a larger one. The key was his absolute willingness to walk away with no regrets whatsoever. You can implement this strategy with the utmost respect for the people with whom you are negotiating. There's no need to appear aggressive or obnoxious. All you need is a don't-worry attitude. Experiment with this strategy and, I believe, you will be well rewarded.

21.

BE WILLING TO CHANGE

In his wonderful book *Success Is No Accident*, Dr. Lair Ribeiro makes a statement that rings true to my ears and has been proven repeatedly throughout history. He says, "If you go on doing what you've always done, you'll go on getting what you've always got." What a powerful message! Sometimes, in order to create positive things in your life, you need to make some changes in the way you do things. The world isn't going to suddenly reward you by changing its conditions. Instead, *you* must alter the way you approach certain challenges.

I have met numerous people who are virtually unwilling to change, even when their current efforts aren't working. People are frightened of change. Sometimes they even argue for their limitations by saying things like: "I've always been that way" or "I'm just not that kind of person" or "I've always done it differently." If something *isn't* working for you, however, statements like these aren't relevant or helpful. It's critical to remember that if you go on doing what you've always done, you *will* go on getting what you've always got!

Maybe you're not the type of person who believes in asking friends and family for favors. And you might even be proud of this fact. Still, there are times when asking for help might be just what you need to succeed. If you're stubborn and insist "I can't do that," you may be missing out on a wonderful opportunity. There are countless other examples of where an unwillingness to try something new, or an unwillingness to do something differently, will interfere with your chances for success. Take an inventory of your own stubbornness: Are there areas in your life where you do things a certain way simply because that's the way you've always done them?

Without doubt, "Keep an open mind" is an overused phrase. Yet relatively few of us actually do keep an open mind. Instead, we are stuck in old, worn-out ways. If you drop your fear, and have the courage to be willing to change, my guess is that you won't have to go on much longer getting what you've always had.

22.

SPEND THE BULK OF YOUR TIME ON THE
"CRITICAL INCH" OF YOUR BUSINESS OR PROJECT

Often, the greatest mistake people make in their quest for success is that they focus on the wrong parts of their business. Too much time and energy are spent doing things that, while perhaps necessary, aren't the critical, absolutely important aspects of the business or project. I've seen people frustrated, claiming they "didn't have time" to make the necessary calls, speak to the decision maker, write the offer, ask for the deal, engage in critical due diligence, write the chapter, make the promotional or marketing effort, or whatever else might be the *essential* task—but somehow they did manage to find the time to clean their desk, make a few social calls, organize their computer disks, plan their weekend, review some files, set up a meeting, and do countless other tasks that have limited relevance to performance and success.

Perhaps, at a given moment, solving a particular problem is the "critical inch" of your business; maybe it's generating additional cash flow, diffusing an interpersonal issue with a colleague, finishing a report, writing a speech, or addressing a technical issue. Part of the solution is asking the relevant question: What's truly most important? More often than not, the answer is quite different from the answer to another question: What seems to be the next logical or convenient thing to do? Frequently, we'll jump from one activity to another without any real thought as to the true relevance of our actions. We'll respond to a mini-crisis, phone call, or something that's been sitting on the desk before taking on the one activity that *truly* makes a difference.

About twice a week I work out at a local athletic club. The same principle seems to apply to working out and getting in shape. It's interesting to watch the different ways people "work out." There is one group of people—I'd like to think I'm one of them—who roll up their sleeves and get to work. They go from machine to machine, exercise to exercise, until they have completed their workout. In thirty minutes or less, they can be in the shower and out the door. Generally, these people are in pretty good shape. They did what they intended to do.

There's another group of people, however, who never quite get to it. They socialize a great deal, take fifteen or twenty minutes to get changed, and walk around the gym looking at the equipment. Sometimes they'll read the paper or take a steam bath. Recently, I overheard a phone conversation between one of these men and his wife or girlfriend. He said to her, with a serious look on his face, "Honey, I just don't get it. I come down here to the club virtually every day, but never seem to lose any weight." Now, I've seen this man at the club on many occasions, but I've yet to see him *actually* work out. He's convinced himself that by being there every day, he's doing something worthwhile; yet he's missing the boat entirely. He never seems to do the critical inch—the exercise!

If we're not careful, it's easy to fall into the same basic trap with our business and moneymaking efforts. We may look busy, and do quite a few things during the course of a day, but we might not be focusing on the one or two things that really make a difference. Some of the most successful people I know work only a few hours a day—but boy, do they understand the concept of the critical inch. When you do what's truly necessary and important, the rest seems to fall into place. Take a moment, each day, to reevaluate your priorities. Make sure you spend your time doing that which is going to create success and abundance in your life.

23.

EXPRESS YOUR GRATITUDE TOWARD OTHERS

When it comes right down to it, there are very few sure things in life. Once in a while, however, we come across an idea that is an absolute, always, no matter what, truism. This is one of them, and a good one to remember: *As long as our expression of gratitude is genuine, other people love it and remember it. This not only makes them feel good, but it also encourages them to help us again and to encourage others to do the same.* The people we remember to thank, in person, with a thoughtful note or gesture, or a phone call, are infinitely more likely to help us again than those we take for granted and/or neglect to thank. It's so obvious, yet so few people really understand how this works.

People are inherently good. Most people love helping others, reaching out, lending a hand, offering assistance. For the most part, people love to be remembered or thought of as the person who gave someone else their big break, or some other form of important, loving guidance. The other side of the coin, however, is that people love to be acknowledged, admired, and thanked. People love to be thanked, not out of any selfish need but simply because it feels good to be acknowledged. And when we are sincerely acknowledged, the acknowledgment acts as a reinforcement that we have done the right thing. Thus, we want to do it again. Because people love to reach out to help others—if we thank them for their kindness—it actually nudges them to encourage others to help us, too. Life becomes infinitely easier when we remember to thank others for their acts of kindness.

Many wonderful people have stepped forward to help me in my career and in my life. Whether I have asked for help or received it without request, I always try to remember to express my gratitude. Although I never thank people in order get something in return, I have found that thanking people from the heart guarantees that more help is just around the corner. None of us wants to be taken for granted. We all love to be thanked!

The next time you do something really nice or helpful for someone and they thank you, take note of how it makes you feel. While it's true there are many instances where you would help again without any thanks (those of us who have children know this), I'll bet you'll find yourself even more willing to help someone who expresses their gratitude, which is, of course, also one of the keys to a joyful life. By engaging in constant gratitude, you'll be guaranteeing success, abundance, *and* happiness.

24.

LEAVE A GREAT IMPRESSION
(NOT JUST A GOOD ONE)

I guess you could say that this strategy is the opposite of the "don't burn any bridges" concept. The feeling others have for you can be a critical element of success. In all cases, when people have a nice feeling toward you, it sets you apart and gives you an ethical, well-deserved advantage in all you do. This doesn't mean you should pretend to be someone you're not, only that you recognize that your presence, behavior, integrity, and kindness will leave a lasting imprint in the minds of those you are with.

I once heard an audiotape from Ken Blanchard called "Raving Fans." In it, he described the importance of setting yourself apart by creating customers who don't simply like your product or service but actually "rave" about it—and you. This strategy is the interpersonal version of creating raving fans. When people think of you, you want them to genuinely want to do business, spend time with, help you. You want your customers, clients, coworkers, colleagues, even competitors, to think and speak highly of you to others.

The way to do this is very simple: Make living your life with absolute integrity and kindness your first priority. Put others first, whenever possible. Be genuinely interested in the lives of other people. Be very present-moment oriented with others. Look them in the eye and really focus on what they're saying. Care about them as individuals. Ask about their families. Listen, listen, listen. Finally, make your actions match your good intentions. Stand out from the crowd. Be the one to thank your customers and the people with whom you work. Send a card or thoughtful note, even flowers if it's appropriate. Make people remember you in a positive light.

If you implement this strategy with your own unique touches and if you are genuine in your thoughts and actions, you will create, over time, a stellar, "one in a million" reputation with virtually everyone you come in contact with. People will be beating down your door for the opportunity to work with or even to spend time with you. What's more, your life will be filled with more joy and loving kindness than you ever thought possible.

25.

MAINTAIN WEALTH CONSCIOUSNESS

Developing wealth consciousness is what this book is all about. Wealth consciousness suggests a complete absence of money worries; an awareness that there is always plenty of money to go around. People who live with true abundance never worry about having enough— they know that creating wealth and affluence is a function of their own mind-set. Worry keeps us from feeling free and joyful. We are never truly free until we break the chains of fear. But once we do, our lives will never be the same. A life without worry is a life of abundance, a life well lived.

That which we focus our attention on expands. If we spend our mental energy worrying, it's difficult if not impossible to create great abundance. Our fear gets in the way of our creativity and traps us in the status quo. In other words, our fear "interferes" with our means of creation. On the other hand, if we are free of worries, if we maintain wealth consciousness, money will flow to us in inexhaustible ways. We will literally create ways to keep money flowing in our direction. Our antennas will be on the lookout for new and exciting opportunities, and our minds will be open to embrace them.

The most important point about wealth consciousness can be summed up with the adage, "Don't put the cart before the horse." Make no mistake about it: Wealth consciousness comes first! You will not suddenly develop wealth consciousness if and when you become "wealthy." It's the other way around. You develop wealth consciousness by eliminating worry, by trusting in the universe and in your own inner resources. Once you secure your wealth consciousness, true abundance is just around the corner.

26.

WAIT FOR INSPIRATION

Ironically, it's often the case that the best use of our time is to do absolutely nothing—to not act, to simply wait for an answer. But in our speeded-up, frentic culture, most of us panic if we aren't actively doing something, even if that "something" isn't wise, productive, or useful. Most of us are so busy, or at least looking busy, that we can't see or hear our own wisdom.

Built into our psyche is a wealth of wisdom. We all have innate common sense at our disposal that can provide us with solutions, inspiration, and guidance. The problem is, we must quiet down enough to hear it. We must wait for inspiration.

To access our innate health takes some humility and getting used to. We must be willing to admit that "we don't know what to do" at a given moment. We must learn to be a little patient; it's worth the wait. The simple act of admitting that you *don't know* an answer, at present, activates your inner wisdom and guidance. By simply being willing to wait for inspiration, you virtually guarantee that it will come—in most cases, rather quickly. Not always, but sometimes, your mind needs a few minutes, occasionally longer, to cultivate the most appropriate answer. The answers you receive, however, will surprise and delight you. Your thinking and instincts will rise to a new level.

27.

USE THE POWER OF REFLECTION

Reflection is one of the most underused yet powerful tools for success. It is a passive way to pinpoint solutions and strategies with the least amount of effort or wasted energy. It's the opposite of "trying too hard," of forcing an answer. Reflection is more a matter of allowing an answer to unfold right before your eyes, often with little or no effort on your part.

One of the benefits of reflection is that it enables us to get our egos out of the way. In a quiet state of mind we are able to see things clearly, including our own contributions to problems, new ways of doing things, and the ways we get in our own way. Reflection allows us to sense our self-imposed limitations and some of the blind spots in our thinking.

Reflection is simply a matter of getting out of your own way. It's about quieting down your mind so that answers can arise within the quietness. Often, when we're looking for an answer, we "turn up the volume" of our thinking. This might be called active problem solving. We think, think, think—and then we think some more. We get personally involved in the process. We take the credit for finding solutions and the blame when we cannot. For the most part, when we are actively thinking, we're thinking about that which we already know, that with which we are familiar. We try to solve a problem at the same level of understanding that initially created it. And often we go around in circles.

People who regularly use reflection, on the other hand, understand that we are connected to, and a part of, a deeper intelligence. This quiet source of wisdom is available to all of us in unlimited doses because it is always present. The only factor preventing us from hearing or being connected to this wisdom is the noise or chatter of our own thinking. When we turn the "volume" of our thinking down, we can begin to sense this deeper intelligence. This is reflection.

Recently I was engaged in an interpersonal conflict with someone I was working with. In my mind, I was blaming him for virtually all of our problems. The more I thought about it, the more convinced I was that the problem was him. It got so bad that I considered breaking up the partnership, which, to that point, had been very successful. My wife, Kris, suggested I stop thinking about it entirely and postpone making any decisions. She suggested instead that I take a drive and spend some time in quiet reflection. I took her advice. As I quieted down, it became clear to me that a great deal of our problems were actually coming from me. I could see how I was contributing to our poor communication and unrealistic expectations.

You may be shocked at how easily most problems can be solved when you simply step out of the way by quieting down. You may also be pleasantly surprised at the ease with which new and creative ideas will flow into your life. Although your mind will be quiet, it won't be turned off. Instead, you will be using a new part of your mind—a softer, wiser part—that understands the path of least resistance and the source of new answers. Success is often a function of doing something exceptionally well or more creatively than it has been done before. Reflection is a powerful vehicle to bring this about.

28.

LAUGH AT YOUR MISTAKES
(AND YOU WON'T REPEAT THEM)

Have you ever noticed that the more seriously you take your mistakes, the more you make them? And the more seriously you take your problems, the more you create them? This is because your behavior follows your attention just as surely as baby puppies follow their mother. Wherever the bulk of your energy lies, your behavior is sure to follow. When your mind is full of confusing or conflicting details, mistakes, and problems, your attention is riveted in a negative direction. Thus, when you make a big deal out of something you have done wrong, when you take yourself too seriously, you are actually setting the stage to repeat the mistake.

Mental energy is a very powerful and potentially useful tool. However, energy cuts both ways. If your energy is directed exclusively toward problems and concerns, that is what you will see and what you will tend to create. If your energy is abundant, however, your mind will be in a more creative mode—searching for solutions, seeing opportunities, building on strengths. Your mind will be open to suggestions to new and better ways of doing things. You will have a winning attitude.

In terms of expending energy, it is far more powerful to be in favor of something positive than to be against something negative—*for* peace instead of against violence, *for* excellence instead of against mediocrity.

A decision to make light of your mistakes, to remain lighthearted, doesn't mean you don't care or that you're not concerned with making an error. It simply means that you refuse to compound a problem by making a bigger deal out of something than is absolutely necessary. It means that you understand the value of keeping your perspective and sense of humor even in the face of adversity.

In every mistake there is the potential for growth. Inherent in every problem there is a solution. When you take the process too seriously, however, you interfere with your ability to see answers. The next time you make a mistake, instead of dealing with it in your usual way, chuckle at yourself instead. You will be surprised at how quickly and easily you are able to resolve the issue.

29.

TAKE YOUR LUNCH

Although you or the person you live with might worry about the effort or time it takes to prepare a lunch, there are some potentially valuable benefits in doing so. Consider this: Suggest to one or more of your friends at work that you would like to do an experiment for a couple of days. The experiment would be that you each bring your lunch and, depending on weather and other factors, plan to go to a nearby park, lake, hilltop, or some other interesting setting to eat it.

The idea is to then combine the lunch group with an investment club where you exchange ideas and investment options. Depending on the structure of the group, members can take turns bringing special food items. Not only can this be a great deal of fun and a lot healthier than eating at a restaurant, but enormously profitable as well. For example, if you stayed on the job for thirty years and substituted a $2 lunch for a $7.50 lunch at a local restaurant, the $5.50-per-day savings deposited in an investment club earning 8 percent over thirty years would amount to around $100,000. And those of us who eat at restaurants frequently know these numbers are extremely conservative.

Even if your investment club met only two or three times per week, the door would be open for some new, "worry-free" ways to create wealth. One of the goals in creating your "club" is to create the discipline and mind-set for regular investing. Once you are thinking in terms of investing instead of spending, you can duplicate this process in other areas. A small bonus from your employer, for example, can be spent on consumer items, *or* it can be invested in your new account to make it grow. The same is true with a tax refund, a surprise gift from a relative, even accumulated pocket change. Anytime you come across a little extra money you may find yourself investing in your future. Over time, your earnings can be extraordinary.

Once you have established this type of wealth-building mind-set, the benefits will continue to grow. You will find yourself making different types of financial decisions that pay off in really big ways. You may decide to buy term insurance instead of whole life and, unlike so many others, you will actually invest the difference! You may choose a more affordable automobile and, rather than feeling deprived, actually feel excited that you get to invest the difference in yourself. You'll discover that investing in this manner is a great deal of fun. Rather than worrying about your future, you'll be making joyful choices to secure a worry-free life. Who would believe that bringing your lunch to work could be such a profitable thing to do?

30.

ASK FOR WHAT YOU WANT

Jack Canfield and Mark Victor Hansen, authors of *Chicken Soup for the Soul,* call this simple strategy "The Aladdin Factor." It's astonishing what you can accomplish by simply asking for what you want—help, a raise, forgiveness, an idea, another chance, a break, or whatever. And not only can you get what you want by asking for it, but often the person you are asking will thank you for taking the initiative.

If it's so obviously helpful and important to ask for what we want, why do so few of us do it? Once again, the answer is fear. We worry about the outcome. We're afraid of rejection or a negative response. We might be worried about offending someone or being perceived of as weak, or of taking advantage of our relationship. We may feel we don't deserve help. For a multitude of reasons, we allow past negative experiences and/or our own made-up fears to taint our present opportunities.

Several years ago I had the realization that one of my own greatest assets was *my* willingness to help others. Hundreds of times, I've returned calls to complete strangers, or written a response to one of their questions. With friends and family, my willingness to help is even greater. Whenever possible, within reason, I'm there to help. I realized that helping others, offering assistance, doing favors, feeling needed and wanted is a deep and important human need. It feels wonderful to be needed.

This being the case, I realized that, for the most part, other people feel the same way. Despite our fears and concerns to the contrary, it's actually quite arrogant and self-righteous to assume that others aren't as willing to help. I'm not the only nice guy around. What in the world was I thinking? The key in asking for something, large or small, is to be sincere in your belief that, deep down, others *want* to help you. You must approach your request by assuming that the person you are asking is just like you—he or she has an inner longing to be of help.

This simple insight about the goodwill of others dramatically speeded up my path to success—as it will yours. It meant that I no longer had to do everything myself. I didn't have to develop all my ideas and projects on my own. There were plenty of others more than willing to pitch in and offer their expertise, assistance, and advice. Today, when I ask someone to sit down with me and share an idea, it often sparks ideas that help them as well. What goes around comes around. Those who are willing to help others are always paid back in one way or another. Obviously, this isn't a prescription to run out and take advantage of people. To think in these terms would be to miss the whole point of this strategy. Your own good judgment will prevent you from doing this. Once you remove the fear of asking for help, your wisdom and common sense will instruct you when and how to ask.

Rather than being afraid to ask for help, remember this: When you ask someone to help you, you are actually doing *them* a tremendous favor by giving them an opportunity to feel needed. Beginning today, rub your magic lamp and experiment with "The Aladdin Factor."

31.

SHORT CIRCUIT YOUR REACTION SPIRALS

It's a rare person who can avoid the trap of reaction spirals. This is the insidious tendency to overreact to something—and then compound the problem by overanalyzing it. Here is a typical example: Someone criticizes some aspect of your work. You overreact to the criticism and become defensive. As if that weren't bad enough, you spend the next half hour analyzing the critical comments, convincing yourself they are incorrect. A whirlwind of thoughts passes through your mind. You focus on them. The more you do, the worse you feel, and the more tired you become.

The question is, how effective are you when you're feeling overwhelmed, defensive, and stubborn? The truth is, in a negative state of mind, we expend unnecessary energy, make very poor decisions, and lose our creativity and sense of joy. Wouldn't it be wonderful if you could nip these reaction spirals in the bud?

You can! The trick is to see them coming and to commit, in advance, to "short circuiting" them. With every negative reaction comes a negative feeling—a feeling of irritation, annoyance, or impatience. We often use these feelings to justify further negativity. For example, we say to ourselves something like, "I have a right to be angry." Now that we're focused on our anger, we think about other instances that make us angry, and so on. This fuels our negative feelings and creates a negative spiral.

If, instead of compounding our negative feelings, we used them as a signal to alert us to potential trouble, we would be in a much better position to stop the cycle before it got out of hand. The other day, for example, I was waiting for an important phone call. I waited and waited. In my mind,

I was certain that the person I was waiting for had agreed to call me at a certain time on a specific phone line. I had canceled other plans to make time for her. Her understanding, however, was that I was to call her. Because I was on the other line while waiting for her call, I didn't phone her either. Finally, she called. And when she did, she was extremely angry at me. Instantly, I became defensive and angry. "How dare she?" I thought to myself. I was enraged. What saved me was my ability to use my negative feelings as an protective alarm! Like a flashing light, I was reminded to calm down, which allowed me to see our mutual innocence. One of us had made a mistake. Big deal. Moments after I became angry, a little voice inside my head said, "Relax. Don't turn this into a big deal." Within a few moments, I regained my perspective and simply apologized. Honestly, I have no way of knowing who was at fault. And who cares? The point is, had I continued in my reaction spiral I would have clearly jeopardized my working relationship with this person. As it turned out, our little misunderstanding was a nonissue. We both were able to get past it in a matter of seconds. No wasted energy, no heated debate, no unnecessary discussion, no defensive or passive-aggressive behavior.

Many potential problems can be averted with this simple strategy. All you really need is the wisdom to understand that negative reactions aren't in your best interest, and the humility and willingness to back off and start over. Abundance is a joyful path. Occasionally, however, we lose our way. Don't waste your precious energy compounding an already negative situation. You'll be amazed how much smoother your life will become and how easily you can get back on track when you short circuit your reaction spirals.

32.

ELIMINATE YOUR MOST SELF-DEFEATING BELIEF

All of us have beliefs that get in our way. And for many of us, there is one in particular—some nagging, habitual tenet that we have come to accept as "just the way things are." For me, it was my belief that "I don't have enough time." Day after day, for most of my adult life, I would remind myself of this limiting concept. Sometimes I would tell myself this many times in a single day.

What possible value could there be in telling yourself this—or any—self-created negative belief? Consider the subtle messages that go along with this idea. After all, if I believe that "I don't have enough time," I must also believe that "I'll never get something done on time," "I'll be under constant pressure," "There's no time to lose," as well as other related, limiting ideas that directly interfere with my success and quality of life. Does this belief help me get things done? Of course not! Does it bring me joy? No. Any effect this belief has is strictly negative.

What's *your* most self-defeating belief? Is it that you believe you aren't good enough, or lucky enough? Maybe you believe you don't deserve success, or that other people control your destiny. Perhaps you believe that people are out to get you, or that you are a victim of circumstance. Whatever it is, it's not worth keeping and it's certainly not worth defending! But each time you remind yourself—by telling yourself—of your limiting belief, you are reinforcing an idea that directly interferes with your own success. It puts a wall between where you are and where you want to be. Each time you say to yourself, "I never get any breaks," or "I can't help it, I've always been that way," or whatever negative message you are sending, it's as if you are saying to yourself, "I don't want to succeed."

Each time I slip into my old habit of telling myself that I don't have enough time, I keep in mind the damage I am inflicting on myself. I remind myself that there is zero value in this, or any, self-defeating belief. I suggest you do the same thing. You may be surprised, even shocked, at how often you repeat self-defeating statements to yourself and/or to others. The good news is that you'll be pleasantly surprised at how easily you can rid yourself of their negative effects. Simply refuse to continue. Make a commitment to yourself to stop reinforcing this—and all—negative beliefs by discussing them, or even thinking about them. As familiar negativity comes to mind, gently dismiss it as you would flies at a picnic. Don't give it your valuable attention. Save your energy for positive ideas and action. Once you get your most self-defeating ideas out of the way, you'll discover that abundance and joy will be right around the corner.

33.

KEEP IN MIND THAT CIRCUMSTANCES DON'T
MAKE A PERSON, THEY REVEAL HIM

It's extremely rare to find a successful person who whines, complains, and frets about her circumstances. This is despite the fact that she may have overcome great obstacles to achieve her level of success. On the other hand, it's extremely common for struggling individuals to continually blame their circumstances for their lack of joy and abundance. The real question is: What came first—the attitude or the success? The answer, in virtually all cases, is that the winning, positive attitude came first, followed by a lifetime of abundance.

Your circumstances are what they are; they were what they were. If you are forty-five years old and were a middle child, you're still going to be a middle child when you're ninety-five. If you're black or white; a woman or a man; or if you were abused, taken advantage of, or bankrupt—these facts cannot change. If your parents couldn't afford to send you to college or if you had to work your way through school, shovel snow in your driveway, or walk ten miles to school—these are all things in your past. It's time to get over them and move on.

You'll find that life will be a lot easier and much more fun when you make the decision to drop your complaining. All it does is make you feel sorry for yourself—sad, angry, victimized, suspicious, and/or self-righteous. When you argue for your limitations, your thoughts and words merely get in your way and greatly interfere with your ability to create. With complaining out of the way, you'll create the space for an explosion of creativity and brilliance. You'll be able to be more focused and oriented to the present moment. Instead of focusing on problems, you'll begin to see solutions. Instead of maintaining an "I can't" attitude, you'll quickly develop a more positive vision for yourself.

All it takes is a simple decision; the decision to stop yourself from falling into the complaining habit. At first it may be difficult—even funny—to observe how often you complain. Habits can be hard to break. But in this case, it's well worth the effort. As an excuse or complaint comes to mind, gently shoo it away like you would flies at a picnic. Don't worry about it too much. You'll quickly get used to the nicer feelings that come from a life without complaints, as well as the success that comes with your new winning attitude!

34.

FORM A WINNING PARTNERSHIP

As you probably already know, the wrong partnership—professional or personal—can be far worse than no partnership. And a winning partnership can be worth its weight in gold. Sometimes, however, fear can keep us from seeking out good partners and forming winning partnerships. Many people worry that they will have to share the profits, decision-making authority, and/or prestige that come with a project or business. A fearful attitude, of course, won't allow us to do this. As always, it's a good idea to overcome this fear so that you will know whether forming a winning partnership is in your best interest.

There are a few important points to consider when deciding if a partnership is right for you. If the members of a partnership do essentially the same thing, it's almost inevitable that one will be harder working and have more commitment than the other. Often, that partner begins to resent pulling the other partner along. Likewise, the partner being pulled resents the other partner's pushing. It's generally *not* a winning partnership. For example, two trial attorneys go into a legal partnership. At the end of the year, one or the other might wonder what benefit he received from the partnership. After all, each is fully capable of doing the other's job. But, if a trial attorney and a corporate attorney go into partnership, usually each one, at the end of the year says, "Thank God for my partner—I don't know what I would do without him."

Ideally, each partner brings to the table different skills and attributes. One might be excellent at details and planning, the other in promotion and public speaking. Or one might be excellent in sales, the other in marketing. A good partnership is like a good marriage—it has to be formed carefully. If you can create the right combination of skills, work ethic, and vision you can create a winning team.

Here's a classic example of a winning partnership. Alan and George each had poor financial years the past few years. Alan is a superb real estate deal maker and has an artistic flair. Although he could negotiate to purchase building lots and negotiate to sell, he did not have any serious product or any true expertise in building custom homes. George is a superior tradesman and building contractor, but he had been working only about half-time. He didn't have the foresight to locate great building sites or the courage to be a tough negotiator. They formed a partnership. Right from the start, their partnership was a match made in heaven. In their very first year of working together, they *each* had their most successful year ever. It's true that they had to split their profits, but their combination of skills *quadrupled* their ability to produce. The key is that the partnership does something that neither could do by themselves. Now, George is busy full-time building custom homes, the thing he does best. Alan is busy negotiating to purchase lots for future building, working on design, subcontracting, and negotiating material pricing. Although it sounds unbelievable, the partnership is able to complete a beautiful custom home, start to finish, in a matter of a few months. This is a winning partnership.

You may be the most talented person on earth, but until you hook up with a good partner, you may never truly unleash that talent. Rather than spending your energy trying to do everything, you and your new partner can each focus on what she or he does best.

35.

LET GO OF FEARFUL THOUGHTS

If you gathered up all the fearful thoughts that exist in the mind of the average person, looked at them objectively, and tried to decide just how much good they provided that person, you would see that not some but all fearful thoughts are useless. They do no good. Zero. They interfere with dreams, hopes, desires, and progress.

Fearful thoughts take many different forms. Sometimes they sound reasonable: "I'm just being careful, so I'm taking my time." Other times they are tied to your past: "I've tried that before and it didn't work." Occasionally, fears are cleverly disguised as being realistic: "Most people fail, so I want to be absolutely sure before I get started." I could fill page after page with other examples. Yet when you take a close, honest look at every fearful thought, there are threads of similarity. All of them are explanations or rationalizations for why something shouldn't or can't work. They are usually justifications for quitting, or for not getting started. To me, fearful thoughts are like a leash on an energetic dog. They hold you back, not some but all of the time.

A critic, especially a fearful one, will look at this advice and say it's unrealistic, simplistic, and/or foolish. The problem with overcoming these objections is that, on the surface, they sound reasonable. Let me assure you that I'm not suggesting you ignore the facts and take unnecessary and/or foolish risks. Nor am I suggesting that you should attempt things you are totally unqualified for. For example, if your dream is to play basketball in the NBA and you're forty-five years old, overweight, and five feet six inches tall, forget it. You're not going to make it!

What I'm talking about here are the fears that clearly and directly interfere with your dreams—the fear of rejection, the fear of failure; thoughts like "What will everyone think of me? I might look foolish," or "I don't think I can do it, I don't have the time, or the experience, or the confidence, or the budget." These common, ongoing fearful thoughts are the dream snatchers of our own making.

For example, I know a person who was working as an independent salesperson. Her goal was to double her income. Her "rational" fear played itself out like this: "I can't call people on the weekends because I might offend them or take away from their family time." The truth, of course, was that she was frightened to make the calls. So, for years and years, she didn't make the calls and she always fell far short of her goals. Then one day she decided to simply drop her fear and pick up the phone. Because more of her clients were home and tended to be more relaxed on the weekends, she discovered that it was the best possible time to call. Once she dropped her fear, it was easy. Her income didn't double, it tripled.

At the risk of being overly simplistic, let me suggest you try something that can change your life. Make a commitment that, for the next month, you will practice dropping and/or ignoring any negative and fearful thought that enters your mind. As fears come to your mind, gently but firmly let them go. As they return (which they will), let them go again. It's easier than you think. It just takes courage and a little practice. Do this again and again until they disappear completely. You'll discover that life is so much easier and more fun without the interference of fearful thoughts.

36.

THINK BIG!

The implications of thinking big are widespread and impressive. Thinking big is a magic door opener that broadens your perspective and allows you to see new opportunities. Thinking big makes life easier and a lot more fun. It also makes large profits more probable.

I've been repeatedly reminded by successful businesspeople in virtually every field that thinking big is one of the keys to success. Let's consider a few examples. Successful insurance salespersons insist that it takes the *identical* amount of time to speak to someone about a million-dollar policy as it does a one-thousand-dollar policy. In the real estate field, the concept of leverage applies whether you're considering a single-family home or a huge apartment building. This doesn't mean that you can't make money in single-family homes, or that your rate of return will necessarily be higher with more expensive properties. It merely suggests that the bigger your vision, the larger your potential for success. If you're trying to sell homes for a living, as an agent, it takes the same amount of energy to ask a wealthy person for their listing as it does a low-end homeowner. You can think small, or you can think big.

In any field where public speaking is in order, this concept is critical. It takes an hour to speak to a single person and the same sixty minutes to speak to a crowd of one thousand or more. The size of your crowd will be affected by the size of your vision. The concept of thinking big also applies to whom you choose to talk to. Are you frightened to go to the top? If so, you're missing out. It's very often the case that the people highest up the ladder are actually the easiest to speak to—and the most willing to help. I've had the owners of car dealerships actually sit in the car and give me a test drive at the same dealership where the salesperson on the floor wouldn't give me the time of day. But in order to make that happen, I had to ask. In the corporate world, the boss is often more than willing to sit down with you, even when middle-level managers treat you with disrespect. It's a strange dynamic, but it's often true.

As usual, the primary reason many people think too small is fear. Thoughts like, "I can't speak to a room full of people," "I can't risk taking on a larger project," and "I couldn't ask the boss to have lunch with me" fill the mind and are taken too seriously. When fearful thoughts enter the mind, try to banish them. You can do it—once you believe you can. The fear you are experiencing is almost always self-created and usually unnecessary.

I have a friend who spent most of his adult life insisting he couldn't write a book. This was very puzzling to me, because not only was he an excellent writer, but he also felt quite comfortable writing articles and chapters! One day I asked him to consider the idea that a book is nothing more than a series of interesting chapters put into sequence. As obvious as this was to me, he had never thought of it in those terms. Instead, he had always focused on his stubborn belief that writing a book was too big a project. This simple shift in his thinking made all the difference. Two years later, he finished his first book.

Take a look at your own vision for abundance. Is your vision too small? Could you be thinking in larger terms? In most cases, the answer is yes! There may be ways that you can reach more people with the same amount of effort. Regardless of the business you are in, the first step is to eliminate any fear or worry that is getting in your way. As your worrisome thoughts gradually disappear and become less appealing, new ideas and insights will begin to emerge.

An acquaintance of mine operates a coffeehouse. For years she did everything herself. She didn't hire a staff because she was concerned that she couldn't afford to expand. The problem was, because she had to do everything herself, her service was rather slow. It hadn't occurred to her that she was losing a great deal of business because of her growing reputation for being slow. She knew that something was wrong, and that people waiting for their morning coffee didn't want to stand in long lines. One day she asked herself, "If I wasn't fearful, what would I do?" The answer was obvious: "I'd hire a few kids to speed up my service." To her absolute delight, this was the answer to her dreams. Her lines speeded up and her profits soared. As is usually the case, there was really nothing to fear—it was all in her mind. Don't worry, make money!

37.

MAKE DECISIONS WITH THE ADVANTAGE OF *LONG-TERM* INFORMATION INSTEAD OF THE DISADVANTAGE OF *SHORT-TERM* INFORMATION

Oh, how tempting it can be to reverse this bit of wisdom and act on impulse. For example, if you looked only at 1996 when the Dow Jones average grew at a 26 percent rate, based on that short-term bit of information, you might be tempted to sell everything you own and invest in nothing other than the stock market! If so, you could always have the experience of a major downward correction over the short term. Or, if you looked at the rates of return that investors were enjoying in the California residential real estate market in the mid-1980s, you may have been tempted to do the same with single-family homes. If you did so, however, and stayed in the game too long, you would have been brought back to earth—perhaps even made homeless—by the end of the decade! You can see that acting on impulse—or on short-term information alone—can be a big mistake.

Instead, make the bulk of your decisions with the advantage of long-term information instead of the disadvantage of short-term information. This wiser way of approaching your decisions gives you a far more realistic outlook. It also takes most of the worry out of investing and business decisions. For example, if you take *any* twenty-year period of time (excluding the disaster of the 1930s), such as the last twenty years, the rate of return in the market was somewhere in the neighborhood of 10 to 15 percent, depending on what particular index or group of stocks you selected. You can be fairly certain that, within reason, this trend will continue.

38.

KNOW WHEN TO BET, WHEN TO HOLD,

AND WHEN TO FOLD

Many people fail to recognize just how important timing really is. Not just the type of timing we usually think of—catching the stock market or a real estate cycle at precisely the right time—but rather the ongoing inner calculations of knowing when to bet, when to stay put, and when to fold or give something up entirely.

Often, the worst (or at least the most unnecessary) thing you can do in a moneymaking venture is to take a significant risk at the wrong time. Or, on the other end of the risk-taking spectrum, to be overly conservative when it's absolutely appropriate to expand, when the wind seems to be at your back, when a certain degree of risk is in order.

There are times when the best possible course of action is to do nothing other than hold on, do essentially nothing, be patient. Other times, of course, it's important or at least appropriate to expand, to grow, to move forward. Occasionally, you're in the "zone"; everything you touch, every decision you make, seems to turns to gold or take you in a positive direction. Other times we can save ourselves a fortune, or a great deal of energy, by simply being willing to take a loss now, to fold, rather than lose everything later.

It's amazing how often problems can be overcome and new opportunities can be realized by simply quieting down "the inner chatter" of our analytical thinking so that we'll know what action (if any) to take. This quieting of the mind allows us to get out of our own way so that we can know how to put the odds in our favor.

Wisdom is knowing when to do what. It's about being flexible and being willing to change, to flow. And while this may sound obvious, many people make the wrong choices simply because their mind is too busy. Thus, they fall into bad habits and are unwilling to consider new ways of thinking—"I've always done it that way" or "I can't close down this office, we've been here for two generations."

My suggestion here is to simply quiet down enough to consider the facts. Sometimes, a nonreturned phone call can cost you a career, a big deal, or a great deal of money. Other times, it's absolutely appropriate to avoid returning a phone call—it can actually be a good idea. The trick is to act from a place of wisdom rather than simply reacting out of habit.

39.

CHANGE WHAT YOU CAN,
ACCEPT THE THINGS YOU CAN'T

This strategy is adopted from the serenity prayer that says, in its entirety: "Lord, grant me the strength to change the things I can, the serenity to accept the things I cannot, and the wisdom to know the difference." What an incredibly powerful message! Can you imagine how smoothly your life would run if you could implement this strategy most of the time?

In every business there are things we *must* deal with. There are things we can change, that we have some power to control. There are other things that are absolutely beyond our control. Yet how often do we spend our time and energy doing absolutely nothing about the things we do have some control over, while whining and complaining about those things we can't do anything about? Often, because we have our priorities twisted in the wrong direction, we end up chasing our tails and wasting time. Once we change gears, put these factors into proper perspective, and focus only on those things that we have some capacity to control, it's easy to get back on track.

A friend of mine recently retired from an extremely successful career in the real estate syndication business. He insists that many of his competitors failed, in part, because of their lack of acceptance of the "way things really are." Instead of focusing on what they could and should have been doing, many people spent their time complaining about bureaucracy and trying to get around the rules and regulations. In his words, "Dealing with bureaucracy is a part of the business. The Securities and Exchange Commission and other government agencies are just part of the game. If you moan, bitch, and complain, you're sunk!" Similarly, builders *must* deal with permits, government agencies, and environmental and safety factors. Farmers must deal with weather conditions and other factors beyond their control. Corporate people must deal with ridiculous memos, interminable meetings, and bad bosses. Inevitably, the most successful people in any field are those who dance with the "what is" part of business instead of struggling against it. Those who fail are often the ones who struggle against the inevitable.

It's tempting to focus on aspects of life that are beyond our control. How often do you hear people complaining about taxes? While no one (myself included) *likes* to pay taxes, and certainly no one should pay any more than he or she is legally required to pay, there is a great deal of wisdom in spending your time creating abundance rather than complaining about taxes.

Go ahead and lobby for lower taxes if you must. Voice your opinion if you choose to do so. But once you have done what you *can* do, let go of it. Know when to quit. Expend your energy doing what you can do— focus on creation, creativity, positive ideas, and solutions. Come up with a new idea—a useful product or service, or a new or improved way of doing something. Improve your existing business, formulate a new relationship, make a phone call you've been avoiding. Stop complaining about taxes; focus, instead, on making so much money that taxes will seem irrelevant! Do something positive, something you have control over. Once you start thinking in these terms, you'll be amazed at how easy and enjoyable it is to create the abundance you desire and deserve.

40.

DEVELOP RELATIONSHIPS WITH PEOPLE BEFORE
YOU NEED SOMETHING FROM THEM

So many of us wait until we desperately need something from someone before we take the time to get to know them. In truth, this is probably the absolute worst time to do so. If you need something from someone and they know it, they may be on guard, even defensive, trying to determine if you are sincere. The truth is, people are so much more pleasant when you don't need anything from them.

How many people have taken the time to actually sit down, or have coffee with, the manager at their bank (before ever needing a loan)? As a percentage, virtually no one does this. Yet how much easier it is to work with people when they already know and trust you, when you know the names of their spouse and children, when they know that you care about their happiness and that you are a sincere, trusting person.

I make it a point to get to know as many people as possible in my own community. I'm friendly with the banker, the owners of the restaurants and coffee shops, the local mechanic, the pharmacist, the florist, and so many others. The result is that, if I need a loan, my banker knows my face and my name. He trusts me. If I wanted one, he'd probably give me a loan over the phone! If one of my children is sick, the local pharmacist will gladly take the time to discuss the issue with me. He's genuinely concerned about my family as I am about his. If I want to send someone flowers, I can call the florist and say, "Can you make this order extra special?" In every case, she'll go out of her way to please me because she knows I care about her. If I have friends in town and want a great seat at the restaurant, my waiter friend at the diner is more than willing to save me a great table.

This has nothing to do with taking advantage of people. It's just the way life works. People love to help those they know and trust. Each of these people, and so many others, know that I'll do (and have done) special things for them as well. In fact, I wouldn't think twice about it.

Although people will do so, no one *really* wants to get to know you—to be the recipient of your kindness—only during those occasions when you need something from them. It can seem disingenuous, as if you're only being nice because you want something. Of course, it's better that you're friendly now than never, but how much nicer it is if the people you need already know that you're a nice, genuine person. Why not show people how wonderful you are, right now?

Obviously, there are some instances when you will need to meet someone under less than optimal circumstances—and you will need something from them. For example, if your car breaks down, you probably won't know the tow-truck driver. In these instances, make the best of it and leave a great impression. But whenever possible, try to meet and enjoy people before you need them. You'll be shocked at how helpful they can be.

41.

BE AWARE OF YOUR UNIQUE "STACKING ORDER"

The idea of a stacking order was introduced to me by a successful computer consultant. What a gift it has turned out to be! Essentially, the concept exists to help you clarify, in your own mind, how much work, or how many projects, you are comfortable working on at any given time.

Over and over again, I've seen incredibly competent people failing simply because they—or their employer—haven't taken this concept into serious consideration.

Everyone is different. We each have different strengths and weaknesses. But, beyond this, we have very unique temperaments regarding an optimal pace to work, how much we can handle, how much is "on our plate," or how many projects we can manage, at any given time.

An area where many people can relate to this concept is in their personal reading habits. Some people love to read one book at a time. They enjoy each page, and won't even think of picking up another until they are completely finished. Other people are just the opposite. They love to have five or six books going at once. They will read a chapter or two in one book, put it down, and perhaps not pick it up again for several weeks. If you forced people to ignore their reading preference (their stacking order), you would take them out of their natural rhythm and ruin their experience of reading. Their comprehension would decrease and their enjoyment level would diminish.

Our work life is very similar, although most people never even consider it to be a factor. Instead, most of us operate as if everyone should work at the same pace and as if we should, or have to, work at someone else's level of activity.

My own preferred "stacking order" is three to four projects at once. This means that I'm most comfortable working on a book, perhaps promoting another one, writing an article, and giving a few lectures a month. If I'm only working on one project, it's simply not enough to keep me engaged. I lose focus, I get a little bored and impatient, and the project doesn't turn out as well as I would like. I love to work a few hours on one project, then shift gears altogether. This may not be the right way to do it, but it's my way. Many people think I'm nuts. I've heard so many people say over the years, "How can you produce so many projects?" The reason it seems nuts to someone else is that their stacking order is different. If I attempted to do it their way, *I'd* go nuts!

Other people love to work on only one project at a time. They focus beautifully on whatever they are working on until they are completely finished. Then, and only then, will they pick up something else. If these people have too many things going at once, they fall apart and look incompetent. It's a shame, because a vast majority of these people are far from incompetent. In fact, in many instances, if these folks were to do nothing other than shift the number of things they focused on at once (i.e., thinking of one or two things or problems or projects, instead of ten) they would begin to look like a genius.

Obviously, there are times when you simply can't work at your preferred pace. You may prefer to work on one project at a time, but be forced by circumstance to work on six or seven. Yet even in these cases, understanding your stacking order can be enormously helpful. You can organize your work in such a way that you can maximize your potential. You can create artificial "time zones" for each of them. For example, you can work on one project for thirty minutes without thinking about anything else whatsoever. Then, after a five-minute break, begin work on project number two. Rather than jumping back and forth, stay focused on one thing at a time.

I hope you'll seriously consider your own stacking order. If you do, you'll discover a pace that's just right for your own temperament. This will make the creation of abundance a much richer experience in every sense of the word.

42.

DON'T PANIC!

Just as Chicken Little was dead wrong when she said the sky was falling, it's important to keep your perspective even when it feels like she was right. Remember, when something is falling, it rarely keeps falling. There are cycles in life.

An excellent example of where huge profits have been realized has been the California real estate market. In my lifetime, the cycle has gone way up and way down many times. Yet the one consistency in the fluctuations has been the tendency for many people to freak out and panic when times are bad, to assume the downturn is going to last forever, that things can only get worse. In retrospect, we can see that, often, the best time to get in is when everyone else is panicking.

In business, people panic about practically everything—missed deadlines, orders not received, comments by others, fear of mistakes, negative trends. You name it and someone has panicked about it. Yet I've never seen even a single instance where the panic actually helped to solve the problem. Instead, panic is neutral at best and greatly interferes at worst. Panic tends to bring out the worst in everyone. It makes others (and you) feel tense and fearful. It increases the likelihood of mistakes, missed opportunities, and miscommunication.

Nothing interferes with the creation of success and abundance like panic. When you make the commitment to stop panicking, you'll notice some incredible things happening. First, you'll notice that a vast majority of what you are most worried about will never happen, or it won't be as bad as you first thought. It was Benjamin Franklin who said, "Some terrible things happened in my lifetime—a few of which actually happened." By avoiding the panic, you won't waste time, anxiety, and energy trying to solve what probably doesn't need solving. Second, when you learn to keep your bearings, your wisdom will come forth. In the absence of worry, answers will emerge. Instead of a head full of concerns, you'll create a head full of solutions. Finally, when you stay calm, you really do bring out the best in others. Many people react to the feelings of others. If you can maintain your bearings, chances are the people you work with will, too.

Life is far too short to worry it away. To bring forth your greatest potential, eliminate panic altogether from your thinking. This will put you on a path toward abundance.

43.

CREATE FROM THE INSIDE OUT

You can work long and hard, be creative, clever, talented, insightful, even lucky—but if you fail to understand the importance of your own thoughts in the process of creation, it will all be for naught.

The single most important factor of success, abundance, and the creation of prosperity comes from within yourself—your thoughts. As James Allen reminds us in *As a Man Thinketh*, "A particular train of thought persisted in, be it good or bad, cannot fail to produce its results on the character and circumstances. A man cannot directly choose his circumstances, but he can choose his thoughts, and so indirectly, yet surely, shape his circumstances."

If you could look into the minds of successful men and women you would discover a wealth of positive energy—thoughts of success and abundance, and a complete lack of doubt. In order to create external prosperity, you must first create *thoughts* of prosperity. You must see yourself as successful, play out your dreams and ambitions in your mind—successfully.

It's tempting to convince yourself that you would become more positive and that your thoughts would become purer and more success-oriented *after* a measure of success. However, this is clearly putting the cart before the horse. The quickest, surest way to riches is from the inside out. Thoughts have tremendous power. Use your imagination to create your dreams, and great changes will quickly follow suit. Once again, James Allen: "Let a man radically alter his thoughts, and he will be astonished at the rapid transformation it will effect in the material conditions of his life."

I've known many successful people in many different fields. Although

99

they have vastly different talents, temperaments, skills, work ethics, and backgrounds, they all have one thing in common. This golden thread of consistency is that each of them sees him or herself as successful. They never question this fact; they can't understand why anyone would question their own level of greatness. It's hard for them to understand why everyone isn't successful because, to them, the formula is quite simple: Success originates in the mind and translates into the material world. It doesn't work the other way around, as so many seem to believe. Successful people know that the one aspect of life that they do have control over is their own thinking. All of us have this same advantage, so let's all start there!

44.

BANISH YOUR DOUBT

In your dreams you are able to do some remarkable things—be two places at once, shift scenes and environments, walk through walls, become rich and famous, overcome great obstacles, get along with your parents, become the CEO, create great abundance, write a bestseller, speak to a million people, to name just a few. And through it all, you never, ever doubt your abilities. In fact, can you imagine how ridiculous it would be to question your abilities while dreaming? Can you imagine saying, "Wait a minute, I can't do that?" And in your dreams, how often do you fail? Rarely. But if you do, it's always for a specific purpose—to learn something, to test your strength, to overcome great odds, to take you to the next level of growth. Because you don't doubt yourself, all things are possible.

Yet in our waking state, most of us spend a great deal of energy every day of our lives, doubting our abilities—to our great detriment. We doubt ourselves at practically every turn; we doubt our abilities to write well, speak to a group, come up with a new idea or solution, overcome an obstacle, create a better mousetrap, market a product or service, or negotiate with a difficult person. We question our self-worth, how much we deserve to be paid, or how valuable or talented we are to an organization or as an entrepreneur. We doubt our ability to overcome rejection, start over, or confront a challenge.

A surefire strategy for success is to banish doubt from your life—all of it. This doesn't mean you should start doing foolish things or making childish decisions. It means you should start trusting in yourself, creating an inner knowing, an awareness that you have everything it takes to be an absolute winner, to make your dreams come true. The only true obstacle lies within the doubt itself—and all doubt lies within your own thoughts.

For years I convinced myself that I couldn't speak in front of groups. I believed this self-imposed limitation with all my heart. I even had concrete evidence that my belief was true; as I mentioned earlier, twice I fainted while trying to speak. Then one day a friend and mentor put me on the spot in front of a large group. Before it was my turn to speak, he turned to me and said, "Richard, the idea that you aren't capable of speaking to a group is absolutely preposterous. Dismiss this crazy notion from your mind and everything will be fine. Get over it, now!" I remember his words as if they were said this morning. He was right. Speaking became effortless the *moment* I banished the doubt from my mind.

You can do the same thing. It's silly to hold on to any doubt in your life. It does no good. All doubt is a waste of energy and interferes with your natural ability to create the abundance and wealth that is your birthright. Whatever doubts are lingering in your mind, let them go. It's far easier than you think, and will produce great rewards.

45.

KNOW THE SECRET OF SILENCE

There is a tendency in business (and in life) to want to actively engage ourselves in the process of creation. We want to know the answers. We want to figure out what to do next. We want to think our way to success. However, in many instances—I believe in most instances—the best answers come not from programmed, memory-based thinking but from the silence within. In fact, I've watched many people (and I've done it, too) think their way out of success by overanalyzing a situation.

Have you ever noticed that when you are quiet and still, calm and silent, you know exactly what to do? Being silent doesn't shut down your mind, it only activates a deeper type of intelligence. No one knows for sure where this deeper intelligence comes from, or what it's called, but all wise cultures are certain that it exists. When we are silent, it's as if we tap into a universal source of wisdom. It's as though our thinking comes to us rather than us having to actively pursue our thoughts. It's as if we get the benefit of "universal thought" instead of having to rely on our own limited thinking.

Learning to trust in silence is simple because, when you do, the results are so spectacular. Once you get the hang of it your life will become far easier and less stressful. Success will sneak up on you. The next time you need an answer that is not readily available, rather than racking your brain over it, try an experiment. Instead of actively thinking about the issue, let it go. The fact that you know the nature of the problem or question is all the information you need. Allow the question to settle, like silt in water. When you do this, something magical begins to happen within your consciousness. Something beyond you, a dimension of thought over which you have no control, flips on. And like the back burner of a stove, the question or problem begins to bubble. In time—it may be a few minutes, hours, or days depending on the issue—an answer will pop into your head. There will be no struggle and no effort. It will just happen. You may be surprised, but you'll certainly be delighted at the wisdom that comes through. Be careful, however, to not take yourself too seriously. The wisdom you experience comes not from you but from the silence. I guess I'm letting the secret out of the bag!

46.

SOCK AWAY TWO YEARS OF LIVING EXPENSES

On the surface, it might seem that the suggestion to scrimp and save, to put money aside for an entire year or two, could be contrary to the message of this book—to not worry. After all, isn't saving for a rainy day based on worry and fear? It all depends on how you look at it.

Several years ago I heard a super-successful financial guru explain that the single most important thing he *ever* did for himself, prior to becoming rich, was to set aside two years of living expenses. Although it required enormous sacrifice, discipline, hard work, and patience—and although it took a full five years to save this much money—it paid enormous dividends, especially psychologically. Essentially, what it did was to give him enormous peace of mind, the freedom he needed to take risks that would be difficult, if not impossible, without this financial cushion. Very simply, socking away a few years of living expenses allowed him to avoid worry, to pursue dreams and interesting opportunities.

I heard a story of a man who was offered a job at a promising and exciting start-up computer company back in the early seventies. Because he had implemented a strategy of having plenty of financial reserve, he was able to accept the job—without fear—which included a relatively small initial salary but a ton of stock, and stock options, in the company. He had no worries whatsoever. If the venture worked out, terrific. If it didn't, it was at least a valuable experience. The man, however, was not the first person chosen for this job. Someone else was the first choice. This man had virtually no savings. He was extremely bright and talented, and making an excellent salary. But, like so many people, he was living paycheck to paycheck. He had a big mortgage and both he and his wife drove very expensive cars, they enjoyed fine restaurants, and their four children attended private schools. They spent most of what they made. Although the job offer sounded like the best opportunity of his lifetime, he decided to decline—too risky! He was too worried. Looking back, he says, "If I'd had enough discipline to save in my early years, it would have been a no-brainer. I would most certainly have taken the job."

To make a long story short: The man who took the risk amassed a huge fortune in less than a decade. His psychological ability to take the risk turned him into a multimillionaire. The other man, who also wanted the job but was too worried, still lives paycheck to paycheck well into his sixties. His abundance was severely limited by his sense of worry.

The moral of the story is obvious. Unless you are extremely lucky, creating abundance usually involves at least some risk taking. However, if you are absolutely, completely dependent on a secure, regular salary, if you are fearful that you are a paycheck away from homelessness, you are probably going to dismiss many opportunities that come your way.

It's well worth the tradeoff—fewer vacations; a less expensive car, home, and clothing; fewer evenings out on the town; as well as many other luxuries, even necessities—for that two years of income in the bank. It's amazing how more creative you can be—appropriately aggressive, and willing to experiment with new and/or unusual opportunities—when your very livelihood isn't dependent on your day-to-day efforts. So, starting today, begin your "rainy day" fund. A few years from now you'll be able to spend it—or give it away. In fact, you'll be able to do just about anything you want to do.

47.

GIVE UP YOUR FEAR OF DISAPPROVAL

How many people choose careers and career directions based on what other people—parents, relatives, professors, friends—think they should do. "You should be a doctor, lawyer, pilot, musician" can be a very powerful message, especially when it's repeated often and associated with status, prestige, social approval, and other psychological accolades.

Here's one simple example of someone I know: Stephen was informed at a very young age that he was going to make his parents proud by becoming a lawyer. He grew up knowing that this was the only way to please Mom and Dad. All the relatives expected this would be his chosen path. The family spoke of the "up-and-coming lawyer" often throughout the years. Two members of the family were lawyers. Both had become very successful, and everyone in the family looked up to them.

In time, Stephen did, in fact, become a lawyer. The problem was, he not only detested the field of law but was also frustrated by his surprising difficulty in making any significant money. Aspects of law that some of his friends and colleagues found intriguing and exciting he found boring and difficult. He struggled for years before he thought he was going to go crazy.

Through a short stint of gentle counseling, Stephen discovered that his fear of disappointing his parents had forced him into a career that gave him no satisfaction whatsoever. His counselor convinced him that the fear of disapproval can interfere with our greatest chance of success.

After his counseling sessions enlightened him as to the source of this fear, he visited a career counselor and discovered through a series of tests that his aptitude for law was among the lowest 4 percent of all lawyers that had been tested. No wonder he was failing in his career! He was barely qualified. The tests showed that he was far more suited to such fields as marketing and promotion. He decided to take a chance and change directions. He not only loved his new field, but he flourished as well. Many of his marketing ideas were real winners and he quickly became a "hot commodity." His financial life quickly turned around to the point where, today, he is quite wealthy and, more important, very happy.

The message of this strategy is enormously important: Our best chance of success is obtained through the elimination of fear. This includes the fear of disapproval from others. Examine the reasons why you entered your chosen field. Was it out of joy and genuine interest? This is where abundance can be found. Or was there an element of pleasing Mom and Dad, or someone else? Did you do it for the attention you thought you were going to get? If the answer to these questions is "yes," it might be time to investigate something new. If necessary, talk to a psychologist or a career counselor who might be able to shed some light on the subject, or offer some helpful guidance. Whatever it takes, it's well worth the effort. If you change direction and do something because you truly love it, instead of because you think it's the "right thing to do," your path toward success might be closer than you ever dreamed possible.

48.

NEVER UNDERESTIMATE THE VALUE OF

GOODWILL

A gentleman who owns a construction business shared with me the following story. He was working with an eccentric client on a huge, profitable job. The client had instructed him to move a large amount of heavy material to a certain location as part of the job. When the work was just about over, the client, for whatever reason, decided he wanted the material moved somewhere else. Everyone agreed that it was a strange request and would take quite a bit of time and effort. But it seemed very important to the client.

A number of people in the owner's company were furious and felt "ripped off," as though the man were taking advantage of the owner. They told him, "Don't do it," and all agreed that if he did do the extra work, he should charge the client a marked-up fee for the hassle.

Although the owner was himself a bit irritated, he decided to give the client the benefit of the doubt with no hassle or complaints. He went ahead and moved the material and didn't charge him extra. It cost the owner a considerable amount of time and money.

He told me that, since then, he has received more work and referrals from that client than from any other single person in his entire career. In fact, that person has become his largest client. He has told the owner, many times, how much he had appreciated his willingness to "go the extra mile." There was a clear relationship between the owner's action and this client's reciprocation.

I've experienced many similar instances in my own business life. I once had a signed contract to do a speaking engagement. Because I had agreed to do the event, I had to turn down several, far more lucrative offers. Then, very close to the date of the engagement, the company cancelled the event and asked if I'd be willing to switch times. Not only had this chain of events cost me a great deal of money and aggravation, but the company was liable for my speaking fee. They were asking me to be extra flexible.

Clearly, I had the ethical and legal right to decline their request and collect my fee. But I didn't. Instead, I agreed to switch dates and to do so without complaint.

You would have thought they had won a contest or something! They were so thrilled and grateful. And, just like the owner of the construction company, my decision has paid handsome dividends. I've received numerous offers since that time that I believe are linked to my willingness to be flexible.

So what is goodwill—having others think highly of you—really worth? I don't think there's any way to quantify it, but it's certainly valuable. The problem is, it doesn't always work so smoothly. Our goodwill efforts are not always appreciated. Some people really do take advantage of others, and you never know if or when your goodwill efforts will pay off. Yet, if you have faith that being fair and ethical and going the extra mile is the right thing to do, then, over time, you will be rewarded. Knowing this is very comforting and helps immensely in your efforts to stop sweating the small stuff about money!

Don't get me wrong. Neither I nor the owner of that construction company are always flexible or willing to deviate from our standard policies. Goodwill is one of those things that requires you to call it as you see it in the moment.

And, again, while it's not quantifiable, goodwill is a valuable commodity. Simply acknowledging this helps us factor it into our decision-making process. So, the next time you're looked upon to be extra flexible or asked to do something special for a client or customer, consider the goodwill factor. Who knows—it just might pay off, big time!

49.

DON'T RELY ON TOO MUCH DATA

It's often the case that when people get worried or frightened, they focus too much on data in an effort to alleviate their anxiety—to make themselves feel better. The assumption is, "If I can figure everything out, everything will be okay." So worried stockbrokers will stare at their computer screens, gathering data instead of making calls and selling stock. Managers in organizations will study reports and financials but will avoid taking actions that will make things work smoother and smarter. And salespeople who are afraid to go out and make sales calls, or who are fearful of rejection in one way or another, will spend countless hours reading sales literature or sending out direct-mail pieces, but they won't go out and take risks, make the calls, or ask for the sale. All this "data gathering" may satisfy their curiosity and buy some time, but it will do little in a positive sense to affect the bottom line.

Of course, it's simple to justify our actions, decisions, and the way we actually spend our time, especially when we're frightened. We can always rationalize that what were doing is necessary and important—the more information we have at our disposal, the better. Right? Sometimes this is true, but not always.

There's a point where excessive information can interfere with going out and actually making money. Too much data can convince us that we're too busy to do what it takes to really succeed; it can convince us that our actions are too risky, too premature. And, of course, sometimes we'll be right. However, this is the exception rather than the rule. More often than not, too much data can fill our heads with worrisome, fearful thoughts that keep us between where we are and where we want to be. A favorite quote of mine suggests that "If we had to overcome every possible objection before we got started, then nothing—absolutely nothing—would ever get accomplished." I have found that excessive data gathering, too much mulling over the same set of facts, is very often the major factor that encourages us to overcome every possible objection before *we* get started, before *we* go out and do what it takes.

The next time you find yourself filling your head with facts and stewing over data, take a step back. See if what you're doing is really going to help you out, make things better—or are you simply postponing the steps that will actually bring about abundance? Be completely honest with yourself. Perhaps, instead of studying facts, you should pick up the phone and make a call. It's very possible you have all the data you need and the simple decision to stop worrying is the most important thing you could be doing.

50.

FIND A MENTOR

It's simple, common sense that if someone wanted to be a journeyman plumber, he or she would be wise to find someone who either has retired or is about to retire from the plumbing field to act as a source of guidance, advice, and inspiration. It's helpful to have someone you can share an occasional cup of coffee with, kick around ideas—someone you can to turn to, ask questions of, seek guidance from, philosophize.

I've never seen or even heard of someone moving backward as a result of finding a mentor. Yet when I ask around, very few people, as an overall percentage, admit to having one.

I have had several mentors in my life who have helped me enormously in many aspects of life—business, money making, investments, marketing, public speaking, even physical fitness. Both the mentor and the student get a great deal out of the relationship, it's an ideal tradeoff. The advantages to the student are obvious: confidence, camaraderie, ideas—a road map to follow. For the mentor, there's the joy of helping, feeling appreciated and needed, the fun of teaching, the privilege of reviewing what he or she did right over the years, the idea of passing the torch. It's a blessing to know that your ideas are being used by someone else.

Often you can find a mentor through your own networking circle—an older friend, someone with whom you have built a relationship over the years, someone you respect and enjoy spending time with. Typically, a mentor is someone who enjoys sharing his or her ideas. It isn't necessary that you formalize your relationship by calling this person a "mentor," only that you have a mutual understanding that you are willing to sit down together or at least talk on the phone, on a somewhat regular basis—once a month, once every other month, whatever. Make it clear that your intention is to learn all you can. These days, it's easier than ever to find a mentor. While nothing takes the place of personal contacts—networking with people who love you and/or care about your success—there are, if need be, mentoring agencies that will help match mentors with students. Don't let anything stand in the way of finding an excellent, caring mentor. You will avoid many unnecessary mistakes and reap the rewards for years to come. Often, the best way to pay back your mentor is to promise him or her that, once you are in a position to do so, you'll do the same for someone else.

51.

DELIGHT IN THE SUCCESS OF OTHERS

Let's be honest here. Have you ever found yourself secretly wishing someone else would fail? I don't mean you wish them any serious bad luck, only that they don't become even more successful than you? Sometimes it's hard to wish others well, particularly those you know well—friends, colleagues, neighbors, family members. It's hard to see a colleague get the promotion you worked so hard for. It's difficult to see your kid sister on television, or your neighbor able to purchase a new car. We're human; we get jealous. I've had clients who were even a little jealous of their own spouse's success.

While it can be seductive, or at least habitual, to secretly desire to keep others at your level, it's absolutely, positively not in your best interest. The way to rise to the top is to wish everyone well, to hope with all your heart that everyone can expand to their greatest potential, to wish that the people you know, and those whom you don't know, can all realize their dreams and achieve greatness.

It's critical to know that there is plenty of success to go around. In fact, as people achieve their goals, the pie gets even bigger for the rest of us. We don't want to see one another at our lowest common denominator, but at our highest common vision. We can *all* succeed and each time someone does—anyone—it helps the rest of us.

When you wish someone well, it creates a momentum within you, an inner environment of success. It reminds your spirit of your loving and deserving nature. It creates the atmosphere within you to help you succeed and create abundance. When you delight in the success of others, it's as if you are sprinkling the seeds for a garden of success.

As you wish others well, notice how good it feels. When your wishes are sincere, they will serve as a reminder that giving and receiving are two sides of the same coin. Truly, it feels as good to see someone else succeed as it does to succeed yourself. Start delighting in the success of others and watch your own level of greatness soar!

52.

ASK YOURSELF,
WHERE IS THIS DECISION LIKELY TO LEAD?

Many of us follow certain paths simply because they present themselves. Often, however, these paths lead you in directions or take you to places you really don't want to be. You can save yourself enormous amounts of time and energy by asking the simple, straightforward question, Where is this decision likely to lead? And then, pay close attention to your answer.

There is a story about "the trip to Abilene," and it goes something like this: There were four friends sitting on a porch in a small town in Texas. It was a really hot day, well over a hundred degrees. Someone mentioned that there was a good restaurant over in Abilene, some two hundred miles away. The road wasn't paved and the car had no air-conditioning. Without knowing why, the four friends somehow ended up in the boiling hot car, headed toward Abilene. It was miserable. The ride was bumpy and extremely hot. All four friends were frustrated and angry.

When they finally arrived in Abilene some five hours later, one of the friends, in a frustrated tone, asked, "Why are we here anyway?" One of the others replied, rather confidently, "I thought *you* wanted to come." "I didn't want to come here, I thought you did," was the response.

To make a potentially long story short, no one had the slightest interest in being in Abilene. Each person thought someone else really wanted to be there. No one thought to ask, Where is this decision likely to lead? No one asked, Why are we really going?

How many family get-togethers or business meetings are like this?

Aren't there times when no one *really* wants to be there but everyone came because each assumed that everyone else wanted to?

Sometimes in business we take our own "trips to Abilene." For example, sometimes therapists or consultants, when opening a private practice, will decide to work on weekends and charge half of what everyone else charges. This way, they believe, they will build up their practice faster and easier. This assumption is far from true. If you ask the question, Where is this decision likely to lead?, you'll get some pretty scary, yet predictable answers. In this instance, you'll begin to fill up your business with people who can only see you on weekends. Your clients will get used to it, and most of your referrals will be people who expect to see you on weekends— probably during the time your spouse is *off* work or the time of your favorite football game. You'll be stuck! As far as the reduced fee goes, again, you're setting yourself up to fail. If you undercharge for your service, your clients will tell all their friends how wonderful and fair you are because you are so incredibly inexpensive! Pretty soon you'll have a full practice— and you'll be going broke! I had a client who couldn't resist the temptation to take on new territory for the product he was selling. What he didn't consider, however, was that if he succeeded (which he did), the quality of his life would suffer (which it did). As he made his decision to expand, he ignored the fact that he would be spending an *additional* twenty hours a week driving in his car. In retrospect, he believes that he would have been far better off focusing on his existing territory and building his business within a reasonable geographic area. Again, the issue would have been easily avoided had he asked himself the million-dollar question.

It's always a good idea to ask yourself, Where is this decision likely to lead? When you do, you can avoid many hassles and mistakes that are otherwise inevitable. By asking this simple question, you can keep your energy directed in areas that will serve you and others well.

53.

REMEMBER THE GOLDEN RULE

Do you remember the golden rule that most of us were taught as youngsters? It goes like this: Do unto others as you would have them do unto you. What are some other ways of saying this magical formula? Let's see. What goes around, comes around. As you treat others, so shall you be treated. If you don't have something nice to say, don't say anything at all. There are many variations of this, and it's one of the first lessons we try to teach our children.

This must be one of the simplest, most easily implementable formulas for the creation of abundance. Simply put, all you have to do to ensure that you will be treated fairly, respectfully, and with kindness—and to ensure that others will reach out to help you and praise you—is to do these things yourself!

Become a thoughtful person. Offer assistance. Be nice. Reach out to others. Become even more generous. Say "Thank you." These, and hundreds of other similar little gestures, are the ways you can reach out and tell the world you care.

Giving and receiving *are* two sides of the same coin. They are different manifestations of the same universal energy. Ultimately, what you offer to the world is exactly what you get back. So, if your goal is to create a joyful life filled with abundance, the most important thing you can do is help others do the same. This is one area of life you can control. You can control how generous you are. You do have the capacity to offer praise and help, to be of service, and to be kind to others.

Don't make the mistake of becoming upset or frustrated if your acts of kindness don't come back immediately. The universe has its own set of rules and its own sense of timing. Be patient and loving. If you are committed to the Golden Rule, it's only a matter of time before your life will be filled with everything you desire.

54.

DON'T BE FRIGHTENED TO ASK FOR REFERRALS

In virtually any type of business that you're trying to expand, referrals are the key. Whether you're trying to build a private practice, grow a business, even build up your nonprofit fund-raising efforts, it's essential to ask for help. It's critical to get others involved, to get people talking about you in a positive way, spreading the word.

Many business experts agree that the single greatest source of failure can be traced to the *fear* of asking for referrals—asking for business, asking for help, or asking for the sale. I would agree. Generally speaking, people *are* frightened to ask for help. They would rather stay small but safe than take a risk and grow. The truth, however, as we know, is that staying frightened is not safe at all. Ultimately, fear will be the downfall of most businesses. Again, to make money, it's critical that you don't worry.

Here's a simple example of how simply asking for referrals would be of tremendous help. My family and I are regular patrons of a local restaurant. We are probably among its most consistent and loyal customers. We praise the owner and the chef on a regular basis. We let them know how much we appreciate their skill and hard work. And we keep coming back. While the food is fantastic and the people are wonderful, the restaurant isn't doing as well as it could be. Its location is questionable in terms of visibility, and they engage in absolutely no marketing.

Here's the interesting part. While we have proven that we are on their side, while we have demonstrated again and again that we want them to succeed, the owner has never, ever asked for our help. He has never asked us to bring in other friends, pass out menus, or even tell others about his fine restaurant.

Can you imagine what would happen to his business if he would simply ask us, and his other loyal customers—people he knows quite well—to help him? My guess is that he would have a waiting list every night of the week; people would be crowding outside the door for a chance to get in! He could, for example, say to me: "Richard, I know you really love this restaurant. The next few times you come in, would you consider bringing in some friends so that more people can try us out? If you do, I'll only charge you half price" (or he could offer a bottle of wine on the house, or a free meal, or a coupon for a reduced-price meal next time, or something else altogether).

There are many people (I'm one of them) who delight in the success of others, and would therefore almost be embarrassed not to be of help once asked. You might be thinking, "If you really wanted to bring friends into the restaurant, wouldn't you do so anyway?" Not necessarily. People go to restaurants for different reasons. One of ours is simply to relax, to be spontaneous. When I'm thinking about a restaurant, I'm usually thinking about my own needs and preferences and those of my family. However, I also love to be of service to someone else if I'm asked, especially if I really like the person.

It doesn't take much effort for me to call a friend or two and ask them to join us. I've probably been looking for an excuse to get together with them anyway. Here's the perfect opportunity. I get to see a good friend *and* help out the owner of the restaurant. By simply using referrals as a source of new business, this owner (and millions like him) could double, even triple his existing clientele in a very short period of time.

This principle applies to virtually any kind of business you are attempting to expand. Not all, but most people really want to help. Go ahead and ask. You'll be amazed at how quickly your business will grow! (P.S. I'm going to give the restaurant owner a copy of this book!)

55.

KNOW THAT THE IDEA "OPPORTUNITY ONLY KNOCKS ONCE" IS A BIG MYTH

It's hard to imagine a belief that is based more on fear than this one. Yet this idea is so common to our collective consciousness that it has turned into a cliché. People actually believe they are being wise by accepting this silly limitation. Yet when they do, it's as if they're saying to themselves and to the world, "My creative days are over. I'm a complete package. My life has been lived out." Nonsense!

When someone says "Opportunity only knocks once," what in the world are they thinking? Opportunity exists virtually everywhere you look. There are thousands of new business opportunities being created as we speak. There are millions more that need to be improved upon, thus an unlimited supply of additional opportunities. There are wonderful jobs being created each day—new partnerships being formed, new projects being started, new products and technologies being invented. There are books that need to be written, children that need to be taught, houses that need to be cleaned and others that need to be built. There are people, in fact entire cultures, who need help—so many people can benefit from and need our unique creativity. We all have gifts and talents to offer. We live in a world of unlimited potential, a world of creative genius. All that is required to succeed is to know, not just hope, that there is plenty to go around.

If you buy into the belief that opportunity only knocks once, you may jump on board too quickly when something that looks like an opportunity presents itself. You may take a job that you don't really like, or move to a location that doesn't suit your temperament. Instead of picking and choosing wisely, from a place of wisdom, joy, and common sense, you may end up reacting impulsively. On the other hand, because fear clouds your vision, you may miss out on wonderful opportunities when they come your way. Your fear may convince you to wait for something else because this one is too risky, or too scary, or beyond you, or whatever. Fear squeezes out opportunity from both ends.

When you let go of the fear that there isn't enough to go around, opportunities will fall into your lap. The absence of fear will clarify your goals and help you see beyond the risks. Knowing that opportunity *isn't* a once-in-a-lifetime event gives you the confidence to explore your options and to keep your mind open to new opportunities. Your eyes will see new ways of doing things; they will see opportunities, even in past failures. You'll realize that your chances have been there all along; you simply haven't seen them.

Let go of your fear. The universe has an infinite supply of opportunity. There is plenty to go around. You may be surprised to see that something is coming your way right now.

56.

STAY AWAY FROM THE BLAME GAME

One of the most insidious, tempting habits in all of life also happens to be one of the surest ways to rob yourself of empowerment, joy, and abundance. I'm referring to the habit of blaming others or external conditions for our failures, mistakes, problems, and lack of success. You might call it "the blame game."

Blaming others is a very easy thing to do. It creeps into our lives in subtle, as well as not so subtle, ways. It shows up in our thoughts and in our conversations. We might, for example, think to ourselves, "I'd be more successful if the products I were selling were of better quality," or "I'd make more money if the economy were better (or if my competition were more ethical, or if I had been luckier, or had taken a different career direction)." We might attribute our lack of fulfillment to changing times, a missed opportunity, or too little education. Or, we might complain to our wife or husband, "I travel too much to consider that new opportunity," or "I can't help it, no one ever taught me how to close a deal." How about this one: "I'd be in better shape, it's just that I don't have time." The habit of blaming can and does happen in almost any situation—we blame our competitors, employer, the government, our personal history, our age, sex, even our parents or current family responsibilities.

It's not that our tendency to blame is without any merit. There usually is a grain of truth in our complaints. But that's part of the problem. We can almost always justify to ourselves why our version of the blame game is valid. But all that does is keep the game going. And in doing so, we move away from the solution, which, of course, is taking charge of our own lives and our own destiny. It's really easy to blame our lack of exercise or family involvement on our schedule—it's a little tougher to admit that we are not prioritizing it. Likewise, it's effortless to convince ourselves that we never get any breaks; far more difficult to commit to making those breaks happen. It's easy to pay lip service to this concept, a little tougher to fully implement it. But when you do, the rewards—financial and otherwise—are great.

Most of the time blaming isn't blatant and obnoxious. It's far more subtle than that. And that's precisely why it's hard to identify—and put an end to. Yet, if you can have the humility to admit that you, too, fall into this habit from time to time—and you can identify those instances—you will have opened the door and paved the way for almost unlimited success and enjoyment in whatever it is that you do. Once you see that you are in charge of your own destiny, your life will become the magical and successful adventure it was meant to be.

I've been amazed at how helpful this concept has been in my own life and surprised by what I have found. The decision to stay away from the blame game has empowered me to live the life of my dreams. I suspect that it will be equally powerful for you if you give it a chance.

57.

NEVER WRITE AN E-MAIL WHEN YOU'RE MAD

I'm borrowing this idea from my wife, Kris, who has written about it in her book, *Don't Sweat the Small Stuff for Women*. It's so pertinent and important to maintaining strong business relationships, making money, avoiding unnecessary conflict, and having a great life, that I couldn't resist writing about it here.

The Internet—specifically, e-mail—has done wonders to increase our capacity to communicate. With lightning speed, we can now write letters, share ideas, even close deals. The benefits are astonishing.

There's a downside to e-mail, however, that's important to be aware of. The problem is, it's tempting, when you're mad or upset, to fire off an e-mail that you might very well live to regret. In a reactive or upset state of mind, or when you're lacking judgment or perspective, it's easy to act impulsively rather than with composure and wisdom. In the blink of an eye, you can confuse someone, hurt their feelings, enrage them, or even destroy a relationship.

The good news is, the flip side of this issue is also true. If you're mad at someone and are tempted to share your feelings via e-mail—but you manage to resist—your restraint can pay enormous dividends. Let me give you a personal example.

In the midst of a hectic week, I received, from someone I had done business with, a rude and somewhat threatening voice mail reinforced by an equally insulting e-mail. With what I hope was a somewhat rare (over)reaction, I was thrown off balance and was furious. In retrospect, it's clear that I was sweating the small stuff.

At any rate, I wrote a lengthy response that made his correspondence seem friendly in comparison. I expressed my dissatisfaction, as well as my desire to cease our relationship. With angry taps on my keyboard, I finished the letter and was about to send it—when, luckily, I saw what I was doing. I realized that I was overreacting and taking his comments personally. Instead of sending the e-mail, I deleted it.

To make a long story short, it was a very good financial decision. The person involved called me the very next day to apologize and to explain his position. Truthfully, he didn't mean what he'd said—he was simply reacting to factors beyond his control. Our relationship stayed intact and was unaffected.

Learning to avoid sweating the small stuff has many practical applications, and this is certainly one of them! Who knows how many business relationships are ruined, or at least adversely affected, every day, by someone clicking "send" instead of simply walking away?

Some practical advice is this: Whenever possible, when you're upset, refrain from sending e-mails. It's dangerous territory. Instead, wait until you cool off. Most of the time, what ends up being said will be more rational and will be better received by the people with whom you do business. In the long run, you'll make more money, maintain good relationships, and have less explaining to do!

58.

TAKE SOME MONEY OFF THE TABLE

Years ago, just after my twenty-first birthday, a few buddies of mine and I were in Las Vegas, Nevada, having our first gambling experience. While none of us knew what we were doing, one of the guys played a game and, somehow, on one of his first tries, ended up with almost $2,000! I had never seen so much cash—and neither had he.

My first reaction was, "That's so great. Now take most of it to the safe-deposit box so that, no matter what, you'll go home with a bundle." His response to me was, "Are you kidding? This is easy." You know the rest of the story. He lost everything and then some.

Years later, I met a man who was very rich. He decided to use his own stock as collateral to buy even more stock in the same company he'd originally invested in. He put all of his eggs into a single basket. He did this not with *some* of his money, but with *all* of it. He was convinced he couldn't lose. He, too, lost everything and then some. There are countless similar stories where the details may differ, but the end result is the same.

While some people would argue that risking it all is a thrill, I disagree. Instead, I think of it more as a way to ensure that you'll be sweating the small stuff, worrying, and feeling anxiety.

Taking some of the money off the table has far-reaching implications, financially and emotionally. Whether you're just starting out, super-rich, or somewhere in between, it's a wise policy to consider. When you know that at least some of what you've earned is safely tucked away, it frees your mind to pursue other ventures. It allows you the emotional freedom to confidently take some risks and try new things. There's no doubt that the feeling of inner security and confidence will ultimately contribute to the abundance and joy in your life.

Taking money off the table can mean anything from opening a simple savings, "rainy day," or money market account, to diversifying your mutual funds or other investments. It can also mean, as we discussed in an earlier chapter, "paying yourself first"—the idea that you want to take money out of your gross receipts and earnings and invest that money in you, before—not after—you pay your other bills. The idea of taking money off the table by paying yourself first is that you don't want to unnecessarily risk all of your investment profits, but neither do you want to "risk" all of your hard-earned money by paying only bills—and not yourself.

One important point is this: making the decision to take some money off the table doesn't mean you become conservative with your money or your career. That's a completely different issue. My friend at the casino could have had a blast—and maybe even won more money—had he gambled only a small portion of his winnings and saved the rest.

There is something very freeing and relaxing about taking money off the table and putting it to use somewhere else. In my own life, it has helped me to not sweat the small stuff. You may have already discovered that, when your mind is free and clear, absent worry and fear, your wisdom will surface, and you'll make wise, appropriate, and profitable decisions.

59.

BUY LARGE DEDUCTIBLE INSURANCE

Very few people would question the value of certain types of insurance. The level of your chosen deductible, however, is essential in a clear-headed financial plan. Generally speaking, you should always select the highest possible deductible that your insurer allows—and invest the difference in yourself. The less you worry, the more you save!

From a certain perspective (and be assured I'm not arguing against insurance), *all* insurance is based on fear. You have an asset—your car, home, business, earning capacity, even your health—and you are afraid that, at some point, something is going to happen to that asset: you will die or get sick, your car will be stolen or damaged, or your home or business will burn to the ground. Insurance is provided to protect you against these and other fears. Of course, some worries are more likely to occur than others. For example, while everyone eventually dies, not everyone will get into a car accident. Or most people will probably need medical attention at some point, but only a tiny percentage will ever be sued. Your job, as a consumer, is to carefully select which worries you most want to protect yourself against.

Since a vast majority of the things you fear the most will never actually happen, it works to your advantage to select the highest possible deductible on all insurance plans—therefore paying the lowest possible premiums. Then, be absolutely sure to invest the difference.

Just the other day I was listening to a radio talk show. The guest was a retired expert on "consumer product insurance." He was discussing the pros and cons of "extended warranties" on vehicles, electronics, and other products. His conclusion was that there were no real "pros" and that, to some degree, the entire industry was a "con." He said that less than 25 percent of the premiums paid were ever actually used. His conclusion was that, statistically, the consumer was far better off sticking the extended warranty premium into a rainy day account where it is likely never to be used. If, for some unlikely reason, you do suffer a loss, you'll still have the money available to make the necessary repairs. If not, you can use the money as a down payment the next time you purchase the item in question.

The math on this type of decision is fairly obvious. Why, then, do most people select a very low deductible and pay outrageous prices on their insurance? Fear is the answer.

When you distinguish between reasonable financial concerns and decisions based solely on fear, you can free up a great deal of financial as well as emotional power. The trick is to be courageous enough to admit that your fear is not working to your advantage and to be truthful about where your decision is coming from. Remember, fear keeps you focused on little details and unlikely events. It's far wiser to assume the best—know that most of the time your fears will not manifest.

60.

WHISTLE WHILE YOU WORK

It's amazing what happens when you act as if you love what you do. The positive energy helps not only you but everyone around you. It's contagious. A positive attitude brings forth creativity and aliveness in your work. It creates a rhythm of harmony and joy. It keeps you curious, interested, and focused on your work.

One of my favorite "Peanuts" cartoon strips was one where Charlie Brown was hanging his head low. He was depressed. While his head was down and his shoulders were slumped over, he was explaining to Linus that if you want to be depressed, it's really important to look depressed; that your negative posture actually helps you remain low. He went on to correctly explain that if you were to lift your head up and smile, it would take you out of your depression and make you feel better!

The idea of whistling while you work is identical, only it's on the opposite end of the attitudinal spectrum. When you appreciate the privilege of doing whatever you are doing, it makes it virtually impossible to feel down. Instead of complaining, you'll notice all the things you love about your work and your life. When your attitude is positive, your perspective is heightened. You will focus less on the irritations and annoyances of your work and more on the aspects that are delightful and nurturing. Your curiosity will encourage you to see new options and new ways of doing things. It will keep your thinking fresh and spontaneous, alive and interesting. The people around you will be affected, too. They will be more likely to offer you genuine, positive feedback. They will actually listen to what you have to say and they will appreciate you more than ever before.

So much of what you've always wanted will emerge—and it all begins with a smile.

Starting today, see if you can incorporate a "whistle while you work" attitude into your daily routine. You'll notice an immediate shift from grumpy and serious to lighthearted and joyful. The creation of abundance is a joyful process. Lighten up and have some fun!

61.

ENCOURAGE CREATIVITY IN OTHERS
AND HAVE FAITH IN THEM

You'd be amazed at what people can (and will) do if you not only give them a chance but also believe in their potential. It's important to know that everyone has unique gifts and talents. It's your job to assist in bringing those gifts and talents out into the world. In other words, rather than sitting back and waiting for people to be perfect—and being frustrated when they are not—take some responsibility in the process by creating an ideal psychological working environment.

There's an old motto in business: Give someone a reputation to live up to and watch them shine. It's really true. Most people, given the right environment, are hard-working, talented, creative, and productive. They want to please others just as you and I want to. Unfortunately, however, most people are hardly ever exposed to an ideal working environment.

What happens to someone when she is insecure, resentful, or frightened? Very simply, she loses most of her motivation to please you as well as most of her other positive work-related qualities. Consider the following example: You have an assistant. Every day when he walks in the door, you remind him how incompetent he is. You point out his weaknesses and flaws. You belittle him in front of other people. Then you walk out the door. The question is, How does your assistant feel? It's hard to know for sure, because people react differently to the same set of facts. But it's a good bet that he's either frightened, insecure, resentful of you, or, most likely, all of the above. His job performance is going to be suspect. If you are disappointed in *him*, you are missing the point! In my book, you haven't done *your* job.

Wouldn't you increase your odds of securing a dedicated, hard-working assistant if you treated him with enormous, genuine respect? Wouldn't your assistant be more likely to work hard and keep your best interests in mind if you were to treat him with kindness, reminding him frequently how much you appreciate him, pointing out to him when he does something right? Ideally, we want everyone to feel good about themselves. We want others to believe in themselves, to feel confident and secure; to feel as if they are talented, competent, and creative. This way, everyone wins.

When you encourage creativity in others and have faith in them, it's analogous to creating the ideal conditions for a garden. You are "planting the seeds" for an environment where success is most likely to occur. When you plant a garden, you want to have the right type of soil, moisture, and sunshine. When you build people up—instead of pushing them down—you create the psychological equivalent. The same principle applies whether you are hiring a housekeeper, an attorney, an accountant, a publicist, or anyone else. It also applies to your children, your spouse, your friends, and your neighbors. It always works: When you believe in someone and when that person knows that you believe in her, magical things can happen. From this point on, see if you can expect great things from people. Do your part by creating the ideal working conditions. Be kind, patient, and supportive. Then, sit back and watch what happens.

62.

DON'T GIVE AWAY YOUR POWER

A major mistake made by many is to give away one's power to perceived experts. We do it all the time—to our doctors, financial planners, insurance salesmen. The assumption is: This person is an expert; I'd better listen to her. And, of course, sometimes this assumption is true and you should listen. But be careful to reserve the ultimate decision making for yourself. Always remember, if *you're* going to make money, *you* must take charge. Abundance and joy come from within you, not from other people.

As usual, the reason we so readily give our power away to others is fear. We worry that if we don't listen to an "expert," then we will surely be making a big mistake. Once you eliminate this fear, you'll realize that the creation of abundance is easier than you thought possible. When you make decisions from a place of wisdom rather than from a place of fear—and when you hold on to your own power—your decisions are usually good ones. They take you in directions that lead you toward your dreams and goals. It's a good idea to surround yourself with experts and to understand where your knowledge and experience are limited. However, the power should remain with you.

Suppose your insurance salesperson insists that what you really need is a million dollars of "whole life" coverage. But you plead with him that "Doing so will take most of my extra income and won't leave anything left for the investments I'd like to make." You go on to explain, "If I bought term insurance instead of whole life, I would have the same coverage at a tiny fraction of the cost." Your insurance salesperson, however, is grounded in fear and is trained to convince you to see life from his perspective. He believes he is giving you unbiased advice and is working in your best interest. "You'll regret it," he insists, attempting to reinforce any fear you may already be experiencing. What now? He is, after all, an "expert."

Whether you are dealing with a pushy insurance salesperson, a timid financial planner, an incompetent physician or attorney, or anyone else, the most relevant and important question to ask yourself is, Who is in charge here? The answer is *you*! Obviously, you want to take into consideration the advice you are getting, especially if you're paying for it. However, always remember that you are the boss. The ultimate decision is yours. Trust in your own instincts and wisdom, and not in the words and fears of experts. If you have a strong sense that your own instincts are the way to go, follow them. Trust yourself.

I went to a doctor once because I was feeling agitated a great deal of the time. The doctor *immediately* assumed that what I needed was antianxiety medicine. I felt this was utter nonsense! I insisted that it must be something else. "Listen here young man," he said in an arrogant tone, "I've seen this a thousand times." His obvious belief was "I know what's best for you! I'm the doctor. You're just the patient." I refused to accept his advice. I knew it must be something else. So I went to a more holistically inclined physician. After about two minutes of asking me questions about my lifestyle, he started to laugh. "Richard, " he said in a respectful and gentle tone, "you're drinking about ten times the amount of coffee you should be. Cut way back on your caffeine consumption and give me a call in about two weeks."

It turned out he was absolutely right. But more important than his good advice was the fact that I listened to my own instincts. Had I simply gone along with the first doctor's advice, I may have been on antianxiety medicine for the rest of my life, while drinking fifteen to twenty cups of coffee per day! My advice to you is this: Don't give away your power. You'll be amazed at the power of your own wisdom.

63.

CHARGE WHAT YOU ARE WORTH

An acquaintance of mine is one of the best professionals in her field. Virtually everyone she works with seems to agree. Why then does she charge between 30 and 40 percent less than her less experienced, less skilled competitors? Her problem, of course, is fear. She is unrealistically worried that, if she charges more, she will lose her clientele and her reputation as a fair businessperson. She believes, as many others do, that the primary reason she is so successful is because of her "reasonable" rates. Nonsense! The reason she is so successful in keeping a full clientele is because she's good at what she does. The truth is, she could probably *double* her fee and keep the vast majority of her clients. There's an old saying that applies not only to the sales of products but to the underpricing of services as well: If you're losing a penny per transaction, you can't make it up in volume.

Undercharging for professional services creates some serious, often unrealized problems. Perhaps the most serious of these is that undercharging keeps your schedule falsely overbooked, thus prohibiting you from having the time and energy to engage in other activities that may work to your greatest advantage—activities that could help create the abundance you desire.

Let's do some simple math. My friend, for example, works on average with six clients a day, six days a week. When you include set up, driving, scheduling, insurance, billing, and other factors, each client takes almost two hours of her time. Realistically, she needs all of her income to make ends meet. Her goal, about which she has been procrastinating for many years, is to go back to school. But, she complains, "I have no time." My argument is that she has it backwards! She doesn't have time *not* to go back to school. This is her dream. Abundance, of course, comes from following your dreams.

Let's assume, for argument's sake, that she doubled her fee from (symbolically) $50 to $100. And let's assume that raising her fee did, in fact, push some of her clients away. To illustrate the point, let's assume a worst-case scenario and that a full 50 percent of her clients left her practice! Look at what would happen: First, she would be making exactly the same amount of money in exactly half the time! Instantly, with one worry-free decision, she would have created the time to pursue her dream of going back to school! But wait, it gets even better. The clients that did stay with her would be the ones who were able to afford her higher fees. Thus, the people that *they* referred to her business would in all likelihood also be able to afford her services. She would be setting in motion an entirely new way of perceiving her work; a perception that would allow her to enjoy her work without worry or resentment, continue to provide a valuable service to her clients, *and* allow her the freedom and joy to pursue her dreams.

I am not advocating lofty pricing practices or greed. Neither am I suggesting that it's always appropriate and/or necessary to raise your prices. I have found, however, that because of fear and worry, many people *under*price their services and/or products. Unfortunately, this can set you up for failure by creating unnecessary demands on your time and energy—making you look and feel very busy but with very little of this energy going toward the creation of abundance. My suggestion is to charge what you are truly worth. This realistic yet confident pricing strategy keeps you free from resentment and pointed toward your dreams.

64.

LISTEN, REALLY LISTEN

Looking back on my life, I'm a little embarrassed to admit that I have been a poor listener. And while I'm a better listener today than I was five years ago, I still have a long way to go. As I look (and listen) to those around me, however, I feel like I have a lot of company.

People love to be listened to. So much so, in fact, that they will pay therapists enormous fees to listen to their stories and complaints. Consumers love to be listened to as well. They will happily pay top dollar for those people who are smart enough to understand that this is what they want—and what they demand. Unfortunately, only a tiny percentage of business persons do understand, or are willing to implement, this important notion.

What does your customer or client really want? Do you know? Are you guessing? Have you asked? If you *have* asked, are you giving her what she wants? Or are you giving her what *you* think she wants or needs? The difference in how you answer these questions may well be the difference between success and failure.

An interesting and eye-opening exercise is this: Pretend that you are a therapist. Listen very carefully to what your customer is saying. Ask probing questions like, What do you really want? and What would make you even happier with this product or service? Be genuine and listen like you've never listened before. Listen from your heart. Make it absolutely clear to your customer that the *only* thing that matters to you is that she is happy and that she is getting exactly what she wants and expects.

If you are running a small restaurant, for example, ask your customers if they would be willing to sit down with you for five minutes. Tell them you want to find out what would make their dining experience a little nicer

143

than it already is. Ask them what they like about your restaurant, what they don't like, why they come in, and so forth. Listen carefully and respectfully.

When you listen in this manner, you may be shocked at the positive response. When people feel that they are listened to, they also feel appreciated and valued. Feeling listened to is such a rare experience that when someone does feel listened to, they tend to tell others about it. When your listening ear is genuine, you'll create raving fans and customers who will love you and will want to do business with you. Listening is like a magic formula that turns ordinary people into loyal, happy customers. One final tip: If you're married and/or have children, the same principle applies. If you want a closer relationship with your spouse or kids, the best place to start is by becoming a better listener!

65.

CULTIVATE HUMOR AND LEARN TO SMILE

Are you as amazed as I am at all the sourpusses out there in the "real world"? A lot of people have lost their perspective and take life so dreadfully seriously. Everything is a really big deal. On the other hand, once in a while you run into someone who is simply a delight. A person who has cultivated a sense of humor and hasn't forgotten how to smile.

This is undoubtedly one of the simplest suggestions in this entire book. Yet very few understand just how important it really is. So often, the difference between one business and another is negligible. In an external sense, it's almost impossible to tell the difference. The groceries and prices at one store are about the same as the one next door. The food at restaurant A is similar to that in restaurant B. The shoes in one establishment are the same ones you find in the store down the block. One example after another points to the simple truth that, in reality, products and services, on the surface and as a whole, look the same.

If I'm completely honest, I'd have to say that my buying decisions—the restaurants where I tend to eat, the places I purchase my clothes, the coffee shops I frequent, the stores I shop at—are virtually all made from the perspective of which employees are the friendliest, have the most genuine smiles and the nicest personalities. The coffee shops I go to are the ones that have the nicest people pouring the coffee. After all, the coffee tastes the same, it costs the same, the cups are the same, the atmosphere and locations are similar, but there is an enormous difference between waking up to a smiling, happy person, and, to use my seven-year-old daughter's words, waking up to "A serious little man." (This is what she calls me when I get too uptight!)

There is a small, family-owned grocery store in our town that is a beneficiary of this philosophy. The owner is one of the nicest men I've ever met. My kids actually *ask* if we can go to his store, and often we do. There is nothing in his store that we can't get elsewhere—and probably less expensively—but we really prefer to visit him. He has a beautiful smile and both my daughters, as well as myself, deeply appreciate it. Over the years he has earned thousands of dollars of our business simply by having a genuine smile. There is no amount of advertising or anything else he could have done to earn our business. His marketing strategy is effective and free! Believe it or not, the same is true, to some degree, when we choose a doctor, accountant, housekeeper, or other professional. Obviously, we want and need competent people to work for us. However, all things being equal (and they often are), what people want is someone who is nice to be around. I've actually avoided certain doctors, especially pediatricians, when they act like "serious little men." I simply don't want my kids to be around that kind of energy unless I have no other options. Why not choose someone who is competent *and* happy?

The benefits of a sense of humor and a nice smile to you extend far beyond greater profits. You'll also have the privilege of feeling better yourself and making others happy as well. I believe that smiling actually gives you more energy, and perhaps even better health. So lighten up and smile. Your payback will be immediate and significant.

66.

DON'T SWEAT THE SETBACKS

The question isn't whether or not we will have setbacks, disappointments, and failures in business (and in life)—we will. Rather, the question is, how will we deal with them? Will we, as so many do, sweat it? Will we become upset, immobilized, frustrated, hopeless, or pessimistic? Or will we take a more positive approach?

With the benefit of hindsight, it's usually easy to see that most setbacks are nothing more than "small stuff" disguised as big stuff. In other words, they can seem significant, even insurmountable in the moment. Yet, once we get through them, we look back on setbacks and even failures as a necessary, even important part of our success. A number of people have told me that being forced to file for bankruptcy was the best thing that ever happened to them. Sure, it was painful while it was happening, but it woke them up and taught them some important lessons.

I once heard a speaker use the example of people driving around looking for a parking place. He said, "It's as if people are driving around looking for no place to park." What he meant was that many people get frustrated because most of the spaces are full. It's easy to forget that you don't need a bunch of spaces—you only need one; the others are irrelevant. Simple as this seems, it's actually an important point to remember—you don't need everything to go perfectly, you only need a few things to go right. And once they do, the setbacks simply fade away. Remembering this takes a great deal of pressure and frustration off your shoulders.

I've spoken to a number of radio and television personalities who've said to me something to the effect that, "I'm glad I was rejected over there because it paved the way for me to be here." I've heard the same story, many times, in the corporate world. Few people are successful immediately, never rejected, perfectly placed the first time around. It's usually just the opposite—trial and error, rejection, setbacks, failures, and so forth.

Perhaps you make sales calls and are rejected over and over again. You can focus on the fact that things aren't working out, beat yourself up mentally, and feel hopeless—or you can learn from your mistakes, improve your skills, let go of the past, and move on.

Is this easier said than done? Of course, but the other options aren't so good. Either way, we are where we are. All the frustration in the world isn't going to change what has already happened—so why sweat it?

An extremely successful financial planner I met was a failure as a builder. He'd hated the work and had lost a great deal of money. Looking back, he attributes most of his success today to that failure. He claims that, had he not hated his former profession so much—and had he not been "so bad" at the critical components of that career—he would never have found his true passion: financial planning.

The trick, I believe, is being able to use not only our past setbacks, but the current ones as well, to help us grow and move on. In other words, when something doesn't work out well, rather than dwelling on it and feeling badly, we let it go, see what we can learn, make any necessary adjustments, and move forward.

Learning to stop sweating our setbacks is a powerful way to live a more successful and abundant life. Without the ongoing nagging and heaviness of self-directed criticism and worrisome thoughts, we free up energy to be creative, hardworking, and successful.

67.

BUILD UP A LARGE "TRUST FUND"

I don't know about you, but I grew up believing that only very wealthy (usually spoiled) people had the privilege and security of a "trust fund." Not true! Each individual—every one of us—has the kind of trust fund that really matters: the trust of other people. The only question is, How large is it? Many people, not knowing how important a trust fund is to their own success, are practically bankrupt in this critical account. Yet others, intuitively aware of its importance, are rich in this category beyond their wildest dreams. Sooner or later, a large trust fund will pay enormous dividends toward your creation of abundance. There is a direct correlation between the size of your trust fund and the desire and willingness of others to work with and help you.

The way to build a large trust fund is simple and straightforward. It involves being accountable for your actions, however large or small, doing what you say you are going to do, delivering on your promises, being on time, and so forth. Anything and everything you do that reinforces your own trustworthiness is like money in the bank. Accountability is derived in both small and large doses. For example, if you tell someone you are going to call them at three o'clock, or pick them up at the airport, and you do so on time, as you say you are going to do, you earn small credits toward your trust fund. Likewise, if you tell someone that you'll send them a copy of a book you've been discussing, and you actually do it, you earn credibility with that person. If you *don't* do exactly what you say you're going to do, while any individual action or inaction may not seem like a very big deal, it decreases your credibility and *reduces* the size of your trust fund. I know people, for example, who will make small promises about

149

things they are going to do practically every time I speak to them. While these are nice, decent people with good intentions, and while nothing they're promising is all that important, they usually don't deliver what they say they are going to deliver. The sad result of this nonaccountability is that I have learned to expect them to renege. In other words, while I may really like them as people, I don't necessarily *trust* them, nor do I take them very seriously. In all likelihood, other people don't either.

Obviously, no one is perfect. We all make mistakes, renege on commitments, show up late, and occasionally forget appointments. I have learned, however, that it's far easier and wiser to avoid making commitments I can't keep than it is to make promises, however small, that may eventually reduce the size of my trust fund.

Starting today, speak and behave with your trust fund in mind. Before you say you are going to do something that someone else is going to depend on, check in with yourself. Ask yourself, Will I be able to keep this commitment? Remember, the size of your trust fund depends on it.

68.

SELL THE SIZZLE, NOT THE STEAK

In any business, it's critical to know what you're actually selling. Very often it's not what it appears to be. If you're selling a house, for example, you're obviously *not* selling wood, brick, or concrete. Instead, you're tapping into a person's dream—his or her perception of how they are going to feel and live once they get into the home.

A good friend of mine was the first to teach me this valuable lesson. He used to own a beautiful apartment complex in a lovely California town. Once, while I was in town, he gave me a tour of the property. It was complete with tennis courts, two beautiful swimming pools, a workout room, and a picnic area. "Wow," was my reaction. "I'll bet everyone loves to use all this great stuff." "Actually, Richard, you may be shocked to know that virtually no one uses the facilities. I wish they would, but the reality is, they don't," was his response. It turned out that less than 10 percent of the residents had *ever* used any of the facilities! And less than 5 percent used them regularly. This came as quite a shock to me as I was always a person who would fall into that 5 percent.

My friend went on to explain that, despite the fact that almost no one uses the facilities, virtually everyone, before they move in, *thinks* they are going to. In fact, it's one of the primary reasons they choose an apartment complex, and one of the only reasons they are willing to pay top dollar for it. The "steak," in this example, is the apartment complex. The "sizzle" is the fancy surroundings and facilities—the sizzle is what's doing the selling, not the steak. So the best way to sell a potential resident on the property was for my friend to be sure to show everyone the complete facilities. Invariably, this would get his potential customers dreaming of how they were going to finally take time to relax, learn to play tennis, swim in the pool, enjoy barbecues with friends, and so forth.

The analogy of selling the sizzle instead of the steak can be extended to many other types of businesses. I have to admit that, often, I've made my decision on which hotel to stay at based solely on the fact that they have an indoor pool and room service. Rarely, however, do I actually take advantage of these luxuries. The same is true with restaurants. Once in a while my wife and I will choose a restaurant because they have an incredible dessert menu—we dream of that decadent piece of chocolate cake—but, except for an extremely rare occasion, we will usually pass on dessert. We either feel too full after the meal or worry about the weight we are going to gain should we choose to eat it. The point is, we enter the restaurant not because of any rational thinking but because we, like most people, are influenced by our thoughts and dreams.

Think of the millions of exercise gadgets that are sold each year. Surveys show that everyone absolutely believes that they are going to become disciplined and use the equipment on a regular basis. New customers dream of flat stomachs and muscular arms. However, statistics show us that 90 percent of consumers stop using the equipment within ten days of purchasing it—and virtually all the rest quit after a month or two. Only a tiny percentage of people continue to use the equipment. The companies making these products know that the best way to sell these machines is to effectively tap into the dreams of the consumer. So they put photographs of beautiful, muscular women and firm, physically fit handsome men on the boxes. The "sizzle" is the possibility that you and I might look like those people in the photograph.

It's important to know that people love to dream. So if you want to sell something, be sure you know what the dreams are. Factor this knowledge into whatever it is you are selling—product or service—and you'll be amazed at how much more effective you will become.

69.

GO AHEAD AND DO IT

I have discovered an amazing secret that works remarkably well. The secret can be summed up in a single sentence that is also the title of Susan Jeffers' wonderful book: *Feel the Fear and Do It Anyway!* I've found that, remarkably, virtually every time I'm really frightened to do something I need to do, and I go ahead and do it anyway, that it almost always turns out okay. It passes. In other words, somehow, despite my worry, I *do* get through it. I always come out the other end. I always survive. What's more, it's almost never as difficult as I make it out to be. In fact, it's usually far easier.

It's very helpful to remind yourself that, despite your fears, here you are. Somehow you have managed to survive it all. In this sense, all your worries have been a mirage—a waste of time, irrelevant.

Think of all the times you've lost sleep over something you had to do. Perhaps you were anticipating a job interview or peer review. Maybe you had a difficult job to do—you had to fire someone or give him bad news. You fretted and worried, sometimes for days, even weeks. But in spite of all the worry, you managed to get through it. In the past, whether you lost your job, felt humiliated, faced a difficult challenge, or whatever else, here you are. You survived. This doesn't mean you haven't had difficult things to do—we all have—but it does mean that the worry we experience is nothing more than a mental irritant. When we set it aside, we can get on with our lives, including our many challenges.

In my career I've felt frightened many times. I've had to speak in front of large audiences and in front of cameras, despite being a very shy person. I've had to create interesting articles and books, after practically flunking high school English. I've faced deadlines that I felt were unreasonable, even impossible to meet. And yes, I worried about it all. Yet when I look back, I realize that, despite the mental anguish I put myself through, I always did get through the situation, one way or another, whatever it may have been. Usually, I'm able to rise to the occasion, and I'll bet you are, too.

There's a lesson here for all of us: We're stronger than our fears and more competent than our worries. The next time you find yourself worrying, step back for a moment and reflect on past worries. Doesn't it seem all too familiar? Is it possible that you're merely repeating a mental exercise? Do you think the worry is going to help? Aren't you going to do whatever you're worried about anyway? What's the point of the worry? I think these are really important questions. And I believe that if you take the time to reflect on them, you'll agree that if you "feel the fear and do it anyway," all will be well. And once you get the hang of it, the worries begin to go away.

70.

BE WILLING TO TAKE ADVICE

Generally speaking, people don't take advice, even good advice. This is true even when the advice is free and when it's offered with love. Think about yourself. How often do you really, honestly take someone else's advice? How often do you say to yourself, or out loud, "That's a great idea. That's a much better way of doing it than the way I have been doing it." This type of humility is almost unheard of in our culture, yet think about the wisdom here. In order to grow, we need to see things differently. We don't want to do the same things over and over if they're not working well. Instead, we want to open our eyes to new and improved ways of doing things. But how can we see things differently if we refuse to take to heart the suggestions from others? It seems so obvious.

Sometimes, the reason we don't take advice is pure stubbornness. We want to do things our own way—even if it's not working! Other times, we avoid advice out of fear. We might be frightened that we're going to look bad in the eyes of someone else, or that we're going to seem incompetent. Or we might be fearful that the advice we get isn't going to help— that if *we* can't figure it out, then no one else can either. Sometimes we've received bad advice or too much advice, and we vow to not repeat that same mistake.

My suggestion in this area is simple and straightforward: Take the advice. Life is so much simpler when you involve the strengths and expertise of others. After all, if you absolutely knew what to do to make your life better or more successful, you'd be doing it already. But if you're struggling in any aspect of your life (and we all do), you need advice.

I'm certain that one of the primary reasons I've had some degree of

157

success in my life is my absolute willingness to seek out, listen to, and often take advice. This makes life so easy that, occasionally, it doesn't seem fair. I love to get advice, especially from competent people. I believe that if someone has worked hard, achieved some measure of success, and is willing to help, I'd be a fool *not* to listen! Plus, as you probably already know, almost everyone loves to give advice. By listening to someone and actually taking their advice, you not only get good results but you also get to contribute to the joy of another person.

Unfortunately, many people miss out on one of the surest shortcuts to success: taking advice. So often, when a person struggles, he or she is very close to a major breakthrough. They are literally "an inch away" from achieving their goals and dreams. If they would just open their eyes to a blind spot, see something they are doing in a slightly different or new way, their success would be phenomenal and certain. I have friends and family members who fall into this category. I believe they are incredibly talented people, on the verge of possible greatness, or on the verge of improving their life in a meaningful way. Yet this one tiny flaw—the unwillingness to listen to anyone else and the absolute unwillingness to take advice—consistently gets in their way. Don't let this minor obstacle get in your way. The advice is out there. People want to help you. Allow yourself to receive help and the quality of your life will soar.

71.

ASK YOURSELF, WHAT HAVE I CONTRIBUTED
TO THIS PROBLEM?

Many people rarely, if ever, ask this critical question. Instead, they automatically assume that any problem they are having must be someone else's fault. If there is a disagreement or argument, it's the other person's fault. If something went wrong, someone else made a mistake. If there's a glitch in the schedule, "someone else must have dropped the ball." It simply never occurs to many people that something is their fault. Or, at the very least, that they may be partly responsible.

On the surface, it might seem nice to believe that you're never to blame. The problem, however, with this "never blame me" philosophy is that you'll rarely be able to pinpoint the one aspect of problem solving that is truly solvable: your own contribution. Once you eliminate the fear associated with admitting that you are, at times, responsible for the parts of your life that aren't working—minor annoyances *and* larger problems— you open a whole new door of possibilities.

Once you're willing to accept responsibility for the problems in your life, you will see obvious solutions that take very minor adjustments to change. Sometimes there's a fine line between doing something really well and doing something really badly. Often, the solution is to simply change something you are doing.

It's really not all that helpful to contemplate the faults and contributions to problems of others. Rarely can you do anything about other people and the way they handle things. It's simple, however (unless you're too frightened), to make changes in your own responses. I try, whenever I can, to see where *I'm* contributing. If, for example, I'm frustrated with the way a business relationship is progressing, I take a look at the way I'm treating that person. I ask myself questions like, Am I being too pushy or demanding? Am I assuming that he or she really understands what I'm asking when they may not? Am I being unclear or unfair? These types of questions are helpful for two reasons. First, I'm almost *always* able to see some contribution on my end. Second, when I do, I can usually make a simple adjustment that can actually help the situation.

Just last week, for example, I was frustrated with someone I was working with over the phone. She was working for me, but nothing seemed to be happening. I was impatient and kept pushing her to perform. Then it occurred to me that she might be angry at me for pushing too hard. I realized that I was terribly overcommitted myself and was, without knowing it, expecting her to operate at my crazy pace. When I called to sincerely apologize, I could sense her relaxation over the phone. I backed off and, as I did, her performance began to improve. Had I continued to blame her for a problem I was clearly contributing to, she would have remained resentful and, in all likelihood, would have continued to perform well beneath her capacity. We both would have ended up losers in the deal.

Obviously, I'm not suggesting that everything is your fault, or that you should spend an exorbitant amount of time and energy thinking about your faults and drawbacks. To do so would be a different type of negative habit. It's critical, however, that you're honest about your contribution to your problems. Don't bury your head in the sand. If you truly want to excel in your life, you must be willing to look in the mirror and, with humility and honesty, reflect on your contributions to what's not going right in your life. That way, you can do something about it.

72.

CONSIDER THAT WISDOM MAY BE
EVEN MORE IMPORTANT THAN IQ

All things being equal, intelligence is a wonderful quality to possess. However, if you had to choose between the two, I'd say that wisdom is even more important than intelligence in your quest for joy and abundance. There are many highly intelligent people who fail to use their intelligence to best advantage. There are also many extremely intelligent people who live very unhappy lives. Sadly, in many cases, it seems that you can fit the wisdom of a highly intelligent person into a tiny thimble.

While you could rank order people in terms of their IQ, the number you assigned to a person would say nothing about their degree of success or happiness. Despite this fact, however, as a society, we continue to revere intelligence, yet barely even stop to consider wisdom at all.

Unlike intelligence, wisdom is a quality that you cannot accurately measure. It's invisible. It includes aspects of life such as perspective, spontaneity, creativity, and social skills. Wisdom is your sense of knowing, an intuitive feeling. William James, often thought of as the "father of modern psychology," said, "Wisdom is seeing something in a nonhabitual manner." It's seeing an old problem in a new, fresh light. As you discover and begin to trust your wisdom, you'll free yourself from your fixed and habitual patterns of thinking and problem solving, and will more easily be able to navigate yourself toward joy and prosperity. In a nutshell, wisdom is the ability to "see" an answer without having to "think" of an answer. It exists outside the confines of your thinking mind. Often, wisdom is seeing the obvious. And unlike the thinking mind, wisdom contains no worry.

One of my favorite stories that demonstrates wisdom is about a giant truck that gets stuck under an overpass. The truck was too tall for the available clearance. The police called out the best, brightest, and most expensive engineers in the city to try to figure out what to do. They brought along their computers, clip boards, and slide rules. They discussed the issue amongst themselves. They racked their brains for hours. They simply couldn't figure out how to remove the truck without damaging the freeway above. It all seemed so complicated. Then a small boy, about seven years old, walked up to the men and tugged on one of their pants legs. "Excuse me, sir," the little boy said in a respectful tone. "Why don't you just let the air out of the tires?" Out of the mouths of babes the problem was solved.

The people who have made the most money, or who have been the most successful in their careers, are certainly not always the most intelligent or the most highly educated. There are plenty of Harvard graduates who have a very difficult time making any significant money, despite their incredible education. Usually, the people who make the most money and who have the most fun doing so are highly creative, highly motivated, have great intuition, solid gut reactions and instincts, and/or the ability to see opportunities. These qualities, and others, stem not so much from intelligence but from wisdom. This is *not* an argument against formal education, or against standard intelligence. Yet it's critical to be aware that you don't need to use any lack of formal education as ammunition against yourself. Education is important and helpful. But don't let anyone convince you that if you aren't formally educated, you are doomed to failure—because you're not.

The best way to access your wisdom is simply to know that it exists and to trust in it. Keep your mind as clear as possible, know that a deeper, more intelligent type of thinking—your wisdom—is available. When you feel that your thinking is too frenetic, overactive, or that you are trying too hard, experiment with backing off. You will find that a softer focus and less effort, not more, will usually result in a better use of the mind. Relax and succeed.

73.

ELIMINATE THE WORDS "I'M NOT A SALESPERSON" FROM YOUR VOCABULARY

Yes, you are! If you have something—anything—to offer someone else, then you are, at least partially, a salesperson. If you ever even attempt to get another person to purchase, try, or even look at what you're offering, then you *are* a salesperson. And that's okay. The point here is that selling is an important part of the web of life. It's okay to sell. It doesn't make you a bad person.

Many people have a self-destructive attitude toward selling, treating it like a four-letter word, thus creating a wall between themselves and their own success. Rather than accepting the fact that we all have something to sell—our time, energy, ideas, products, vision, dreams, or services—they choose to deny the fact that they have anything to do with selling. I have seen this silly belief interfere with virtually every type of business venture, from network marketing to personal service businesses, to running a bakery. Whenever you set yourself up as a person who is against selling, you create a difficult environment to succeed.

The bigger the deal you make out of it, the more you interfere, energetically, with your own success. Keep in mind that your energy follows your attention. If your attention is busy being a nonsalesperson, all that will happen is that you will become ineffective at selling—even though you are selling. Thus, any attempt to convince yourself that you aren't selling anything is counterproductive and unwise.

74.

CONSIDER THAT BUSYNESS GETS IN YOUR WAY

Tom Hanks, one of the best actors of our time, was being interviewed on television when he responded to a question by saying, "More isn't always better." He was attempting to get across the message that busyness gets in your way, that too many things going on at once, too many projects or details to attend to, can be a distraction that keeps us from being our best; when your head is too full, there's little room left for freshness and creativity. He is absolutely right!

Many of us are so busy that we lose sight of which end is up. We rush around, looking and feeling very busy, but, in actuality, we are getting very little of substance done. Our creativity and wisdom are lost in our busyness. We lose sight of what's truly relevant and most important. New ideas are hard to come by.

Often, in business decisions, a single moment of thoughtful reflection is all that is needed to make the best possible choice. However, if you are too busy, scrambling around, frantic, you'll often miss that precious, all-important moment. You'll see all the chaos, but you won't see the obvious solutions. For example, I met a real estate buyer who purchases properties that others had attempted, but failed, to renovate and resell at a profit. He told me that, in most cases, the failure was the result of acting too impulsively with a very busy mind. "You see," said this successful businessman, as he pointed to a project he was working on, "all this property really needed was a cosmetic tune-up. The people who owned it before me went broke trying to make it perfect. There were indeed a lot of problems with the property, but they weren't nearly as serious as they believed them to be. They were rushing around so frantically that they lost sight of the obvious."

Somewhere along the line, most of us got the message that looking, acting, and being really busy is a virtue. Certainly there are times when we truly are busy and can't do much about it. Ironically, however, when we stop worrying so much about getting everything done; when we stop looking and telling others how busy we are, we are better able to determine what's most important. We calm down and see what really needs to be done.

A critical aspect of success is to schedule time in your day when absolutely nothing is going on. Even if you can only spare a few extra minutes a day, you need to have "down time." Rather than overlapping your meetings and appointments, and running them together, see if you can allow a little extra time. Create some space. Stop worrying that you won't get everything done. What you'll find is that when you have a little more space for yourself and a little less hurry, many of your best ideas will begin to surface. This has certainly proven to be the case for me. Most of my best ideas come not when I'm overwhelmed in my busyness, but during the moments between the busyness when I have a few quiet moments to myself and my wisdom has a chance to surface. Starting today, see if you can become a little less "busy." You'll be surprised at what occurs to you.

166

75.

THINK ABOUT PURPLE SNOWFLAKES

I'll bet you read that sentence twice. Of course, that's the whole idea—to get your attention. I've found that many people are a little timid, even frightened, to stand out, to do things a little differently. They worry about what people are going to think, or what they are going to say, or that their efforts will be perceived as foolish, or that they won't really work. In marketing, however, the whole idea is to get someone, or a group of people, to take a look at what you're selling, asking for, or offering.

The notion of purple snowflakes is a metaphor for standing out in the crowd. In our world of incredible competition and sheer volume, it's more important than ever to stand apart. You certainly don't want to fade into the background. As long as the product or service you are marketing is at least as good as everyone else's, standing out—offering purple snowflakes— will often make the difference.

When I really want someone to open the mail I'm sending them, for example, I send it via Federal Express or some other overnight delivery service. Obviously, this is a much more expensive route, but think about the tradeoff for a moment. Suppose you're sending a request to a famous and/or super-busy person who receives dozens of requests each day. If you, like virtually everyone else, simply send your request in a regular business envelope, the chances are excellent that it will be days, perhaps even weeks, before the person even opens your letter. Yet very few people, irrespective of how famous or busy they are, can resist opening an overnight delivery package. Now that they have opened your mail, there's a chance they will respond favorably. In this case, your "purple snowflake" was the Federal

Express package itself. I can assure you that if your request is granted, you'll be sold on the idea of purple snowflakes.

A friend of mine, in my eyes a marketing genius, wanted to get an ex-professional football player to invest in his business. The business was solid and an excellent opportunity. The problem was that this particular ex-athlete, known in part for the wealth he had been able to amass, was approached by all sorts of credible entrepreneurs on a daily basis. It was fairly common knowledge that he had essentially stopped reading the request letters.

My friend, adept at creating purple snowflakes, wanted to overcome this obstacle because he knew that if he could just get the athlete to read his reports, that he would seriously consider the investment opportunity. So here's what he did: He taped his request to an actual NFL football and sent it to the man. Needless to say, the former football star recognized the shape of the package, was curious, and opened it immediately. Within a few days my friend received a personal call—not from a secretary, from the athlete himself—congratulating him on his incredible creativity. The athlete asked my friend to dinner, telling him that, as long as the numbers checked out, and everything was ethical, as it seemed to be, he would be honored to do business with someone who was so clever.

Obviously, not every purple snowflake is going to be so well received. But instead of giving up, and without becoming obnoxious about it, see if you can create another purple snowflake. Drop your fears about how your snowflakes will be received. As they say in Hollywood, any attention is better than no attention.

76.

STAY OUT OF REVERSE

Reverse, in a psychological sense, works the same as the reverse gear in your car—it takes you backward. And, like your car, if you want to change direction and begin moving forward, you must shift gears completely. It's impossible to move forward in reverse gear.

The way reverse sounds in day-to-day living is this: "Can you believe what happened yesterday? Those guys were jerks. Every time I work on something, it gets messed up. That's the sixth time this week our deliveries were delayed. I'm still mad at what she said to me." There are an unlimited number of possible examples. Anytime you are fixated, immobilized, absorbed in, or even overly concerned with something that is over—whether it happened this morning or ten years ago—constitutes reverse gear. I challenge you to take an honest look at how often you (and probably most people you know) are focused in reverse. You may be shocked.

The way you can tell if you are in reverse gear is simple. It will feel heavy and serious. You won't be moving forward; you might even be moving backward. You'll be stagnant, stuck in emotional quicksand. You'll be making references to the past, to yesterday, last week, last year, or to your childhood. You'll be complaining about things, people, circumstances, events, rules, problems, and concerns that are, for the most part, over and done with. Being in reverse saps the joy out of whatever you are doing. It's boring, unforgiving, and counterproductive.

The reason people find it so difficult to get out of reverse gear is that they can so easily justify being there. In other words, they argue for their "right" to be in reverse by saying things like, "But he *did* sabotage the deal," or "She *did* criticize me in public." People will use the fact that

169

events actually took place as evidence to support their anger and frustration. What they usually fail to see, however, is that right now, in *this* moment, the event they are frustrated about is over. The only factor keeping it alive is their memory, their own thinking.

Obviously, it's important to learn from our past, from our mistakes. I can assure you, however, that being in reverse gear will not help you do so. To learn from our past experiences, it's helpful to gently reflect on the way we have done things. Reverse gear isn't gentle. In fact, it's harsh.

The way *out* of reverse is to notice how it feels to be *in* reverse. If you can observe yourself—your mind, your thoughts, your attention—focused on past events, or past frustrations, you can gently bring your attention back to the present. Training your mind to stay out of reverse can be a little like training a puppy to stay at your side. The puppy will stay for a minute, then dart away. Your mind is like that, too. It can stay focused for a minute or two, then dart backward to an annoyance from this morning or a frustration from yesterday. The most effective way to train your puppy is to gently lead him back to your side. The same approach works with your mind as well. As you notice your thoughts drifting backward, remind yourself that the past is over and done with. Then, gently and easily, guide yourself back to the here and now. All it takes is a little patience and some practice. Pretty soon, your tendency to be in reverse gear will be a part of your past.

77.

LET GO OF THE FEAR THAT IF YOU'RE RELAXED
OR HAPPY, YOU'RE GOING TO FAIL

I was recently interviewed on a radio station located in Cincinnati, Ohio. We were discussing my assertion that "sweating the small stuff" interferes not only with your sense of well-being but with your productivity as well. The two people—a man and a woman—conducting the interview were exceptionally confrontational and suspicious. I could sense a complete lack of joy and a very serious nature. Life, to them, was clearly an emergency. The gentleman, in particular, was convinced that if a person was to follow my "program," as he put it, they would surely become apathetic, if not homeless! "If you're not uptight," he insisted, "you'll lose your drive."

Sadly, many people believe that if you aren't uptight and serious, you are doomed to failure. In my entire lifetime, I've never been more convinced that something is not true. Let me give you an analogy:

Think back to last year's Thanksgiving dinner. Remember how you felt after eating all that food. If you're anything like most Americans who are privileged enough to enjoy a feast such as this, you were stuffed. And along with feeling stuffed, you felt tired. Am I right? When you eat too much, the energy that is usually directed toward normal body functions—healing, cell division, metabolism, and all sorts of other good stuff—must go toward digestion. This makes you feel sleepy and lethargic. You lose motivation and energy.

There is an emotional equivalent. You can extend this same metaphor to your tendency to be overly serious and immobilized over little things.

When you are angry, bothered, and annoyed, virtually all the mental and emotional energy that could otherwise be used for creativity, spontaneity, and mental ambition is taken away. When you focus on things that irritate you, like the gentleman who was interviewing me, it interferes with the process of creation. It keeps you down, stuck, focused not on the wonder and mystery of life and its many possibilities but on what's lacking, what's wrong, and all that makes you mad and frustrated.

To argue for, to even suggest that, going with the flow is the same as burying your head in the sand is, quite frankly, foolish. It's wrong. In fact, I've found the opposite is almost always true. As you lighten up, relax, and unwind, you open the doors of creativity and joy that were previously hidden. You discover new interests and new possibilities. So, starting today, remind yourself that it's okay to relax—in fact, it's more than okay, it's downright important.

78.

BE AWARE OF POSITIVE BURNOUT

Burnout is a major topic of conversation in the business world. We discuss it, dread it, and have theories about why it exists. Estimates are that seven out of ten of us feel burned out at any given time, and virtually everyone will experience burnout at some point in their career. The most common reaction to burnout, however, is our fear surrounding it. We worry and wonder, When will it happen to me?

But have you ever stepped back far enough to see the *positive* side of burnout? Often, burnout is a signal that something new, exciting, and profitable is just around the corner! After all, why would you make major changes in your life in the absence of these types of feelings? You probably wouldn't. If you always felt great about your career and current direction, you may spend the rest of your life doing the very same thing.

There was a time in my life when I thought I was going to make it as a professional tennis player. Yet after many years of aches and pains, as well as some noticeable shortcomings in my game, I began to feel burned out. Had it not been for these feelings, I surely would have continued on the same path, which included a great deal of struggle, frustration, and little chance of major success. If not for my burnout, I would have been missing out on a great education and a personally fulfilling career. As I look back on my life, I can see that virtually every positive fork in the road was preceded by a certain degree of burnout. And in retrospect, it was all positive burnout.

The point here is that it's not at all necessary to freak out or worry when you feel burned out. Instead, try to keep things in perspective. Remember that negative feelings can be deceptive. Often they are positive signals disguised as negative feelings. As you worry less, two things will happen. First, you'll discover that most burnout is nothing more than a bad mood taken too seriously. If you don't worry too much about it, it will probably go away and you'll regain your enthusiasm for your work within a short period of time. Second, the less you worry about burnout, the less energy you give it, the clearer you will be about any needed changes in your life. In other words, you'll know what to do.

Worry gets in the way of your wisdom and common sense. As you let go of fear, as you investigate your feelings of burnout, you may discover that your feelings are trying to tell you something, point you in a new direction, redirect your energy—or something else that is *positive* in nature. As you learn to trust your inner resources by letting go of fear, you'll discover that your wisdom will tell you exactly what you need to be doing at any given point in your life. Try putting a positive slant on your feelings of burnout and watch them fade away.

79.

DIVE IN

If you're going to do something important, the best time to start is right now. Not later, tomorrow, next week, next month, or next year. Right now. The best strategy is to "dive in." I know there's always an important reason to put off doing today what you are planning or hoping to do tomorrow. In fact, there are usually many good reasons to wait. Despite these good reasons, however, I urge you to get started now. The pure and simple fact is that the individuals who start *now*, who dive in, have a far better track record and enjoy much greater degrees of success than those who wait. They also tend to be more engaged in their lives and have a lot more fun.

About a year ago I attended a business meeting with my wife, Kris. There was a woman at the meeting who seemed to be bright, well educated, and talented. The purpose of the meeting was to help people get started in an exciting new business. This particular woman decided to wait. Despite being "certain" (her word) that she wanted to get involved, she wanted to "think about it" for a while. She wanted the time to be right.

A few months later, we attended a different meeting where my wife was one of the speakers. Who did we see? The same woman. We urged her to get started. "Not quite yet" was her response. She was "really committed" to the program but didn't want to "dive in" (again, her words). Well, the story continues and gets even worse. As of this writing, the woman still hasn't gotten started.

The good news is that several of the people who did get started at that first meeting are well on their way to building very successful businesses. They knew that the key was simply to get started and not to put it off.

These people, the ones who *did* get started, have the same obstacles, if not more, than the woman who hesitated. They have children to take care of, jobs to go to, responsibilities, bills, houses to keep clean, lawns to mow, trips to take, school plays and other family-oriented things to attend to, relatives to visit, new babies on the way, and everything else imaginable. The secret to success is to understand that, despite all of these responsibilities, the best time to begin is now.

You don't have to do everything in one day to succeed, but you do have to get started. Just getting off the ground, getting started, is, for most people, the most difficult part. Once you do, the rest will usually fall into place. If you are interested in, or considering, a new venture, as long as it's something that you are truly committed to, my advice is simple: dive in.

80.

JUST ONCE, TRY SOMETHING DIFFERENT

Many of us do the same things, day after day, for most of our adult lives. We have the same habits, go to the same places, hold the same opinions, get upset over the same things, think the same thoughts, meet with the same people, do things in the same way. And for the most part, we get the same results. How boring!

It took years for me to understand the obvious: If I keep doing the same things, making the same mistakes, and having the same expectations, I'm probably going to keep getting the same results as well as the same frustrations. I finally realized that if I wanted something different, something more, I was going to have to try something different. I did, and it worked. And I've seen it work over and over again for virtually everyone who is willing to try. Most people are stuck right where they are. The reason they're stuck, however, isn't usually due to circumstances, incompetence, or lack of opportunity, but a simple unwillingness to change, to try new things.

I'm not necessarily talking about trying a different job or career (although that might be a good idea, too). Instead, I'm referring here to smaller, inner changes that you can make on a day-to-day, moment-to-moment basis—changes in your attitude, reactions, and expectations. I'm talking about being willing to meet new people at new places, take new risks, and face old fears. Perhaps you can, for once, listen to someone else's opinion or read a periodical that you usually disagree with. Over and over again I hear people saying things like "I've always done things that way" or "That's just the type of person I am." These things are said as if they are carved in stone, as if there is something other than their own thinking and attitude that is holding them in place. There isn't. It's amazing what you can learn by simply opening your mind and trying new things.

Starting today, tell yourself that you are going to do something, however small, a little differently. Perhaps you can be more friendly to the people you work with. Maybe it's never occurred to you to invite your boss to lunch. Perhaps you've never stayed late or arrived early at the office. Maybe it's not too late to overcome your fear of asking others to help you, or for their advice. Whoever you are, whatever you do, there is always something you can do a little differently. Experiment with newness. You may find that you love the tiny changes you make and that you can open exciting new doors by making relatively small adjustments. Just once, try something different. If you're okay with the changes, which I suspect you will be, you might want to try some other changes as well.

81.

HELP SOMEONE ELSE SUCCEED

It's been said that the absolute best way to learn something is to try to teach it. I've found that not only is this assumption true, but that the learning curve I experience when I teach is often astounding. I have, for example, agreed to give a lecture to an entire student body of more than 3,500 people on a topic I was familiar with but was by no means an expert on. I knew, however, that by agreeing to teach others, I would force myself to "own" the material. Teaching others helps us pinpoint our knowledge and the way we express it. It also helps us to raise our standards of excellence by encouraging us to think in creative, articulate ways. Most of us want to practice in our own lives what we teach. So, if we teach someone how to be more successful, we will invariably help ourselves in the process.

There are probably many people in your life you are in a position to help. Perhaps you're an expert or very experienced in your field. Maybe there is someone who could use some feedback, advice, or encouragement. Could you possibly meet a younger, less experienced person for lunch or coffee? Is there someone in your immediate family or circle of friends who is struggling? If you look around, I'll bet you can find someone who would really appreciate your help.

I'm not suggesting that you overwhelm someone with your presence, or with your ideas. You don't have to change a person's life or get overly involved. Sometimes, all a person needs is a little jump start. A friend, for example, might need some help with a personal issue—quitting smoking or drinking. You can help them succeed in this goal by being a source of support or a good listener. Or you may have some clever marketing ideas

179

for a friend starting or struggling in his or her small business. Your ideas could make the difference between that person quitting or helping them turn the corner. You can help them succeed.

My only word of caution is to be sure to get permission before offering your help. Be gentle and patient. Not everyone wants or is ready for help. And that's okay. Don't take it personally. Everyone is at a different place in their life.

As you help others succeed, even in very small ways, it helps you redefine and reflect on your own goals, assumptions, and ways of doing things. If you suggest to someone else, for example, that they think of education as a lifelong process, it might remind you that *you* haven't taken a class in years. I'm often amazed at how my advice applies to my own life and my own success. Just the other day, someone asked me for advice. Upon reflection, I suggested that he desperately needed a break or else he might burn out. That evening, I realized that I had been working way too hard and that *I* needed to slow down! I think you'll find that one of the shortcuts to success is to help others succeed.

82.

PERSEVERE

When I was just getting started in business, my father said something to me that, at first, sounded a little superficial. After being around for a while, however, I realized that he was right. He told me that part of being successful was just hanging in there and sticking with it. He said that many people quit too early, get impatient, fail to defer any gratification, and move around too much.

I had the advantage of loving what I was doing. So, in my early years, I didn't move around too much. I did defer plenty of gratification, I wasn't very impatient and I certainly didn't quit too early. And you know, my dad was absolutely right. After a while, people start to know who you are and what you do. You develop a reputation. And if people like you and you're competent, they begin to think of you as someone to do business with.

If you start a business but fail to stick around very long, you might not give your customers enough time to help you out. You won't have adequate time to develop your skills, learn the ropes, or develop a healthy reputation. If you get impatient and move around too much, or keep changing careers because you get bored or itchy for success, you may be quitting too early. You may not be giving your efforts enough time to show results. You may never quite get off the ground. But "getting off the ground" is often the most difficult part of the process, especially in entrepreneurial efforts. Often, when someone is very successful and it appears, on the surface, that they perform without effort, what you fail to see are the hundreds or even thousands of "presuccess" hours that created that sense of ease.

My wife, Kris, works in a networking business that serves as an excellent example. She knows that virtually anyone can be successful in her business, but that most people fail to give it a fair try. If they have one or two disappointments early on (which most do), they allow their fear or impatience to enter into the equation and they're on to something else. In a nutshell, they quit too early. They lack perseverance. Instead of saying, "This is going to take some time and work and I'm going to do what it takes," they believe that there is something out there that is going to be much easier. There isn't. Sometimes people will say to Kris, "You make it look so easy." What they don't realize is that it took a great deal of work to get to that point. Any new venture that is destined for success is going to take work and perseverance. If it didn't, your success wouldn't be as rewarding.

I've found that there is a delicate balance between being willing to stick something out and a willingness to make changes. You need the wisdom to know when to quit and when to stay right where you are. So, if you feel like quitting, don't do so impulsively. Instead, check in with your wisdom. If you're quitting too early, remind yourself to persevere.

83.

CONSIDER THE WISDOM OF OPTIMISM

There are essentially two types of people: optimists and pessimists. The question is, Which is wiser? Pessimists, of course, will tell you that they are being "realists." They insist that life is hard, things often don't work out, and it's not a good idea to set yourself up for disappointment. Pessimists believe that if you expect things to go wrong, you won't be let down when they do.

It should come as no surprise to you that pessimists experience far more disappointments than optimists. The reason is simple: They are looking for failure. They want verification that they are correct in their negative assumptions. They use negative experiences as ammunition and proof against the wisdom of optimism. They believe that optimists are burying their heads in the sand and that they simply don't understand the realities of life.

Optimists, however, understand that no one has a crystal ball and that no one can accurately predict the future. Along these lines, they know that although pessimists feel confident that things won't work out, they are only guessing and assuming that this is true. Optimists believe that, because no one *really* knows what's going to happen, it's far wiser and makes for a more pleasant and joyful experience of life if one is optimistic, if one assumes the best.

One of the most basic laws of success is that your energy follows your attention. This is true for every person on earth, optimists and pessimists alike, and whether you like it or not. If your energy is primarily negative; if you are looking for flaws, problems, and verification that life is essentially bad, that's where the bulk of your energy will lie. Your ability to manifest abundance will be severely limited because your energy will be directed, focused, and grounded in negativity and limitation. We create what we see and what we expect to see. If we enter into a situation with negative expectations, we will tend to create negative results.

Here's a simple, everyday example: I've been hired on numerous occasions to intervene in an argument. Invariably, the person who has hired me tells me all the negative qualities of the other person—he's stubborn, unwilling to listen, defensive, and obnoxious. He expects that our conversation will be heated and difficult. The person who has hired me enters the situation as an absolute pessimist, in every sense of the word. If you ask him, however, if he's being pessimistic, he would probably laugh at you. He feels he's simply being realistic.

I, on the other hand, enter the situation as an optimist. I've seen many situations like this and know without any doubt whatsoever that most people want to get along with others, and most people are capable of change. I enter into the situation looking for incremental improvement, areas of agreement, and common ground. I expect miracles.

The question is, Who has a better chance of success? Obviously, I do. The truth is that you not only *find* what you are looking for, you're *creating* it as well. When you're looking for answers and expect to find them, you usually do. Does this mean you'll always succeed? Absolutely not. But unlike the pessimist who will say, "See, what did I tell you? People are difficult and stubborn," the optimist will simply chalk it up as another learning experience. When I experience a failure in an interaction such as this one, I simply assume that it will be all that much easier next time because of all I have learned. There is a great deal of wisdom and joy in optimism. Give it a try.

184

84.

HOLD ON TIGHTLY, LET GO LIGHTLY

This is one of my very favorite sayings. "Hold on tightly, let go lightly" is a motto that encourages you to obtain the optimal balance between productivity and inner peace. "Hold on" suggests that you want to work hard, stick with things, give it your best shot, persevere, pursue your goals and never give up. The "let go lightly" side, however, suggests that you shouldn't hold on too long, and that when it is time to give in, give up, or let go, that you do so gracefully. Hold on tightly, let go lightly covers two very important aspects of success: the achievement of goals and the joy of happiness.

An excellent example of holding on tightly and letting go lightly exists in parenting. When we raise our children, most of us want to hold on tightly when they're young. We work very hard to protect them, to expose them to varied experiences. We defend their safety and their honor. We do all we can to steer them in the best possible direction. But then there comes a time when you need to "let go," when you need to set them free, to step aside and allow them to live their own lives. Letting go has nothing to do with ceasing to love our children. In fact, letting go is one of the ultimate expressions of a parent's love.

In business, and in all forms of competition, the same principle applies. It's appropriate and often necessary to do all we can to put the odds in our favor. Sometimes we need to negotiate hard, work in our best interest, expend effort like our life depends on it. We do everything we can to succeed. But then there comes a time when the season changes. Change is inevitable. Perhaps we have won—or lost—the game. Maybe we've played the game too long. Perhaps the industry has outgrown us, or we have

185

outgrown our previous interests. This is when it's time to let go. If we do it gracefully, with perspective, we will remain peaceful and grow from our experience. Like opening a tight fist, we will feel free and energized. When the time does come to say good-bye, or to make a change, try doing so with grace. This will keep you pointed in the direction of your dreams. Instead of looking back, it will keep you focused on your next great adventure.

85.

BE WILLING TO APOLOGIZE

Whenever you are in business—or when you are taking risks, making things happen, interacting with others, or in the public eye—you are bound to make mistakes. At times you are going to use bad judgment, say something wrong, offend someone, criticize unnecessarily, be too demanding, or act selfishly. The question isn't whether you will make these mistakes—we all do. The question is, Can you admit to them? If so, the question becomes, Can you apologize?

Many people never apologize. They are either too self-conscious, self-righteous, stubborn, or arrogant to do so. The unwillingness to apologize is not just sad, it is a serious mistake as well. Almost everyone expects others to make mistakes. And with a humble and sincere apology, almost everyone is willing to forgive. However, if you are a person who is either unable or unwilling to apologize, you will be branded a difficult person to work with. And over time, people will avoid you, speak behind your back, and do nothing to help you.

The ability to apologize, to admit mistakes, is a beautiful human quality that brings people closer together and helps us succeed. By simply acknowledging our humanness and saying "I'm sorry" when appropriate, we bond with others and increase their trust in us.

On a live television talk show once I was discussing one of my books about happiness. I was in a terrible mood and was dealing with some pretty serious stuff myself. There was a guest on the show who was asking for my advice. Normally, this is where I'm at my best. I love talk shows and I love helping others when I can. I can't remember what I said on that particular day, but whatever it was, it offended him and hurt his feelings.

The producer contacted me with a rather nasty letter telling me that as far as she was concerned, I wasn't welcome on her show again! In years past, I think I would have become defensive, and offered an explanation in an attempt to make her a part of the problem. Instead, I simply offered my most sincere apology. I told her that I was wrong and that she was right. I really meant what I said. I even offered to call the guest I had offended if she could get me his number.

A few weeks went by and I received another letter from the producer. This time, however, the letter was quite different. She said that in over ten years as a producer, she had never received such a sincere and nondefensive apology. She asked if I would come back as a guest again real soon. By apologizing, I had corrected my mistake.

Obviously, you must never apologize as a tool of manipulation, to try to get a response like this or to get something out of it. I tell you this story to remind you of how forgiving people can be when you admit you're wrong. When you apologize from your heart, you keep most of your existing doors open. Occasionally, you may even open doors that had previously been closed.

86.

IF YOU FIND YOURSELF IN A HOLE, STOP DIGGING

The great football coach Vince Lombardi once said, "Just because you're doing something wrong, doing it more intensely won't help." What a powerful statement.

Yet, how often do we do just that? We are making a mistake, getting ourselves into trouble—and, instead of backing off, reflecting, and doing it differently, we roll up our sleeves and do the very same thing even more intensely! Seems to me like a guaranteed way to encourage yourself to sweat the small stuff and to stress yourself out!

How many commercials have you heard where the proposed solution to being in serious financial debt was to get a credit card line so that you can consolidate your loans and use the extra money to buy even more things—especially really expensive things like a swimming pool or a new car? It's absolutely amazing, yet people do it all the time. That would be like saying, if you want to lose weight, double your food intake and stop exercising! I've even met people who have searched for the best credit card interest rates so that they can, in their own words, "afford" to get into even greater debt. Obviously, the real problem is overspending, too many desires and not enough self-control. To want more "stuff" or more experiences or whatever is simply compounding the problem. It's like being in a deep hole, struggling to get out, and all you can think of doing is to continue to dig!

The same pattern exists in many areas of our lives. Many people have a great deal of conflict to manage. Whenever a potential new conflict arises, or the environment or circumstances seem to be encouraging that development, instead of backing off and looking for new ways to defuse the situation, they charge straight ahead, as always—repeating their identical patterns and responses, taking the adversarial approach—and, once again, find themselves in the middle of another drama or conflict. Then, frustrated and stressed, they assume the world is to blame, or that they need to find more effective and more aggressive ways to deal with things. This is the essence of being in a vicious circle. The same essential problems come up over and over again, unless and until you see your own contribution—and vow to do something differently.

The solution is simple, but not always very easy. The trick is to recognize when your part of the pattern is being repeated; for example, "I'm living over my head again," or "Here I am, arguing again," or "I'm upset by the very same things—this sure feels familiar." Then, rather than clenching your fists, feeling frustrated, filling your mind with stressful thoughts, and trying the same old thing, you instead relax, back off, and empty your mind. Soften and try to see the situation in a whole new way.

I've met people who used to be aggressive and adversarial who have become much more patient. I've met others who, for years, lived well beyond their means and who are now able to control their spending and lifestyle. And I've known still others who used to blame anyone and everything for their troubles—who now understand their own contributions to the problems in their lives. The one major trait all these people have in common now is that they are much happier than before and less stressed. Each of them was in one type of a hole or another until they wised up and stopped digging!

87.

REMEMBER THAT EVERYTHING IS USED
THE DAY AFTER YOU BUY IT

There's something special about buying a brand-new item. Whether it's a new car, a special piece of clothing, a new lawn mower, or any other consumer good, it's always nice to purchase it new. Unfortunately, however, there's often a huge price to pay. That price is what's called opportunity cost. Simply put, this is what you *could* have done with the money instead.

Everything is "used" the day after you buy it—and therefore less valuable. In the auto industry, they say a new car is no longer "new" the moment you drive off the lot. Have you ever bought something new and decided you didn't really want or need it and then try to sell it? If you're lucky, you'll get fifty cents on the dollar. I once bought a piece of exercise equipment for almost $1,000. I tried for weeks to sell it and was only able to get $300! I had only used it once. The truth is, you can usually buy a reasonable facsimile of an item—a car or anything else—and pay 30 to 50 percent less for it if you're willing to buy it used. And while it's not always critical to do so, and perhaps not as initially satisfying, there are a few ideas worth considering.

Consider a brand-new car. Let's assume you can purchase a new car for about $20,000. The moment you drive it off the lot, it loses a great deal of its so-called value, probably 10 to 15 percent, and continues to decline each month you own it. In addition, you'll probably be concerned about your hefty monthly payments, which will last for around five years, possibly even longer. That's sixty months of payments for something that

191

is guaranteed to lose significant value each and every month. In addition to the payments you'll worry about damaging, scratching, and cleaning your new beauty, and there's always the possibility of theft. Then, there's insurance, registration, and maintenance to think about. In the end, there's a lot of money tied up in your new car. And perhaps a lot of unnecessary worry.

Your option, of course, is to purchase a used vehicle. Remember, everything is "used" the day after you buy it anyway. Nothing stays new very long. In addition to not worrying so much about theft and damage, your down payment, monthly payments, sales tax, insurance and registration costs will be far less with a used vehicle. If you are somewhat disciplined, and would like a worry-free investment, you could invest your savings (which would be simple to determine) in an appreciating asset. This way, with zero effort, you could save hundreds of dollars every month, guaranteed. Over your adult lifetime, this single decision made repeatedly, could help fund your retirement needs. I urge you to calculate the exact numbers or, if you don't know how, talk to someone who does. Your opportunity cost will surprise, perhaps even shock you!

I've met many people who have very little money at retirement. Yet some of these same people did manage to drive fairly nice cars, usually new ones, over the years. I wonder what would have happened if, instead of driving new cars and purchasing other new things, they would have invested their money more wisely.

88.

KEEP IN MIND THAT CHEAPER IS NOT
ALWAYS BETTER

The other side of the coin, however (from strategy #87), is that cheaper is not always better. Sometimes purchasing a used item (despite the potential advantages) is not worth the added time that's involved and the additional aggravation. The most obvious example might be the decision to purchase a "fixer-upper" house that is far cheaper than a newer one down the street. It might seem great that you're saving 30 percent (or more) on the initial cost. But unless you are qualified to fix things yourself and really love doing so, the cheaper home might drive you crazy. Older houses can, and often do, fall apart. And the repairs involved can be a real pain (and very expensive in the long run). Did you guess that I've made this mistake myself?

The same principle also applies to far more ordinary purchases. For example, it might be nice to save some money by purchasing a used computer instead of that brand-new one you like. However, if you can't use it very often because it's in the repair shop, you might *regret* the savings instead of appreciate them. Then there's the time involved in getting to and from the repair shop. Do you really want to spend your time attending to your used purchases?

It is not always simple to compute the actual cost of something. For example, at first blush, it seems like a $100 automobile tire that will last for 50,000 miles is exactly the same cost as a $50 tire that will last for just 25,000 miles. However, the devil is in the details. Consider, for example, the out-of-pocket cost of interest, of providing the additional $50 in tire investment for the length of time that you drive on the tire. Before you rush out and buy one $50 tire and replace it with another $50 tire, you have some other considerations. What is the value of your time in going in for one additional tire change? Then there are safety considerations. The point is, cheaper might be better, but then again, it might not be. Consider these decisions carefully.

Perhaps the best way to analyze the cheaper versus more expensive decision is to be completely honest about what you will do with the savings if you choose the cheaper version. Are you going to spend the savings? Are you really going to invest them? These decisions are more important than they appear on the surface. Over time, you can amass a fortune by making the best decision, most of the time.

89.

DON'T BE AFRAID TO TAKE BABY STEPS

Often, people worry about taking baby steps. They worry that the steps they are taking aren't big enough or significant enough. Or they worry that others will laugh at them, or see them as weak. Many people are so frightened to take baby steps that they end up doing nothing at all.

If success were easy, we'd all be successful. But while the strategies (like the ones in this book) that can take you toward success are simple, they aren't always easy. These strategies are only a road map; you must walk the path yourself.

I've had many people ask me the best way to write a book. My answer is almost always the same: just start writing. Don't wait. Even if you can only write a single paragraph, even a sentence, it's far better than nothing. There is a common misconception that if you wait to begin, someday you'll wake up with tremendous inspiration and take a giant step. I can assure you that this *is* possible, and it can happen to you. However, you greatly increase the likelihood of taking "giant steps" if you begin with baby steps. Both of my children started taking "baby steps" at around one year of age. Today, I can hardly keep up with them. Every process, be it personal or professional, begins with baby steps.

My wife and I decided a number of years ago to run a marathon together (yes, I'm proud of this). Our training began with twenty minutes of jogging per day—baby steps. It would have been crazy for us to wait to start our training program until we were able to run an hour. We never would have been able to do it; we needed our baby steps to succeed.

We've all heard people say, "I don't have enough money to start a savings plan. I can only afford to put $20 a week into my savings, or even $20 per month." My answer is: Great! Get started. Commit to putting 5 percent of your earnings into your savings. Take a baby step. Then, as you make more money, you'll be in the habit of saving. Your baby steps will have trained you how to do it. Chances are, if you avoid the baby-steps stage, you'll never take the bigger steps.

To become successful, it's critical to focus on what you can do, not on what you can't do. Baby steps are the vehicle, an essential part of the journey toward abundance. Maybe you'd like to start a business but feel you don't have the time to do everything that's required. No problem. Take some baby steps. Do something. Make that first phone call to City Hall about the license, or go to the library and pick up one book on some aspect of the business so that you can do some research. Or meet with one person a week—a mentor, perhaps—to get some ideas. Before you know it, those baby steps will become big steps.

90.

REMIND YOURSELF THAT YOUR LIFE ISN'T YOUR ENEMY, BUT YOUR THINKING CAN BE

At times, it can seem like life is our enemy, as if things never quite pan out the way we would like them to, as if there's a secret conspiracy against us. However, it's critical to remember that, in reality, life *isn't* our enemy. There is no conspiracy. Life is just life. It is what it is. The factor that can make life *seem* like our enemy, however, is our thinking. Nothing more, nothing less. Life wants you to succeed just as much as it does the next person.

As obvious as this insight may seem, the implications are enormous. The truth is, life isn't going to accommodate any of us by giving us fewer demands, less traffic, people who are easier to get along with, or a smoother path toward success. If we want a different experience of life, a more peaceful outlook, we are the ones who must change.

If you're angry, you're the one having angry thoughts. If you're stressed, you're the one having stressful thoughts. If you're feeling sorry for yourself, again, you're the one having thoughts of self-pity. The good news, of course, is that while you can't alter life very often to suit your needs, you do have a fair measure of control over your own thinking. You can change the way you think, and you can change your reactions to life. It's entirely up to you. You can go on hating the many inconvenient aspects of life or you can relax and commit to changing your reactions to them.

It's very helpful to remind yourself (daily) that your life isn't your enemy. While you're at it, remind yourself of the tremendous power of your own thinking, that your world is shaped by those thoughts you choose to focus on the most. You have the power to change your reactions, expectations, and outlook. You have the power to become anything you want to become. But to do so, you must realize that life is not your enemy; it's your friend.

91.

EMBRACE ALL ASPECTS OF YOUR JOB

I was in San Francisco doing a daylong seminar with my good friend and colleague Joe Bailey. After the event was over, I went to the parking lot to pick up my car.

As I was about to pay my parking fee and exit the facility, the strangest thing happened. The parking fee was around $20. The only bill in my wallet was a $100 bill. What's the big deal, you might ask?

Well, to the parking attendant, it was a really big deal! Rather than express his concern politely or gracefully, he blurted out, "You must have something smaller," to which I replied, "Unfortunately, sir, I don't. I'm really sorry." In a near rage he yelled out, "Oh, that's just great! I'm going to have to go see my manager—I don't have that much change. You're going to have to sit here. God help me. I can't believe it."

I found the experience a bit amusing. After all, one of the major parts of this man's job was to give change to customers. Obviously, if there wasn't enough change for any single transaction, that would have to be dealt with, but, after all, that was part of the job. As with every other job on the face of the earth, there are aspects of it that simply go with the territory—parking cars and having change seem to go hand in hand. It seemed to me that his being so upset was a bit like a snow-shoveler complaining about snow that needed to be shoveled, or a telephone operator complaining about the number of calls coming in from customers needing help with their phone calls!

This employee, like so many of us, thinks of most of the things he does as if they were items to be checked off a list. I call this tendency being "list-oriented." Someone who is list-oriented feels good when something

199

is taken off his list—and feels annoyed or frustrated when there is an obstacle that prevents him from doing so. The parking attendant, for example, probably saw me as just another part of his list. As he saw it, his job was to take my money and get me out of the garage. The fact that he didn't have enough change became his obstacle—it came between him and his list completion.

The problem with this type of mentality is that inherent within it is a great deal of frustration. If you're list-oriented, for example, and you're working on a project or trying to make a sale, you're going to feel good only when the project or sale is complete—and then, only if it meets your expectations. But what if things don't work out according to plan? And, even if they do, what about all the time between the start of the project and the end result? The work itself, including the hassles, obstacles, and disappointments, is what life and work are all about. Therein lies the bulk of your time.

Yet, sadly, I've met so many people who don't ever seem to enjoy the process. They work and work, negotiate and struggle, make things happen and take risks and so forth, but never enjoy a single moment. Then, when the process comes to an end—they evaluate whether or not they did well enough and either feel good or bad, depending on their perception. What pressure!

The option is to view your day-to-day experiences, tasks, and responsibilities not only as items to be checked off your list, but rather as part of a process; to see it all as necessary and interesting.

This alternate way of looking at your activities might be called being "process-oriented." In other words, rather than focusing on and being driven *only* by the end result, you become interested in the entire experience—however it happens to unfold. It all becomes, as philosopher Ram Dass calls it, "grist for the mill," or part of the overall story. Obviously, you will always prefer that your daily activities go smoothly, successfully, and without a hitch or hassle—but when you become process-oriented, you're no longer dependent on that occurring. You end up enjoying the process as well as the result.

When life is looked at this way, you become far less likely to sweat the small stuff! In addition, of course, this makes for a far more interesting experience of life. Being more process-oriented allows you to embrace each aspect of the experience—whatever you're doing—without feeling like it's a great big hassle. You'll be less annoyed by the people you work with as you embrace all aspects of your job.

So whatever it is that you do for a living, see if you can become less attached and zeroed in on the end result or outcome, and, instead, become more engaged in each moment along the way. My guess is that you'll not only enjoy your work more than ever—and experience far less stress—but, in addition, you'll actually become more effective and successful as well.

92.

RESIST THE TEMPTATION TO CONTINUALLY RAISE

YOUR STANDARD OF LIVING

Philosophically, there are two very different ways to become rich: (1) make more money, and (2) have fewer wants. In reality, there is a middle ground. I have found that the easiest way to assure an abundant life is to go ahead and make more money—and have a blast doing so—but avoid believing that, along with every pay increase, you must also raise your standard of living. To do so can be a foolish mistake.

Many people make more money than they ever dreamed possible, yet are more financially stressed than ever before. How can this be? Simple: What a vast majority of people do as they earn more money is to continue to spend as much if not more than they make. They buy a bigger home and a nicer car. They go on more expensive vacations, wear more expensive clothing, and eat at finer restaurants. They spend, spend, spend. Some go into foolish investments or silly tax shelters that don't hold up. Before you insist that you would never do this, I urge you to consider that you probably will—unless you consciously make a vow not to.

Making money is often easier than keeping it. The more you make, the more things you see that you want. The problem with material desire is that, unless you are extremely cautious, it is insatiable. Remember, more isn't necessarily better.

If you raise your standard of living to match your current income, it forces you to keep producing at the same level, whether you want to or not. And you may not want to. Never feeling as if you have "enough" causes several obvious problems. First, if you run into difficult times (which most people do at some point in their lives), pulling yourself out of a rut can be very difficult if you're spending everything you earn. If, however, you keep your spending and your desires in check, running into bad times will not cause an emergency. You'll simply make adjustments. The other major problem is that raising your standard of living, always wanting more, more, more, tends to keep you on the treadmill being busier and busier. The more things you have, the more things you have to take care of, insure, look after, protect, and worry about! Pretty soon, your life is filled with "stuff" and unnecessary demands on your time. You become "a servant to your servants."

This doesn't mean that you shouldn't have nice things or that you don't deserve them. But keep in mind that you also deserve a peaceful and happy life, and that material things don't necessarily make you happy! Happiness comes from within, by the way you relate to what you have, not from your actual possessions.

If you can manage to keep your desires in check, to live at or beneath your means, you'll discover a different type of abundance—peace. You'll be able to stay calm and relaxed. To me, this is among the greatest gifts in a lifetime.

93.

STOP SWEATING THE SMALL RISKS

Often, without even knowing we are doing so, we make a big deal out of relatively small risks. We treat small risks like big risks. And by doing that, we pay a huge price.

One of the best ways I know to create more abundance, while simultaneously reducing your stress, is to learn to differentiate between those risks that are small and those that are truly significant. Then, once you do, to make the decision to worry less about those risks that, in reality, aren't so risky!

Some decisions really would be quite risky. Gambling with your kids' college savings fund, of course, would be extremely risky. The same could be said about putting all your money into a single, unproven stock. Screaming at your employer would be risky, as would driving without a seatbelt! To me, these are all legitimate things to worry about.

There are many other activities, however, that we tend to worry about, often obsessively, that maybe we shouldn't. Things like asking for a raise, whether or not to take certain advice, or worrying about how someone will react to us. These activities may, in fact, frighten us, but there is very little actual risk associated with them. In the same way, many people worry their heads off about looking foolish—so much so that they avoid activities that could very well enhance their success: speaking in public, taking a stance that isn't popular, aggressively marketing their product or service, and so forth. It's not that there isn't any risk in doing these things, it's just that the cost of treating them like big risks is exceptionally high.

205

There would certainly be some degree of risk in dollar-cost-averaging investing in the stock market, but probably not enough to worry about. There are certain inherent liabilities in many businesses. But if there is an extremely small likelihood that you will be affected, and you are acting with integrity, then why sweat it? I've met people who can't sleep nights for fear of being sued when, in reality, it will probably never happen. And, even if it did, they would probably win anyway.

Likewise, it's true you could be audited, and many people are really worried about that possibility. Yet, if you are conducting your business legally and ethically, what's the point of spending even one minute concerning yourself about the possibility? We worry about all sorts of relatively common things over which we have little or no control.

Something that can be quite helpful is to create a list of truly legitimate risks, things that could adversely affect your life or ruin you financially. You'll probably find that, while there are legitimate things to worry about, the list you create is going to be quite short. Next, jot down the more subtle things that you tend to worry about. You'll probably create a much longer list of these perceived risks.

When you see the "real" risks next to the others, right there on paper, it's often pretty easy to convince yourself to let go of the ones that are less severe.

I was talking to a woman who was afraid to expand her business for fear of taking on too much overhead. From an outside perspective, there appeared to be very little actual risk. It seemed obvious that her fear was holding her back in a very big way. We discussed the difference between real risks and make-believe risks, and she agreed that hers was mostly in her head. It's not that her fear had zero merit; rather, she was turning it into something much bigger than it actually was. To her credit, she decided to stop sweating it! A year or so later, I received a nice thank-you message from her saying that the business was doing great.

When we're dealing with business and money, there are many ways that we allow small risks to get the best of us. By learning the difference between legitimate worries and less significant ones, we pave the way to a far more abundant life.

94.

HAVE A PLAN

It's quite difficult to get somewhere if you don't know where you're headed. Yet a huge percentage of us have no plan. We don't really know where we're going or how we're going to get there. It's easy to look and feel extremely busy when we don't have a plan, but in reality we're just spinning our wheels, putting out fires, or chasing our tails.

The other day I asked a gentleman who was working for a corporation in San Francisco, "Where would you like to be and what would you like to have accomplished a year from now?" His answer was somewhat typical. He said in a flustered tone, "I can't think that far ahead. I guess I'd just like to get through this mess." His "mess," of course, was his "in basket," his list of things to do. Unfortunately, getting through your daily task list doesn't necessarily lead you anywhere. In fact, it often leads you in circles. The very nature of an in-basket is that it's supposed to be full; items that are taken care of are constantly being replaced with new ones.

A plan is like a road map. It tells you where you are and points you in a direction. It helps you strategize about how you are going to get from point A to point B. For example, if your goal is to increase your productivity or sales volume by 50 percent, your plan would be a daily reminder of the steps necessary to achieve that goal. Part of your plan, for instance, might be to make phone calls to five new potential customers daily, rather than simply returning the phone calls that come your way. Or part of your plan might be to take three new courses to increase your knowledge base before the end of the year. Without this predetermined plan, it is probable that you wouldn't find the time to take any courses. Like the gentleman I spoke to from San Francisco, you'd be too busy putting out daily fires. You'd keep thinking, "I'll get to it later." But somehow you never will.

When you have a predetermined plan, something magical happens: Your plan helps you to draw out your inner strength, creativity, and discipline. In some mysterious way, you are usually able to stick to your plan, once you have one in place. A few years ago, I suggested to a single mom who was struggling with her finances that she needed a financial plan. She hadn't been able to save a dime for her eventual retirement. She said she had been waiting for the right time to start saving, but there never seemed to be anything left over at the end of the month. The plan she came up with took her about five minutes to create, but was among the most significant five minutes of her life. She decided that if she didn't start saving now, she may never begin. So she committed to pay herself first. She said that her "plan" was to save 10 percent of every dollar she earned and put it toward her retirement. I bumped into her a while ago and asked her how it was going. She reported that she was well on her way toward financial freedom. Her plan had, in her words, saved her life. She insisted that, once she had a plan in place, following it was easy.

With a plan in mind, the sky's the limit. As long as you can visualize a way to implement your plan, your dreams—however big—can become a reality. Your plan may be to become a multimillionaire, to run a marathon, to spend an extra day each week with your children, or to open an ice-cream shop. It doesn't matter what your plan is, but it does matter that you have one. Make a plan today.

95.

DON'T GET LOST IN YOUR PLAN

On the other end of the spectrum from *not* having a plan is someone who gets *lost* in their plan. This, too, is easy to do. It's easy to become focused, even obsessed with your plan or your goals. You can become so engrossed in your plan that you forget to enjoy the process. One of my favorite quotes says, "Life is what's happening while we're busy making other plans." What a powerful message!

Many people get lost in their dreams of becoming successful. So much so that they sacrifice their relationships with family members, friends, even themselves. They are focused on the end result, not on the steps along the way. The steps, however, are where you find the joy.

There are several reasons why people become obsessed with their plans and future goals. Perhaps most important is that people worry too much about their success and the direction of their lives. Keep in mind that worrying interferes with your ability to create abundance; it gets in the way and clouds your vision. Becoming successful is not difficult. In fact, creating success is virtually inevitable when you get *out* of your own way. And as we have been discussing throughout this book, worry and lack of faith are your greatest obstacles. When you take worry out of the picture, your plan will have a chance to unfold.

Keep in touch with your sense of knowing, that inner awareness that any goal or dream you have, as long as you know what it is, is within your grasp. An important aspect of a successful life is achieving a balance between these two seemingly different messages (having a plan, but not getting lost in it). My advice is for you to know exactly where you'd like to go and exactly how you plan to get there. But at the same time, let go of

211

your goal and enjoy the ride. Each step of your journey is an important part of your unique curriculum. Each hurdle you face and problem you overcome is part of your divine plan. So don't get lost in your plan. If you do, you'll not only interfere with the very goals you'd like to achieve but you'll also miss out on all the fun.

96.

STOP COMMISERATING

Commiserating is a socially accepted form of complaining. Yet in reality it's exactly the same thing. We all do it, only to different degrees. People commiserate for several reasons. First, it's a habit. Everyone else is doing it, too. Next, many people feel they are getting somewhere or getting some benefit when they do it. Finally, some people think "getting things off their chest" or allowing others to do so is a positive action. They associate the familiarity of commiseration with a feeling of relief.

Unfortunately, commiseration is a bad habit and it detracts from your success and from the success of others. Our actions follow our energy, which includes our thinking and our conversations. Negative conversations, complaining and commiserating are expressions of negativity.

The next time you're at a social gathering listen carefully to all the commiseration in the room. Listen to the ways people share their misery and wallow in their problems. Feel the energy of it all. Then, when you get home, sit quietly for a few minutes and consider what just happened. Try to tally up, in your mind, all the commiserating and all the complaints. Now ask yourself: How much good does it all do? How far does it go toward solving problems, creating opportunity, expressing joy, and bringing forth creativity? The answer is none, zero, zip. It does no good. But it's actually far worse than that. The amount of energy the average person spends in commiseration is awesome! Listen to the conversations around you—at work, over lunch, at home. It's everywhere and it's a rare person who chooses not to participate. However, the one person in twenty who makes this decision has a tremendous advantage over everyone else.

Consider the amount of mental and emotional energy expended in commiseration. It's a lot. This is energy that could be spent in creative ideas or quiet reflection. This is energy that might be used to solve a problem, implement an idea, or market a product. This energy is the source of your abundance. It's yours, and it's free. When you make the decision to stop commiserating, you free up this energy—instantly. New thoughts begin to emerge; new, exciting ideas rise to the surface.

Make no mistake about it: Breaking this habit is difficult. It takes time, but it's worth it. The only way to quit is to notice yourself in the midst of commiseration or when you're about to commiserate. Gently remind yourself that, while it's tempting to join the others, you've got better things to do and dreams to pursue. As you avoid the tendency to commiserate, your rewards will be swift and certain.

97.

WORK AT IT

You probably haven't found anything in this book too difficult to understand. Perhaps, for the most part, you have had the feeling of "Oh, I already know that." So one of my concluding thoughts as we near the end of this book is something you may not already know.

Perhaps the most difficult insight about how to save money, create abundance, have a wonderful life, and accumulate wealth is that, although it's fun and simple, you do have to work on it. These dreams, although within the grasp of anyone, do not necessarily come naturally.

We can break tasks into two basic categories: There are those tasks we know we have to study and learn, and then there are those we believe just come naturally. To build a suspension bridge obviously requires a lot of specific learning, and to breathe comes naturally from birth. Now, here's the question: Does abundance come naturally like eating and breathing, or is it a task that must be learned and worked? I think it's a little of both.

Let's take an analogous issue. Does parenting come naturally or is it something that must be learned and worked? Often a parent produces a rebellious, angry child—a child that cannot maintain relationships, survive in school, keep a job, and so on. There are very few parents, however, who would admit they did a bad job of parenting, and I'm almost sure that there is no parent who sits up late at night planning how to be a bad parent. I believe that every parent would be sincere in a statement that he or she was a good parent, even if their child is sitting out a sentence in a juvenile detention facility. Certainly, the economic and industrial situation is a contributor in the difficulties we face as parents, but another big contributor is that many parents just don't know how to parent! So, if parents can be misled about their ability to parent, is it possible that parents can be equally misled about their ability to save money, make dreams come true, and accumulate wealth?

I believe that the pursuit of an abundant life includes a little of both. It's a natural process, but it does take some work. The best and most empowering ideas are simple, but they require implementation. I believe I am empowering you when I tell you that it's *your* choice. If you fail to save money and accumulate wealth, you can blame others and the world. Or you can gain some insight about your own contribution. Once you have insight about your part in the process, you can open the door and have the opportunity to do something about it. This is a powerful and important door to open. You have the power to create the life of your dreams. Go ahead and make it happen!

98.

CREATE YOUR OWN LUCK

Some people seem to get all the luck. Upon closer examination, however, you'd be shocked at the amount of "luck" that is self-created. The truth is, while luck is a factor of success from time to time, "lucky people" share some very consistent characteristics.

Lucky people are constantly putting themselves in the position to be lucky. In other words, they step up to the plate, they participate, they tell others that they are willing to accept help. I was "lucky" in a finance course I took at Pepperdine University many years ago. My friends couldn't believe that the professor gave me an A for the course when it seemed like I probably deserved a B at best. What they didn't know was that I visited the professor and solicited his help *every single day* that he had office hours. The professor knew, with no doubt whatsoever, that I was trying hard and that I knew the material. Was I lucky? Sure I was, but had I not demonstrated a burning desire to learn, I wouldn't have been nearly so lucky. The professor wouldn't have even known me, much less cared if I succeeded. As it was, however, my professor really liked me. He wanted me to succeed. In fact, it was almost as important to him as it was to me. He knew I was sincere, not only in my efforts to learn but also in my fondness for him as a person and in my respect for him as an instructor. Obviously, I was in a position to be lucky.

Since that time, I've been lucky hundreds of times. I've been really lucky, for example, to get on certain radio and television shows around the country to promote my work. But while others complain about their lack of promotion and/or wait for the phone to ring, I'm busy sending books, press kits, and show ideas to producers all over the country, sometimes several times a day for months and months at a time. Am I lucky? You bet I am! But I create a great deal of that luck myself by letting people know I'm ready and willing to be lucky.

I have an acquaintance who just got his "big break" in the corporate world. "He's so lucky," everyone said. And they're absolutely right: He was lucky. But was it blind luck or did the fact that he arrived at the office before most people had gotten out of bed, or that he remembered his boss's birthday (and his children's), or that he was willing to apologize when he was wrong, shared the credit when he deserved all of it, said "thank you" when something nice came his way, and persevered long after others gave up have something to do with it? I think both are true. He *was* lucky, but he also put himself in the position to be lucky. Creating your own luck is sort of like planting a garden in an ideal environment. You'll be "luckier" with your plants if you provide the best soil, water, sunshine, and growing conditions. If you don't do these things, you might still get lucky and have a bumper crop, but the odds are far less likely.

The strategies in this book are designed to put you in a position to become lucky. As you look back and reread the various sections, you'll notice that most of the strategies are designed to give you an edge, improve your attitude, help make you a kinder or less reactive person, sharpen your wisdom, or deepen your perspective. The truth is, you never really know where your lucky breaks are going to come from. Lucky people know this, so they always act as if luck is just around the corner. Perhaps the person you choose to smile at or help, instead of frown at and ignore, is in a position to help you—or will be some day. You never know. As you take the advice in this book to heart, you'll notice that luck will begin to come your way. Then others will be calling you lucky.

99.

DON'T FORGET TO HAVE FUN

Obviously, this hasn't been a book on how to improve the rate of return in your investment portfolio. It's not an investment strategy book, or a book on finance or economics. It's a book on how to create abundance, how to manifest your dreams. I believe that the advice in this book can help you much more than any book on finance or economics. I wrote this book not only to help you make your dreams come true, but also to help you maximize enjoyment, the quality of your life, and the potential for fun. I want you to succeed, and I know you can. But just as important, I want you to have fun. And the more fun you have—when mixed with wisdom, creativity, and a little hard work—the more you are going to succeed.

When you look back on your life, perhaps on your deathbed or toward the end, it's very likely that you *won't* be asking yourself how much money you made or how many possessions you managed to collect. Nor will you see the purpose of life as being the collection of achievements or even the fulfillment of your goals. What you will see, I believe, is that the purpose of life was to have been kind and loving, to grow and to give back to others. You will have plenty of regrets if you forget to have fun, and probably none if you do not.

Realizing your dreams—whatever they are—can be a blast. It's certainly enjoyable to feel financially secure, but even more so to use your mind, attitude, charm, wisdom, and genuine kindness to create great abundance in all aspects of your life.

As you reflect on the strategies in this book, accept them into your life in the spirit in which they are offered—lighthearted, helpful, and fun. The more fun you have, the more you are likely to succeed. Don't listen to the so-called experts who tell you that creating wealth is a serious venture. Sure, it's hard work, but that's a different matter entirely. This is your life. You have the right to enjoy it. So be successful and create great abundance, but don't forget to have fun!

100.

DON'T WORRY, MAKE MONEY

One of the indicators that lets you know that you love what you do is that you'll be slightly saddened when you finish your project. You love it so much, you hate to see it end. I feel that way now.

This book was originally published as *Don't Worry, Make Money*. When I first heard Bobby McFerrin sing his classic song, "Don't Worry, Be Happy," I felt as if he were singing my thoughts to the world. I've always known that when we are happy and worry-free, we not only enjoy our lives more, but we are also more competent, creative, wise, and productive. We bring out the best in others and in ourselves. Without the internal distractions of stress, sweating the small stuff, anger, frustration, and worry, our relationships flourish, stress is diminished, new doors are opened, and our lives run smoothly.

I've learned that there is often a fine line between success and failure, or winning and losing. And so often, the difference between the two lies in overcoming worry. We worry about all sorts of things; some obvious, others more subtle. We worry, for example, about making or repeating mistakes or looking foolish. We worry about what others will think if we ask for help or ask for a raise. We worry about being ourselves, speaking to groups, or asking for a sale. We worry about our future, and we worry about the past. But when all is said and done, what good does worry really do us? Some would argue that it's "wise" to worry, that it somehow proves that you're able to anticipate problems. Yet while being able to anticipate problems is certainly useful, I disagree that doing so requires worry.

I'm now certain that, in most instances, any success or abundance we enjoy is *despite* our worry, not *because* of it. Far from being wisdom-filled, worry is actually a dream-snatcher. It takes an enormous toll on your spirits and on your emotions. Worry adversely affects your decisions and your judgment, keeping you on-edge, uptight, and heavyhearted. It's no fun to be a worrier—and it's not much fun to do business with one.

If you know super-successful people in any field, you'll find a thread of consistency that runs through virtually everyone—they don't worry about money. Interestingly enough, however, the lack of worry preceded their success and was not a by-product of it. Successful people share an inner unshakable confidence that is free from excessive worry.

Part of overcoming worry is to see it as a distraction rather than as a necessity. As worries enter your mind, try to give them less significance and less of your attention. In doing so, you may find it easier than you imagine to shoo them away as you would flies at a picnic! That way, you can concentrate on more important things that will help you deliver your dreams.

It's hard to adequately put into words how wonderful life can be when worry is diminished. For me, abandoning worry has made accessible so many possibilities for both my inner and outer worlds. Life without worry has opened new doors and created freedom that, in previous years, I didn't know was possible. So, "don't worry," I know this can happen for you, too. I hope this book has been and will be helpful to you in the creation of your dreams. I wish you the best of everything.

Treasure yourself and the gift of life,

Richard Carlson

SUGGESTED READING

Allen, James. *As a Man Thinketh*. New York: Barnes & Noble, 1992.

Carlson, Richard. *You Can Be Happy No Matter What*. San Rafael, Calif.: New World Library, 1992.
———. *You Can Feel Good Again*. New York: Plume, 1993.
———. *Short Cut Through Therapy*. New York: Plume, 1995.
———. *Don't Sweat the Small Stuff*. New York: Hyperion, 1997.

Carnegie, Dale. *How to Stop Worrying and Start Living*. New York: Pocket Books, 1984.

Cates, David. *Unconditional Money*. Willamina, Ore.: Buffalo Press, 1995.

Chopra, Deepak. *The Seven Spiritual Laws of Success*. San Rafael, Calif.: New World Library, 1994.
———. *Creating Affluence*. New York: New World Library, 1993.

Covey, Stephen R. *The Seven Habits of Highly Effective People*. New York: Fireside, 1989.

Day, Laura. *Practical Intuition*. New York: Villard, 1996.

Dyer, Wayne. *Real Magic.* New York: HarperCollins, 1992.

Givens, Charles. *Wealth Without Risk.* New York: Simon & Schuster, 1991.

Gross, Daniel. *Forbes Greatest Business Stories of All Time.* New York: John Wiley & Sons, 1996.

Hansen, Mark Victor. *Out of the Blue.* New York: HarperCollins, 1996.

Hill, Napoleon. *Think and Grow Rich.* New York: Fawcett Columbine, 1937.

Jeffers, Susan. *Feel the Fear and Do It Anyway!* New York: Fawcett Columbine, 1987.

Kushner, Harold. *When All You've Ever Wanted Isn't Enough.* New York: Pocket Books, 1986.

Machtig, Brett. *Wealth in a Decade.* Chicago: Irwin Professional Publishing, 1997.

Mandino, Og. *The Greatest Salesman in the World.* New York: Bantam, 1972.
———. *Secrets of Success and Happiness.* New York: Fawcett Columbine, 1995.

McCormack, Mark H. *What They Don't Teach You at Harvard Business School.* New York: Bantam, 1984.

Novak, Michael. *Business as a Calling.* New York: The Free Press, 1996.

Phillips, Michael. *The Seven Laws of Money.* Boston: Shambhala, 1997.

Ribeiro, Lair. *Success Is No Accident.* New York: St. Martin's Press, 1996.

Shinn, Florence Shovel. *The Secret Door to Success.* Marina Del Rey, Calif.: DeVorss & Company, 1940.
———. *The Game of Life and How to Play It.* New York: Fireside, 1986.

Sinetar, Marsha. *To Build the Life You Want, Create the Work You Love.* New York: St. Martin's Griffin, 1995.

Sternberg, Robert. *Successful Intelligence.* New York: Simon & Schuster, 1996.

Toppel, Edward Allen. *Zen in the Markets.* New York: Warner, 1992.